Robert Barnes received his PhD from the London School of Economics and Political Science in 2011. He was the Masters Programmes Senior Tutor in the Department of International History at the LSE before being appointed a lecturer in History at York St John University in 2013. He has published a number of articles and chapters in collections relating to the Korean War. This is his first monograph.

For my Mum and Dad.

THE US, THE UN AND THE KOREAN WAR

Communism in the Far East and the American Struggle for Hegemony in the Cold War

ROBERT BARNES

I.B. TAURIS

LONDON · NEW YORK

Published in 2014 by I.B.Tauris & Co Ltd
6 Salem Road, London W2 4BU
175 Fifth Avenue, New York NY 10010
www.ibtauris.com

Distributed in the United States and Canada
Exclusively by Palgrave Macmillan
175 Fifth Avenue, New York NY 10010

Library of Modern American History 3

ISBN: 978 1 78076 368 2

A full CIP record for this book is available from the British Library
A full CIP record is available from the Library of Congress

Library of Congress catalog card: available

Typeset in Garamond Three by OKS Prepress Services, Chennai, India
Printed and bound by CPI Group (UK) Ltd, Croydon, CR0 4YY

CONTENTS

ACKNOWLEDGEMENTS

For providing much invaluable insight regarding the content and style of my book as well as pointing me towards innumerable important books and sources, I would like to thank my doctoral supervisor, Dr Steven Casey, my temporary doctoral supervisor, Dr Antony Best and my advisor, Professor David Stevenson. Without their assistance my research would not have got beyond the embryonic stage. Many thanks, moreover, to Professor Matthew Jones and Dr Chi-Kwan Mark who gave me guidance on how to turn my doctoral thesis into a book. On my many research trips I have also been given considerable assistance by a number of archivists who have pointed me towards documents I very much doubt I would have unearthed myself. In this regard, I would especially like to thank the friendly and knowledgeable staff at the Harry S. Truman Library, the Dwight D. Eisenhower Library and the UN Archives and Records Management Section. I have also received sage advice and words of encouragement from my patient family members, particularly my mother, father, brother and sisters, and many of my close friends and colleagues, including John Millar, Dougal Squires, Ewan Gault, Benjamin Roberts, Marvin Fried, Andrew Watkins and Raquel Campos.

I would also like to thank the various institutions that have provided me with the financial support necessary to complete my book. I have received a number of generous grants from: the

Department of International History, the Research Studentship Scheme and the Postgraduate Travel Fund at the London School of Economics and Political Science; the University of London Central Research Fund; the Royal Historical Society Postgraduate Research Support Grant; the Harry S. Truman Library Institute Research Grant; the Rajiv Gandhi Travelling Scholarship; The Mercers' Company Educational Trust Fund; and the Gilchrist Educational Trust Travel Grant. Finally, the publication of this book was made possible by the support of the Scouloudi Foundation in association with the Institute of Historical Research.

LIST OF MAPS AND ILLUSTRATIONS

LIST OF ABBREVIATIONS

AMC	Additional Measures Committee
ANZUS	Australia, New Zealand, United States Security Treaty
CAB	Cabinet Office
CM	Cabinet Meetings
CP	Cabinet Papers
CPVA	Chinese People's Volunteer Army
DDE	Dwight D. Eisenhower Library
DEFE	Defence Ministry
DO	Dominions Office
DPRK	Democratic Peoples' Republic of Korea
ECOSOC	Economic and Social Council
EDC	European Defence Community
FO	Foreign Office
FRG	Federal Republic of Germany
FRUS	Foreign Relations of the United States
GOC	Good Offices Committee
HST	Harry S. Truman Library
ICF	Indian Custodial Force
ICRC	International Committee of the Red Cross
LAC	Library and Archives Canada
MAAG	Military Assistance Advisory Group
MAC	Military Armistice Commission

MEA	Ministry of External Affairs
MHS	Massachusetts Historical Society
MNLA	Malayan National Liberation Army
MSC	Military Staff Committee
NAA	National Archives of Australia
NAI	National Archives of India
NARA	National Archives and Records Administration (United States)
NATO	North Atlantic Treaty Organisation
NKPA	North Korean People's Army
NMML	Nehru Memorial Museum and Library
NNRC	Neutral Nations Repatriation Commission
NNSC	Neutral Nations Supervisory Commission
NSC	National Security Council
PLA	People's Liberation Army
PREM	Prime Minister's Office
PRC	People's Republic of China
PUL	Princeton University Library
RLS	Royal Library of Sweden
ROK	Republic of Korea
ROKA	Republic of Korea Army
SACEUR	Supreme Allied Commander in Europe
SCAP	Supreme Commander for the Allied Powers
SEATO	Southeast Asia Treaty Organisation
UKNA	United Kingdom National Archives
UN	United Nations
UNARMS	United Nations Archives and Records Management Section
UNC	United Nations Command
UNCOK	United Nations Commission on Korea
UNCURK	United Nations Commission for the Unification and Rehabilitation of Korea
UNGA	United Nations General Assembly (Official Records)
UNKRA	United Nations Korean Reconstruction Agency

UNSC	United Nations Security Council (Official Records)
UNTCOK	United Nations Temporary Commission on Korea
US	United States'
USAMGIK	United States Army Military Government in Korea
UVL	University of Vermont Library
WEU	Western European Union
YUL	Yale University Library Manuscripts Collections

INTRODUCTION

To describe the Korean War as 'forgotten' or 'unknown' is now an unwarranted cliché. The significance of this short but intense conflagration in shaping the post-war world, not to mention the risks of a global conflict that it entailed, especially in the winter of 1950–51, have long been appreciated by political, international, military, social and economic historians alike. While the Cold War clearly existed prior to 1950, the Korean War set in motion a chain of events that shaped international relations until 1989 and beyond. As a result, over the previous three decades a proliferation of research has been conducted into a wide array of aspects of this complex confrontation. Yet one crucial aspect has been almost entirely overlooked and will be addressed in this book.

Throughout the Korean War relations between the United States and members of the Commonwealth of Nations[1] at the United Nations (UN) oscillated between long periods of amicability and a series of tense crises. Publicly, few questions were ever raised against US policy. But behind-the-scenes the Commonwealth occasionally challenged US dominance of the UN. This book will highlight and explain the level of disharmony that existed between these states as they struggled to formulate an acceptable UN response to the Korean War. In doing so, it will demonstrate that the Commonwealth was able, at least to some degree, to constrain the policy of the US government at the UN when its members acted in unison. But this raises the further questions: when and why did the Commonwealth unite? I demonstrate that such unity only occurred when the risk of a global conflict was at its greatest, when key Commonwealth personalities were prepared to exercise their influence, when coincidence brought the Commonwealth members together, and when the US government was willing to bow to Commonwealth pressure. Conversely, when these conditions were removed the Commonwealth became disjointed and its members put their other allegiances ahead of Commonwealth loyalty. In these circumstances, no single Commonwealth country, not even Britain, had sufficient influence to alter US policy.

Washington found it very difficult to ignore a united Commonwealth because its members represented key allies in vital Cold War theatres. Given the closeness of their wartime alliance and Britain's continued, if diminishing, worldwide influence, London was the US's closest ally. This was especially the case in Western Europe where the British were expected to play a leading role in strengthening the political, economic and military situation in the face of a direct Soviet threat. Canada, as its northern neighbour and long-standing economic and security partner, was also a close ally. US relations with Australia and New Zealand were more recent but had been bound in blood during the Second World War and Washington had come to see these two countries as its most dependable friends in the Pacific. South Africa, as with most of that continent, featured less in American thoughts but its staunchly anti-communist position was appreciated and friendly relations existed. Of more difficulty was the role of India and Pakistan in US planning. Although the US government was extremely wary of India's position of neutrality both countries were considered of great strategic importance in the Cold War. Furthermore, Washington appreciated the influence India had over the emerging Third World. Efforts were made, therefore, to win these countries over to the Western camp.

The Commonwealth's importance was most clearly evident in the UN where it represented a numerically significant voting bloc and wielded much moral authority because of its multiethnic nature, its liberal democratic traditions, and its close ties to various groups of other members. The 'Old' Commonwealth countries—Britain, Canada, Australia, New Zealand and South Africa—were an integral part of the Western bloc. But the 'New' Commonwealth members—India and Pakistan—were part of the loosely connected 'neutral' bloc. India, in particular, had assumed the extremely difficult task of mediating between the two superpowers at the UN. Despite these differing perspectives, common ground was occasionally found between the Commonwealth members and they were able to act as a pseudo-bloc to achieve their temporary shared goals.

The UN, moreover, provided a location in which Commonwealth representatives could meet regularly to coordinate policy. Such contact was more problematic through normal diplomatic channels given the vast distances between member states. So while the United States was the hegemonic power at the UN in the early 1950s, it still relied on the votes of its allies to exercise its will and so had to pay attention to Commonwealth concerns when raised.

The following pages are structured to emphasize and clarify these points. The Prologue will provide extensive background detail on the international and peninsular origins of the conflict and the nature of relations between the United States and the Commonwealth at the UN leading up to the eruption of fighting. The necessary contextual information to make sense of subsequent decisions will thus be established. Each of the seven main chapters will then examine relations between the United States and the Commonwealth members at the UN during a specific phase of the conflict. The goal of each chapter is to establish whether the Commonwealth members were able to unite and constrain US policy and what factors led to this outcome. Because decisions regarding UN policy were not taken in a vacuum but were heavily dependent on the military situation in Korea, domestic developments in the United States and each of the Commonwealth countries, and international events connected to the Cold War, each chapter begins by setting the context.

The opening two chapters cover the tense and fluid early months of the Korean conflict between June 1950 and February 1951. Chapter 1 examines the UN Security Council's establishment of its first collective security action and the General Assembly's endorsement of the unification of Korea by force. Throughout this period US dominance of the UN remained largely unchallenged by a Commonwealth that was disunited. Only India voiced any significant criticism but could not rally its Commonwealth partners behind its position. In contrast, during the winter crisis following Chinese intervention outlined in Chapter 2 the Commonwealth did unite for a sustained period and acted as a constraining agent upon Washington. President Harry S. Truman and his Secretary of State Dean Acheson were determined to have Beijing branded an aggressor, but the Commonwealth members feared such action would lead to an escalation of the conflict. In consequence, they acted together to force the Americans to accept a number of UN attempts to bring about a ceasefire. Only after considerable delay and after Washington had granted many concessions did the Commonwealth agree to OK calls to have the People's Republic of China (PRC) punished.

Chapters 3 and 4 cover the often overlooked middle 18 months of the Korean War. The first of these chapters focuses on the UN's continuing unsuccessful attempts to bring the fighting to an end while at the same time considering what sanctions to impose upon China. During this time the Commonwealth unity that had existed during the winter crisis slowly disintegrated as the military situation improved and Washington adopted a more moderate course. Still, much friction existed, especially between the Americans and the British, over the timing and nature of sanctions. Chapter 4 then reveals that the Commonwealth became almost entirely subservient to the Americans during the first year of the armistice talks that commenced in July 1951. With representatives from the UN and Communist commands meeting directly and making slow but steady progress, all the Commonwealth members were content to postpone consideration of the Korean question at the UN hopeful that a ceasefire was forthcoming.

The next two chapters then cover the final tumultuous year of the Korean War. Chapter 5 examines the second half of 1952 when the UN resumed its efforts to bring about a ceasefire after the breakdown of the armistice negotiations. At the root of these problems was the fate of prisoners of war. In contrast to the US government, the Commonwealth members were not prepared to allow this one outstanding issue to prolong or lead to the escalation of the conflict. During weeks of deliberations the Commonwealth members, emboldened by the unprecedented weakness of the Truman administration, worked closely to find a compromise resolution sponsored by India in the face of US opposition. Yet, as Chapter 6 demonstrates, this challenge to US hegemony did no lasting damage to relations between Washington and the Commonwealth capitals. In the final months before the signing of the Korean Armistice Agreement the Commonwealth members were generally supportive of the new US President Dwight D. Eisenhower's decision to avoid further debate at the UN. They accepted that the best way to bring about a ceasefire was through direct negotiations with the terms of the Indian Resolution providing acceptable parameters.

The final chapter of this book examines the UN's efforts to establish a political conference to bring about a peaceful settlement of the unification question. This issue caused much antagonism between the United States and the Commonwealth members, as the latter firmly believed that neutral countries, especially India, should be represented. The Eisenhower administration, however, insisted that only belligerents should participate. But this time Common-wealth unity buckled under pressure and Washington had its way. Yet the Communist countries opposed the composition proposed by the UN and it took bilateral discussions beyond the UN to finally agree to the Geneva Conference. And even then, no means to unify Korea could be agreed and the talks were prematurely terminated. The Epilogue then briefly examines the subsequent fates of the Korean question at the UN, of the nature of the Commonwealth and of the Commonwealth's relationship with the United States. As such, it demonstrates that with the Korean ceasefire holding, other crises emerging and decolonization accelerating, the Commonwealth was no longer able or willing to unite to constrain US policy at the UN.

From what I have outlined above this topic evidently falls within the broad sphere of international history since it examines the diplomatic interaction of a number of states within the context of two very different international organizations. Furthermore, this book is concerned principally with the top echelons of foreign decision-making within the US and Commonwealth governments. Throughout, it emphasizes that issues of power, national interest and security governed the actions taken by the United States and the Commonwealth members at the UN during the Korean War. Yet this is not to say that other factors were unimportant. Clearly, the key individuals involved had very different conceptualizations of how best to achieve these goals. As will be discussed in more detail below, the Commonwealth members shared a set of liberal democratic values that formed the bedrock of the organization. But this vague ideological notion did not provide a blueprint for meeting the multifarious Cold War problems faced by each of the Commonwealth governments. In consequence, the vast majority of Commonwealth leaders, even those from nominally socialist political parties such as British Labour Prime Minister Clement Attlee and his Foreign Secretary Ernest Bevin, saw their national interests as being best served by siding with the United States in its hostile campaign against the Soviet Union. Only Indian Prime Minister Jawaharlal Nehru adopted a contrary course, championing the policy of non-alignment.

At the same time, racial prejudices caused the greatest ruptures within the Commonwealth even though it was precisely the multiethnic composition and liberal traditions of the organization that gave it such great moral authority at the UN. The staunchly conservative governments of Winston Churchill in Britain, Robert Menzies in Australia and Sidney Holland in New Zealand, as well as that of Dr Daniel Malan, the architect of apartheid, in South Africa, viewed the New Commonwealth countries as racially inferior and found it very difficult to work with them as equals. For their part, Nehru and his Pakistani counterpart Liaquat Ali-Khan, despite their continued admiration for many British and European practices, still harboured much resentment towards their 'white' former colonial masters. Even so, the factors that did unite the Commonwealth in its effort to constrain US policy at the UN tended to be a product less of these 'soft' issues and more to do with very real 'hard' issues of power.

Moreover, in the tradition of international history, the research conducted for this book has focused on a number of national archives in the United States and Commonwealth countries. It also looks beyond these formal records at a variety of private papers in an attempt to discover the motivations behind the views and actions of a number of the key decision-makers. In addition, this book draws from the abundant secondary literature written on the Korean War. Specifically, three categories of historical study are closely related to its subject matter: international histories of the Korean War; national histories of the role played by the United States and individual Commonwealth countries in the conflict; and histories of the two international organizations under consideration, the Commonwealth and the UN. This book shares many significant similarities with each of these groups of work. But, as will be demonstrated, crucial differences exist.

William Stueck is the only true international historian of the Korean War. In his two more recent major books, *The Korean War* and *Rethinking the Korean War*, as well as in a number of articles, Stueck has provided by far the most extensive examination of the conflict's impact on global politics. He also provides the most considered analysis of activities at the UN and the influence wielded by some of the Commonwealth members within this forum and in Washington.[2] Even so, he is principally concerned with the roles played by the three largest powers involved in Korea—the United States, the Soviet Union and China—and he does not consider the impact of the Commonwealth as a united bloc. Moreover, while he does note occasional tension between the United States, Britain, Canada and India, he largely sees the Commonwealth members as playing a part in support of US policy at the UN. He does not think the Commonwealth members had the ability or will to significantly constrain US policy because of their small military contribution and desire to maintain close relations with Washington.[3] In contrast, this book argues that Washington was much more susceptible to Commonwealth pressure when its members were united.

Compared to the limited number of international histories of the Korean War, numerous national histories have been written focusing on the role played by an individual state. While American-centric accounts dominate, Rosemary Foot has provided the most complete national history of the US experience in Korea in *The Wrong War, A Substitute for Victory* and numerous articles. Foot provides a similar argument to my own in that she states that Washington's allies, particularly Britain, did have a moderating influence on US policy at the UN. But the similarities end there since Foot fails to identify the Commonwealth as an agent of constraint. She also understates the level of allied influence on US decision-making, claiming it did little but reinforce cautious views that already existed. Foot, moreover, spends relatively little time considering the UN context, concentrating almost exclusively on activities in Washington.[4]

With regards to Commonwealth countries, the role of Britain has received by far the most attention. Anthony Farrar-Hockley's two-volume work *The British Part in the Korean War*[5] and Callum MacDonald's *Britain and the Korean War*[6] are the most complete examples. Peter L(owe)[7] and Michael Dockrill[8] have also written a number of important works on the British experience. Two excellent national histories of Canada's role during the conflict have also been written: Denis Stairs' *The Diplomacy of Constraint*[9] and John Melady's *Korea: Canada's Forgotten War*.[10] Easily the most far-reaching study of Australia's role is Robert O'Neill's two-volume book, *Australia in the Korean War, 1950–53*,[11] but Gavan McCormack's *Cold War, Hot War* provides another valuable contribution.[12] The only national history of New Zealand's role is Ian McGibbon's detailed two-volume study *New Zealand and the Korean War*.[13] And the best account of India's experience during the Korean War remains Shiv Dayal's somewhat dated book, *India's Role in the Korean Question*.[14]

This book is inherently linked to these national histories in the sense that it too examines the decision-making processes in each of these Commonwealth countries. Yet the following pages are different in two crucial ways. First, none of these works has examined in any detail how the Commonwealth members interacted with each other and under what circumstances they were brought together. Second, none of these texts truly considers why the UN proved such a fruitful forum for the Commonwealth to act in unison and constrain US policy. The UN dimension receives relatively little attention throughout, as each historian prefers to focus on bilateral relations. It is this book's contention that due to its size, multiethnic composition and shared values, the Commonwealth wielded much influence in the UN and could not be ignored by the dominant power, the United States.

The final cluster of works connected to this book is that dedicated to the two international organizations in question, the Commonwealth and the UN. In terms of the former, a number of studies have examined its general workings and evolution. The best examples of these are H. Duncan Hall's *Commonwealth*[15] and Patrick Gordon Walker's *The Commonwealth*.[16] Other studies have considered relations between the Commonwealth members and the United States during the Cold War, including Ritchie Ovendale's *The English-Speaking Alliance*[17] and A.P. Thornton's article 'The transformation of the Commonwealth and the "special relationship"'.[18] These works do place the Commonwealth at the forefront of attention, stressing the importance of the organization in the post-war world. But none of them concentrate specifically on either the Korean War or the role of the Commonwealth at the UN. Ovendale's work also only examines the perspectives of the 'white' former British Dominions. The only partial exception is Graeme Mount's study of the Korean War, *The Diplomacy of War*.[19] Still, Mount's narrative is weighted too heavily in favour of his native Canada and he dedicates very little space to the complex interaction between the Commonwealth members in formulating UN policy. And, like Ovendale, he focuses only on certain Commonwealth countries, completely ignoring even India's crucial role.

On the UN, the most thorough works are Evan Luard's *A History of the United Nations*,[20] Paul Kennedy's *Parliament of Man*[21] and Bertrand Maurice's *The United Nations: Past, Present and Future*.[22] These studies cover lengthy periods and a whole range of problems that came before the world organization. Despite briefly examining the role of the UN during the Korean War, none of these historians provides in-depth analysis and they focus too heavily on American activities. No consideration whatsoever is given to the influence of the Commonwealth. To be sure, Tae-Ho Yoo's *The Korean War and the United Nations*[23] is dedicated solely to the role of the UN in the conflict. But he is much more concerned with the legal nature of the collective security action than the diplomatic activity that went on behind the scenes. He thus pays scant attention to the activities of the Commonwealth members. Likewise, Leland Goodrich's *Korea: A Study of US Policy in the United Nations*,[24] as the title suggests, concentrates solely on the US experience and does not recognize the unique role played by the Commonwealth.

This book thus makes an innovative and essential contribution to historical knowledge. It not only provides a new and unique perspective on the Korean War; it also examines two other issues that have come under far less scrutiny by historians of the Cold War: the roles of the Commonwealth and the UN. As it demonstrates, behind-the-scenes alliance diplomacy played a crucial part in shaping the course of the Korean War. While the United States sought to use its dominance of the UN to legitimize its policies, this process was far more complicated than usually assumed and Washington often had to make concessions to its Commonwealth allies. Most significantly, the Commonwealth, when united, was able to constrain US policy, to some degree at least, at the UN. Even in the deeply polarized world at the height of the Cold War the Commonwealth mattered to its members, at the UN and beyond, and was more than just a symbolic group of states bound by a common history.

PROLOGUE

Before first light on 25 June 1950 ferocious fighting erupted in Korea at various points along the 38th parallel. The North Korean People's Army (NKPA)—supported by Soviet-made tanks, artillery and aircraft—pushed south across the de facto border quickly gaining ground from the ill-prepared Republic of Korea Army (ROKA). Very few precise details exist regarding what actually took place during these initial exchanges but it soon became apparent that this was more than another minor skirmish. While there had been concerns in New York, Washington and the Commonwealth capitals that such an eventuality might take place, few had predicted the timing and scale of the North Korean invasion. By the time the UN Security Council convened in an emergency session later that day—the point where this book commences its narrative—North Korean forces were bearing down on Seoul.

These events marked the beginning of the Korean War but this conflict had been a long time in the making.[1] To understand the outbreak and course of this civil and international conflagration it is first necessary to outline briefly the recent history of Korea. After losing its independence to Japan in 1910, Korea experienced 35 years as a colony in which the indigenous population was, in general, treated brutally. Numerous resistance movements sprang up but were violently suppressed and forced into exile in neighbouring China, the Soviet Union and beyond. Korea received very little international

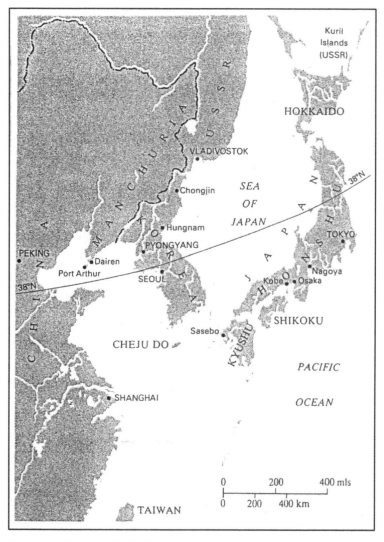

Figure 1   Korea and neighbouring areas.
Source: Lowe, Peter, *The Origins of the Korean War* (Basingstoke, 1997), p. 266.

attention until the 1943 Cairo Conference where the United States, Britain and China agreed that after the defeat of Japan, Korea should regain its independence 'in due course'. Then, in the dying days of the

Second World War, the US government, fearing that the Soviet Red Army would occupy Korea after Moscow had declared war upon Japan, proposed dividing the peninsula at the 38th parallel. Soviet forces would be stationed in the north and US forces in the south. Somewhat surprisingly the Soviet Union accepted this plan even though it left two-thirds of the Korean population and the capital city, Seoul, in the US occupation zone while US forces were unlikely to arrive for a number of weeks.[2]

The two occupations had very contrasting experiences. In the south, the US Army Military Government in Korea (USAMGIK) abolished the Korean 'people's committees' formed after the Japanese surrender fearing they had communist sympathies. Instead, the Americans retained Japanese and Korean collaborators in official posts creating friction with the local population. With little direction or funding from Washington as the Truman administration focused on the recovery of Western Europe and Japan, USAMGIK worked closely with the unpopular local elite, especially Syngman Rhee, a right-wing nationalist who had campaigned for decades in exile in the United States against Japanese rule. In the north, the Soviet Civil Authority worked closely with the people's committees instigating a programme of land collectivization and nationalization, forcing wealthy landowners and industrialists to flee south. Kim Il-sung, a former anti-Japanese guerrilla fighter and officer in the Soviet Red Army, was hand-picked by Soviet leader Joseph Stalin to be Chairman of the Provisional People's Committee for North Korea but quickly proved to be a popular choice with the peasantry due to his energetic leadership.[3]

Meanwhile, the work of the US-Soviet Joint Commission, established at the Moscow Conference of Foreign Ministers in December 1945 to bring about Korea's independence, became stalemated. The US government, eager to terminate its costly military occupation, consequently brought the problem of Korean independence to the UN General Assembly hoping to use its dominance of the world organization to find an acceptable solution. This ploy initially proved effective since on 14 November 1947 Resolution 112 (II) was adopted stating that the UN's objectives were to establish a 'united, independent and democratic' Korea and establishing the UN Temporary Commission on Korea (UNTCOK) to oversee the creation of a proportionate National Assembly. The Soviet Civil Authority, however, refused to recognize UNTCOK or hold elections in the north.

Nonetheless, elections were held in South Korea on 10 May 1948. With left-wing parties boycotting and corruption much in evidence, Rhee gained victory and on 15 August 1948 the Republic of Korea (ROK) was declared, USAMGIK was terminated, and US forces began to withdraw. In retaliation, less than a month later the Democratic People's Republic of Korea (DPRK) was established in North Korea with Kim appointed Premier. On 12 December 1948 the General Assembly then adopted Resolution 195 (III) endorsing the elections in the south and the sovereignty of the ROK, and establishing the UN Commission on Korea (UNCOK) to use its good offices to bring about the unification of Korea. But the work of UNCOK proved futile since both Rhee and Kim claimed authority over the entire peninsula. They also threatened to use force to unify the country, while a number of bloody clashes took place along the 38th parallel. UNCOK thus devoted much of its energy to observing the developing military stand-off.[4]

At the same time, Cold War tensions reached a new high. Nineteen forty-nine witnessed the formation of the North Atlantic Treaty Organisation (NATO), the successful testing of the first Soviet atomic bomb and the Communist victory in the Chinese Civil War leading to the proclamation of the People's Republic of China (PRC) in October. The last of these events had the most profound impact on Korea. The Truman administration, facing an enormous domestic backlash for the 'loss' of China, adopted an ambiguous policy. It continued to recognize Chiang Kai-shek's Nationalist rump regime on Taiwan and opposed the seating of the PRC at the UN but it did not offer military protection to Taiwan. In stark contrast, Moscow recognized the PRC and walked out of the UN Security Council when that body failed to do so in January 1950. Yet Stalin was worried that China, and Chairman Mao Zedong in particular, could threaten Soviet interests in East Asia and his own pre-eminence in the Communist world. In February 1950, therefore, Stalin, with only a little reluctance, signed the Sino-Soviet Treaty of Friendship, Alliance and Mutual Assistance.[5]

The Communist victory in China also influenced other events in Asia. Close ties were forged between the Chinese and Vietnamese Communist parties and the Chinese Military Advisory Group was sent to Indochina to provide advice and financial and military assistance to the Viet Minh, the independence movement led by Ho Chi Minh. As a result, the United States directly provided financial and military assistance to the French in Indochina for the first time.[6] More limited assistance was also given to the ethnic-Chinese dominated Malayan National Liberation Army (MNLA) in its efforts to oust the British. In reaction to these worrying developments the new British Director of Operations in Malaya, Lieutenant-General Sir Harold Briggs, improved the coordination of the counterinsurgency and established 500 'New Villages'—guarded communities to replace illegal Chinese squatter camps on the edges of the jungle. The Briggs Plan intended to deprive the MNLA of recruits, food and supplies thus forcing the guerrillas into open combat.[7]

In this dangerous climate Kim asked Stalin to authorize and provide support for a military invasion of South Korea, assuring him that this would inspire the people to rise up against Rhee. The Soviet leader had previously rejected similar requests on the grounds that such action might lead to war with the United States. But this time he assented. The Soviet leader felt emboldened by recent Cold War developments and dared to make this move after Acheson, speaking at the National Press Club on 12 January 1950, had excluded Korea from the US defence perimeter in the Pacific. Furthermore, Stalin was eager to trigger a conflict in Korea that might embroil China in a drawn out conflict with the United States, distracting Washington away from Europe while making the PRC more dependent on Moscow. Stalin did give Mao the final go-ahead on the invasion but the Chinese leader had little choice but to accept this fait accompli even though it disrupted his plans for conquering Taiwan. The Soviet Union thus provided Kim with material assistance and advisers to plan the operation.[8]

When news of the North Korean invasion reached Washington very late on 24 June 1950 local time, the US government was ill-prepared to meet the emergency. Truman was at his home in Independence, Missouri, and a number of other key decision-makers were away from the capital. Acheson rushed back to the State Department from his farm in Virginia and, after very brief discussions, telephoned the President recommending an emergency session of the Security Council be held to take action. Truman agreed without question.

The reasons why the Truman administration made this apparent snap decision to intervene in the Korean civil war have long been debated. The official reason given was that it could not ignore an open act of aggression since this would encourage Soviet adventurism elsewhere. But other factors were also at stake. Strategically, a Communist victory in Korea would jeopardize the security of Japan. Economically, the loss of South Korea would deprive Japan of much-needed resources and markets. And internationally, the United States had to act tough to reassure its allies, particularly in Europe, that it took its security commitments seriously. Political factors also played a role in the US decision to intervene in Korea. By mid-1950, 18 months after his shock victory in the 1948 presidential elections, Truman's domestic popularity had again begun to decline and Congressional bipartisan support for his foreign policy was disintegrating. The loss of Korea after China, therefore, was unthinkable, especially as the United States had invested heavily in the ROK and the fledgling country had become a symbol of containment in East Asia.[9]

What has been less discussed is why the US government opted to intervene in Korea through the UN. This action was perhaps surprising seeing as the Truman administration had purposefully bypassed the UN and acted unilaterally when dealing with earlier European issues, such as Greece, Turkey, Berlin and Western European economic recovery and security. Behind these earlier decisions was the knowledge that the Soviet Union would use its veto in the Security Council to block US policy in this vital Cold War theatre. Now, though, a number of other factors were in play that made the US decision to intervene through the UN almost inevitable. To start with, Truman had overseen the creation of the world organization in 1945 and since then had publicly insisted that working through the UN was the central tenet of US foreign policy. At some level he also held idealistic convictions about the value of the UN. Demonstrating this most visibly was the fact that since a young age he had carried in his wallet a hand-written copy of a section of Alfred Lord Tennyson's utopian poem *Locksley Hall* stating:

> For I dipt into the future, far as human eye could see
> Saw the vision of the world, and all the wonder that would be;
> Saw the heavens fill with commerce, argosies of magic sails,
> Pilots of the purple twilight, dropping down with costly bales;
> Heard from heavens fill with shouting, and there rain'd a ghastly dew
> From the nations' airy navies grapping in the central blue;
> Far along the world-wide whisper of the south-wind rushing warm,
> With the standards of the peoples plunging thro' the thunder-storm;
> Till the war-drum throb'd no longer, and the battle flags were furl'd
> In the Parliament of Man, the Federation of the World.

The President and many of his subordinates thus worried that if the UN did not implement collective security measures to meet this first flagrant act of aggression since 1945, then the future of the organization would be jeopardized. He did not want the UN to share the fate of the League of Nations, which he partly blamed on the United States' failure to become a member.[10]

Working through the UN also made practical sense. Truman and Acheson were confident that the United States' global political, economic and military strength made it the dominant power at the UN, particularly in the General Assembly where it did not have to contend with the Soviet veto. Whatever policy it put forward in this forum invariably received the majority of votes since it could generally use its influence to command the support of all Western and Latin American members as well as most of the nominally 'neutral' countries. In contrast, the Soviet bloc numbered just five and only a few neutral members were willing to stand up to Washington.

With this knowledge the Truman administration had, in fact, utilized the world organization on a number of occasions prior to the North Korean invasion to deal with less vital non-European matters. Most famously, Washington had used its dominance of the UN to facilitate the creation of the state of Israel. More significantly, the US government had also referred the problem of the independence of Korea to the General Assembly in 1947 and used the UN to establish the ROK a year later. In consequence, the Truman administration considered Korea a UN matter. In his oft-criticized and notorious speech to the National Press Club in January 1950, Acheson had tried to spell this out. Although he excluded Korea from the US defence perimeter in the Pacific, he also stated that if South Korea came under attack Washington would invoke 'the commitments of the entire civilized world under the Charter of the United Nations'. Acheson's sincerity may be questioned in the context of his earlier lack of faith in the organization and his preference for negotiating with those states directly involved in specific issues, rather than small disinterested countries.[11] Even so, while clearly designed principally to deter Soviet aggression, Acheson's comments indicate that the US government did have a contingency plan ready for use if the ROK came under attack. In these circumstances the United States would seek to intervene in Korea through a UN collective security action. The speed with which the Truman administration decided to refer the Korean question to the Security Council suggests it was simply putting into effect this long-standing plan. Indeed, not to have utilized the UN would have been hypocritical.

Yet the US decision to intervene in Korea through the UN was also opportunistic. If Moscow had not been boycotting the Security Council over the Chinese representation question then Washington would surely have avoided the UN, realizing it could achieve little due to the Soviet veto. Truman hoped as well that a vigorous UN response would rekindle the American public's faith in the world organization that had been blunted by the inability of the Security

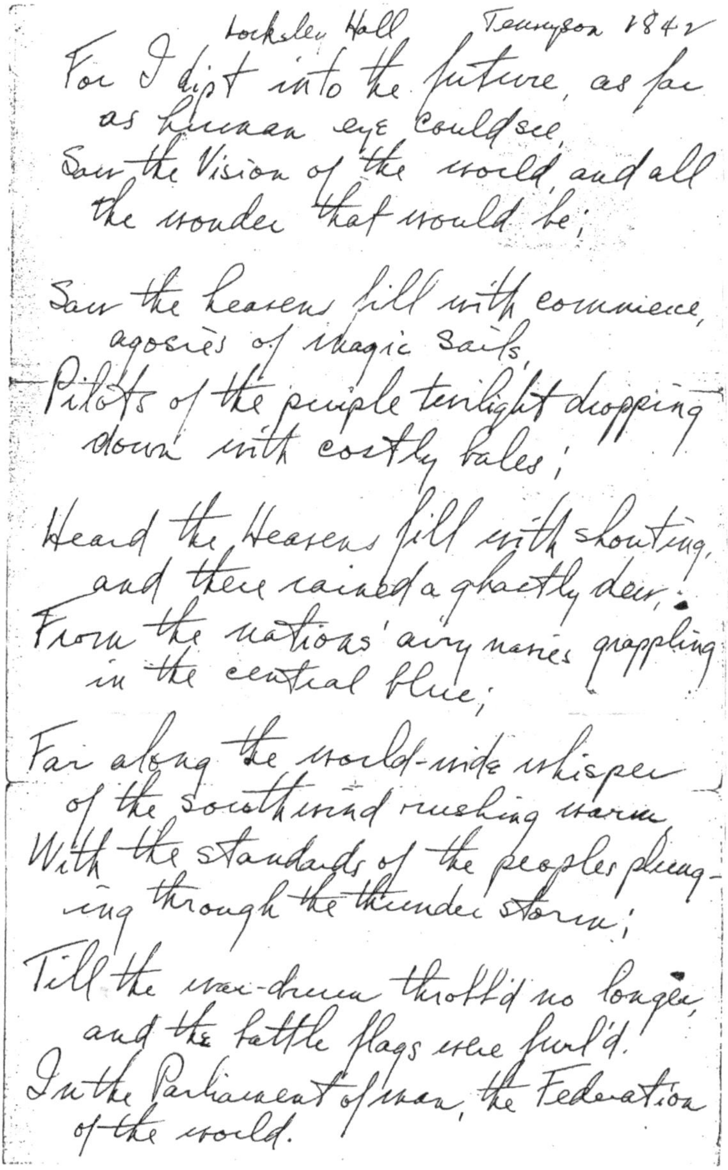

Lockesley Hall   Tennyson 1842

For I dipt into the future, as far
   as human eye could see,
Saw the Vision of the world, and all
   the wonder that would be;

Saw the heavens fill with commerce,
   argosies of magic sails,
Pilots of the purple twilight dropping
   down with costly bales;

Heard the Heavens fill with shouting,
   and there rained a ghastly dew,
From the nations' airy navies grappling
   in the central blue;

Far along the world-wide whisper
   of the south-wind rushing warm
With the standards of the peoples plung-
   ing through the thunder storm;

Till the war-drum throbb'd no longer,
   and the battle flags were furl'd
In the Parliament of man, the Federation
   of the world.

Figure 2   Truman's handwritten copy of Tennyson's *Locksley Hall*.[12]

Council to act. Furthermore, the President also realized that intervening through the UN was still very important in persuading Congressional and public opinion that the United States was not alone in its endeavours to contain Soviet imperialism and that not only US soldiers would be fighting and dying in Korea.

* * *

While the origins of the Korean War have received an abundance of historical attention, the fate of the Commonwealth in the years preceding the conflict has received much less scrutiny. To understand its functioning at the UN during the Korean War fully it is essential to outline the nature of the organization, how its members perceived it and how they viewed their role in the UN. In doing so, it will become evident that the Commonwealth meant different things to different parties at different times. Still, the Commonwealth was not simply a symbolic organization based on a shared history. For all its members, to a greater or lesser extent, the Commonwealth continued to be an important means for furthering national interests and providing security.[13]

Before the Singapore Declaration of 1971 the Commonwealth had neither a formal organizational structure nor a set of unifying principles. It remained largely defined by its founding document, the 1931 Statute of Westminster. This effectively established the legislative independence and equality of the six Dominions—Australia, Canada, the Irish Free State, Newfoundland, New Zealand and the Union of South Africa—that became known as the 'Old' Commonwealth members. The Statute also defined the Commonwealth as being 'a free association . . . united by common allegiance to the Crown'. From the outset, therefore, the Commonwealth was a loosely-defined intergovernmental organization of independent states united by a shared Head of State. The only official contact its members had was at sporadic meetings on specific issues and roughly bi-annual Commonwealth Prime Ministers' Conferences held in London at which common problems were dealt with informally. Yet in the Commonwealth capitals the High Commissions of the other members held privileged positions and were kept in much closer and constant contact by the host government than the embassies of other countries. These ties were often strengthened by close personal relationships between Commonwealth diplomats and military figures present in other Commonwealth countries.

The Second World War undoubtedly marked the pinnacle of Commonwealth cooperation. Although Britain's inability to offer adequate protection led to periodic spats, for the most part all the Commonwealth members, with the exception of Ireland, united against the dire threat posed by the Axis Powers, and London became the focal point of wartime planning. At war's end the Commonwealth members optimistically hoped that the fledgling organization would continue to play an important global role. But the post-war world soon proved more complex. The composition of the organization expanded with India, Pakistan and Ceylon[14] accepting Common-wealth membership when they gained independence. These states became known as the 'New' Commonwealth members. Then in 1949 two members left the Commonwealth. Newfoundland joined Canada while Ireland became a republic, a path that India seemed likely to follow. With the onset of the Cold War, however, India was considered too important to lose by the Old Commonwealth members, especially Britain, due to its strategic position and influence in Asia. Both factors made India vital to preventing the spread of communism. And so when it became a republic, the Commonwealth Prime Ministers agreed on the London Declaration. This allowed the inclusion of members who simply recognized the British Sovereign as Head of the Commonwealth, and not their Head of State, while also dropping the word 'British' from the organization's title.

These actions demonstrated the flexibility of the Old Common-wealth members, not to mention their strong desire to retain close relations with their new partners. Such sentiments were given further expression in January 1950 when the Commonwealth Foreign Ministers met in Colombo, Ceylon, to discuss raising living standards in Asia to prevent the spread of communism. This meeting resulted in the Colombo Plan, a framework for intergovernmental arrangements for the economic and social development of the region. Although not officially launched until July 1951, the Colombo Plan quickly gained momentum as the developed Commonwealth members began providing aid, assistance, investment and training to the developing members. The Colombo Plan was the clearest indicator prior to the Korean War that the Commonwealth members were able and sincere in their efforts to work closely with each other to overcome international problems.[15]

Still, the importance of the Commonwealth to each of its members depended greatly on their specific foreign-policy priorities. The British Labour government was not overly sentimental towards the Empire. But Attlee, Bevin and Secretary of State for Commonwealth Relations Patrick Gordon Walker realized that a united Commonwealth under nominal British leadership helped to perpetuate Britain's Great Power status, in spite of growing indications of post-war decline. London also wished to incorporate Commonwealth forces into its global strategic plans, particularly in the Middle East, and maintain close economic relations to aid Britain's recovery. Moreover, the British hoped that by maintaining close relations with the New Commonwealth members, especially India, it could continue to influence events in the emerging Third World. Britain clearly had not abandoned all hope of maintaining a position of relative equality with the United States and USSR in world affairs.

Bevin, though, was wary of using the Commonwealth as a counter-weight to US influence. Since the end of the Second World War the Labour Left, including influential figures such as Minister of Health Aneurin Bevan, as well as some right-wing Conservatives, had been calling for Britain to use its global influence, specifically its connections to the Commonwealth and Western Europe, to act as a 'Third Force' between the two superpowers.[16] Despite some sympathy for the Third Force concept, Bevin's overriding focus, however, was on securing from Washington aid and military support for Europe and he was unwilling to take any measures that might jeopardize the achievement of these goals. Partly for this reason, along with its lack of faith in the utility of the organization following the breakdown of the wartime Grand Alliance, the Attlee government was generally content to follow the United States' lead in the UN and had not attempted to use its nominal leadership of the Commonwealth to challenge US dominance. Even so, prior to the Korean War some debates at the UN had strained Anglo-American relations. For example, Britain had been reluctant to support the formation of Israel and it believed that the PRC should be seated at the UN. London was also much more eager than Washington to maintain the support of the neutral members whenever possible, believing that it had a better understanding of these Arab and Asian countries than the less experienced Americans.[17]

After Britain, Australia and New Zealand were the most emotionally attached members of the Commonwealth. The Australian and New Zealand Prime Ministers, Robert Menzies and Sidney Holland, were both fervent Anglophiles and looked to Britain to provide leadership. They also recognized that Australia and New Zealand remained closely tied to Britain in a number of ways. Until the late 1940s their foreign policy bureaucracies remained under British dominance. Economically, too, the sterling area continued to be of great importance to these countries since Britain was their main trading partner. And the Australian and New Zealand armed forces were closely tied to Britain, as demonstrated by their continued commitment to defend the Middle East in a global conflict.

Yet there were limits to their Commonwealth attachment. Menzies and Holland disliked the admission of non-white Commonwealth members. Their Ministers for External Affairs, Percy Spender and Frederick Doidge, also placed greater emphasis on courting US support for a Pacific security pact than on Commonwealth loyalty. Inside the UN, then, Australia and New Zealand, recognizing they were smaller powers that could not decisively influence events, rarely sought to discuss matters with their Commonwealth partners. Instead, they tended to support US policy without raising too many questions and complaints.[18]

In comparison, since the end of the First World War Canada had displayed much greater political, economic and military independence from Britain and it did not hold the Commonwealth in as high esteem. To begin with, Canada had its own 'special' relationship with the United States, while its Francophone population, including Liberal Prime Minister Louis St Laurent, had few emotional ties to the British Empire. St Laurent's Secretary of State for External Affairs Lester Pearson also thought the Commonwealth anachronistic.

Still, the post-war Canadian government supported the Commonwealth partly because of its new multiethnic composition. St Laurent had, in fact, been instrumental in drafting the 1949 London Declaration, determined to retain Indian membership. Pearson also wished to maintain close relations with his Commonwealth colleagues since he realized that by itself Canada lacked the ability to influence global events but that it might punch above its weight by operating as part of a united Commonwealth. Pearson was particularly confident about the possibility of acting this way in the UN, where he hoped that Canada, as a middle power, could combine with other likeminded members to play a useful mediatory role between the two superpowers. Even so, with the intensification of the Cold War Canada's room for manoeuvre had lessened, and recently it had offered consistent support for US policy in the world organization.[19]

For its part, the Nationalist South African government of Prime Minister Dr Daniel Malan had little desire to promote a multiethnic 'British' Commonwealth. Since its election in 1948, the Malan government had focused on establishing the *apartheid* system. These reforms heightened existing tensions between South Africa and the other Commonwealth members, particularly India, but even Malan was not prepared to turn his back completely on the organization. During his election campaign, in a ploy to win votes from the English-speaking community, he had dropped calls to make South Africa a republic. More importantly, with Cold War tensions mounting, Malan, as a staunch anti-Communist, sought to maintain close relations with the Old Commonwealth members, especially Britain, for security reasons. In addition, the South African economy was closely linked to Britain and the Empire. Malan also found working within the Commonwealth preferable to the UN, where South Africa generally played a passive role except when its domestic policies came under attack.[20]

Unsurprisingly, the New Commonwealth members did not wish to overtly promote an organization that reminded them of their former colonial status. In fact, both Prime Ministers Jawaharlal Nehru of India and Liaquat Ali-Khan of Pakistan wished to assert their independence. Nevertheless, the governing elites in India and Pakistan retained close cultural and personal ties with Britain, respected the British liberal democratic tradition and realized that their shaky economies and precarious external security were inextricably connected to the Commonwealth. Ironically, with Kashmir a constant threat to regional stability and a source of friction within the Commonwealth since the Indo-Pakistani War following partition in 1947, India and Pakistan also used Commonwealth membership as a means for building bridges and keeping an eye on each other.

But naturally these two states approached the Commonwealth from very different perspectives. Nehru hoped to use the Commonwealth to counter-balance US dominance of the non-Communist world, increase India's global standing and promote Asian issues and his message of non-alignment. Like Pearson, he saw the UN as a particularly important venue, since here India could play a decisive mediatory role, using its Commonwealth connections and nominal leadership of the Arab-Asian neutral bloc to counterbalance the influence of the two superpowers. In stark contrast, Liaquat Ali-Khan increasingly saw Commonwealth and UN membership as a way to build closer security relations with the United States and increase Pakistan's international status vis-à-vis India. By 1950 this policy was bearing some fruit, with Washington gradually coming to view Pakistan as a vital link in its containment chain ringing the Soviet Union. Partly as a result of this development, Nehru became increasingly suspicious of the United States, fearing that the support it was giving Karachi was boosting Pakistan's position in Kashmir.[21]

* * *

On the morning of 25 June 1950, then, even before the Security Council met, a degree of inevitability existed about what would transpire. The US delegation would almost certainly take the lead in

Acid Test

Figure 3   Korea: the UN acid test.
Source: *Washington Evening Star*, 1 July 1950.

discussions and that it would press for a stiff response. What was less clear was whether US policy would meet any significant resistance. Washington's concerns on this matter focused on whether the Soviet delegation would end its boycott and return to the Security Council to block any collective action. Given the Commonwealth's past record at the UN, the Americans did not foresee this organization playing a significant role. In fact, the Truman administration took Old Commonwealth support for granted. This analysis was not surprising since previously the cleavage—based on the questions of race and differing Cold War perspectives—between the Old and New

Commonwealth members, particularly India, had prevented them from uniting. Yet the Commonwealth had the potential to constrain US policy at the UN. Because of its multiethnic composition and its liberal democratic values, the Commonwealth was held in high esteem by many UN members, particularly in Western Europe and the Third World, and could wield much moral authority at the UN. All that was needed were the correct conditions to unite its members.

CHAPTER 1

THE UN COLLECTIVE SECURITY ACTION, JUNE–OCTOBER 1950

On the night of 24–25 June 1950 frantic activity was not only taking place in Korea and Washington. That night in UN circles New York lived up to its reputation as the city that never sleeps. At approximately midnight UN Secretary-General Trygve Lie was awoken at his home by a telephone call from US Assistant Secretary of State for UN Affairs John Hickerson. In a brief and agitated conversation Hickerson informed the shocked Secretary-General of the reports Washington had received regarding the North Korean invasion and the indications that this was more than another border clash. Lie immediately requested a report from UNCOK on what had taken place. At 2 a.m. US Deputy Permanent Representative to the UN, Ernest Gross, then made a formal request for an Emergency Session of the Security Council. Realizing the gravity of the situation Lie immediately obliged, setting a meeting for 2 p.m. that day. While the Secretary-General returned to bed for a few more hours of sleepless rest, hurried phone calls were made to the missions of those member states represented on the Security Council who relayed the news to their respective governments. Even though the morning newspapers were published too early to report the outbreak of the Korean War, by daybreak word of the North Korean invasion had spread across the globe.[1]

Over the following two weeks the Security Council established the UN's first collective security action. The driving force in this process was the US government. It took the lead in formulating the various draft resolutions that were adopted while the US delegation dominated proceedings in New York. For the most part the Commonwealth members played a passive role at the UN during this opening phase of the conflict, giving their unquestioned support to US policy. India was the partial exception, only temporarily abandoning its position of neutrality to give tacit approval to the Korean action. While the Old Commonwealth members did coordinate their response to the call for military assistance, no comparable effort was made to bring about a united Commonwealth position at the UN. Furthermore, the Commonwealth members had no significant desire to constrain Washington's policy since they generally agreed with it and had no alternative suggestions to make.

The Commonwealth remained disunited because none of the necessary conditions for unity were present. To begin with, while its members saw the North Korean invasion as a threat to global peace, they strongly believed that the UN decision to intervene was a necessity and not one that would in itself lead to an escalation of the conflict. The Korean action was intended to repel aggression and throughout the first months of the conflict all the Commonwealth members except India thought it very unlikely that either the Soviet Union or China would become directly involved. The other Commonwealth members, therefore, saw no need to try to constrain US policy at the UN, especially once military fortunes improved. Nor did many opportunities exist to coordinate a united policy. Only Britain and India were members of the Security Council and they had little time to consult with each other, let alone the other Commonwealth governments. Even when a number of key Commonwealth personalities assembled for the Fifth General Assembly they preferred to support rather than challenge the US position. In addition, the Truman administration consistently showed little willingness to consult with the Commonwealth members let alone bend to their wishes. Washington considered Korea its responsibility and it would not have altered its position even if the Commonwealth had raised objections.

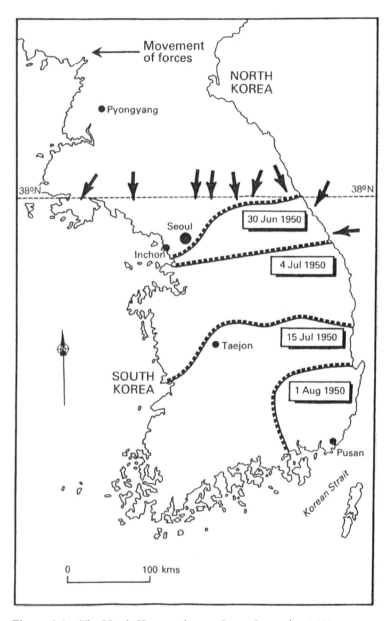

Figure 1.1 The North Korean advance, June–September 1950.
Source: MacDonald: *Korea*, p. 202.

But to understand the course of the early UN debate on Korea fully it is first necessary to set the context by outlining the military situation on the ground, relevant domestic developments in the United States and each of the Commonwealth countries, and international events connected to the Cold War during this period.

Military situation

Within days of their invasion, the NKPA had won a number of victories, capturing Seoul, against the numerically inferior ROKA that had only received light arms from the United States for fear Rhee intended to launch an assault of his own. Even the intervention of US air and sea forces on 27 June 1950, under the command of General Douglas MacArthur, Supreme Commander of the Allied Powers (SCAP) in Japan and Commander-in-Chief of US Forces in the Far East, did little to slow the North Korean advance. Three days later the US Eighth Army, under the UN banner and commanded by Lieutenant-General Walton Walker, began arriving from Japan. Bolstered by his sense of both destiny and racial superiority, MacArthur was confident that the North Koreans would be easily defeated. But over the following weeks the UN forces in Korea were overwhelmed and pushed back. The Eighth Army's ineffectiveness was the result of post-1945 cuts in the military budget which had produced an under-strength, poorly-equipped, trained and officered force. After nearly five years of occupation duties in Japan, these American soldiers were also ill prepared for combat.

Yet just as it appeared that the Eighth Army might be driven out of Korea the tide slowly began to turn. A strong defensive position was hastily established in the southeast of the country in what became known as the Pusan Perimeter. Behind this shortened line the ROKA was able to regroup while the Eighth Army was greatly strengthened by the arrival of reinforcements from the United States. The port of Pusan was also crucial in bringing in supplies from Japan. In addition, US air, naval and artillery superiority was successfully employed to interrupt the overextended North Korean supply network. Then in late August 1950 the first contributions from other

UN members arrived. Throughout the following weeks the fighting was brutal, but slowly the UN position improved as the North Korean forces tired, and many of its experienced soldiers and better equipment were lost.

The crucial turning point of the early conflict then took place in mid-September 1950. MacArthur, now Commander-in-Chief of the UN Command (UNC), had long called for an amphibious counteroffensive at Inchon near Seoul. The Department of Defense, however, opposed this suggestion on the grounds that Inchon had formidable natural and manmade defences and had treacherous tides and currents. Still, on 23 August at a meeting in Tokyo, MacArthur convinced the Joint Chiefs of Staff of the wisdom of his plan by stressing the element of surprise. On 15 September the landings took place and went spectacularly well with little resistance being encountered. A week later the US X Corps under Major-General Edward Almond moved on Seoul. Despite continued fighting Almond claimed the city's liberation three days later. Meanwhile, the UN forces, including the 27th British Commonwealth Brigade, staged a massive breakout from the Pusan Perimeter, using its air and naval forces to sever the enemy's supply lines. By the end of the month the North Korean forces had been decimated and pushed back to the 38th parallel.

The question now facing the US government was whether to pursue the enemy north over the former border. The Pentagon and the State Department had some apprehensions that this might lead to Soviet or Chinese intervention in the conflict. But intelligence estimates stated that this was very unlikely and MacArthur was tentatively granted authority to employ forces north of the 38th parallel. As a result, some ROKA units did cross the frontier but neither Washington nor Tokyo wished to employ non-Korean forces in North Korea without UN legitimization. As will be discussed in detail below, on 7 October 1950 the General Assembly then took the crucial decision allowing the UN to unify Korea by force. Before this happened MacArthur had sent a message to the North Korean Command calling on their forces to lay down their arms, cease hostilities and cooperate with the UN efforts to unify and rehabilitate

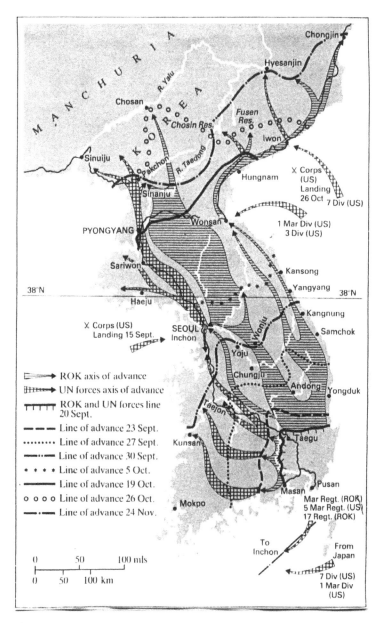

Figure 1.2   The UN Command's counter-attack, September–October 1950.
Source: Lowe: *The Origins of the Korean War*, p. 269.

Korea. Nevertheless, UN forces almost immediately crossed the 38th parallel and the enemy was quickly overrun. By late October 1950 US troops had reached the Yalu river despite Truman's explicit instructions to only use ROKA units in the frontier region. The Korean War appeared to be drawing to a close.[2]

Domestic developments

The first four months of the Korean War witnessed the most tumultuous period of Truman's presidency to date as he struggled to sell the 'police action'—as he had labelled the UN intervention in Korea, to circumvent a Congressional declaration of war—to the American people. The public's initial response to the decision to intervene in Korea had been generally enthusiastic and the majority of the population saw the conflict as a necessity to prevent Soviet aggression elsewhere. The public perception of the UN also improved dramatically with the successful establishment of the organization's first collective security action. But the popularity of the war soon declined with the early military setbacks. Criticism mounted, especially from the right wing of the Republican Party led by Senator Robert Taft of Ohio, over the government's handling of the conflict. A growing sense of uncertainty developed in Congress and the public domain as to why US soldiers were dying in a distant land of little strategic value. Moreover, the UN came under renewed attack since so few other members had contributed forces and the work of the Security Council had again become deadlocked following the return of the Soviet delegation. Nonetheless, the popularity of both the conflict and the UN radically improved following the Inchon landings and the military turnaround on the battlefield.[3]

Inside the administration, meanwhile, the Korean War created much friction. Acheson, a long-standing target of the Republican press in general, and Senator Joseph McCarthy in particular, became the butt of Grand Old Party (GOP)[4] attacks as the mid-term election campaign heated up. Truman, however, remained loyal to his most trusted adviser. Acheson's rival, Secretary of Defense Louis Johnson, however, was much more vulnerable. He was an easy scapegoat since he had aggressively overseen the military budget cuts ordered by Truman over the previous 18 months. By the middle of September Johnson's position had become untenable and Truman forced him to resign. He was replaced by General George Marshall, the former Army Chief of Staff and Secretary of State, who was particularly close to Truman.[5]

A quite different relationship existed between Truman and MacArthur. The president appointed the general to lead the UN forces in Korea due to his experience, prestige, popularity, and because he was on the spot in Tokyo. But friction between the two men surfaced in late July 1950 when MacArthur made an unauthorized visit to Taiwan to consult with Chiang Kai-shek. Truman cautioned MacArthur for acting beyond his authority but, a month later, the general publicly criticized US policy in East Asia in a written statement to the Veterans of Foreign Wars. Truman reacted angrily and demanded that MacArthur withdraw his statement. Relations then remained strained until MacArthur's military masterstroke at Inchon. Consequently, when they met for the first time at Wake Island on 15 October 1950, both men were cordial and MacArthur reassured Truman that neither the Soviet Union nor China would intervene to prevent the unification of Korea and that the war would be over by Christmas.[6]

In contrast to these US upheavals, the outbreak of the Korean War had a much less disruptive political impact in the Commonwealth countries. Generally, the Commonwealth governments, and their domestic audiences, did not believe that an act of aggression by such a small power as North Korea, looking to simply reunify the peninsula, could trigger a global conflict. Furthermore, they saw Korea principally as a US issue and they did not think it was their position to meddle too deeply. Yet in the Commonwealth countries a consensus view emerged that the Korean situation could not be ignored. Memories of appeasement were strong and the vast majority of Commonwealth governments realized that the Soviet Union lay behind the North Korean invasion. They thus agreed with the Americans that Moscow had to be taught that aggression would be resisted anywhere in the world. Support for the UN intervention, therefore, was widespread even if it led to few public outpourings of emotion. When it came to the question of sending ground troops to Korea, however, a number of prominent critics were opposed on the grounds that their countries could not afford to send soldiers to such a distant theatre. Nevertheless, post-Inchon these voices were soon hushed.[7]

Behind this moderate reaction to the Korean War was the fact that most Commonwealth governments were popular. St Laurent in Canada, Menzies in Australia and Holland in New Zealand had all been recently elected and their domestic and foreign policies enjoyed widespread support. Likewise, in India and Pakistan, Nehru and Liaquat Ali-Khan were enjoying periods of relative domestic stability and their respective leadership positions were secure. Britain and South Africa were the exceptions. In London, even though the Conservative opposition largely backed Attlee's Korean War policy, the Labour government was in a precarious position. Since the February 1950 general election it held a majority of just five seats and had become increasingly divided over Bevin's pro-American foreign policy. Unity prevailed in support of the initial UN intervention in Korea but the pre-existing fissures gradually widened following the decision to contribute British ground forces.[8] The situation in South Africa was even more tumultuous as Malan continued to push through *apartheid* legislation in spite of much internal and external opposition. More than in any other Commonwealth country, Korea remained an extremely peripheral issue for South Africa.[9]

International situation

The eruption of the Korean conflict created immense international shockwaves. Although many governments shared US fears that the North Korean invasion might be a precursor to further acts of Soviet aggression, the US reaction only heightened these anxieties. On 27 June 1950 Truman issued a controversial statement announcing that the US Navy's Seventh Fleet would be positioned in the Taiwan Strait. The President stressed that he was trying to prevent the PRC taking advantage of the situation in Korea to launch an invasion of

Taiwan. Beijing and its Soviet bloc allies reacted angrily to this decision and accused the United States of committing aggression against China. India also publicly criticized Washington, while the other Commonwealth members privately complained that the US government was confusing the Chinese and Korean situations.

In this same statement Truman announced that the United States would provide massive assistance to the State of Vietnam (a decision actually taken over a month before) and the Philippines in their efforts to quell communist insurgencies. As a result, in September 1950 the Military Assistance Advisory Group (MAAG) arrived in Vietnam, constituting the first physical US presence in that country. Soon after, the US government agreed to support France politically, logistically and financially to defeat the Viet Minh. Nonetheless, the situation in Indochina continued to deteriorate as the PRC simply increased its assistance to the insurgents and the French failed to win the support of the indigenous population.[10]

Chinese actions in Tibet also intensified the crisis in Asia. On 7 October 1950 the People's Liberation Army (PLA) invaded the region that had claimed independence since 1912. In less than two weeks Tibetan forces had surrendered and the PLA set about the 'peaceful liberation' of what Beijing claimed had for centuries been an integral part of China. This involved entering into negotiations with the Tibetan government headed by the Dalai Lama. While Lhasa had little option but to agree, they asked the UN to intervene. But the matter was quickly dropped by the Security Council as its members soon realized that nothing could be done due to the Soviet veto. Still, the invasion of Tibet concerned India. Nehru had only recently dropped his calls to make Tibet a buffer state between India and the new PRC and no longer opposed China's claim of sovereignty as long as Tibet was granted significant autonomy. He believed this policy would eliminate a possible contentious issue between New Delhi and Beijing, allowing for ever-closer relations between the two capitals. The Indian Prime Minister, therefore, was not only annoyed that Mao had failed to consult him in advance, especially as India was trying hard to champion Beijing's cause in the UN; he was also worried that India now shared borders with a potentially dangerous neighbour.

However, this point of friction was partially removed in early 1951 when the 'Seventeen Point Agreement for the Peaceful Liberation of Tibet' was signed permitting the retention of Tibet's feudal and theocratic system and the Dalai Lama to remain as leader.[11]

Establishing the collective security action

All these factors had a direct impact on the UN debate during the initial months of the Korean War. Returning to the North Korean invasion, with the emergency meeting of the Security Council set for the afternoon of 25 June 1950, the US government immediately set about formulating its policy. The State Department created a draft resolution condemning North Korea's act of aggression and calling for an immediate ceasefire and all troops to be withdrawn to the 38th parallel. Gross then discussed this proposal with a number of Security Council members. This meeting included the only two Commonwealth countries currently represented on the Security Council, Britain and India. While all present were in general agreement that the US proposal was an appropriate initial response, British Acting Permanent Representative Sir Trevor Shone and Indian Permanent Representative Sir Benegal Rau, the current President of the Security Council, questioned the use of the term 'act of aggression'. They argued that it was still unclear from the limited information available whether all blame should be attributed to North Korea.

Significantly, Gross was prepared to bow to this Commonwealth pressure and for the phrase 'act of aggression' substituted 'breach of the peace', a slightly lesser charge in the UN Charter but one that did not restrict the retaliatory action of the Security Council.[12] The British and Indian delegations accepted this concession following the arrival of an interim report from UNCOK concluding that North Korean forces had crossed the 38th parallel in large numbers without provocation. UNCOK's members also warned that a serious situation was developing which was assuming the character of a full-scale war that might endanger the maintenance of international peace and security. This evidence convinced the Indians in particular that the

UN was dealing with a clear-cut case of aggression and failure to respond would have amounted to overt approval of it.[13] So while this episode did not amount to the Commonwealth constraining US policy, it did demonstrate that Washington was sensitive to Commonwealth opinion.

A couple of hours later the Security Council met to discuss the item 'Complaint of aggression upon the Republic of Korea'. Gross took the lead, proposing that the ROK be invited to send a representative to participate in the debate as the victim of the North Korean aggression. As no objections were raised the ROK Ambassador to the United States, John Myun Chang, was seated. Gross then tabled the US draft resolution and received the wholehearted support of Shone. However, Rau remained silent and the Egyptian and Yugoslavian representatives stressed that not enough information had been received to cast judgement. At this point, Gross called for the meeting to be adjourned and a closed session was held.[14] The Egyptians were brought round but the Yugoslavian delegation had no instructions and could not vote in favour of the US proposal.[15] When the Security Council reconvened, therefore, Yugoslavia tabled a draft resolution proposing North Korea be invited to send a representative since it was the Council's duty to hear both parties in a dispute. Despite these arguments, the US draft resolution was adopted by nine votes to zero, with Yugoslavia abstaining, becoming Security Council Resolution 82 (see Appendix 1, p. 256–7). Importantly, both Britain and India backed the US proposal. The Yugoslavian draft resolution was not put to the vote.[16]

Still, this resolution had done little more than identify a breach of the peace and issue a verbal warning to North Korea. It did not constitute a collective security action. Predicting that the North Korean forces would not halt while they were in the ascendancy, Truman thus instructed his top advisers to consider what retaliatory measures the Security Council should take.[17] The consensus view that emerged in Washington was that military sanctions would have to be imposed because economic and political measures would not prevent North Korea from rapidly conquering the entire peninsula.

As a result, the State Department formulated a draft resolution recommending that members furnish such assistance to the ROK as necessary to repel the invasion and restore international peace and stability to the area.[18] This proposal was discussed first with the British. Bevin, though, was concerned that the wording of the draft resolution would compel all members to render military assistance and cause much embarrassment to those who could not provide forces.[19] Washington accepted this argument and assured the British that contributions would be voluntary. With this concession won, the Attlee government agreed to support the US draft resolution.[20]

Nevertheless, before the Security Council next met the situation was complicated by the rapid fall of Seoul and Truman's contentious statement on 27 June 1950. As well as linking Korea to other Asian issues as discussed above, the President revealed that he had already granted MacArthur authority to use air and sea forces to support the retreating ROKA without explicit UN approval, claiming that these orders had been made in the spirit of Security Council Resolution 82.[21] It was in these inauspicious circumstances that the Security Council met later that day. Undeterred, US Permanent Representative Warren Austin, returned from his holiday in Vermont, tabled the US draft resolution. The British delegation quickly indicated its support for the proposal. But Yugoslavia tabled a rival draft resolution calling on both sides to cease fire and return to the *status quo ante bellum*. What is more, the Indian and Egyptian representatives claimed that they had not received instructions from their governments and could not vote. Consequently, the US draft resolution was adopted with a minimum of seven affirmative votes, with Yugoslavia voting against, and Egypt and India not participating. It became Security Council Resolution 83 (see Appendix 2, p. 258). No vote was taken on the Yugoslavian proposal.[22]

This narrow result worried the United States and Britain, particularly because India, after supporting the initial decision to intervene in Korea and appearing to have dropped its neutral stance, had now failed to endorse military action. Washington and London saw India as a key partner in winning Asian support, while the Attlee government was also sensitive to the image of a divided

Commonwealth. Even so, with events unfolding so quickly the US and British delegations had not had time to consult with their Indian colleagues prior to the 27 June 1950 Security Council meeting, assuming Nehru had now fully committed to the idea of a collective response to the North Korean invasion. Once this postulation proved incorrect the US and British governments, through their representatives in New Delhi, made a concerted effort to win India's retroactive support for Security Council Resolution 83. Nehru revealed to US Ambassador Loy Henderson that he thought the resolution a 'natural corollary' of the initial UN action but regretted that the decision had been taken so quickly before North Korea had responded to the first resolution.[23] In response, Acheson stressed that it had been necessary to act precipitously before North Korea was victorious and presented the UN with a fait accompli.[24] British High Commissioner Archibald Nye also warned Nehru that India should not adopt a neutral policy when it came to aggression.[25] In Washington, the same arguments were presented to the Indian Ambassador, Nehru's sister Vijaya Lakshmi Pandit.[26] Under this intense Anglo-American pressure Nehru eventually announced that he 'accepted' Security Council Resolution 83 as a necessary measure, but reasserted India's neutral foreign policy.[27]

While this resolution was vital in establishing the UN's first collective security action, it failed to specify a machinery to utilize the assistance rendered. According to the UN Charter, plans for the application of armed force should be made by the Security Council with the assistance of a Military Staff Committee (MSC) composed of the chiefs of staff of the five permanent members. But negotiations to establish a MSC had been abandoned in 1948 due to disagreements between the United States and the Soviet Union. The Security Council thus had to establish an ad hoc mechanism and do so quickly seeing as the advanced elements of the Eighth Army were faring so badly. Again, the US government took the lead in this process. Recognizing that it was the only country present in the region with the resources to resist the North Korean invasion, the United States wanted to be made the operating agent of the UN action. This feeling was especially strong since US domestic support for the conflict was waning and it was felt the public would not understand if the US military did not command its own forces.[28]

When this policy was suggested to the British and French delegations they generally agreed that the United States would have to assume overall control of the military action since they could not do so. However, the French thought it important that the Security Council play a visible role by establishing a committee to coordinate offers of assistance.[29] Bevin, on the other hand, instructed the new British Permanent Representative to the UN, Sir Gladwyn Jebb, to oppose this proposal since such a committee would be composed of smaller members, giving them too much say, while the United States and the Commonwealth members would inevitably have to bear the military burden.[30] Acheson was glad of this British support and ignored France, formulating a draft resolution recommending that members make their assistance available to a unified command under the US government that would, in turn, designate a commander-in-the-field.[31] The Secretary of State was even more grateful once the British offered to co-sponsor this draft resolution, sparing Washington from having to table a proposal that bestowed so much authority upon itself.[32] The French then dropped their proposal and grudgingly followed the British lead.[33]

In spite of the anxieties caused by India's failure to vote in favour of Security Council Resolution 83, the US and British delegations again made little effort to consult their Indian counterparts on their latest proposal. The Indian delegation, for its part, made no suggestions as to how the UN force would be constituted.[34] However, Nehru made it clear to Henderson that India would not vote for a proposal that gave so much responsibility to the United States, preferring the appointment of a non-American commander who would report directly to the Security Council. The Indian Prime Minister was particularly worried that MacArthur, whom he considered far too belligerent and controversial in Asia, would be appointed the UN commander.[35] In addition, Nehru hoped that concurrent British and Indian bilateral proposals in Moscow and Beijing for an immediate ceasefire might bear fruit since Stalin and Mao had indicated they might support this course if the PRC was granted a seat at the UN. The Truman administration, though, refused to reward aggression and these peace feelers petered out.[36] Evidently, Nehru's patience was wearing thin at this time as he wrote to his sister claiming that he was already becoming weary of the Korean problem and questioning whether India had made the right decision supporting the UN action.[37]

When the Security Council met on 7 July 1950 Jebb tabled the Anglo-French draft resolution and the majority of members immediately expressed their support for it. Still, when the vote was taken the proposal was only narrowly adopted with seven affirmative votes, with India, Egypt and Yugoslavia abstaining, becoming Security Council Resolution 84 (see Appendix 3, p. 258–9). Following the vote, Austin made a long statement that the US government would accept the great responsibilities and heavy burden it was assigned.[38] The next day, it was announced that the Commander-in-Chief of the UNC would be MacArthur.[39] Security Council Resolution 84 thus marked the end point in the establishment of the Korean collective security action.

As has been seen, during the first critical fortnight of the Korean War US hegemony at the UN went relatively unchallenged. While the US and British governments conducted much discussion on policy, the latter generally accepted the will of the former. Nevertheless, Washington did demonstrate that it was sensitive to the views of its chief ally and was willing to amend the language if not the substance of its proposals. Yet the Commonwealth made very little effort to constrain US policy. Minimal communication took place between Britain and India. And when this did happen it took the form of British pressure on New Delhi to accept rather than resist US policy. Clearly in the Security Council, where the permanent members were dominant, India's position as the leading neutral power had little clout. Furthermore, the other Commonwealth members not represented in the Security Council were absent from the UN decision-making process. With events moving so fast, their representatives in Washington, London and New York were briefed on what was going on but their views were generally neither asked for nor given. These members simply offered their moral support for the decisions taken and no coordinated opposition was formed.

Implementing the collective security action

Even while the Security Council was establishing its first collective security action, thoughts in Washington turned to how the moral indignation of the vast majority of UN members at the North Korean invasion could be translated into material support. As the unified command, the US government was unsurprisingly most concerned with this matter and was determined to avoid the image that it was merely using the UN's cloak of legitimacy to pursue its own interventionist policies in Korea. The Truman administration, therefore, placed enormous political pressure on its allies to make military contributions. Due principally to the shared experience of the Second World War, where they had proved their military worth, and close political relations, forces from the Old Commonwealth members were considered most desirable.

Almost instinctively Washington appealed first to London for support, believing the other Commonwealth capitals would then follow. Despite the British Chiefs of Staff's warnings that Korea was of little strategic value, Attlee was conscious that a refusal to contribute would damage Anglo-American relations. He also realized that if North Korea was victorious the future of the UN might be at risk. As a result, he immediately placed all the Royal Navy ships in Japanese waters at the disposal of the Americans. Attlee correctly judged that this limited measure would not be opposed by the British public. The British government, as predicted by the Americans, also took it upon itself to try to extract offers of assistance from the other Commonwealth members.[40] New Zealand was first to respond, announcing it would make available two frigates.[41] Australia quickly followed suit, committing two naval vessels[42] and later adding the Royal Australian Air Force squadrons based in Japan.[43] As with the British decision, these offers were mainly made for political reasons, since both the Australian and New Zealand governments wished to nurture close relations with the United

States. St Laurent, on the other hand, was only willing to contribute if a Canadian force would be militarily useful.[44] It was only after Pearson warned that a Canadian refusal to commit would impact upon Ottawa's relations with Washington that St Laurent finally agreed to send three naval vessels.[45] Of the Old Commonwealth countries, the only negative response came from Pretoria, which argued that Korea was far beyond its sphere of interest.[46]

Washington welcomed these contributions. But State and Defense Department pressure quickly mounted for ground troop offers as the military situation deteriorated and domestic criticism of the other UN members increased. Predictably, the US government again directly targeted the Commonwealth countries, starting with Britain. Foreseeing this move, the British Cabinet had already begun considering the possibility of contributing ground forces. Attlee was very reluctant since he feared that the public and the left wing of the Labour Party would oppose sending British troops to a far-flung corner of the world at the behest of Washington. The chiefs of staff also warned the Prime Minister that no forces were available, given Britain's global commitments and problems in Malaya.[47] Nevertheless, serious divisions emerged within the Attlee government when the Americans made their formal approach. Bevin was most in favour of contributing ground forces in an effort to maintain US goodwill, especially towards NATO. But Aneurin Bevan argued in the opposite direction. After much heated debate Attlee reluctantly agreed with his trusted Foreign Secretary. The British government thus told the Americans that it could contribute a 'self-contained unit' of three infantry battalions, an armoured unit and artillery, but this would not be ready for two months.[48]

The Australian and New Zealand governments, however, announced that they would contribute ground forces at an unspecified point in the future the day before the British government made its decision public.[49] For both governments this decision had not been taken lightly. Their respective military chiefs argued that resources were limited and the Middle East rather than East Asia was held as the priority. Menzies and Holland were also concerned with the public reaction to the sending of forces to Korea. Yet Spender and

Doidge argued that contributions should be made to aid their attempts to gain US support for a Pacific security pact. Action was only taken, nevertheless, after finding out that Britain was going to make an offer without consulting them in advance.[50] This was their attempt to steal the limelight and strengthen their independent ties with the United States.

Still, neither Australia nor New Zealand had a clear idea of what their contributions would entail. Menzies told Truman while visiting Washington that he could give no indication of troop numbers and warned that it would take considerable time before the Australian contribution could be deployed. He explained that the limited permanent Australian armed forces were needed exclusively for national defence and legally any forces operating abroad had to be specifically recruited for this task. This technicality explained why the Australian troops serving as the British Commonwealth Occupation Force in Japan could not be used in Korea.[51] Similarly, Holland could say little more than that a force of approximately 1,000 New Zealand troops would be recruited to join with the British and Australian contingents at some point in the distant future.[52]

The Canadian government was more cautious still, since its military chiefs warned that all its forces were needed for the defence of North America in case of a direct Soviet attack. Like Menzies, St Laurent was also concerned that, due to Canadian legal restrictions, Parliament would have to authorize any decision to recruit a force designed solely for operations in Korea. Since Parliament was currently in summer recess a decision to recall it at short notice would be difficult and unpopular. In addition, the Prime Minister worried that the Francophone population would oppose sending Canadian forces as part of an Anglo-American coalition. Pearson, on the other hand, was sympathetic to Washington's desire to have other countries contribute forces for psychological and propaganda reasons.[53] The Secretary of State for External Affairs and Minister of National Defence Brooke Claxton thus pressed their Cabinet colleagues for a brigade to be raised specifically to fight in Korea. But the other ministers preferred to give the question more consideration.[54] Pearson then went to Washington to discuss

Canada's problems with Acheson, who strongly urged Ottawa to reconsider its position.[55] Under this pressure, the Canadian Cabinet decided on 7 August 1950 to commit a Special Field Force of 5,000 men recruited over the next six months to fight in Korea.[56]

The other Commonwealth members, however, did not succumb to US influence. The South African government stated plainly its unwillingness to contribute ground forces to a conflict of little strategic interest.[57] Even so, Pretoria did later announce that it would make available a fighter squadron.[58] Likewise, Liaquat Ali-Khan made it clear that Pakistan had no forces available, stressing it only had a small defensive force designed to deal only with its troubles with India and Afghanistan.[59] Unsurprisingly Nehru, given his lack of support for Security Council Resolution 84, also announced that India would not contribute forces, citing the same reasons as Pakistan. Even so, the Prime Minister did offer an Indian field ambulance unit, again demonstrating his general support for the UN action in Korea.

Although pleased with the Old Commonwealth response, and unsurprised by the reactions of the New Commonwealth members, the US government was greatly concerned that no additional troops would arrive in Korea for some time, especially as the Eighth Army was now pinned back behind the Pusan Perimeter. Truman was sympathetic that the British had their own troubles in Malaya but he was convinced that they could find a brigade for Korea without having to train one from scratch.[60] Consequently, Acheson stressed to Bevin the urgency of the situation and that for propaganda reasons it was better to immediately despatch any available units.[61] In mid-August 1950 the Attlee government, after much soul-searching in London, eventually agreed to send two infantry battalions from Hong Kong.[62] This decision was extremely controversial given that the security of this colony was under constant threat from the PRC.[63] The 27th British Commonwealth Brigade, therefore, arrived in Pusan on 29 August 1950. These forces constituted the first non-American troops to participate in the UN action and provided an important morale boost at the same time as the North Koreans began to tire.

In addition, the British strongly urged their Commonwealth partners to accelerate the despatch of their ground force commitments.[64] As a result, Australia agreed to send its troops by the end of September 1950.[65] But New Zealand refused to make any firm promises.[66] and Canada refused to speed up its recruitment process.[67] American pressure for the Old Commonwealth governments to hasten their commitments then lessened after the success of the Inchon landings. At the same time the Commonwealth members began to ask whether they would need to send any more troops once the defeat of North Korea appeared imminent.

Stalemate in the Security Council

Meanwhile, the members of the Security Council saw little reason to tinker with the machinery they had established throughout the remainder of July 1950, despite the deteriorating military situation in Korea. Evidently, these governments were prepared to give the UNC time to repel the North Korean aggression. Nonetheless, behind-the-scenes discussions took place concerning the humanitarian needs of the Korean people. The US delegation believed that the UN should establish a relief programme that would allow members who could not contribute militarily to offer much needed non-military assistance instead.[68] Acheson backed this plan, believing it would give the action more of a 'UN' flavour.[69] But Bevin argued that few countries were in a position to give relief assistance and full focus should be placed on the military situation until the fighting had ended.[70]

Disagreement between the Americans and British meant that discussions on relief remained in the background until the Soviet Permanent Representative, Yakov Malik, announced that he would take up the rotating Presidency of the Security Council for August 1950. Acheson was now determined to have a resolution on relief adopted before the end of July to avoid the Soviet veto. He proposed a draft resolution granting the UNC responsibility for determining relief requirements and providing this in the field along with the Secretary-General, the Economic and Social Council (ECOSOC) and the UN specialized agencies. Acheson thought this would provide a sufficient 'UN umbrella' for the programme.[71] Bevin was concerned that the relief operation had not been fully thought out[72] but Britain, France and Norway agreed to co-sponsor the proposal.[73] After a very short debate on 31 July 1950 this draft resolution was then adopted by nine votes to zero, with Yugoslavia abstaining, becoming Security Council Resolution 85 (see Appendix 4, p. 259–60).[74] India, struggling to retain its position of neutrality, remained silent throughout but voted in favour of the resolution on humanitarian grounds. The Americans and British were greatly pleased by this Indian support since they hoped this resolution would silence critics in Asia who claimed that the UN action simply masked US imperialism in Korea.

Acheson was also inspired by the news of Malik's imminent return to seek further measures against North Korea before the Soviet veto came into play. The Secretary of State formulated a draft resolution condemning Pyongyang for its continued defiance of the UN while calling upon all states to use their influence to have North Korea comply with the existing resolutions. The Soviet Union was clearly the target of this second provision.[75] However, the US delegation warned that other members, particularly India, might object to the proposal and prevent its rapid passage. As a result, Austin decided to table the draft resolution on the final day of the month so that it held priority over any Soviet proposal when the Security Council next met.[76] Bevin welcomed this ploy since he thought the US proposal added nothing of substance and was untimely given MacArthur's recent Taiwan trip.[77]

As it turned out, the US draft resolution was not discussed for the whole of August 1950. Before his first meeting as President of the Security Council, Malik tabled a provisional agenda, with the top item being Chinese representation, and retitling the Korean item 'Peaceful settlement of the Korean question'. On hearing this news, the US and British delegations met and agreed that the Chinese representation issue should not be allowed to interfere with the Korean problem and the original title for the Korean item should be retained.[78] When the Security Council met on 1 August 1950 a bitter procedural debate thus ignited between Malik, Austin and Jebb. The US and British permanent representatives dismissed the provisional agenda and demanded that the outstanding US draft resolution be discussed immediately. Malik responded that he was not obliged to include any items that had been discussed when two permanent members of the Security Council—the Soviet Union and the PRC—had not been present.[79] This squabbling continued for another two days before the US delegation tabled a motion giving priority to the original Korean item. This motion was adopted with all the members except the Soviet Union voting in its favour.[80]

Nevertheless, the procedural debate did not end there. At the next meeting Malik refused to invite a ROK representative to participate and tabled a draft resolution inviting representatives from the PRC and 'the Korean people'. Austin and Jebb immediately attacked this manoeuvre, arguing that the ROK had been invited to participate in the entire Korean debate and proposals inviting North Korea had already been rejected. The debate was then adjourned for five days.[81] The United States and Britain used this interval to consider their tactics. Acheson was determined to force Malik to rule that the decision to invite the ROK did not stand so that this ruling could be challenged. He was prepared to talk out the whole month to achieve this goal, believing that a tough stance in the Security Council was the best method to win back the American public, which was becoming disillusioned with the conflict and the UN.[82] Bevin agreed that a drawn-out procedural debate could do no harm to the collective security action since no pressing decisions had to be taken, especially now that the UNC appeared secure behind the Pusan Perimeter. But he recognized that a propaganda battle was being waged, particularly in Asia, and he did not want the US and British delegations to be seen to be taking an entirely negative position.[83]

However, Malik further complicated matters by tabling a draft resolution calling for 'US forces' in Korea to stop their 'inhuman and barbarous methods of waging war'. The US position instantly hardened with Austin publicly alluding for the first time that the Soviet Union was assisting and influencing the North Korean aggressors.[84] Acheson, moreover, decided that the Security Council debate should be used solely for propaganda purposes aimed particularly at an Asian audience.[85] Bevin now fully agreed with this course.[86] Yet Nehru was not impressed with the dilatory tactics of both the Western allies and the Soviets and wanted some kind of positive action taken.[87] Consequently, Rau suggested that a committee composed of the non-permanent members, including India, be established to consider all the proposals so far made on Korea. Rau argued that these members would be able to make a more reasoned evaluation of the problem since none of them had special interest in the future of the peninsula.[88]

Acheson was unimpressed by the committee proposal, believing that the priority was bringing about North Korea's compliance with the existing Security Council resolutions and having the proposals on the table voted upon. He felt that a committee of non-permanent members would only delay this process and that the matter had to be decided by the most interested parties.[89] Importantly, Bevin concurred with this analysis.[90] Still, Rau hoped that the United States and Soviet Union would abstain on his proposal, estimating that the six non-permanent members would definitely support his proposal leaving Britain, India's Commonwealth partner, with the crucial casting vote.[91] But Bevin was not prepared to allow Commonwealth loyalty to get in the way of his policy and he refused to vote in favour of Rau's proposal.[92] Following this response Rau was instructed to pursue his plan only if it received the positive support of the permanent members.[93] Gross was then quick to state that while a US abstention had been a possibility, voting in favour of the proposal was very unlikely.[94] Rau grudgingly abandoned his proposal, therefore, when Malik also gave an 'unfavourable' response.[95]

In the meantime, Malik, Austin and Jebb's propaganda statements in the Security Council were becoming increasingly acrimonious. While this wrangling was largely unproductive, on 17 August 1950 Austin made one statement of future importance. He suggested that a UN body be established to assist in the creation of a democratic government for a reunified Korea. He hinted that to make this possible, UN forces would have to first occupy the area north of the 38th parallel.[96] Austin's words were soon to prove prophetic. But during the final days of the Soviet presidency the Security Council descended even further into chaos as Malik introduced a number of other items not directly linked to Korea, sparking bitter procedural wrangling.[97]

When Jebb succeeded Malik as President of the Security Council in September 1950 the situation temporarily improved. Jebb's first action was to immediately invite the ROK representative to participate and this ruling was upheld with only the Soviet delegation voting against it. The members then overwhelmingly rejected the Soviet draft resolution calling for representatives of the 'Korean people' to participate in the debate. The procedural problem that had dogged the Security Council for the whole of the previous month had thus been dealt with in one day.[98] The substantive debate then finally got underway and was also dealt with surprisingly quickly. Within the space of one meeting the US draft resolution condemning North Korea was discussed and put to the vote. It gained nine affirmative votes, with India abstaining, but failed to be adopted due to the Soviet veto. A Soviet draft resolution calling for the withdrawal of all foreign forces was then firmly rejected.[99] The following day the Soviet draft resolution concerning 'barbarous acts' employed by 'US forces' only received the vote of the Soviet Union. Crucially, throughout these brief deliberations Jebb stood loyally by Austin while Rau remained quiet.[100]

After these decisions had been taken, however, the Korean debate again degenerated into a propaganda contest. The highlight of this period occurred on 18 September 1950, in the aftermath of the Inchon landings, when Austin famously accused the Soviet Union of supplying North Korea with weapons and pulled out from under his desk a Soviet-made machine-gun captured on the battlefield. In response, Malik dismissed Austin's 'evidence' claiming that Soviet machine-guns were readily available.[101] Malik then tabled a draft resolution calling upon the US government to cease its atrocities against the Korean people in an attempt to regain the initiative. But the majority of the members ruled against discussing these charges until the final day of Jebb's presidency, when the Soviet proposal was rejected by nine negative votes, with India abstaining.[102]

August and September 1950 had witnessed the pinnacle of Anglo-American cooperation during the early debates on Korea. With a live nationwide television audience of approximately 20 million viewers, Malik's scathing propaganda statements and diversionary tactics made him a hate figure across the United States. In stark contrast, the seemingly more defensive retorts made by Austin and Jebb transformed these two men into modern folk heroes. According to Secretary-General Lie, the styles of the two men perfectly complemented each other and it appeared that they were singing from the same hymn sheet throughout the debate. Austin was emotional and full of righteous indignation while Jebb had an urbane and sophisticated wit.[103] For Austin, a former senator used to making impassioned public speeches, this was a role he relished.[104] However, for Jebb, as a career diplomat used to operating behind the scenes, this was something he found rather uncomfortable.[105] But there was a cost to this unity. India was increasingly marginalized as its attempts to play the role of mediator were shunned by both sides and the British showed little concern for its Commonwealth partner.

The Fifth Session of the General Assembly

With the Security Council deadlocked, American and Commonwealth thoughts soon turned to the Fifth Session of the General Assembly due to commence in mid-September 1950. The US government saw this as an opportunity to reclaim the initiative in the Korean debate, since it was confident it could dominate the General Assembly where it normally had the support of the Western, Latin American and many nominally 'neutral' members. In comparison, the Soviet bloc consisted of just five members and did not have the benefit of the Soviet veto. The opening of the Fifth Session of the General Assembly was also very significant for the Commonwealth since now all its members could take a direct role in formulating UN policy for the first time. Whether the Commonwealth would take advantage of this fact, though, to unite and attempt to constrain US policy, remained to be seen.

Before the opening of the General Assembly discussions between the US and Commonwealth delegations in preparation for the Korean debate were limited. The first effort to coordinate policy took place in late August 1950 between the US, British and Canadian delegations. But the representatives of the first two countries had very little to say as they remained preoccupied with the propaganda battle in the Security Council.[106] Then when Acheson, Bevin and French Foreign Minister Robert Schuman met in New York just days before the Fifth Session commenced they did not discuss Korea and it was left to their delegations to work out policy on this subject.[107] It was only after the Inchon landings that discussions really got going.

With military victory now a real possibility the crucial question was how could the UN achieve its long-standing political objective of establishing 'an independent, democratic and unified Korea'.[108] The US delegation, headed by Acheson, had in mind a resolution recommending the creation of a UN commission to supersede UNCOK to bring about the UN's political objectives through elections and establish a programme of relief and rehabilitation.[109] But Acheson, on the advice of John Foster Dulles, currently a bipartisan Republican Special Consultant in the State Department, insisted that this commission could only be effective if UN forces were permitted to cross the 38th parallel and occupy the whole of the peninsula. The problem was finding a suitable provision permitting this action that would win widespread support since the Security Council resolutions had only called for North Korean forces to be repelled, not destroyed, and an offensive north of the 38th parallel risked Soviet and Chinese intervention.[110]

It was the British delegation, under Bevin's leadership, that found the means to permit this action. Equally buoyant after the military successes, the British were eager to align with US policy and to find a lasting answer to the distracting Korean question.[111] Bevin's draft resolution added to the US proposal by naming the new body to be established the UN Commission for the Unification and Rehabilitation of Korea (UNCURK). More importantly, it added a provision recommending that 'all appropriate steps be taken to ensure conditions of stability throughout Korea'. While appearing innocuous within this long and detailed draft resolution, this short phrase implicitly permitted the crossing of the 38th parallel. The US delegation jumped at this suggestion.[112]

With US support attained, Bevin set about convincing his Commonwealth partners to co-sponsor the draft resolution, realizing that it would be embarrassing for the Americans to table such a far-reaching proposal. Yet the initial reaction of the Commonwealth members was ambiguous. The New Zealand and South African delegations readily supported the proposal but were wary of becoming directly involved in a Korean settlement and would not act as co-sponsors. The Canadian delegation headed by Pearson was even more cautious, fearing that if UN forces crossed the 38th parallel the Soviet Union and China might intervene to secure their borders.[113] Still, under pressure from Acheson and Bevin, Pearson agreed to support, but not co-sponsor, the British draft resolution.[114] In contrast, the Australian delegation, led by Spender, with a Pacific pact as ever in mind, eagerly agreed to co-sponsor the proposal.[115] Equally keen to court US friendship, the Pakistani delegation made the same commitment.

The only Commonwealth member that adamantly opposed the British draft resolution was India. Realizing this fact, Bevin wrote a personal message to Nehru stressing the necessity to occupy North Korea to fulfil the UN's political objectives.[116] Nevertheless, Nehru replied that he opposed crossing the 38th parallel since this went beyond repelling aggression. He proposed instead a draft resolution recommending that North Korea immediately cease hostilities and declaring that the UN's political objectives should be achieved through all-Korea elections under UN auspices.[117] At the root of Nehru's attempt to find a compromise solution was the warning he had received through the Indian Ambassador in Beijing, K.M. Panikkar, from Chinese Premier Zhou En-lai stating that the PRC would intervene in Korea if UN forces entered the area contiguous to the Chinese border. Zhou En-lai stressed that Beijing could not accept hostile US forces on its doorstep. Nehru firmly believed that these words had to be taken at face value.[118]

While Bevin argued with Nehru that China would not dare attack a UN force,[119] clearly the Commonwealth members were affected by the Indian warning. Bevin suggested that the US delegation make a statement reassuring the Chinese that the UNC had no hostile intentions and the British delegation would then propose inviting a Chinese representative to New York to explain Beijing's concerns.[120] And Pearson recommended that a second resolution be tabled calling for North Korea to surrender before the 38th parallel was actually crossed.[121] Yet Acheson opposed both these measures on the grounds that they would create delay, allowing North Korean forces to regroup, and thus put UN soldiers' lives at risk and endanger Korean unification. He also dismissed the Chinese threat of intervention as a 'bluff', believing MacArthur and US intelligence estimates over the reports of Panikkar, whom he saw as sympathetic towards communism. Moreover, Acheson insisted that military plans were already in place and it would be impossible to halt them now. As a result, Bevin and Pearson hurriedly dropped their proposals.[122]

The only question that still needed to be settled, therefore, was the composition of UNCURK. Acheson believed that none of the permanent members of the Security Council should be represented or else the Commission would be unworkable. He also felt that India should not be a member since the ROK would oppose its inclusion.[123] Bevin agreed with the first point but thought it essential that UNCURK have the strongest possible Asian representation, including India.[124] Pearson concurred with Bevin and was opposed to US suggestions that Canada be a member if India was not included.[125] Still, a crisis between the US and Commonwealth delegations was avoided when Nehru announced that India was unwilling to serve on UNCURK since he was against crossing the 38th parallel.[126] The US and other Commonwealth delegations thus persuaded Pakistan to serve in India's stead while Australia, at the insistence of Spender, was granted membership ahead of Canada.[127] In the end, the seven members of UNCURK were Australia, Chile, the Netherlands, Pakistan, the Philippines, Thailand and Turkey.

In the meantime, the 'Problem of the independence of Korea' item came up on the agenda of the First Committee, the General Assembly committee composed of all member states and devoted to political and security questions. British Minister of State Kenneth Younger took the lead and tabled the draft resolution, which now had eight sponsors: Britain, Australia, Brazil, Cuba, the Netherlands, Norway, Pakistan and the Philippines. Interestingly, when outlining the draft resolution, Younger concentrated on the provisions regarding UNCURK and Austin took up the point regarding crossing the 38th parallel. The US Permanent Representative stated that since 25 June 1950 this line had become 'imaginary' and North Korea should not be given sanctuary behind it. Instead, UN forces should be permitted to bring about the unification of Korea.[128] Over the following days the Old Commonwealth members then stated their support for the Eight-Power draft resolution. In retaliation, the Soviet bloc tabled a rival proposal recommending an immediate ceasefire; the withdrawal of all foreign forces; and all-Korea elections under UN supervision to bring about unification. This was clearly designed to win the support of the neutral bloc and was partially effective since Rau, seeking to act as a mediator, informally suggested that the General Assembly establish a sub-committee to try to find a compromise between these two draft resolutions.[129]

The US and Old Commonwealth delegations gave an entirely negative response to this suggestion, however, arguing that the two proposals were incompatible. But the Indian Permanent Representative remained unperturbed and formally tabled a draft resolution embodying his proposal. The US and Old Commonwealth delegations remained solid though and, while publicly expressing appreciation for the Indian effort to bring about reconciliation, argued that it would create delay and no compromise could be found. In consequence, the Indian draft resolution was narrowly rejected by 32 votes to 24 with three abstentions. Notably, the US and other Commonwealth delegations all voted against this proposal but the Soviet bloc and most Arab-Asian members supported it. The Soviet bloc draft resolution was then decisively defeated, with only the five sponsors voting in its favour. Finally, the Eight-Power draft resolution was overwhelmingly approved with only the Soviet bloc voting against it. In an effort to remain neutral India abstained on both these proposals.[130] The Eight-Power draft resolution became General Assembly Resolution 376 (V) (see Appendix 5, p. 260–3).[131]

On the same day the PRC launched its invasion of Tibet, demonstrating that Beijing was prepared to use force to achieve its goals. But this warning did little to alter the course of events at the UN or in Korea. Within a matter of days UN forces had flooded across the 38th parallel and North Korea was quickly overrun, leading MacArthur to conclude that the war would be over by Christmas. As a result, attention in New York shifted to the course of action to be taken once victory had been achieved in Korea. The Interim Committee of UNCURK tentatively considered how to bring about a political settlement while the ECOSOC considered the relief and rehabilitation programme. These discussions eventually led to the establishment of the UN Korean Reconstruction Agency (UNKRA).[132] Obviously very few members expected that the work of these two subsidiary organs would be put on hold indefinitely, as the worst crisis of the early Cold War period was about to begin.

Conclusion

Throughout the early months of the Korean War the Old Commonwealth members played little more than a supporting role to the hegemonic United States at the UN. During the initial crisis following the North Korean invasion some minor tactical disagreements emerged between the US and British delegations but no major strategic rifts occurred concerning overall policy. Publicly in the Security Council, this bond went even further as Austin and Jebb worked closely to undermine the Soviet Union. The Old Commonwealth members also demonstrated their support for US policy by committing military forces to the collective action in Korea despite their own military limitations. Furthermore, at the Fifth General Assembly the Old Commonwealth members whole-heartedly backed American plans to unite Korea by force. Only India bucked this trend. Despite having initially supported the UN response, Nehru was prepared to upset Washington if this was necessary to maintain India's neutrality and prevent China's intervention in the conflict.

The Commonwealth members failed to unite in opposition to US policy because all the necessary conditions were absent. The need to act through the UN to halt the North Korean aggression was accepted by all and the Commonwealth had few concerns that the US policy at the UN would lead to an escalation of the conflict beyond Korea. Apart from Nehru, the key Commonwealth personalities, especially Bevin, Pearson and Spender, also saw an opportunity at the UN and by providing military forces to build closer ties with the United States. They did not, therefore, have any desire to attempt to constrain US policy since this could only lead to a souring of relations. In addition, with the early crucial UN decisions being taken in the Security Council the Commonwealth members were unable to come together and act as a voting bloc. And even when the debate shifted to the General Assembly where all the Commonwealth members were represented and many of the key personalities, such as Bevin and Pearson, were present, there was little desire to coordinate policy. Finally, if the Commonwealth had opposed US policy it was very unlikely that Washington would have altered its position. The Truman administration was determined to take a hard line due to a combination of domestic and international factors and only consulted the Commonwealth members when absolutely necessary. In these circumstances, the most the Commonwealth members could hope to achieve was to moderate the language of the proposals put forward by the United States.

CHAPTER 2

BRANDING AN AGGRESSOR, OCTOBER 1950–JANUARY 1951

China's intervention in the Korean War in late October 1950 precipitated the biggest crisis of the early Cold War period. Because of its importance, historians have lavished enormous attention on both the Truman administration's political and military responses and the diplomatic manoeuvring that occurred inside the UN.[1] But they have largely overlooked the role played by the Commonwealth. This is a significant gap, for during this crisis the Commonwealth not only challenged US hegemony at the world organization but also directly influenced UN actions. From late November 1950 onwards Washington was determined to have the PRC branded an aggressor and for the UN to take retaliatory action in an attempt to force the Chinese out of Korea. However, for almost two months the Commonwealth was able to constrain US policy at the UN, allowing cooler heads within the Truman administration to prevail, despite the rapidly deteriorating military situation and the American public's ire. This was the first instance of the Commonwealth coming together in such a way since the inception of the UN.

Essential to the Commonwealth's success was the unity of its members as all the conditions necessary to produce this were present. To begin with, the Commonwealth capitals shared the fear that the policy being pursued by Washington at the UN risked escalating the Korean War into a global conflict. Unlike in the earlier phase of the conflict the key Commonwealth personalities were also now prepared to exercise their influence and coordinate a position in opposition to the United States. The fact that a series of coincidences brought the Commonwealth members together both in New York and in London made this possible. Working in such close proximity the Commonwealth representatives could hold frank discussions that were impractical through normal diplomatic channels. In addition, throughout this period the US government showed a surprising willingness to heed Commonwealth pressure at the UN if this meant it would eventually garner unanimous Commonwealth support. Washington also cleverly utilized the delay in New York created by the Commonwealth response to dampen calls for extreme military retaliation from both within and outside the administration. Nonetheless, after these conditions were removed, the majority of Commonwealth members put their other allegiances ahead of Commonwealth loyalty and supported the US position, albeit in a diluted form. Crucially, this episode demonstrated that no single Commonwealth country, not even Britain, had sufficient influence to constrain US policy. But as a unit the Commonwealth wielded considerable moral authority, not to mention influence, in Washington and New York.

The calamitous debate at the UN over Korea was symptomatic of a larger crisis during the winter of 1950–51. To understand exactly why the Commonwealth united to constrain US policy and why Washington reacted in the way it did, knowledge of the military, domestic and international contexts is first needed.

Military situation

On 25 October 1950 Chinese forces launched their limited First Phase Offensive in Korea. Although this action came as a complete shock to the UNC, which had estimated that the fledgling, weak and divided PRC would not risk conflict with technologically superior forces, the Chinese decision to intervene had been a long time in the making. Mao had considered sending troops into Korea since the outbreak of the conflict for a number of reasons. Firstly, he saw intervention in Korea as necessary to prevent China's principal external foe, the United States, becoming a hostile neighbour. He also saw Korea as an opportunity to employ his 'people's war' military methods and demonstrate the PRC's strength, speed up the revolution at home and abroad and inflict a serious blow upon the United States, especially after Washington had frustrated his plans to invade Taiwan. Yet Mao was only willing to intervene with Soviet moral and material support. A series of complicated exchanges between Mao, Zhou En-lai and Stalin followed. Mao tried to appear cautious and reluctant to intervene but appealed for backing and stressed the need to prevent the defeat of North Korea. Stalin, refusing to enter the conflict on behalf of North Korea due to the risk of direct combat with the United States, urged the PRC to send forces but procrastinated on whether to supply the arms requested. The Soviet leader evidently did not want to strengthen Mao's hand too much. Eventually, however, Stalin agreed to provide limited assistance even though he later reneged on his promise to provide Soviet air support for the Chinese invasion. In spite of this setback Mao surged ahead with his plan and Stalin did eventually provide Soviet aircraft for use in the border areas.[2]

Large numbers of Chinese forces marching under the banner of the Chinese People's Volunteer Army (CPVA), commanded by General Peng Dehuai, then began passing into North Korea undetected on 15 October 1950, under the cover of darkness. These forces first targeted ROKA positions ten days later before encountering UN forces on 1 November 1950, pushing them south. However, just as quickly as they had appeared, the Chinese forces retreated into the mountains leading MacArthur to conclude that the new enemy had limited objectives and numbered only 30,000 troops. As a result, MacArthur refused to alter his plans to complete the unification of Korea by force. Importantly, Washington continued to give the UN Commander overwhelming support since it was determined to see Korea unified and to not appear to be appeasing the PRC. The UN 'end-the-war' offensive, therefore, was launched on 24 November 1950.[3]

What MacArthur did not realize was that the Chinese Second Phase Offensive, composed of some 200,000 troops, had commenced simultaneously. The two offensives met head on with the CPVA coming out on top over the unsuspecting UN forces. Consequently, MacArthur famously concluded that 'we face an entirely new war' and immediately ordered the retreat. This withdrawal took place in disarray over the following weeks even though contact with the enemy was quickly lost.[4] At the same time, MacArthur put pressure on Washington to authorize retaliatory action against the PRC, such as the bombing of military bases in Manchuria and the bridges crossing the Yalu river, and even hinting at the use of atomic weapons. By mid-December 1950 the Chinese advance had halted at the 38th parallel. But any thoughts that Beijing had achieved its objective were quickly dashed with the launching of the Chinese Third Phase Offensive on New Year's Eve. The UN forces again retreated in a state of confusion leaving Seoul to be recaptured with little resistance.

In this atmosphere, MacArthur stepped up his demands and recommended that UN forces be withdrawn from the peninsula as rapidly as it was tactically feasible to do so. Clearly, the general had it in mind to then drop atomic bombs on China. The US public and Congress also widely called for such a strategy. Still, the Truman administration, determined to limit the war to Korea, refused to authorize such action even though serious discussions did take place in Washington regarding the possible tactical use of nuclear weapons. This course was only eventually dismissed due to the lack of suitable targets, costs and the fear of alienating allied and Asian opinion.[5] Furthermore, the Chinese offensive soon petered out south of the capital as its forces outran their supply lines. The new commander of the US Eighth Army, Lieutenant-General Matthew Ridgway, replacing Lieutenant-General Walton Walker, who had been killed in an automobile accident, seized upon this opportunity. Ridgway had been chosen for this command by MacArthur and was given much freedom of action. He used this license to launch Operation Thunderbolt, an effective defensive move taking advantage of the UNC's aerial and artillery advantage to inflict heavy losses on the Communist forces. He also, with great personal zeal, quickly set about restoring the confidence of the battered UN forces by

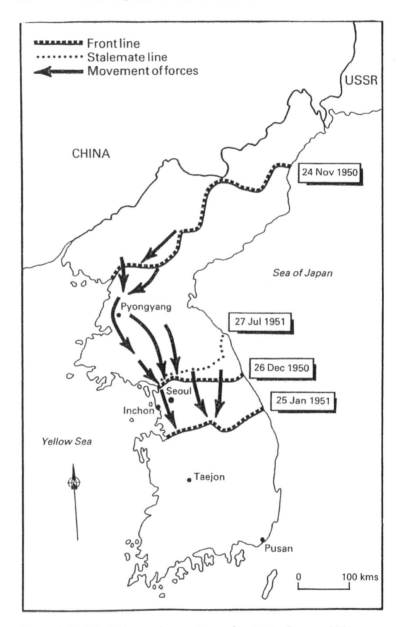

Figure 2.1   The Chinese advance, November 1950–January 1951.
Source: MacDonald: *Korea*, p. 214.

reorganizing the command structure and demanding much from his officers and troops. By 19 January 1951 the Army and Air Force Chiefs of Staff, Generals J. Lawton Collins and Hoyt Vandenberg, returning from a tour of the Korean front, reported that evacuation need no longer be considered. The Chinese advance halted a week later.

Domestic developments

In the United States the domestic situation following Chinese intervention was highly fraught. On 7 November 1950, the concerns of the public with this development were made abundantly clear in the mid-term elections. In the House of Representatives, the Democrat Party lost 28 seats and saw its majority cut to just 36. In the Senate, the Democrats fared even worse with the Republican Party gaining five seats, leaving them with a majority of just two. Evidently, the popularity of Truman was in freefall with a large section of the US population now opposed to the Korean War. The Chinese Second Phase Offensive made this situation even worse since grave fears emerged that the UN forces might be defeated and that a global conflict was imminent. On 30 November 1950 Truman further increased these worries when, in a press conference, he infamously made an off-the-cuff comment that the use of atomic weapons was under constant consideration and that the commander-in-the-field would decide what weapons would be employed. The domestic situation did then improve slightly in late December 1950 as the fighting in Korea temporarily stabilized at the 38th parallel. However, the Chinese New Year's Eve offensive brought on the greatest wave of panic, which lasted until the last week of January 1951.

Throughout this crisis the Truman administration struggled to sell the Korean War. Surprisingly, the President and his advisers remained quiet during the first fortnight following massive Chinese intervention, except for his disastrous press conference. The US government adopted this policy because it was wary of stirring up public calls for direct action against the PRC and the Soviet Union.

But finally Truman declared a state of national emergency on 15 December 1950, essentially outlining the administration's new Cold War strategy embodied in the paper NSC-68. The President stated that the United States was under threat from the Soviet Union and for the first time openly accused Moscow of being behind the Korean War. Truman announced that in response the US defence budget would be massively increased, its armed forces would be doubled in size and the production of equipment would be rapidly accelerated. He warned that these steps would necessarily involve increased taxation, but the US public generally accepted this fact given the apparent Communist threat. Even so, discontent with the conduct of the Korean War continued to mount.[6]

Despite these efforts, the Republican Right in the Senate went on the offensive, criticizing all aspects of Truman's interventionist foreign policy and massive rearmament programme in what became known as the 'Great Debate'. The President triggered this controversy when he announced that the United States would send an additional four army divisions to Europe without consulting Congress. The Republican Right responded by tabling two bills. One bill stated that Congressional authorization was needed to send troops to serve under NATO. The other bill stated that Congressional authorization was needed to send troops abroad during peacetime. In response, Democrat and Republican internationalist senators, as well as Truman and his advisers, vociferously defended the need to send additional forces to Europe and the President's right to do so. After three months of bitter wrangling, the Senate decided to support Truman's decision but the President was obligated to go back to Congress if he wanted more troops and on the condition that the European members provided the majority of NATO's forces.[7]

Troubles within the Truman administration also intensified as civil–military relations disintegrated. MacArthur became increasingly frustrated as his repeated requests to take more drastic measures were refused. In consequence, the general made a number of public statements criticizing the limited war strategy being pursued by Washington and hinting at the need to take the fight to China. On 6 December 1950 Truman tried to nip these comments in the bud by ordering all officials to consult with the State Department before making any public statements on military or foreign policy matters. Yet MacArthur became ever more outspoken and his insolence went unchallenged. Once Ridgway began to enjoy military successes this problem became even more pronounced, since the Pentagon increasingly consulted with him directly, pushing MacArthur further to the sidelines.[8]

The news of the Chinese intervention also set alarm bells ringing in all the Commonwealth countries. Widespread anger was aimed towards Beijing as well as Moscow.[9] But a degree of sympathy for the Chinese initially existed as many Commonwealth politicians thought that China had intervened solely to safeguard its borders and the hydroelectric power stations on the Yalu river that supplied much of Manchuria. Instead, considerable opposition to the unified command's conduct of the war soon emerged. In India, condemnation was focused squarely on Washington for ignoring its warnings. The public in the Old Commonwealth countries also criticized the United States but focused their attacks on their own governments for being complicit in the decision to cross the 38th parallel. These feelings grew in intensity with the military collapse in late November 1950. Now it was clear that the Chinese were in Korea for more than defensive purposes, grave fears were kindled that the United States would extend the conflict to China forcing the Soviet Union to enter the conflict under the terms of the Sino-Soviet Treaty. Truman's gaffe regarding the use of atomic weapons then exponentially heightened these worries. Throughout the winter crisis, therefore, public demands were placed on the Commonwealth governments to do everything in their power to prevent escalation.[10]

Yet domestic developments in the Commonwealth countries were not so closely tied to events in Korea as they were in the United States. Korea was a major issue but other events were also of great importance to each Commonwealth country. In South Africa, the establishment of the *apartheid* system remained the priority. In New Zealand, Holland sought to bring about the abolition of the Legislative Council, the second parliamentary chamber. In Australia, Menzies tried in vain to bring about the dissolution of both Houses of

Parliament so that elections could be held in the Senate to overcome the Labor Party majority there. And in India, Nehru's thoughts were increasingly dominated by a famine caused by flooding during the previous monsoon season. It was only in Britain that the news of Chinese intervention threatened the stability of the government. Attlee himself was greatly worried by developments in Korea but he also faced the most serious challenge to his position as Prime Minster when 76 Labour Members of Parliament threatened to withdraw their support for the government if US policy in Korea led to an escalation of the conflict. Consequently, the British government had to exercise whatever influence it had over the US government or face collapse.[11]

International relations

Widespread concern erupted in Washington and the Commonwealth capitals following Chinese intervention in Korea that the Soviet Union would take advantage of the fact large numbers of Western forces were pinned down in East Asia to make gains in Europe. This triggered a radical reassessment of NATO. Many of its members were deeply disappointed with the development of the organization since its establishment in 1949. A year on, NATO continued to lack a command structure, only two divisions of US combat troops had been made available, no specific forces had been raised by the European members and its members were divided over allowing West Germany to rearm. It was clear to the Western European members, and particularly to Bevin, who had been the driving force behind its creation, that NATO was at present not a true deterrent to Soviet expansion, since Moscow enjoyed a massive conventional military advantage. Containment could thus only be achieved if the United States agreed to play a greater role.[12]

The Truman administration, under strong domestic pressure for fiscal prudence, had been reluctant to step up its commitment to NATO prior to the Chinese intervention. But its reactions were swift following the events in Korea and the adoption of NSC-68. In December 1950 Truman appointed General Dwight Eisenhower the first Supreme Allied Commander in Europe (SACEUR). Eisenhower then immediately set about establishing an integrated military structure for NATO and called for four more US army divisions. Truman controversially fulfilled this request, triggering the Great Debate. In return, the European members agreed to step up their own contributions, massively increasing defence spending in spite of the obvious economic strain this had on their still brittle economies. These countries also tentatively accepted the eventual rearmament of West Germany although French Prime Minister René Pleven proposed the creation of a European Defence Community (EDC), a pan-European military force, instead of Bonn joining NATO as an equal member. Moreover, of the European members of NATO, Britain continued to hold a privileged position as Field Marshall Bernard Montgomery was appointed Eisenhower's deputy and Britain was given a key role in the command structure.

In addition, the Chinese intervention in Korea sparked major concerns in the West that Beijing might become more directly involved in Southeast Asia. In Vietnam in January 1951 these fears appeared to be becoming a reality when the Viet Minh launched a massive offensive in an attempt to take Hanoi. Nonetheless, the previous month General Jean de Lattre de Tassigny had been appointed the French commander and he had immediately set about building a strong defensive line around the city. As a result, when the Viet Minh attacked 20 miles from the city they were defeated.[13] Likewise, the Briggs Plan appeared to be having little impact in Malaya. While much of the Chinese population came to accept the better facilities and protection provided in the New Villages, the MNLA's campaign of violence continued and intensified.[14]

The Security Council response

It was not until 6 November 1950, over a week after first contact had been made, that the Security Council received a special report from MacArthur revealing limited Chinese intervention in Korea.[15] Nonetheless, the US response at the UN to this news showed an unexpected level of moderation, especially since Acheson privately considered that China's actions amounted to aggression.[16] The Secretary of State formulated a draft resolution that simply called on the Chinese forces to cease their activities in Korea and withdraw to allow the UNC to complete the unification of the peninsula. This proposal also emphasized that the UN had no aggressive intent toward China and would withdraw as soon as conditions for international peace and stability had been restored.[17]

The British delegation agreed that while the Chinese intervention was limited and the risk of escalation remained minimal there was no need to take more serious action. Britain, therefore, co-sponsored the US draft resolution along with four other members of the Security Council. But divergence between the Commonwealth members and the United States had already begun to surface. Jebb, with the support of Rau, insisted that as a preliminary measure the PRC should be invited to send a representative to clarify China's objectives in Korea. Behind this request was the belief held by many of the Commonwealth governments that China had intervened solely to protect her interests in the border zone. Implicit in this conclusion was a sense that the United States was in some way responsible for the alarming turn of events in Korea. Acheson was aware of these sentiments and was thus opposed to inviting a Chinese representative to the Security Council in case this led to US embarrassment. Still, he was sensitive to Commonwealth wishes and the US delegation abstained on the British draft resolution, which was adopted with the support even of the Soviet Union, becoming Security Council Resolution 88 (see Appendix 6, p. 263–4).[18]

Even so, Zhou En-lai swiftly rebuffed this Anglo-Indian overture and announced that the Chinese representative visiting the Security Council in late November 1950 to discuss the Taiwan question would not be authorized to speak on Korea.[19] This response greatly alarmed the Commonwealth members. Nehru was resigned to the fact his fears that the war might spread beyond Korea were being realized and had no suggestions to make in the Security Council.[20] Bevin shared these worries, believing that Beijing was planning a large-scale invasion of Korea. But he thought he could head this off by proposing to the United States the creation of a buffer zone south of the Korean–Chinese border that would be supervised by the UN.[21] The Foreign Secretary hoped this would avoid a costly war without having to make any significant territorial or political concessions to the PRC.[22] Acheson, however, was opposed to taking any action that would hinder MacArthur's forthcoming 'end-the-war' offensive.[23] Bevin grudgingly backed down, but this episode demonstrated that he was already more willing than Acheson to placate Beijing, which was hardly surprising given that Britain wanted to establish diplomatic relations with the PRC, had strong economic interests in China and was concerned with Hong Kong's precarious position.[24]

These divergent positions came to the fore, however, when MacArthur reported massive Chinese intervention. The Truman administration's reaction in the UN to this news was emphatic as Acheson was determined to 'uncloak' Chinese aggression.[25] Austin openly accused the Chinese Communists of committing aggression in Korea and pressed for an immediate vote on the outstanding Six-Power draft resolution.[26] Nevertheless, Bevin was concerned with the speed of events and feared that were this moderate proposal rejected by Beijing, then the US government would press for a much harsher draft resolution.[27] The British delegation, despite these worries, voted with eight other members of the Security Council in favour of the Six-Power draft resolution though its adoption was blocked by the Soviet veto. Interestingly, India remained quiet in the short debate and abstained in the vote.[28]

Transfer to the General Assembly

This vote made it plain to everyone that the Security Council would not be able to respond to the Chinese intervention. As a result, the US government transferred the debate to the General Assembly by tabling the item 'Intervention of the Central People's Government of the People's Republic of China in Korea'.[29] This action was made possible under the terms of the 'Uniting for Peace' Resolution adopted a month earlier in response to the deadlock in the Security Council following the return of the Soviet delegation. The Truman administration had decided that such a situation had to be avoided in the future and so it had presented this wide-ranging proposal, including the provision that if the Security Council failed to exercise its primary responsibility for the maintenance of international peace and security due to a lack of unanimity among the permanent members, the General Assembly would immediately consider the matter and make recommendations.[30]

Crucially, by transferring the Korean item to the General Assembly all the Commonwealth members were again brought into play. But rather than meekly following the US lead, as they had done in September–October, this time the Commonwealth swiftly united in an attempt to constrain US policy and prevent the General Assembly from taking precipitate action. What brought the Commonwealth states together was their shared fear that a US effort to brand China an aggressor would result in the implementation of the UN Charter's collective security provisions and escalate the conflict. From the Commonwealth perspective, such an outcome would be utterly disastrous. Although the various members had different global strategic priorities, none relished the prospect of a wider war. India and Pakistan, for instance, feared that another global conflagration would create both external and internal threats to their recently won independence. Australia and New Zealand thought that such a war would leave them further isolated in the Pacific region. Canada felt more secure due to her proximity to the United States but was unwilling to increase its military spending or deploy large numbers of troops overseas unless this was absolutely essential. And in London, Attlee's government thought that any collective security measures against the PRC would divert resources away from Europe, trigger Chinese retaliatory action against Hong Kong and Southeast Asia and drag the Soviet Union into the fight. The Attlee government was acutely aware that Britain, due to its proximity and Soviet technical limitations, would likely be Moscow's primary nuclear target in a global conflict.

Determined to restrain the United States, the Commonwealth states employed various techniques. Initially, the Indian and British delegations sought to find out through General Wu Hsiu-chuan, the Chinese representative who had recently arrived in New York to discuss Taiwan, whether Beijing had intervened in Korea for aggressive purposes or simply to defend its borders. But when he addressed the Security Council, Wu gave no indication of flexibility, claimed that the Chinese soldiers in Korea were volunteers and stated that the only peaceful solution to the Korean problem was the withdrawal of all US forces from East Asia.[31] When Jebb then managed to meet him privately, the Chinese representative remained intransigent and simply reiterated these points.[32] Meanwhile, Rau was scarcely more effective. Though he got to see Wu on a number of occasions, taking advantage of India's favourable relations with the PRC, Rau was given no indication that China would support a cease-fire.[33] Gross later revealed that the joke at the UN at the time was 'that Rau Wued and Wu Raued'.[34]

Stymied here, the Commonwealth players switched their attention to the Truman administration. In early December, in the wake of Truman's press conference comments regarding the use of atomic weapons, Attlee flew to Washington to meet with the President. The British Prime Minister was alarmed by the apparent shift in US thinking and made the snap decision to embark on this trip after facing a barrage of questions in the House of Commons and to stave off the mounting backbench rebellion.[35] In addition, before leaving Attlee consulted with the other Commonwealth members and a number of Western European governments, including French Prime Minister René Pleven. He discovered that British fears were widespread, especially regarding the impact the use of atomic weapons would have on European security and Asian opinion towards the West. Nonetheless, once in Washington Attlee was unable to convince Truman to agree to an immediate ceasefire at the 38th parallel, let alone a commitment to discuss other East Asian issues such as China's admission to the UN or the future of Taiwan after the fighting had ended. Instead, the two leaders simply agreed to back in the General Assembly the Six-Power draft resolution that had been vetoed by the Soviet Union in the Security Council. The only vague concessions Truman did make were at his last meeting with Attlee when he agreed that the US government would seek to limit the conflict to Korea, not to abandon the peninsula unless forced out and to try to consult with Britain before using atomic weapons. Important to these allowances was the report written by General Collins on his return from Tokyo claiming that the situation was not as dire as MacArthur had indicated.[36]

The focus then shifted back to New York where the plan agreed to by Truman and Attlee was put in place. Austin tabled the Six-Power draft resolution and the British delegation gave it a ringing endorsement.[37] But behind-the-scenes the Heads of the Commonwealth delegations were decidedly unimpressed with this stance. Meeting on 6 December 1950, they concluded that the Six-Power draft resolution was outdated, divisive and would inevitably be rejected by the PRC. The Commonwealth representatives feared that in such circumstances the United States would press for an aggressor resolution, with all that this entailed. The Commonwealth members thus launched their most important diplomatic gambit. They agreed to formulate a rival resolution calling for a ceasefire now that military contact with the enemy had been lost.[38]

A number of efforts were made to produce an acceptable proposal. To start with, Bevin called for a resolution that set out a specific line and date for a ceasefire.[39] In response, the Australian government proposed a resolution calling for an immediate ceasefire and reaffirming the UN's peaceful objective to reunify Korea.[40] But Nehru took up the mantle with most zeal since he was most determined to end the conflict and least concerned with American ire. His draft resolution proposed a ceasefire at the 38th parallel and the creation of a demilitarized zone, and promised negotiations with the PRC on the future of Korea and Taiwan after the cessation of hostilities.[41] This proposal garnered general support from the other Commonwealth members.

Acheson's immediate reaction was to oppose Nehru's draft resolution but the Commonwealth's leverage over the United States was beginning to take hold. The Secretary of State recognized that Britain was Washington's only true global partner, while the other Commonwealth members represented its key allies in North America and the Pacific, together with the leading voice in the emerging neutral bloc. Indeed, Acheson was in a difficult position. On one hand, he was convinced that the West ought to hold fast in response to Chinese aggression and was acutely aware of the intense domestic political pressure, stirred up by MacArthur's public remarks, to have China branded an aggressor. He also recognized, on the other hand, that a united Commonwealth was difficult to ignore at the UN because of the moral authority it possessed due to its multiethnic composition and liberal democratic traditions. Decisively, therefore, in an effort to maintain Commonwealth support, Acheson proposed that the President of the General Assembly, along with two people he would designate, be empowered to confer with Washington, as the unified command, and Beijing to determine the basis for a ceasefire.[42]

The Indian delegation seized upon this opportunity with alacrity. Within days it had convinced all 13 Arab-Asian members to co-sponsor a draft resolution incorporating Acheson's proposal.[43] The Heads of the Commonwealth delegations wholeheartedly supported this conciliatory first step,[44] while the US government, in light of the united Commonwealth position and the fact that Acheson had originated the resolution's provisions, was willing to give it priority over the Six-Power draft resolution.[45] The 13-Power Arab-Asian proposal was thus adopted, with only the Soviet bloc voting in opposition, becoming General Assembly Resolution 384 (V) (see Appendix 8, p. 265–6).[46] Furthermore, in fulfilment of the resolution's provisions, President of the General Assembly Nasrollah Entezam of Iran asked two Commonwealth representatives to join him on the Cease-fire Committee, Rau of India and Pearson of Canada. The Commonwealth thus had a special interest in the work of this newly-formed body.

In the confusion following massive Chinese intervention, the Commonwealth had united against any attempt to push the UN into hasty action. Its unity, which was to prove vital in exerting leverage over the United States, stemmed from a variety of factors. One was the dire nature of the crisis, which convinced the Commonwealth governments that any condemnatory action taken by the UN against the PRC would inevitably lead to an escalation of the conflict. Another was the role of key Commonwealth personalities, especially Bevin and Nehru, who took it upon themselves to defuse the situation. Finally, the US government had shown a willingness to be flexible to maintain Commonwealth support. These concessions had been made easier by the fact the fighting in Korea had temporarily ceased and domestic pressure for drastic action had decreased. For the first time during the Korean conflict the Commonwealth had thus coordinated its policy and achieved its goal of constraining US policy at the UN. But Bevin remained wary that the Truman administration was simply 'building up a case for the record' with a view to branding the PRC an aggressor.[47]

The Cease-fire Committee

By the second week of December 1950, with the UNC's reports clearly indicating that the Chinese offensive had halted north of the 38th parallel, the Commonwealth members optimistically hoped that Beijing had achieved its war aims and that a ceasefire could be arranged. Yet the Cease-fire Committee's work got off to an unpromising start. Its members sent a message to Wu asking to meet him or another Chinese representative at a location of Beijing's choosing as soon as possible to discuss ceasefire conditions. But this note went unanswered.[48] Rau, however, was able to communicate informally with Wu and was told that the Chinese government did not recognize the 'illegal' Cease-fire Committee, formed without its consent, and would not negotiate until the UN agreed that all foreign forces would be withdrawn from Korea; that Beijing's sovereignty would be extended over Taiwan; and that the PRC would be admitted to the UN. Wu also revealed that he would be returning to China in a matter of days. In response, the Cease-fire Committee sent Wu a letter urging him to stay and talk, but this approach was again ignored.[49] Wu then made his views publicly known in a press statement, making any future negotiations impossible.[50]

In contrast, the US government, acting as the unified command, had cooperated with the Cease-fire Committee in as much as it had revealed its conditions. These were a ceasefire at the 38th parallel, the creation of a demilitarized zone and the establishment of a commission representing all belligerent parties to oversee the truce.[51]

But the domestic pressure on Truman to adopt a tough stance was mounting following his declaration of a state of national emergency. This only served to heighten tension and further jeopardized the work of the Cease-fire Committee. And, to make matters worse, in New York the US delegation also snubbed Pearson and Rau, who were trying to push for the adoption of a 12-Power draft resolution sponsored by the Arab-Asian members, excluding Washington's ally the Philippines, recommending that the representatives of several unnamed governments meet as soon as possible to make recommendations for the peaceful settlement of all outstanding East Asian issues. The Cease-fire Committee hoped that such a resolution would meet China's preconditions but the US government would not agree to such a commitment until the fighting had stopped.

In spite of the toughening US stance, the Cease-fire Committee turned its attentions to Beijing. It sent a cable directly to Zhou En-lai stating that as soon as a ceasefire had been arranged it planned to proceed with the 12-Power draft resolution.[52] Nevertheless, the UN was again caught between the two belligerents. After much delay, Zhou En-lai firmly rejected General Assembly Resolution 384 (V) arguing that it was meaningless without the 12-Power draft resolution.[53] In response to this development, Acheson once again began to press hard for the adoption of the Six-Power draft resolution.[54] With the bargaining position of both sides as far apart as ever, the Cease-fire Committee's two Commonwealth representatives realized little hope existed of brokering a deal through the UN.[55] Its members, therefore, made no recommendations. Still, Rau told the First Committee that his colleagues had made a valuable attempt to find a solution.[56]

During the Cease-fire Committee's brief efforts to find a solution, the Commonwealth governments had remained quiet. With the lull in fighting the US government did not press for any drastic policy at the UN risking escalation and so the Commonwealth members saw little need to coordinate their views. Moreover, the Commonwealth members appreciated that the unified command had shown flexibility and had cooperated with the Cease-fire Committee, which was in marked contrast to Chinese intransigence. Nonetheless, the Commonwealth remained united behind the effort to find a ceasefire and gave much encouragement to Canada and India to persevere in their efforts. On a more personal level, Rau and Pearson showed great determination and used their connections with both the PRC and the United States in their attempts to bring about a ceasefire. Yet their efforts were not enough to bring the positions of the belligerents any closer and the threat to international peace continued to ensure that the Commonwealth did not disunite.

The Commonwealth Prime Ministers' Conference and the ceasefire principles

Despite disappointment with the failure of the Cease-fire Committee, battlefield events led to the Commonwealth's most serious challenge yet to US hegemony at the UN. The Chinese New Year's Eve Offensive across the 38th parallel led the Truman administration, under huge public pressure, to now openly demand that China be branded an aggressor. Acheson warned that if the UN failed to take the same action it had done six months earlier in response to the North Korean invasion then the organization would lose all credibility.[57] The Commonwealth members were equally disturbed by the radical change in nature of the crisis, but they believed that the US proposal risked escalating the conflict and alienating the Arab-Asian members. The Commonwealth, therefore, called for another intermediary step in the hope of convincing the Chinese to accept a ceasefire. Significantly, the US government again agreed to put its own desires to one side, largely because Acheson believed that Beijing would inevitably reject all UN calls for a settlement, giving the Commonwealth members time to 'return to comparative sanity'.[58] The Secretary of State was thus willing to accept a limited delay if this proved necessary to have an aggressor resolution adopted by an overwhelming majority, including the votes of Washington's Commonwealth allies.

The Truman administration, however, underestimated the unity of purpose of the Commonwealth in searching for an acceptable

intermediary step. Pearson and Rau remained at the forefront, using
the continued existence of the Cease-fire Committee to formulate a
statement of ceasefire 'principles' to propose to the PRC. These
principles were: an immediate ceasefire followed by the staged
withdrawal of all armed forces from Korea; the creation by the UN of
machinery whereby the Korean people could express themselves
freely; agreement to interim arrangements for the administration of
Korea and the maintenance of peace pending the establishment of the
new government; and affirmation that the United States, Britain, the
Soviet Union and China would seek a peaceful settlement of all
outstanding Far Eastern issues after the cessation of hostilities. The
Cease-fire Committee had intended to table these principles
alongside its report to the General Assembly but Rau had been
unable to obtain instructions from Nehru in time. Even so, Pearson
told the First Committee of the intended statement and the debate
was adjourned for 48 hours to allow the principles to be submitted.[59]

In the meantime, and more vitally to Commonwealth unity, a
Commonwealth Prime Ministers' Conference, called by Attlee when
the winter crisis had just begun, opened in London on 4 January
1951. For the first time at such a conference the government leaders
sought to formulate a united policy and thereby take the initiative in
the Korean debate. Bevin summed up the sentiment of the
Commonwealth when he stated at the opening meeting that the
nature of the organization's membership—spanning the globe and
various races as well as representing both the Western and neutral
camps—meant that it could exert great moral influence at the UN
and over US policy.[60] The Foreign Secretary then tabled a
memorandum suggesting that a ceasefire occur simultaneously
with settlement of the Korean question, the admission of the PRC to
the UN and for Taiwan to come under Beijing's sovereignty.[61] Bevin
was aware that this suggestion would be unacceptable to the United
States but he was evidently trying to gauge how far his
Commonwealth colleagues were prepared to go to bring the Korean
War to an end. He found that, on one hand, Nehru predictably
supported the idea of settling all East Asian issues, arguing that
China would accept no other course. The Old Commonwealth Prime

Ministers, on the other hand, warned that the US government would only accept political negotiations after a ceasefire had commenced.[62]

In consequence, St Laurent, after receiving a strongly-worded telegram from Pearson in New York,[63] urged his colleagues to support the Cease-fire Committee's principles. He argued that they might be acceptable to Washington and Beijing but, if not, their adoption would at least postpone the submission of an aggressor resolution. This course won favour with the Australian, New Zealand and South African representatives. Nehru, though, revealed that Panikkar had been informed by the Chinese government that the principles were unacceptable. The Indian Prime Minister thus suggested a simplified version of Bevin's plan merely mentioning rather than promising the settlement of outstanding issues at the same time as a ceasefire.[64] Interestingly, Nehru's rival, Liaquat Ali-Khan, made a similar proposal recommending that representatives of the United States, Britain, the Soviet Union and China meet at the earliest moment to resolve all outstanding East Asian issues.[65] After this muddled meeting Attlee took it upon himself to send a message to Truman stressing that the Commonwealth was principally concerned with Washington's intentions at the UN after the PRC was branded an aggressor.[66] But the President's reply was evasive, only stating that the UN should not shirk from stating the truth.[67] In response, Bevin suggested to the Commonwealth Prime Ministers a resolution 'disapproving' of Chinese intervention, calling for Chinese forces to be withdrawn and for the Great Powers to meet in order to deal with issues threatening world peace. Nehru worried that this proposal was too vague but the consensus view in London was to support this new plan.[68]

Meanwhile, events beyond the Commonwealth Conference worked to unite the Prime Ministers. In New York, at the behest of Rau under instruction from Nehru, the Cease-fire Committee sought to revise its ceasefire principles in an effort to make them more acceptable to the Chinese. Pearson, wary of Rau's zealous efforts to appease the Chinese and willingness to overlook the Truman administration's difficult domestic position, took this task upon himself. After close consultation with the US delegation, and taking into account the reports he had received from St Laurent regarding

The Shape of Things to Come?

Figure 2.2 The shape of things to come?
Source: *Washington Evening Star*, 24 January 1951.

the discussions in London, Pearson revised the principles so that negotiations on other East Asian issues, specifying the questions of Taiwan and Chinese representation, would take place 'as soon as a cease-fire had been agreed on'.[69]

Initially, the US delegation indicated that its government would 'sympathetically acquiesce' with the principles but was unsure if it would vote affirmatively.[70] The next day, however, the Truman administration once more proved willing to compromise, despite domestic uproar, and instructed Austin to vote in favour of the cease fire principles.[71] In light of this development, Bevin dropped his proposal and the Commonwealth Prime Ministers agreed no longer to consider an alternative policy since the United States had accepted a moderate course. Only Nehru indicated that he might change his position if the Chinese made it clear they did not support the principles.[72] With the US and Commonwealth positions aligned, the Cease-fire Committee tabled its supplementary report and the General Assembly approved the principles even though the Soviet delegation warned they were unacceptable.[73]

The Chinese New Year's Eve Offensive had clearly heightened the crisis and rekindled the Truman administration's demand for China to be branded an aggressor. This reaction effectively united the Commonwealth in opposition to Washington's policy. Furthermore, the Commonwealth Prime Ministers used this opportunity to try to formulate an alternative UN policy, realizing that the very nature of their organization made it difficult to ignore. The fact that the US government remained silent at the UN for over a week while the Commonwealth leaders discussed this matter in isolation dramatically highlights this point, especially as the military situation worsened and the US public increasingly turned against its President.

Still, the Commonwealth Prime Ministers' Conference had also demonstrated that its members were not as united as they had hoped. Attlee and Bevin were preoccupied with trying to appease Nehru who, in turn, was most concerned with placating China. In contrast, St Laurent, Menzies and Holland were more sensitive to the Truman administration's desperate domestic position. These fissures within the Commonwealth were soon to open into a gaping chasm. Yet for the meantime, the Commonwealth was united by the clear-sightedness displayed by Pearson and Rau on the Cease-fire Committee and the US government's continued willingness to meet the Commonwealth's viewpoint.

The 'aggressor' resolution

The Prime Ministers' Conference represented the pinnacle of Commonwealth coordination during the winter crisis. After this point in time, the conditions for unity were removed one by one. Most significantly, the US government's willingness to compromise evaporated. On the same day as the ceasefire principles were adopted, Acheson, predicting that Beijing would reject this peace overture, formulated another draft resolution branding China an aggressor and calling for the UN Collective Measures Committee, a 14-member body created by the 'Uniting for Peace' Resolution, to make recommendations accordingly.[74] Then after 17 January 1951, when Zhou En-lai rejected the ceasefire principles and made a counter-proposal for a conference to be held in China composed of the PRC, the Soviet Union, the United States, Britain, France, India and Egypt to negotiate all outstanding East Asian issues before a ceasefire, the Truman administration's patience finally snapped.

This development was expressed in a number of ways. First, the President told the press that the US government would seek to have China branded an aggressor 'with everything that we could bring to bear'.[75] Next, in the General Assembly Austin stressed that the UN had explored every possibility for a peaceful settlement; now the time had come to take firm action or face ruin.[76] In addition, Acheson told the British that the US government's support for the ceasefire principles had brought it 'to the verge of destruction domestically' and it was unwilling to make any further compromises.[77] The US delegation, therefore, was instructed to search for sponsors for the aggressor resolution, starting with the Commonwealth members, but if none could be found then it was authorized to table the proposal alone.[78] Hickerson explained to Austin that this course was necessary since it was essential that the US government made it swiftly known that it considered the Chinese counter-proposal 'unacceptable' and to 'avoid any confused thinking, about our being a bunch of appeasers'.[79]

Under this pressure the Commonwealth alliance began to splinter. The New Zealand and South African governments were the first to capitulate, agreeing to support the US draft resolution. Even so, Spender proposed adding a provision establishing an ad hoc body to use its good offices to bring about the cessation of hostilities.[80] In stark contrast, Bevin was more convinced than ever that an aggressor resolution would divide the world organization and lead to its break-up. He also felt that no military, economic or political measures existed that the UN could effectively impose upon China without resources being diverted away from Europe and Hong Kong being sacrificed.[81] The British Cabinet thus called for the US draft resolution to be divided into two stages. The first stage would be to have the PRC condemned for rejecting a ceasefire. If this stage did not bring about a cessation of hostilities then, as a second stage, the question of additional measures would be dealt with. Bevin believed that this method would provide time for the United States and Britain to consider in private the sanctions the UN could effectively impose upon China.[82] The Canadian Cabinet had come to a similar conclusion.[83] Nehru, meanwhile, was encouraged by the Chinese response and sought further elucidation of Beijing's position before committing to any UN policy.[84] Importantly, the Indian Prime Minister was encouraged in these efforts by both Attlee[85] and St Laurent.[86]

Even now, despite his aggressive posturing, Acheson remained sensitive to Commonwealth pressure. He soon agreed to revise the US draft resolution by incorporating the Australian provision for an ad hoc body to seek a peaceful solution to the conflict. Acheson named this body the Good Offices Committee (GOC) and decided that it would be composed of the President of the General Assembly and two persons designated by this officeholder. The US government hoped that the addition of this clause would allow the Commonwealth governments to co-sponsor the proposal and avoid the embarrassment of tabling its draft resolution alone. But Acheson's ploy was only partially successful. Although Australia was a willing co-sponsor, Britain and Canada continued to insist that the paragraph referring to additional measures be deleted.[87] Still, under intense pressure from both houses of Congress, which had overwhelmingly adopted resolutions demanding the PRC be branded an aggressor, the Truman administration decided to table the revised draft resolution alone. Austin argued that this approach was better than having a number of smaller countries sponsor it, amplifying the division within the Western camp.[88] The Australian delegation, however, felt it had been 'dumped' because the State Department did not feel that enough 'respectable' sponsors were forthcoming.[89]

Washington's determination to demonstrate the strength of its convictions was not shaken by the arrival of a communication from the Indian government containing a set of 'clarifications' to the earlier Chinese counter-proposal. Zhou En-lai had told Panikkar that after the Seven-Power conference had commenced its work Beijing would use its influence to bring about the retirement of the Chinese volunteers alongside the withdrawal of all foreign troops; at the opening meeting of the conference a ceasefire would be agreed; and that the conference would decide the principles under which Korea's internal political problems would be solved. In a footnote the Indian Ambassador added that China also narrowed its demands on Taiwan to the withdrawal of US forces and called for the conference to merely affirm the PRC's legal status but not its admission to the UN.[90] Nehru was greatly encouraged by these clarifications and sent a personal message to Zhou En-lai urging the Chinese government to state officially that it desired negotiations to bring about a peaceful settlement.[91] But the Truman administration viewed the Chinese concessions as nothing more than a propaganda ploy designed to delay the work of the UN.

The US reaction thoroughly divided the Commonwealth, but not along the familiar Old–New cleavage. On one side, Britain, Canada and Pakistan joined with India in concluding that a window of opportunity had been opened and needed to be pursued. Australia, New Zealand and South Africa, on the other side, were against any attempt to constrain the United States, especially now that Washington had clearly signalled that it would stop at nothing less than an aggressor resolution. On 22 January 1951 Commonwealth disunity was then made public when the British, Canadian and Pakistani delegations supported a motion tabled by Rau to have the Korean debate adjourned for 48 hours so that the clarifications could be examined. In contrast, the Australian, New Zealand and South African delegations abstained to avoid voting in opposition to their Commonwealth partners. Notably, in spite of a negative American vote, this motion was narrowly adopted demonstrating that the majority of the UN members also feared precipitously branding China an aggressor.[92]

Nonetheless, during the adjournment Commonwealth unity disintegrated completely. The vote on the Indian motion had exposed the rift within the Western alliance and finally brought home to a number of Commonwealth members that they might find themselves voting against a US draft resolution. In addition, it had become increasingly clear to the Commonwealth governments by this time that the severity of the crisis had lessened in the preceding weeks. Under Ridgway's operational command the UN forces had halted the Chinese offensive and restored confidence that a line could be held across the peninsula. Moreover, the international situation had stabilized with the strengthening of NATO and the improved fortunes in Indochina and Malaya. In these conditions the Truman administration, with a slight easing of public pressure, felt less need for the UN to immediately impose additional measures upon the PRC while the Commonwealth members were less worried that the conflict would escalate if China was branded an aggressor.

As a result, the key personalities within each Commonwealth government reassessed their positions in light of their long-term relations vis-à-vis Washington. With a possible Pacific security pact uppermost in his mind, Spender gave the Australian delegation final instructions to vote in favour of the US draft resolution.[93] This decision was taken while Menzies was still in London suffering from influenza and in spite of the Australian Prime Minister's instructions not to diverge from Britain.[94] Yet Menzies retroactively backed Spender's policy.[95] Similarly, Doidge, equally desirous of a US security guarantee for New Zealand, convinced Holland to support the US draft resolution against his own pro-British convictions.[96] Furthermore, Pearson grudgingly recognized that if Ottawa wished to maintain its special relationship with Washington it would have to vote for the draft resolution.

Bevin still felt that time was needed, however, to explore the Chinese counter-proposal and was greatly angered by the US 'steamroller tactics' that he felt risked dividing the UN.[97] But Bevin was gravely ill in hospital and his deputy, Minister of State Kenneth

Younger, formerly an ardent critic of US foreign policy during less tense times, warned the Cabinet that if Britain did not support the US draft resolution it would become isolated from its key allies. Initially, the majority of the Labour Cabinet remained firmly opposed to branding China an aggressor and Attlee agreed that Britain would have to vote against the US proposal unless the provision concerning additional measures was deleted.[98] What is more, the British Prime Minister tried to rally the support of the Commonwealth by writing a message to all his colleagues urging them to support the British efforts to have the Americans revise their draft resolution.[99]

Nehru's convictions, nevertheless, were little affected by concerns of voting against the US proposal. In fact, the Indian Prime Minister had become greatly disillusioned with the Commonwealth precisely because the majority of its members had folded under US pressure at this critical moment. India, therefore, turned its attention to the neutral bloc where it continued to hold much sway. Rau had consequently been able to persuade the Arab-Asian members to revise their outstanding draft resolution to incorporate the Chinese proposal for a Seven-Power conference. The rift within the Commonwealth was then made public as the British delegation called for more time for consideration, while the other Old Commonwealth members agreed that the US proposal should be voted upon.[100]

Even though the Commonwealth was thoroughly disunited and the majority of its members had endorsed the US position, at the eleventh hour the Truman administration proved willing to make a final concession to avoid a split with Britain. Acheson was supremely confident that, now the united Commonwealth front had been broken up and the moral influence of this organization over the other UN members had evaporated, the aggressor resolution would be overwhelmingly adopted. Still, the Secretary of State recognized that London represented Washington's closest and most powerful ally. He was thus prepared to go one step further to perpetuate this long-term partnership. He also realized that without British support the Western alliance would appear acutely divided even if the other Old Commonwealth members voted for the US draft resolution. The

Secretary of State feared the domestic response to this act of British insubordination—especially with the 'Great Debate' intensifying—and how Communist propaganda would take advantage of this situation.[101]

Taking all this into account Acheson agreed to amend the US draft resolution so that the committee for additional measures would defer its report if the GOC reported satisfactory progress in its work. On first glance this concession appears to be considerable given the domestic pressure Acheson was under to have the PRC promptly punished. But the Secretary of State was convinced that the US public would accept a delay before sanctions were imposed since he predicted that the GOC would soon fail and the postponement would be very short. Moreover, he was confident that the UN members would then be more willing to take harsher action once Beijing had proved itself totally intransigent.[102] The British Cabinet, on their part, were content that the Commonwealth had forced Washington to make a number of significant concessions and, realizing that they could wring no more now the Commonwealth was disunited, finally agreed to vote in favour of the aggressor resolution to avoid being alienated at the UN.[103]

In the meantime, India continued to oppose any attempt to condemn the Chinese intervention in Korea since Nehru maintained that no good purpose would be served by branding China an aggressor.[104] In addition, Mrs Pandit told Acheson that the US draft resolution should be withheld. She warned that it risked escalating the conflict and Beijing would not come to the negotiating table once tarnished with this label. Acheson replied that the door to negotiations would remain open and, while he had faith in Nehru's motives, stressed that the US government was 'tied hand and foot' to public opinion that demanded action and was more resentful of India than ever before.[105] In a last-ditched effort to win support Rau thus revised the 12-Power draft resolution so that the first action of the proposed Seven-Power conference would be to arrange a ceasefire. He then informed the General Assembly that the Indian government had received information from the 'highest sources in Peking' that the Chinese government regarded this proposal as 'providing a genuine basis for a peaceful settlement'. Yet these efforts were not enough to reunite the Commonwealth.[106] When the Arab-Asian proposal was put to the vote it was rejected, with a large number of members abstaining, including all the Old Commonwealth countries. In comparison, the US draft resolution was overwhelmingly adopted, becoming General Assembly Resolution 498 (V) (see Appendix 8, p. 265–6), despite Pakistan abstaining and India finding itself in opposition with the Soviet bloc.[107]

Conclusion

In the crisis following Chinese intervention in Korea, the Commonwealth, by remaining united for a prolonged period, had been able to force the US government to make a number of significant concessions. This created the delay necessary to expose China's insincerity and bring about the overwhelming support of the UN members for the aggressor resolution. As Stueck points out, this delay came at a crucial time: had the United States been able to push through an aggressor resolution in early January 1951, when the battlefield situation was so bleak that a UN defeat seemed distinctly possible, then it was possible that such a resolution might have been used to give legitimacy to some of the escalatory measures briefly considered in Washington. But by February 1951 the military situation on the ground was already starting to improve. The Commonwealth had thus bought some valuable time.[108]

Meanwhile, the Old Commonwealth members were generally pleased that their challenge to US hegemony at the UN had brought them closer together than they had been since the Second World War, and this helped to ensure that the Commonwealth remained a significant aspect of their foreign policies. More importantly, these Commonwealth members were relieved that this act of resistance, though serious in the short-term, had not jeopardized their long-term relations with the Western superpower. On the debit side, however, for India the adoption of the aggressor resolution dented its belief in the Commonwealth as a counterweight to US influence. Events in January 1951 convinced Nehru that his Commonwealth partners were only willing to push Washington so far. The Indian Prime Minister, therefore, increasingly placed his allegiance with the neutral bloc even though he did not completely abandon the Commonwealth at this point. Still, it was a paradoxical consequence of the high-water mark of the Commonwealth's influence on international politics.

In terms of broader importance, this episode demonstrated that the Commonwealth was more than a symbolic group of states bound by a common history. With the risk of a global conflict at its greatest, the key Commonwealth personalities prepared to exercise their influence, coincidence bringing the Commonwealth members together, and the US government willing to bow to Commonwealth pressure, its members were able to coordinate a united position and wield influence over the United States at the UN. When these conditions were removed towards the end of January and the Commonwealth members acted independently, none of them, not even Britain, could constrain US policy.

CHAPTER 3

RESPONDING TO CHINESE AGGRESSION, FEBRUARY– JULY 1951

The winter crisis following China's intervention in the Korean War had witnessed the most tumultuous period in the relationship between the United States and the Commonwealth members at the UN since its inception. During this period the Commonwealth members had overcome their internal differences and united to an unprecedented degree to effectively constrain Washington's wishes to take quick punitive action. In comparison, the spring and early summer of 1951 were characterized by the gradual fragmentation of the Commonwealth's challenge to US hegemony at the UN. Although many areas of friction had to be resolved, particularly between Washington and London over the nature of the sanctions to be imposed upon China, the Commonwealth did not unite in opposition to the United States. Still, it took almost six months before the Commonwealth fully resumed its traditional role compliantly supporting the US position at the world organization.

Crucial to this period of relative harmony between the United States and the Commonwealth at the UN was the absence of the conditions necessary to unite the Commonwealth members. Firstly, the risk of the Korean War escalating into a regional or global conflict appeared far less likely than during the previous months. The steady improvement in the military situation in Korea and the limited war strategy employed by the Truman administration were responsible for this situation. Secondly, due to domestic and international developments the key Commonwealth personalities had little desire to resist US policy at the UN. Thirdly, few opportunities arose to coordinate a united Commonwealth policy. Finally, the Truman administration, facing unparalleled Congressional and public criticism of its foreign policy and management of the UN action in Korea, both before and after MacArthur was sacked, refused to bow to the relatively insignificant Commonwealth pressure at the UN.

Once again, the nature of the discussions on Korea at the UN during the first half of 1951 reflected the military, domestic and international environments they took place in. This background information, therefore, will be briefly outlined below.

The military situation

Between February and July 1951 the military situation in Korea gradually stabilized around the 38th parallel, albeit with considerable fluctuations in battlefield fortunes. On 5 February 1951 Ridgway seized the initiative launching Operation Roundup advancing as far north as the Han River. More importantly, this operation met the Communist Fourth Phase Offensive head on. This assault was minor compared to its predecessor, involving just 18,000 Chinese troops and, although it made some initial territorial gains, the Communist advance was halted by mid-February. Crucial to this success was the strengthening of the UN forces in Korea with reinforcements arriving from the United States and from other UN members, including Canada and New Zealand.[1]

With the momentum of the Communist attack broken, Ridgway launched Operation Killer to inflict maximum casualties upon the enemy by taking full advantage of the UN's ground and aerial firepower. This strategy proved to be a great success and in early March the UN forces began slowly but steadily to progress north. Next, the UNC made great territorial advances through a series of ground and air operations entitled Ripper, Tomahawk, Courageous,

Rugged and Dauntless. Between early March and mid-April 1951 Seoul was recaptured and the UN forces advanced across the peninsula to positions on or slightly north of the 38th parallel. Throughout this process the UNC also expended considerable effort building defences at Line Kansas along the Imjin River and Line Wyoming further north.

These preparations were essential because the Communist forces were far from beaten. Ridgway estimated that the Chinese had almost unlimited manpower reserves and intelligence reports indicated that the Communist armies were massing for another drive south, possibly being supported by aircraft concentrated in Manchuria. The Chinese Spring Offensive, with its first phase commencing on 22 April 1951 and the second on 17 May 1951, thus came as little surprise to the UNC. These actions were on a far greater scale than that of February, involving approximately 250,000 Chinese troops, and pushed the UN forces to the 'No Name Line' just north of Seoul. The fighting was extremely intense and both sides suffered significant casualties. However, unlike in the previous large-scale Communist offensives, the UN forces fought a well-organized defensive action, inflicting 70,000 losses upon the enemy and only suffering 7,000 casualties themselves. No large-scale 'bugging out' occurred this time now that MacArthur had been replaced by Ridgway, as will be outlined below, and Lieutenant-General James Van Fleet was leading the US Eighth Army.

Moreover, once the Spring Offensive had ground to a halt Van Fleet immediately went on the counteroffensive. In late May and June, under operations Detonate and Piledriver, the UN forces pushed the Communists back to near the previous battle line. In fact, Van Fleet pressed for further amphibious landings behind enemy lines and an advance to the narrow 'waist' of Korea at the 39th parallel between Pyongyang and Wonsan. He claimed this action was militarily feasible and would win a decisive victory, forcing the Communists to accept an armistice. Whether this represented a genuine opportunity is contentious, but Van Fleet's superiors in Tokyo and Washington thought such a move would be reckless and were convinced that seizure of territory north of the 38th parallel would be unpopular at the UN after the military debacle of the previous winter. In addition, Ridgway, the Joint Chiefs of Staff and the State Department remained convinced that a ceasefire at or near the 38th parallel remained the best course of action.[2]

Notably, the Commonwealth forces in Korea played their most important role during the early stages of the Communist Spring Offensive. Central to the Communist plan was a swift assault on Seoul, outflanking the UNC along Korea's west coast. This area was defended by the 29th British Infantry Brigade, who fought an impressive defensive action at the Battle of Imjin River in the first two days of the attack. The British forces blunted the momentum of the offensive and bought enough time to allow other UN units to establish a more defensible line north of Seoul and repel the Communist advance. Although inflicting much heavier losses upon the enemy, the Commonwealth forces were ultimately defeated. But this action has long been lauded in British and US military circles.[3]

Military parity had existed in Korea since February 1951, with UNC technological superiority cancelling out the Communist's massive manpower advantage, but it had taken these events to convince both sides of this fact. The UNC now believed that the current position should be held since any advance further north would only stretch its supply lines while shortening those of the enemy, and place its forces in a less defensible position. The Communist High Command came to a similar conclusion, realizing that it could not defeat the UNC at least until it had reinforced its own forces. With the battlefront stabilized both sides commenced a largely defensive war of attrition. The risk of the Korean War escalating had thus reached its lowest point since the outbreak of fighting a year earlier.

Domestic developments

Despite the improved military situation in Korea, the Truman administration witnessed its most fraught period domestically. Hot on the heels of the 'Great Debate' was an even stiffer challenge to the

President's authority. On 11 April 1951 Truman took the courageous yet exceedingly controversial decision to dismiss MacArthur on the grounds of insubordination. Two incidents gave the President little choice but to take this action. The first incident took place in early March when, on hearing that the President was preparing to issue a statement expressing his willingness to negotiate a ceasefire, MacArthur released a pre-emptive statement of his own demanding that the Communists accept the unification of Korea under UN terms. The general also vociferously accused China of weakness. MacArthur must have known this demand would be rejected by Beijing, increase public pressure for action against China and scupper the chances of a presidential statement regarding a ceasefire. The second incident took place just a few weeks later when MacArthur responded to a letter from the Republican House Minority Leader, Joseph Martin of Massachusetts, criticizing Truman's limited war policy and demanding victory in Korea to prevent further Communist aggression in Asia and Europe. Martin went on to read this letter on the floor of the House of Representatives, to Truman's great embarrassment.[4]

Truman had decided to only reprimand MacArthur after the first incident, realizing that the dismissal of the general would be deeply unpopular and it would be difficult to find a replacement able to assume his multiple commands. Even so, after the second incident the administration was unanimous that MacArthur had to be removed. Behind this decision was the Pentagon's fear of an imminent Communist offensive in Korea based on intelligence that Communist air forces were being concentrated in Manchuria. The US military believed that if these aircraft were used to support a ground offensive and positions behind the UNC's lines were attacked, then it would be necessary to give the field commander the authority to take immediate action such as 'hot pursuit' and the bombing of air bases in China. Neither the Pentagon nor the White House was willing to assign these powers to MacArthur. So on Marshall's advice Truman decided that the UN Commander had to be replaced by the more trustworthy Ridgway.[5] In connection to this, Truman also authorized the stationing of bombers armed with atomic weapons in the western

Pacific which could be used for tactical use on the battlefield if the UN position in Korea became untenable. Again, the administration had worried at having these weapons in such close proximity to MacArthur.[6] Furthermore, throughout this period Washington's allies, notably Britain, increased their pressure to have MacArthur relieved since there held grave fears that the general would drag the UN into open conflict with China and potentially the Soviet Union.[7]

MacArthur's dismissal was thus widely welcomed internationally. In stark contrast, in the United States the public and Congressional backlash against the decision was unprecedented. Truman's approval ratings slumped to a record low while MacArthur received a hero's welcome when he returned home. In light of these developments, the President reluctantly accepted a joint Senate Armed Services and Foreign Affairs Committee hearing on his entire foreign policy starting with MacArthur's dismissal. These hearings lasted a number of weeks and, although the Republican senators involved heavily criticized Truman's foreign policy, the Democrat senators, along with the members of the administration questioned, especially Acheson, provided a strong defence. What is more, MacArthur's dismissal appeared to be vindicated. The committee manoeuvred the general into admitting that as a field commander he was not in a position to criticize the global policy of his superiors. Marshall and the Joint Chiefs of Staff also emphasized that despite MacArthur's claims they disagreed with his proposals to escalate the Korean conflict. And the administration produced evidence revealing that MacArthur had disobeyed a direct presidential order to consult Washington before making any public statements. Nevertheless, the Truman administration was never able to recover fully and remained deeply unpopular with the public, who by and large favoured the escalatory measures proposed by MacArthur.[8]

A number of Commonwealth countries also faced serious domestic problems in early 1951. In Britain, the Attlee government's position was greatly weakened. To begin with, Bevin was dying and in March 1951 was replaced as Foreign Secretary by Herbert Morrison. Deputy Prime Minister and Leader of the House of Commons since 1945, Morrison was a very senior figure in the Labour Party, seen by many as heir-apparent to Attlee. Despite these attributes, Morrison had no experience in foreign affairs and was almost unknown outside Britain. Consequently, he lacked Bevin's high standing in Washington and his predecessor's courage to challenge US policy for fear this would irreparably damage Anglo-American relations. Morrison's principal concern, therefore, was developing close bonds with the US government by demonstrating Britain's loyalty.[9] Furthermore, in April 1951 Aneurin Bevan, now Minister of Labour and the leading figure of the Labour Left, resigned from the Cabinet in protest at cuts from the healthcare budget to pay for British rearmament. Divisions within the Cabinet were now very much out in the open.[10]

In Australia, the Menzies government was also going through a period of transition. In April 1951 Percy Spender, satisfied that his ultimate aim of securing a Pacific pact had been achieved, as will be outlined below, decided on the grounds of ill health to step down as Minister for External Affairs. Spender's successor, Minister for National Development Richard Casey, had been a distinguished diplomat during the Second World War, serving as both the Australian Ambassador to the United States and British Minister Resident in the Middle East. In terms of foreign policy, Casey more closely shared Menzies' sentimental attachments to the Common-wealth than had Spender, but he also recognized that the relationship between the United States and the Commonwealth was more important than ever before. In particular, Casey believed that the smaller Commonwealth countries, such as Australia, had a special opportunity to influence London, Washington and the UN. Meanwhile, Spender had accepted Menzies' request that he become Ambassador to the United States. By sending such a high-profile pro-American figure to deal directly with Washington the Australian government had made a clear statement that it desired to strengthen its relationship with the United States.[11]

The domestic situation in Australia was also complicated by Menzies' decision to bring about a double dissolution of both the House of Representatives and the Senate and to call a general election for 28 April 1951. The election campaigns of both Menzies and the leader of the Opposition Labor Party, Ben Chifley, focused on the domestic and international threat of Communism. Nonetheless, Menzies' solid Liberal-Country Party coalition had the upper hand throughout, emphasizing its role in Korea, at the UN and at the Commonwealth Prime Ministers' Conference in January, and boasting of a formal US security guarantee. It thus won comfortable majorities in both Houses. But during these months the Menzies government had naturally been preoccupied with the election and the Prime Minister had consciously avoided taking any controversial decisions.[12]

In New Zealand, the Holland government faced its most serious challenge to date. On 21 February 1951 the Prime Minister declared a state of national emergency as a result of the 'waterfront dispute'. This crisis had erupted over demands by waterside workers for higher wages as the economy boomed and the cost of living increased. The shipping companies, however, were not bound by the Arbitration Court's decision to award 15 per cent pay increases to public sector workers and offered an increase of only 9 per cent. The militant Waterside Workers Union thus ordered its members to refuse to work overtime, the companies refused to hire workers if they insisted on these conditions, and the ports ground to a halt. Holland responded by introducing a number of Emergency Regulations restricting the civil liberties of the waterside workers and those who helped them while ordering the military to ensure the continued operation of New Zealand's ports. These measures led to much friction between the government and large sections of the sympathetic workforce who disapproved of these draconian actions. Consequently, a number of violent clashes took place between the strikers and the military. Still, the waterfront dispute never developed into a national strike since the majority of workers disapproved of the union's militant tactics and strike-breakers soon returned to the ports. By mid-July 1951 the dispute was over.[13]

In India, Nehru had become preoccupied with the famine now affecting large swathes of the country. The Prime Minister greatly feared that this problem would ignite social unrest and religious clashes that might lead to the breakup of the country. In his efforts to find food aid, therefore, Nehru was forced to court Washington and in late January 1951 requested two million tonnes of US wheat grain. This appeal was ignored for over a month before Truman, hoping to persuade India to abandon its neutral foreign policy, sent a special message to Congress urging it to meet the request. Yet a large number of senators, aware of the public's distrust of India, were unwilling to provide aid unless it was administered by the US government and India provided strategic materials in return. Initially, Nehru rejected these proposals but when the Senate shelved the Indian aid bill he agreed to all the conditions except supplying materials that could be used in the production of atomic weapons. After this, rapid progress was made and on 15 June 1951 Truman finally signed the bill. Although Nehru immediately expressed his deep gratitude, this episode only heightened tensions between Washington and New Delhi.[14]

International relations

Following on from the strengthening of NATO during the winter crisis, Australia and New Zealand had become increasingly anxious that the US security umbrella be extended to the Pacific. As a result, when Spender, Doidge and Dulles met in Canberra in February 1951 to discuss a peace treaty with Japan, the question of a defence pact soon dominated proceedings. The Australian and New Zealand representatives desired a formal tripartite mutual security treaty and made this a condition of their agreeing to a non-punitive peace treaty permitting Japan many freedoms, including Japanese rearmament, claiming they still feared a resurgent Japan. Initially, Dulles claimed that he was not authorized to agree to a formal pact and suggested an informal 'off-shore' linkage of Asian countries stretching from Japan to New Zealand. Spender and Doidge, however, opposed a loose alliance with weak Asian countries and refused to accept the draft Japanese peace treaty. Under this pressure, Dulles admitted that he was authorized to agree to such a Pacific pact if this was necessary to gain agreement over Japan. After this breakthrough, rapid progress was made and Dulles left

Canberra with an initialled copy of the Australia, New Zealand and United States Security Treaty (ANZUS).[15]

While this agreement greatly pleased both Spender and Doidge, they realized that these arrangements still had to be accepted by the Truman administration, including a reluctant Acheson, and then ratified by Congress. This meant that throughout the following months Australia and New Zealand had to be extremely careful to retain Washington's goodwill. These two countries, moreover, were made aware of the British government's anger at its exclusion from ANZUS and its concern that Australia and New Zealand would no longer be able to fulfil their Commonwealth commitment to defend the Middle East. Australia and New Zealand remained sensitive to British views but were determined to secure a US security guarantee. For that reason Canberra and Wellington were greatly relieved that the Attlee government reluctantly announced its support for the Pacific pact. Still, as a concession to the British, at a Commonwealth Defence Ministers' Conference held in June 1951 Australia and New Zealand accepted that the Commonwealth's security priority remained the Middle East.[16]

The Good Offices Committee

As these military, domestic and international developments unfolded, the US and Commonwealth governments considered how best to implement the terms of General Assembly Resolution 498 (V). Publicly, these countries gave their full support to the UN's efforts to bring about the cessation of hostilities by peaceful means through the GOC. Difficulties arose immediately for the Commonwealth, however, regarding the composition of this body. The resolution asked the President of the General Assembly, Nasrollah Entezam of Iran, to 'designate forthwith two persons who would meet with him at any suitable opportunity to use their good offices'. Entezam, therefore, wished to simply resurrect the Cease-fire Committee and again work alongside Pearson and Rau.

But the Canadian and Indian governments were far less eager to become directly involved in the conciliatory efforts of the UN this time. In New Delhi, Nehru was still smarting from the defeat of the 12-Power Arab-Asian proposal in the General Assembly and did not want India to be associated with a body established under a resolution it had opposed. Nehru also doubted that the GOC would have any success in making contact with the Chinese until the Americans accepted Beijing's 'reasonable' demands for a ceasefire in the framework of a general East Asian settlement.[17] In addition, the Indian Prime Minister was sensitive to the negative reports he was receiving from his sister in relation to India's request for food aid. Mrs Pandit noted that US public opinion was 'being whipped up against us because of our independent policy in the UN'.[18] Nehru responded that while US criticism of India did not affect him personally and would not alter Indian policy, he thought it best, given India's dire need for wheat, to 'keep our heads down ... and refuse to enter into a bitter controversy with the US'.[19] In Ottawa, Pearson told his Cabinet that he had no specific objections to serving on the GOC but since India was not participating he felt that Canada should also decline. In addition, Pearson was concerned with the state of Canadian relations with the United States after Canada's very public reluctance to support the 'aggressor' resolution. The Secretary of State for External Affairs thus thought it better to avoid membership of the GOC since this would only place Canada in another potentially controversial position vis-à-vis Washington.[20]

Following these negative responses Entezam designated the Swedish Permanent Representative to the UN, Sven Grafström, and the Mexican Ambassador at the UN, Luis Padilla Nervo, to serve on the GOC. Thoughts then quickly turned to the course of the committee's work. Naturally, Entezam looked first to the US government for advice and Acheson suggested that the sooner the Committee approach Beijing the more likely it was that it would be successful. Behind these views was the US fear that the military successes of the UNC might be short-lived since the CPVA had just launched its February offensive. The Secretary of State also expected the GOC's approach to be snubbed by the Chinese, which would allow the consideration of additional measures to commence swiftly.[21] The Commonwealth members, on the other hand, adopted a more relaxed attitude to the work of the GOC, believing that a military stalemate was the likely outcome of the conflict and the Communists would eventually agree to a ceasefire. Bevin thus argued that the GOC should carry out its work unhurriedly and unobtrusively, pursuing all available avenues.[22] In concurrence, Spender believed that to maintain a common front in the UN the GOC had to be given every opportunity.[23]

When the GOC did at last get down to work the Truman administration instantly became frustrated with its efforts to communicate with the Chinese. On a number of occasions during February 1951 the Committee sent notes to both the Chinese Ambassador in Stockholm and the Chinese government via the Swedish Embassy in Beijing suggesting talks should be held between the GOC and Chinese representatives at a place of their choosing. But the PRC gave no indication of its willingness to discuss a peaceful settlement. Despite this apparent failure, the GOC continued to call for more time, arguing that Beijing's delayed response suggested a division of opinion within the Chinese government.[24] Washington was unconvinced by this argument, however, and suspected that the Chinese were delaying their answer while they prepared for a renewed military offensive. In consequence, Acheson became impatient with the GOC and pressured its members to issue their final report to the General Assembly.[25] At the same time, the Commonwealth's support for the GOC evaporated. In March Bevin was replaced by Morrison, who was less willing to challenge the US position and accepted the view that the work of the GOC would come to nothing.[26] Both Spender and Pearson also lost patience with the GOC and realized that its refusal to admit failure was causing much annoyance in Washington.[27]

Still, unlike the Americans, the Commonwealth members remained opposed to consideration of additional members and favoured trying to find a peaceful solution through channels beyond the GOC. They thus rallied around a proposal made by Morrison that they hoped would placate the US government. The British Foreign Secretary suggested that the UN members contributing forces to the Korean action issue a public declaration restating the UN's political objectives and the ceasefire principles to reassure Beijing that the UN had no aggressive designs.[28] This proposal did gain considerable sympathy in the State Department but the Truman administration preferred that the President issue a vague statement of aims as a report of the unified command to the UN.[29] After much discussion the Commonwealth members were willing to give way on this point, but this concept quickly fell out of favour in Washington following MacArthur's unauthorized statement demanding that the Chinese accept the unification of Korea under UN terms. The Commonwealth members urged reconsideration of this proposal after MacArthur's dismissal but Truman, under intense public and Congressional pressure, was not prepared to make any further appeals. The Commonwealth members then finally accepted that this window of opportunity had been firmly closed when the Communists launched their Spring Offensive. Instead, the US government now concentrated its efforts wholeheartedly on punishing the Chinese through the UN.

The Additional Measures Committee

As well as the GOC, General Assembly Resolution 498 (V) had established an ad hoc committee to consider additional measures to meet the Chinese aggression in Korea. This committee was only to report its findings if the GOC made no progress in its mission to bring about the cessation of hostilities by peaceful means. The body was also to be composed of the 14 member states represented on the UN Collective Measures Committee: Australia, Belgium, Brazil, Britain, Burma, Canada, Egypt, France, Mexico, the Philippines, Turkey, the United States, Venezuela and Yugoslavia. The ad hoc committee, therefore, included both the United States and a strong Commonwealth contingent. Partly because of this fact the question of additional measures generated considerably greater friction between Washington and the Commonwealth capitals than that of good offices.

At one extreme, Acheson sought to have the ad hoc committee meet as soon as possible and give full and sober consideration of sanctions even though the GOC had yet to conclude its work. The Secretary of State believed that this course would put pressure on the Chinese to comply with the efforts of the GOC.[30] Bevin, at the other extreme, gave the British delegation clear instructions to delay for as long as possible any discussion of additional measures, believing that this could only prejudice the work of the GOC.[31] With the Australian general election in mind, Spender also saw no need to rush consideration of additional measures while the work of the GOC stood a chance of success.[32] Interestingly, during February and March 1951, while the military situation in Korea and the US domestic dimension were relatively stable and the GOC had not yet completely failed, the Truman administration was content to bow to Commonwealth pressure and accepted that meetings of the ad hoc committee should be postponed.[33]

In the meantime, the US government considered what possible additional measures could be imposed upon the PRC. The State Department ruled out all military or political sanctions believing they would be too controversial, risk escalation or would be ineffective. It thus decided that the 'irreducible minimum' a General Assembly resolution could contain was a non-binding recommendation for the imposition of a selective embargo on strategic goods with each state determining what commodities it would restrict, applying its own export controls and reporting its implementation to the ad hoc committee.[34] Evidently, the Truman administration realized the difficulties they would have convincing its allies as well as a two-thirds majority of UN members to support harsher measures than these in the current tense atmosphere in New York. The proposal for a selective embargo, then, represented much self-restraint and willingness to compromise on the part of the US government.

Nevertheless, the British government was reluctant to go even this far. The Chiefs of Staff believed that a selective embargo would have little military impact on the enemy since China's limited sea-going trade could be easily offset by overland trade with the Soviet Union.[35] The Colonial Office was also concerned that economic sanctions against Beijing would undermine Hong Kong, whose viability relied on trade with China.[36] This would in turn weaken the British economy.[37] In addition, all the Old Commonwealth members argued that they had already privately imposed trade restrictions on strategic exports to the PRC since its intervention in Korea. India and Pakistan also highlighted that they had very little trade with China, especially when it came to strategic materials. A UN embargo would thus not affect them.

In this climate progress on additional measures remained slow. The ad hoc committee did hold a number of administrative meetings agreeing to rename the body the Additional Measures Committee (AMC) and to continue to give priority to the work of GOC.[38] The only concession made to US calls to proceed immediately was the appointment of a subcommittee consisting of the United States, Britain, France, Australia and Venezuela to draw up a shortlist of possible additional measures when word had been received from the GOC.[39] The work of the AMC was then left in suspended animation for the rest of March as the military situation and the work of the GOC took their course. The US and British governments did try to use this opening to find an agreed position on sanctions but their respective views only diverged further. London revealed that to prevent confusion and abuses it would only accept a selective embargo that included lists of specific strategic items.[40] Acheson argued, on the contrary, that it would be difficult and time-consuming to compile a list acceptable to the majority of UN members.[41]

Of the other Commonwealth countries, those represented on the AMC unsurprisingly took by far the keenest interest in this subject. But no consensus existed among them. On one hand, the Australian government was sympathetic to the US proposal but shared the British view that a decision on economic sanctions was not immediately necessary. Canberra's cautious approach was a direct result of the upcoming Australian general elections. Menzies was unwilling to make foreign policy decisions that meant taking sides between Washington and London given the Australian public's sentimental attachment to Britain.[42] Canada, on the other hand, was less prepared to voice its opposition to action in the AMC if this risked friction with its southern neighbour. The other Old Commonwealth members not represented on the AMC generally supported the British position but remained content to let the two senior Western powers settle their differences among themselves. Significantly, India was not consulted by its Commonwealth partners on these matters and remained almost silent on the sanctions issue while Nehru's appeal for US wheat remained pending.

In April 1951, however, with tensions reaching fever pitch in the United States following MacArthur's dismissal, Acheson's patience with the Commonwealth wore thin. He believed that now the threat of escalation posed by the General had been removed as the Commonwealth had wished, these countries should accept the need for tougher action against China.[43] With the Communist Spring Offensive, the Secretary of State's willingness to delay action on additional measures ran out completely. Acheson told the British government in no uncertain terms that this act ended all prospect of negotiation for a peaceful settlement and made it imperative that the General Assembly impose a selective embargo on China to demonstrate that the UN could not be intimidated by aggression.[44] Furthermore, Acheson informed the US delegation that as damaging as disharmony among allies in the UN may be, still greater damage would be done at home if the US government did not publicly take a stand on additional measures.[45]

With the hardening of the US position, the limited Commonwealth resistance that had existed up to this point soon fragmented. The Commonwealth capitals all realized that to call for further delay before imposing additional measures would place them in an impossible position with Washington. A selective embargo on strategic goods was thus accepted as a necessary minimum in light of the continued Chinese aggression. This view was coupled with the fact that the resultant UNC defensive action and counteroffensive helped confirm that the Truman administration wished to avoid escalating the conflict unless UN forces were about to be driven out of Korea. Notably, at this time the Commonwealth members contributing forces dropped their earlier concerns, now MacArthur had been replaced by Ridgway, and readily accepted Truman's decision to authorize the UNC to take retaliatory action against Manchurian air bases and engage in 'hot pursuit' if Chinese and Soviet air forces became actively involved in the Spring Offensive.

The first clear signal of this change of position within the Commonwealth came from Britain. Morrison had already dropped Bevin's objections to a selective embargo but had been adamant that the GOC should be given every chance to succeed before the AMC began its formal consideration of additional measures.[46] Yet after the turn of events in Korea Morrison had written to Acheson stating that the British government appreciated the domestic difficulties the Truman administration faced and agreed that the AMC should meet immediately. He emphasized, all the same, that his freedom to manoeuvre was restricted by the British government's own domestic difficulties, specifically the divisions within the Labour Party regarding foreign policy, its increasingly tenuous position in Parliament and the growing anti-US fervour in Britain that would be intensified by the imposition of sanctions.[47]

Following the British lead, the other Commonwealth members expressed their support for a selective embargo. After his landslide victory in the Australian general election Menzies revealed to Attlee that the Australian government would support the US proposal since its opposition would have an adverse effect on discussions concerning the ratification of the ANZUS Treaty taking place in Washington.[48] Wellington had similar concerns regarding the ANZUS Treaty and now openly came out in support of a selective embargo.[49] The Canadian Cabinet, moreover, accepted Pearson's analysis that a UN embargo on strategic materials was desirable since it would standardize the restrictions on trade already imposed by Canada and others.[50] Even the Indian delegation hinted at its support for the US proposal, stating that it might make Nehru's tentative proposal for a resolution calling for a ceasefire along the 38th parallel unnecessary.[51]

Despite this apparent narrowing of differences, friction between Washington and London re-erupted in early May 1951. Morrison's views on a selective embargo had not reflected the majority opinion of the British Cabinet, which was eager to adopt a more independent foreign policy after Bevin's death in an attempt to win back the

Labour Left. Accordingly, the British delegation informed their US counterparts that Britain was not prepared to vote for a selective embargo until a declaration of UN aims in Korea had been issued and the AMC had decided upon a specific list of items to be embargoed.[52] In the AMC Jebb then called for more time to study the implications of a selective embargo on strategic goods and cast doubt on whether such measures would impact upon China's ability to wage a war.[53]

In the face of this British reversal, Acheson went on the offensive. He wrote a personal message to Morrison stating that the failure of the GOC had demonstrated that the inaction of the AMC was far from helping to bring about negotiations for a peaceful settlement. He also stressed that such indecision suggested timidity on the part of the UN in responding to the continued Chinese aggression.[54] What is more, the US Ambassador to Britain, Walter Gifford, stressed to the Foreign Office the wave of anti-British feeling that had emerged in the United States, first over Britain's alleged role in MacArthur's dismissal and now London's resistance to additional measures. Gifford claimed that many Americans believed, rightly or wrongly, that Britain was allowing strategic materials to reach China via Hong Kong.[55] Yet Acheson did write again to Morrison stating that he remained sensitive to British concerns and reassuring him that, barring military disaster in Korea, the US proposal was not designed to be an 'opening wedge for [a] complete embargo'.[56]

The Secretary of State's carrot-and-stick policy proved effective. Morrison, greatly concerned that Anglo-American relations were being severely damaged, strongly urged his Cabinet colleagues to agree to a selective embargo. After intense debate, this policy was agreed upon although a number of Cabinet ministers continued to fear that the Americans intended a complete economic embargo of China in the future that would risk general war and economic disaster for Hong Kong.[57] With Anglo-American differences resolved at last a united position took shape in the AMC. The British, Australian and Canadian delegations accepted a selective embargo in principle and the US draft resolution went through a number of editorial revisions until the text was acceptable to all. On 14 May 1951 the work of the AMC concluded with its members unanimously deciding to recommend a selective embargo on strategic goods to the General Assembly.[58]

In the First Committee, nonetheless, while the US and Old Commonwealth members rallied around the AMC's report, both the Indian and Pakistani delegations revealed they would abstain in the vote. Rau explained that India had opposed General Assembly Resolution 498 (V) in the first place and now doubted the positive effect of a selective embargo, believing such measures might create additional obstacles to a peaceful settlement. Still, neither of the New Commonwealth members made any attempt to propose an alternative resolution or to convince their Arab-Asian colleagues to oppose the AMC's report. With the second phase of the Communist Spring Offensive now underway the vast majority of UN members saw little choice but to support a selective embargo. The First Committee, therefore, approved the AMC's report by 47 votes to zero with five members not participating and only India and Pakistan abstaining with the Soviet bloc.[59] This vote was reproduced in the Plenary and General Assembly Resolution 500 (V) (see Appendix 9, p. 266–8) was adopted.[60]

Implementing General Assembly Resolution 500 (V)

Over the next few weeks, as the military situation in Korea stabilized near the 38th parallel once the Communist Spring Offensive petered out, attention shifted away from the UN. The implementation of General Assembly Resolution 500 (V), however, was not without controversy. The resolution explicitly requested the AMC to: report on the general effectiveness of the selective embargo; report the desirability of continuing, extending or relaxing it; continue its consideration of additional measures to meet the aggression in Korea; and receive within 30 days the reports sent by each UN member on the measures it had taken to prevent the export of strategic material to the PRC. This last point proved most contentious since Washington and London bickered over the timing and content of these reports.

Acheson wanted to send the US report providing an extensive list of materials it considered of strategic value without delay to act as a guide for the other UN members.[61] For the majority of the Commonwealth members the US example was unproblematic since they had already imposed widespread restrictions on exports to China or, in the cases of India and Pakistan, had very limited trade of any kind with the PRC. This question was much more difficult for the British as an all-embracing definition of strategic materials might have dire economic consequences. Due in large part to Hong Kong's and, to some extent, Malaya's, dependency on trade with China, the Attlee government maintained that rubber was not of sufficient strategic value to justify a full embargo and preferred suitable quantitative controls.[62] Even so, Acheson violently opposed this interpretation. He stressed that the British position could not be defended against public criticism in the United States and would undermine the US government's statements regarding allied cooperation in implementing the UN resolution.[63] In light of these arguments, Morrison convinced his reluctant Cabinet colleagues to back down and rubber, along with another 50 strategic items, was included in Britain's report to the AMC.[64]

US and Commonwealth thoughts then tentatively turned to what other measures the AMC could take if, as was expected, the selective embargo proved ineffective. Eager to deflect attention away from a complete economic embargo, the British suggested that the AMC make an appeal for additional troops from members not yet contributing.[65] Acheson agreed that a request for further ground forces was a logical corollary to the economic measures but he feared that such discussion in the AMC would lead to undesirable debate concerning the entire Korean situation. The Secretary of State preferred instead that the unified command make a unilateral appeal through Secretary-General Lie.[66] Although the British had doubts regarding its efficacy, they accepted this course and Lie duly sent an appeal to all the members who had expressed support for the UN action but not contributed forces. Acheson's moderate approach to additional measures can be explained by the ever-improving military situation and the fact the MacArthur controversy was finally beginning to die down. Little domestic pressure thus existed for extra punitive action against China in this brief moment of relative calm.

General Assembly Resolution 500 (V) also reaffirmed the continued UN policy to bring about the cessation of hostilities and the achievement of its objectives in Korea by peaceful means, requesting the GOC to continue its good offices. By this time, though, the prospects of the GOC appeared bleaker than ever. Its members simply wanted to issue their final report to the General Assembly conceding failure. But they also wished to include a draft resolution providing that upon some clear indication by the PRC or North Korea that they had no intention of advancing south of the 38th parallel that the UNC would make a similar commitment not to cross the line. It was hoped such an agreement would bring about a de facto ceasefire allowing a more permanent armistice to be found by negotiation.[67]

For once the US and British governments were completely united in their opposition to this proposal. Acheson doubted that a contentious General Assembly resolution would provide the best vehicle for opening negotiations with the Communists and preferred discreet efforts made through private diplomatic channels.[68] Morrison agreed that a fresh initiative made in the General Assembly could only be divisive.[69] The Foreign Secretary also did not want the GOC to report failure and be wound up, leaving the AMC alone. He was concerned that this would give the false impression that all hope of a negotiated settlement had been abandoned and that the UN was determined to impose additional measures.[70] In response to this Anglo-American opposition the GOC grudgingly dropped this proposal from its report and remained officially active.

By mid-June 1951 the work of the AMC and the GOC had ground to a halt. Members of both committees had accepted that they could contribute little towards finding a peaceful solution to the Korean conflict for the moment. Nevertheless, with the halting of the Communist Spring Offensive the military situation on the ground was at its most stable since the original North Korean invasion. The stalemate near the 38th parallel had effectively reproduced the *status quo ante bellum*. Consequently, both sides came to accept that they could no longer achieve their ends by military means in the present circumstances. Efforts were thus made beyond the UN to bring about ceasefire negotiations. The first such attempt was made in early May at an informal function in New York when Malik had hinted to Austin that Korea should be settled by direct discussion between the United States and the Soviet Union.[71] A few weeks later State Department Counsellor and Soviet expert George Kennan, currently on leave, sent a message to Malik at Acheson's behest stating his 'unofficial' view that it would be useful if they 'could meet and have a quiet talk some time in the future'.[72] As a result, the two men met at Malik's home but the Soviet Permanent Representative remained cagey, only revealing that the Soviet government desired a peaceful settlement to the Korean problem at the earliest possible moment.[73]

Just as these private ceasefire efforts were beginning to appear stillborn a major breakthrough occurred. On 23 June 1951 Malik, talking on the UN radio programme 'Price of Peace', delivered a speech stating that the Korean problem could be settled and calling for the belligerents in Korea to meet to discuss an armistice providing for the withdrawal of forces from the 38th parallel. Importantly, Malik indicated that any talks would be of a purely military nature and did not mention any of the political preconditions for a ceasefire formerly listed by the Chinese.[74] While Malik refused to make further comment on this issue, the US Ambassador in Moscow, Alan Kirk, spoke with Soviet Deputy Foreign Minister Andrei Gromyko who stated that the Chinese might agree to purely military ceasefire talks.[75] Ridgway then made a public statement indicating to the Communist commanders that a meeting could be arranged to discuss a ceasefire.[76] Within a matter of days Kim Il-sung and Peng Dehuai agreed to a meeting at Kaesong, just north of the battlefront. On 11 July 1951 the Korean armistice negotiations commenced between a UN team, consisting solely of US military personnel acting on behalf of the unified command, and a Communist team composed of representatives from the NKPA and CPVA.

Conclusion

The six months following the winter crisis witnessed the gradual fragmentation of Commonwealth unity as its members were unwilling and unable to constrain the policy of the United States.

This is not to say that relations between the United States and the Commonwealth members were harmonious throughout this period since a number of issues did arise, especially between Washington and London, regarding the UN's response to Chinese aggression. Yet at no time did the Commonwealth members feel the need to try to seize the initiative at the UN away from the Truman administration. Instead, the Commonwealth resumed its traditional role in support of US policy. Regarding the GOC, differences did arise over the pace of the Committee's work and the means employed to achieve its goals. But these issues never risked developing into a split since all the Commonwealth members, at varying speeds, came to accept the US analysis that the GOC's efforts were futile. As the chances of establishing a ceasefire faded, however, more serious tension emerged between Washington and the Commonwealth capitals over the question of imposing additional measures upon China. Although the Commonwealth members had only minor reservations regarding the US proposal for a selective embargo on strategic goods, they still had grave concerns over the timing of such action. Still, Commonwealth resistance to additional measures dissolved as battlefield events and US intransigence made this a very risky policy. At the same time, domestic constraints within the Commonwealth countries were either lifted or ignored.

The Commonwealth became largely disunited during the spring and early summer of 1951 since the conditions for unity that had existed over the winter were removed. Most importantly, despite much bloodshed, throughout these months the battlefront did not move far from the 38th parallel. Under these conditions, the Commonwealth members steadily became convinced that an escalation of the conflict was much less likely and were, in the main, content that the Truman administration had accepted the military stalemate and would not seek to expand the fighting to China. The replacement of the erratic MacArthur with the more reliable Ridgway was extremely important to this shift in viewpoint. Key Commonwealth personalities were also unwilling or unable to resist US policy at the UN. After the tension of the previous months all these figures preferred to mend fences rather than burn their bridges with Washington. Furthermore, no formal meeting brought the Commonwealth leaders together to coordinate policy since none were present in New York and no Prime Ministers' Conference was held at this time. And ultimately, the Commonwealth failed to unite due to the Truman administration's lack of willingness to compromise. Under intense domestic pressure the President and his advisers were placed in a foreign policy straightjacket and all attempts by the Commonwealth to modify the US position were bluntly rejected. Luckily, the Commonwealth members recognized the extremely complex position the US government found itself in and backed down in the interest of bilateral relations with Washington.

CHAPTER 4

FROM PANMUNJOM TO PARIS AND BACK AGAIN, JULY 1951–JUNE 1952

Between July 1951 and June 1952 the UN was notable by its absence from answering the Korean question. Unlike in the previous 12 months, the world organization did not provide the main forum for attempts to bring about a peaceful end to the Korean War. The focus of these efforts, instead, rested with the armistice negotiations being conducted between the UN and Communist negotiators on the battlefront. For the vast majority of this period the world community was generally united in the view that the UN could do little to precipitate the end of the conflict now that the belligerents had sat down together to discuss a ceasefire. Moreover, at the UN there remained for many months a strong sense of optimism that an acceptable truce could be found despite the fluctuating fortunes of these talks. Evidently, the majority of UN members firmly believed that the UN negotiation team, composed solely of US military personnel, could restore peace to the peninsula.

In this atmosphere of relative calm and confidence all the Commonwealth members, even India, supported the US policy at the UN and felt no need to try to constrain the Truman administration. Since late January 1951 the Commonwealth's challenge to US hegemony at the world organization had fragmented and by July its members were once again pursuing largely independent policies. Over the next year this pattern persisted—even hardened—since the conditions necessary for Commonwealth unity were completely deficient. At the root of the Commonwealth's relative indifference to the Korean question was the stability of the military situation on the ground. The stalemate near the 38th parallel coupled with the existence of the armistice talks convinced the Commonwealth members that an escalation of the conflict beyond the peninsula was a distant possibility. In addition, due to domestic and international pressures upon each government, key Commonwealth personalities were much less inclined to focus on the Korean question or challenge US leadership at the UN. Coordinating a united Commonwealth position was also made difficult since no opportunities arose for the leading figures to gather for this purpose. Finally, the Truman administration, under intense public scrutiny, was unwilling to make any concessions regarding its Korean policy at the UN. In contrast to the previous winter, the US government was much more interested in complying with the views of American voters than with its allies.

As indicated above, the general lack of activity at the UN concerning Korea and the specific failure of the Commonwealth to unite to constrain US policy at this time had much to do with simultaneous military, domestic and international events as well as the course of the truce talks. The following pages, therefore, will provide the necessary contextual details to gain a full understanding of the UN debate.

Military situation

Even though the armistice negotiations had commenced in early July 1951, bitter fighting continued in Korea and casualty figures mounted. Yet the military situation was very different from the dynamic ebb and flow that had existed since the outbreak of the conflict. From this point on the Korea War witnessed a classic military stalemate in the vicinity of the 38th parallel comparable to the Western Front during the First World War. With the *status quo ante bellum* restored both sides employed largely defensive strategies and constructed strong, in-depth positions in the mountainous terrain. The UNC and the Communist High Command had both concluded that a massive mobile infantry offensive to win an outright victory was now impossible and preferred to use artillery barrages and, for the UN side, aerial bombardment to wear down the enemy's capacity and will to fight. In Washington, under public and Congressional pressure, consideration of the use of atomic weapons to find a breakthrough continued, but with the crisis abating this thinking did not get far. The Truman administration appreciated that to take such drastic action now that peace talks had begun would be widely opposed by America's allies and in Asia.[1]

Still, limited strategic advances were made by the UNC. In August and September 1951 Van Fleet wished to seize a series of hills in the Punchbowl area in central Korea that formed a ridge overlooking UN positions. Although UN forces eventually achieved their objective, this operation cost 2,700 UN and approximately 15,000 Communist casualties. For obvious reasons this event became known as the Battle of Bloody Ridge. To make matters worse, the enemy simply pulled back to a similarly well-defended ridge just 1,500 m further north, leading UN soldiers to dub this 'Heartbreak Ridge'. Another costly battle took place here as the UNC launched operations Commando, Nomad and Polar to gain control over this important strip of land. Eventually, victory was won and Line Missouri was reached, but only after 3,700 UN and 25,000 Communist casualties had been inflicted. After these minimal territorial gains were bought at such a heavy price, Ridgway ordered the UN forces to cease all offensive operations. At the same time, the Communists decided to abort plans for an offensive of their own.[2]

Domestic developments

In the United States the political situation remained very tense after the controversies surrounding the dismissal of MacArthur in April 1951.[3] Truman and Acheson had lost the support of the vast majority of the electorate and were under considerable Congressional pressure as McCarthyism reached its zenith. On top of the unpopularity of the government's limited war strategy in Korea, the Republican Right continued to criticize US policy in Europe and East Asia, and the administration was plagued by a number of corruption scandals. By February 1952 Truman's approval ratings were at a record low of 22 per cent, a figure not surpassed by any other president until 2008. As a result, on 29 March 1952, after being defeated in the New Hampshire Democrat primary election, Truman announced that he would not stand for re-election. Although a great surprise at the time, in hindsight it is understandable why Truman did not believe he could pull off another shock victory as he had done in 1948. But by choosing not to run the President made it very difficult to pursue any new course of action since he would not be in a position to implement his policies. He also did not want to adopt any radical foreign policy position that might prejudice the Democrat nominee's chances of success.[4]

The domestic political scene in Britain was equally unsettled. With the Labour government's position becoming increasingly untenable, Attlee called a snap general election for 25 October 1951 even though the previous election had been held only 18 months previously. The contest that followed was bitterly fought on a range of domestic issues, but few marked differences existed between the foreign policies of the two major parties. In the end, the Conservatives, with the support of the National Liberal Party, won with a majority of just 16 seats even though they received a quarter of a million fewer votes nationally than Labour.[5]

The new Prime Minister, Winston Churchill, did not, however, let this narrow victory deter him from his efforts to resume his role as one of the world's great statesmen.[6] Foreign Secretary Anthony Eden, Churchill's heir-apparent, also wished to reassert his position on the international stage.[7] The cornerstone of the new government's foreign policy, therefore, was Churchill's concept, first made public in 1948, of Britain being positioned at the centre of three interlocking circles: the British Empire and Commonwealth, the 'English-speaking world' including the United States and a 'United Europe'. It was London's responsibility to carefully maintain the connections between these three groups of states. But foremost in Churchill's and

Eden's minds was guaranteeing British security through close relations with Washington. Both men wished to resurrect the wartime alliance and it was Churchill, after all, who had coined the phrase the 'special relationship' in his 5 March 1946 'Sinews of Peace Address' in Fulton, Missouri. In their efforts to court the US government, Churchill and Eden were generally willing to play a secondary role at the UN, especially as both men had little faith in the organization, believing that the Great Powers should resolve their differences through summitry. Furthermore, Churchill and Eden were anxious to avoid raising small points of disagreement with the Americans on Korea since they recognized that Britain was bearing only a small fraction of the military burden. Yet soon after coming into office Churchill made it clear to Eden that he believed that Korea was of little strategic importance and that the conflict should be terminated at once so resources could be concentrated elsewhere.[8]

The election of the Churchill government, nevertheless, met a mixed response in Washington. Many were relieved that the socialist Labour government had been replaced by the Conservatives, and Churchill's personal standing remained as high as ever. But Truman did not have the same close relationship as his predecessor, Franklin Roosevelt, had had with Churchill. Dealings between them at the Potsdam Conference had been limited and Truman had been wary of being manipulated by Churchill. As a result, no initial rapport developed between these two very different men even though Churchill, based mainly on their discussions regarding the atomic bomb, did think Truman would be more resolute with Stalin than Roosevelt had been at Yalta. Also, despite the fact he had seen and approved the text in advance, the President still harboured animosity towards Churchill after his comments regarding an 'iron curtain' in his 'Sinews of Peace Address'. Truman had invited Churchill to Fulton that day and was greatly annoyed that the former British Prime Minister's comments had led to much public questioning of his then policy of cooperation with the Soviet Union. In the meantime, the two men had also clashed privately when the United States decided to ignore the Quebec Agreement and cut Britain off from post-war nuclear collaboration.[9] Finally, Truman had some concern that he might be overshadowed by Churchill as a global statesman.[10]

Relations between Acheson and Eden were even more fraught despite their later claims to the contrary. The personalities of the two foreign ministers clashed, since both men were confident to the point of arrogance, were very reluctant to make concessions and even dressed and spoke in a similar manner. Peter Lowe accurately described the two men as 'prima donnas of haughty approach'.[11] An example of this friction occurred in early 1952 when the UN discussed the fate of the Trusteeship of Eritrea. Eden eventually conceded that Eritrea should be merged with Ethiopia but the damage with Acheson had already been done.[12]

Close behind forging the 'special relationship' in the Churchill government's list of foreign policy priorities was strengthening the Commonwealth. The Prime Minister and his Foreign Secretary firmly believed that the organization represented the great legacy of the British Empire, and hoped that its members would enjoy the close relationship that had existed during the Second World War under British leadership. Churchill thus urged his Commonwealth colleagues to maintain strong connections with Britain and to cling to the liberal democratic traditions that gave the organization enormous moral authority in international affairs. Nonetheless, privately, the Prime Minister, on racial grounds, was not enthusiastic about Britain dealing as equals with India, Pakistan and Ceylon, whose independence he had opposed. These views, however, were counterbalanced by those of Eden and Secretary of State for Commonwealth Relations Lord Ismay. Eden and Ismay better realized Britain's diminished position in the world since 1945 and believed that if Britain was to continue to play a major role in the emerging Third World it had to maintain close relations with these countries. Still, Ismay was replaced in March 1952 by Churchill's close friend Lord Salisbury, a hard-line imperialist.[13]

The Commonwealth members themselves reacted in a variety of ways to the election of the Churchill government. Due in very large part to his record during the Second World War, Churchill was held in very high esteem throughout the Commonwealth. This sentiment was felt most strongly in Australia and New Zealand where the Anglo-centric conservative governments hoped for ever-closer bonds with Britain.[14] On the contrary, Pearson feared that Churchill would try to restrict Canada's more independently-minded foreign policy and he thought Churchill and Eden's traditional views were not suited to contemporary Cold War problems.[15] Pearson was also concerned with Churchill's age and ability to withstand the rigours of leadership at this critical juncture.[16] In South Africa, the Nationalist government, and the Afrikaner population as a whole, also viewed Churchill with suspicion given his emphasis on the Empire. And the New Commonwealth countries were least enthusiastic about Churchill's election. The new Prime Minister's views on race and decolonization were well documented and these members understood that Churchill did not truly accept them as equals and was not keen on coordinating policy with them. In particular, the vast majority of members of the ruling Indian National Congress, including Nehru, as well as many politicians in Pakistan, distrusted and disliked Churchill because of his long-held opposition to Indian independence.[17]

Beyond Britain, important developments were taking place in other Commonwealth countries. In India the first general election held in the country since independence took place. The election campaign began in late 1951 and was completed with the formation of the first House of the People, or 'Lok Sabha', on 17 April 1952. Nehru's Indian National Congress Party won a massive majority of 364 of the 489 seats and received almost 45 per cent of the popular vote while the second largest party, the Communist Party of India, won just 16 seats and a little over 3 per cent of the vote. Throughout this period, therefore, the Prime Minister had been preoccupied with electioneering and trying to make sure that India's first general election ran smoothly and was not marred by sectarian violence. Consequently, Nehru was much less proactive on the international scene than previously.[18]

In Pakistan the political situation was even more unstable. On 16 October 1951 Liaquat Ali-Khan was assassinated by an Afghan assassin in retaliation for his tough policy towards the Pushtun tribes in the border area. This action sparked a period of political instability within Pakistan with the focus of attention being firmly fixed on domestic rather than international issues. In the short term, however, the Governor-General of Pakistan, Khawaja Nazimuddin, stepped down to assume the premiership without an election and was eager to consolidate his position at home. Nazimuddin's principal objectives were to avoid the disintegration of Pakistan by trying to address the problems of lawlessness in the tribal lands in the north and, more significantly, the serious rifts that were emerging between West and East Pakistan.[19]

Furthermore, in New Zealand, with the waterfront dispute fresh in the memory, Holland called a snap general election, held on 1 September 1951. Holland was concerned that many New Zealanders opposed the emergency measures he had implemented to put down the labour unrest and he sought a mandate for these actions. This ploy proved very successful as the National Party increased its majority in Parliament by four seats. The general election thus strengthened Holland's position. Another significant development in Wellington also took place at this time. With the ANZUS Treaty all but signed, Doidge decided to retire as Minister of External Affairs and become the New Zealand High Commissioner to Britain. In his stead, Holland appointed the Attorney General and Minister of Justice, Thomas Clifton Webb. Webb was a senior figure within the government very close to the Prime Minister and had played a major role in the waterfront dispute. Nonetheless, he had no experience in foreign affairs. Partly because he had no ties to the Anglo-centric diplomatic bureaucracy, Webb had few emotional ties to the Commonwealth and put more emphasis on building close relations with the United States.[20]

International relations

During the second half of 1951 by far the most important international issue was the conclusion of a Japanese peace treaty to bring the Pacific War to a formal end. This question was very complicated since over 50 countries, including the United States, the

Soviet Union, China and all the Commonwealth members were still technically at war with Japan. The US government, as the Occupation Power, had inevitably taken the leading role in trying to resolve this issue. The Truman administration, determined to make Japan its Cold War ally, wished to conclude a peace that restored Japanese independence and allowed the country many freedoms—including the right to rearm for national defence—but required Japan to forsake its imperial possessions and assets, pay compensation to the Allied territories it had occupied, pay compensation to Allied prisoners of war and accept the decisions of the Tokyo War Trials. Truman had appointed John Foster Dulles, despite his Republican loyalties, to act as his negotiator with the Japanese government and the other interested countries to try to sell this solution before the San Francisco Conference of September 1951.[21]

However, Dulles' efforts were dogged from the outset by a number of serious problems. To start with, there was little agreement over who would actually attend the conference. Much disagreement between Washington and its allies erupted over whether the PRC or the Chinese Nationalists should be invited. The US government would only accept the latter while the Commonwealth was divided. Britain, India and Pakistan strongly favoured the former, but the other members would not deviate from the US course. Similar but less intense disagreements also arose between these countries over whether the ROK or the DPRK should represent Korea. In the end, no invitation was sent to any Chinese or Korean authority. The Soviet bloc complained against this glaring omission but, interestingly, did not make the inclusion of the PRC a condition on their participation. Nonetheless, three of the 54 countries invited—India, Burma and Yugoslavia—refused to attend the conference for this reason and because they claimed the US draft peace treaty illegally limited Japanese sovereignty. Nehru was also annoyed that Dulles had not come to New Delhi for discussions.[22]

At the San Francisco Conference itself the US delegation, headed by Acheson, dominated proceedings, with the vast majority of states represented, including the Commonwealth members present, quickly accepting the US proposal.[23] In opposition, the Soviet

Union, Czechoslovakia and Poland argued that the treaty: was invalid without the concurrence of the PRC; would not prevent the re-emergence of Japanese militarism; illegally granted the United States the right to station forces in Japan and occupy Japanese islands; was designed to turn Japan into a military base directed against the Soviet Union; and did not recognize Soviet sovereignty over South Sakhalin and the Kuril Islands that had been granted at the Yalta Conference. Still, on 8 September 1951 the Treaty of Peace with Japan was signed by 48 Allied nations and Japan. Moreover, on the same day the Japanese-American Security Alliance was signed in San Francisco, providing a mutual defence agreement between Japan and the United States.

As explained in Chapter 3, the fate of ANZUS was closely linked to the Japanese Peace Treaty. Canberra and Wellington had waited patiently since the terms of this document had been agreed in February 1951 while the US government and Congress deliberated upon it. This policy finally paid off when, on 1 September 1951, during the San Francisco Conference, representatives of the three countries signed the ANZUS Security Treaty. ANZUS was not as tightly bound as NATO since its members were only required to consult each other whenever one of them was threatened in the Pacific area. The organization also lacked an integrated defence structure and its members were not obliged to dedicate specific forces. Moreover, rather than having joint military coordination at the highest level, the ANZUS Treaty provided for an annual Council of Foreign Ministers. This point was particularly disappointing to the Australians but the United States would only accept regular consultations between respective field commanders in the Pacific region.

The evolution of NATO also continued during this period. At the Lisbon Conference in February 1952 the post of Secretary-General was established to run all the civilian agencies of the organization and serve the North Atlantic Council. With an American-appointed SACEUR, it was decided that a British official should hold this new position. As a result, Lord Ismay was appointed the first NATO Secretary-General on 12 March 1952. As an experienced general during the Second World War, close confidant of Churchill and with much experience in international affairs, Ismay was a popular choice. Besides, this appointment brought the United States and Britain even closer together in NATO as the countries now dominated the military and civilian wings of the organization. NATO also expanded in 1952, with Greece and Turkey joining at Washington's insistence despite Western European, particularly British, fears that the inclusion of two relatively weak and distant countries risked conflict with the Soviet Union. Finally, on 28 April 1952, after barely a year in the post, Eisenhower stepped down as the SACEUR to be replaced by Ridgway after his exploits in Korea.[24]

Alongside these NATO developments, Washington, ever eager for greater European integration and for its allies to contribute more effectively to the containment of the Soviet Union, was pushing forward discussions for the formation of the European Defence Community first proposed by France in 1950. This issue was to prove highly controversial, though. To begin with, French and other Western European fears persisted over West German rearmament. Furthermore, the EDC was intended to be supranational in nature, with centralized military procurement and a common budget, arms and institutions. To US chagrin Britain, therefore, refused to join while the other countries found it difficult to find agreement on such measures. And for the Federal Republic of Germany (FRG) the fact that its forces would report directly to the EDC while other national forces reported to their own governments was a bitter pill to swallow. Yet after months of painstaking talks a treaty was signed in May 1952 by France, the FRG, Italy and the Benelux countries.[25]

Another international development that diverted British attention away from Korea was the assassination by the MNLA of Sir Henry Gurney, the High Commissioner in Malaya, in October 1951. This high profile act of terrorism had an important impact on local politics as most of the Malay population disapproved of such methods and felt it hampered rather than furthered their calls for independence. More significantly, Gurney's assassination sparked a major shake-up of the British counterinsurgency effort. To begin with, the newly-appointed Conservative Colonial Secretary, Oliver Lyttleton, went to Malaya to examine the deteriorating situation first-hand. Soon afterwards

Lyttleton appointed Lieutenant-General Gerald Templar as High Commissioner and gave him responsibility for both civilian and military operations. Templar continued the Briggs Plan but adopted a 'hearts-and-minds' policy, promising the ethnic Chinese population the right to vote, providing improved services, and offering financial rewards to civilians for detecting guerrillas. At the same time, he stepped up the military campaign against the MNLA, improved intelligence, and accelerated the development of the Malayan Army. These reforms proved successful in the long term in blunting the insurgency. In his vigorous pursuit of his goals Templar thus gained the nickname the 'Tiger of Malaya'.[26]

The armistice talks

The Korean armistice negotiations commenced at Kaesong on 10 July 1951 in an extremely tense atmosphere. Kaesong itself had been made a neutral area but the city was within territory occupied by Communist forces, who sought to use this fact to their advantage. In a blatant attempt to intimidate and infuriate the UN delegation travelling to and from the truce tents, the Communists established a number of heavily guarded checkpoints. At the negotiating table the Communists also attempted to seize the psychological advantage through various underhand tactics. For example, the head of the UN delegation, Vice-Admiral C. Turner Joy, was given a much shorter chair than his Communist counterpart, General Nam Il of North Korea, so that the American's greater height was not noticeable. The UN delegation was also seated at the southern end of the negotiating table since traditionally in East Asia this position would be assumed by the loser. The Communists, moreover, allowed their press to attend the talks but would not permit access to Western journalists.[27]

These problems, however, were nothing compared to those experienced once discussions got underway. It took over two weeks even to agree to an agenda, since Nam Il insisted on the inclusion of the question of the withdrawal of foreign forces from Korea. In opposition, Joy argued that this was a political issue and should be decided only after a military armistice had been concluded. But after much deliberation, it was eventually agreed that the agenda would consist of four substantive items. First, a suitable demarcation line and buffer zone between the two sides would be found. Second, concrete arrangements to end the shooting and supervise the ceasefire would be arranged. Third, arrangements would be made for the exchange of prisoners of war. And finally, recommendations would be made to the governments concerned on both sides. This vague last item was designed so that the Communists could recommend the withdrawal of all foreign forces.

Nonetheless, the demarcation line issue immediately created disagreement between the two sides. On one hand, the Communists called for a return to the *status quo ante bellum* and the restoration of the 38th parallel. The UN delegation, on the other hand, demanded a line north of the current line of contact, arguing that this would compensate for the loss of the UNC's aerial advantage after a ceasefire. But before this issue could be seriously discussed the talks broke down. On 5 August 1951 the UNC unilaterally suspended the negotiations after armed enemy troops were seen in the neutral zone. After Communist reassurances were given the talks temporarily resumed until, on 23 August 1951, the Communists claimed that UN aircraft had bombed the neutral zone. They then unilaterally adjourned the meetings until the UNC accepted responsibility for these acts. Yet Ridgway vigorously denied ordering these bombings and protested that the Communists had prevented an investigation of the supposed targets.

Efforts were made to have the talks resumed as soon as possible but neither side was willing to back down. Eventually, after 63 days involving much heavy fighting, the two teams agreed to resume negotiations at Panmunjom, a small village located exactly on the line of contact between the opposing forces. The Communists continued to be based at Kaesong while the UNC had its headquarters at the village of Munsan-ni, just south of the battlefront. The practical and psychological advantages enjoyed by the Communists at Kaesong were thus removed. Under these conditions the negotiations ran more smoothly. On 27 November 1951 the two sides agreed that the demarcation line would be the line of actual contact at the time of the ceasefire, with both sides withdrawing two kilometres to form a demilitarized zone.

Following on from this success some points of agreement were found between the two sides on the second item. The negotiators accepted that after an armistice both sides should not be able to reinforce their forces or stockpile weapons but should be able to rotate troops and update armaments. They also agreed that a Military Armistice Commission (MAC) composed of representatives from both sides should be established to monitor the ceasefire. But this is where cooperation broke down. The Communists insisted that the MAC only operate in the demilitarized zone while the UN negotiators wanted the body to have power of inspection throughout Korea. Furthermore, serious friction developed over the question of reconstructing airfields. Nam Il stressed this would be necessary for the rehabilitation of his war ravaged country but Joy claimed this would place the Communist forces in an advantageous position to launch another invasion.

Even so, in February 1952 further progress was made at Panmunjom on these contentious issues. Both sides agreed that the MAC should only monitor the demilitarized zone but that a Neutral Nations Supervisory Commission (NNSC) composed of Swedish, Swiss, Czech and Polish representatives would be established to carry out inspections throughout the peninsula. In addition, the UN delegation grudgingly dropped its demands regarding the reconstruction of airfields. Behind this concession was an agreement made by all the contributing UN members to issue a 'warning statement' after an armistice had been signed, threatening that if the Communists violated the agreement then the signatory countries would use everything within their power to end the aggression, including escalating the conflict beyond Korea. The US government hoped that this would be a sufficient deterrent to render the airfields question obsolete. Finally, as regards item four, both sides agreed to recommend to all interested parties that within three months of an armistice, a political conference be held for settling the question of the withdrawal of all foreign forces, finding a political settlement for Korea and any other questions.

Yet in the meantime the ceasefire negotiations had entered their most troubled phase as attention shifted to the prisoner of war item. This issue had been under consideration in Washington since November 1951, when Truman had argued on humanitarian grounds that after an armistice only those prisoners willing to be repatriated should be exchanged. Joy had then raised this point at Panmunjom in January 1952, asserting that some 5,000 North Korean, 11,500 Chinese prisoners and 30,000 civilian internees (South Koreans who had been coerced into the North Korean Army) out of the approximately 132,000 prisoners of war and 37,000 civilian internees held in its custody would violently resist repatriation in the fear that if they returned home they might face the death penalty. In stark contrast, Nam Il demanded that prisoners be exchanged on an 'all-for-all' basis arguing that according to the Third Geneva Convention, relative to the treatment of prisoners of war, all prisoners without exception should be repatriated after the cessation of hostilities.[28]

The level of scorn levelled by the Communists as well as the strength of their legal arguments did temporarily shake the confidence of the US government in its position. But in February 1952, after consulting his advisers, Truman decided to remain firm even though this risked prolonging the conflict indefinitely. Playing to the President's strong humanitarian beliefs, Acheson had written a memorandum arguing that the forcible repatriation of Communist prisoners was repugnant to US principles on the importance of the individual. He also claimed that in future wars this principle would encourage Communist soldiers to defect to the US side. Acheson thus championed the principle of 'no forcible repatriation', believing this would gain strong domestic and international support. The new Secretary of Defense Robert Lovett, Marshall's former deputy, and the Joint Chiefs of Staff, however, warned that this policy would lead to the prolongation of hostilities and the length of time the 3,000 US prisoners of war would spend in Communist custody. Still, the Pentagon supported the principle of non-forcible repatriation on military grounds since it would limit the number of soldiers being returned to the PRC and North Korea who would be able to fight if the war reignited, especially since comparatively few UN and ROK troops would be returned.[29]

The Communists were so intransigent on this question because they were deeply concerned with the psychological and propaganda blow they would suffer if thousands of their own soldiers refused to return home. For the PRC this problem was particularly acute since it was desperate to portray itself as the legitimate government of China as well as the revolutionary vanguard in Asia. In addition, Beijing was determined that no Chinese soldiers end up in Taiwan strengthening Chiang's armies. Matters were then made worse for the Communists in late March 1952 when the UNC decided to rescreen the prisoners of war in their custody, basing its estimates more on conjecture and coercion than accuracy. The Communists did not initially protest against this action as they hoped that if it was found that approximately 100,000 prisoners were willing to be repatriated they could agree to this figure. However, the re-screening found that only 73,000 prisoners and civilian internees wished to return home. As a result, the Communists' protests resumed, the negotiations at Panmunjom became rigidly deadlocked for the remainder of this period and discussions became dominated by vitriolic propaganda statements.

One matter about which the Communist negotiators consistently complained was the treatment of North Korean and Chinese prisoners in the custody of the UNC. As well as claiming that coercion was used when these prisoners were screened, the Communists alleged that the UN guards inflicted violence upon the prisoners, resulting in a number of deaths. These accusations were denied by the UNC but in the spring of 1952 a number of riots at the prisoner of war camps on Goje Island had broken out while screening was taking place. These events seriously undermined in many countries, particularly in Asia, the UN claims regarding the numbers of prisoners who would resist repatriation and the principle of non-forcible repatriation. The situation became even worse on 7 May 1952 when the new camp commander, Brigadier-General Francis Dodd, sent in to quell the unrest, was taken hostage by a group of Communist prisoners who demanded he admit that UN guards had used violence in the camps.

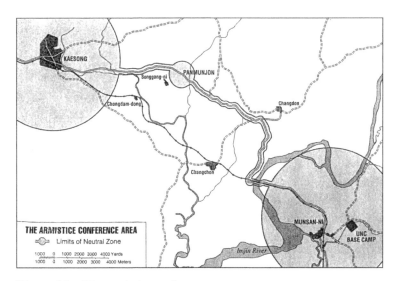

Figure 4.1   The armistice conference area.
Source: Stueck: *Rethinking the Korean War*, p. 155.

After 72 hours Dodd's deputy made such a statement and the camp commander was released unharmed. While this incident achieved little it did highlight the problems experienced in the prisoner of war camps.[30]

Premature post-armistice planning

With the opening of the armistice negotiations in July 1951 the UN's role in answering the Korean question soon faded into the background. The consensus view in New York was that the UN could do nothing more until an armistice had been arranged and that the resumption of the General Assembly debate would only complicate and delay the ceasefire talks. What is more, the Truman administration, as the unified command, had sole responsibility for formulating the negotiating position of the UN delegation and no longer had to take into account the varied and often contradictory views of the other UN members. After the difficulties encountered at the UN during the previous months in having its policies adopted, the Truman administration was unwilling to voluntarily share these powers, even with its closest allies. Luckily, the Commonwealth members, now that an end to the fighting was within sight, accepted this situation and did not press for debate in the General Assembly. They recognized that the United States was bearing the brunt of the military burden and did not wish to incur animosity by infringing on this area.

This did not, however, prevent the US and Commonwealth governments considering what course the UN should take if and when an armistice was concluded. As was customary, the US government took the lead on post-armistice planning. Acheson thought that when the fighting had ceased the General Assembly should adopt a resolution noting the armistice, reaffirming the UN's political and military objectives in Korea and permitting the retention of UN forces in South Korea to maintain international peace and stability. The Secretary of State stressed that a resolution was needed that would 'set the record straight' and demonstrate the conviction of the whole UN membership not to allow the Communist aggression to go unnoticed.[31]

Morrison, in contrast, wanted the Security Council—where the Korean action had originated—to adopt an 'anodyne' resolution simply noting the armistice, thus avoiding the Soviet veto. The Foreign Secretary desired this course since he feared that debate in the General Assembly on Acheson's proposed draft resolution would likely be acrimonious and ruin the progressive 'atmosphere' created by an armistice.[32] Importantly, the British plan was favoured by the other Commonwealth delegations over that proposed by the Americans.[33] As this question was purely theoretical at this stage, Acheson was willing to compromise. He agreed that first a Security Council resolution along the lines envisaged by Morrison should be adopted as long as the Commonwealth then agreed to support a General Assembly resolution of the kind he desired.[34]

At the same time, US and Commonwealth attention was being given to what the UN could do to bring about a Korean political settlement after an armistice. Washington believed that the UN should deal directly with the Chinese and felt that the General Assembly should appoint a small UN delegation, composed of the

United States and possibly Australia and Thailand, to make contact with the Chinese. This delegation would then try to set up a conference in which its members, the ROK, North Korea and the PRC would participate.[35] But the British expressed sympathy for Secretary-General Lie's suggestion that a UN mediator be appointed to hold talks with both sides to try to find acceptable terms for a peaceful settlement. Furthermore, the Indian delegation argued that no definite opinion could be formed until the terms of the armistice agreement were known and the function of a mediator clearly defined. Finally, the Australian delegation stated that UNCURK, on which its government was represented, already existed to fulfil such a mediatory role.[36]

Still, post-armistice planning was cut short by the Communists' unilateral decision to adjourn the negotiations at Kaesong. In this climate hopes of an early armistice were shaken. Acheson, in particular, was increasingly pessimistic regarding the future of the talks, believing that the enemy were trying to buy time before launching another offensive. This negativity was demonstrated when he met with Morrison in Washington after the San Francisco Conference and argued that if the armistice negotiations did not resume quickly then it would be necessary for the General Assembly to impose additional political, economic and military sanctions against China. These measures would include: recommending that members withdraw their recognition of, or diplomatic relations with, the PRC; a complete economic blockade; and a request for members to make further troop contributions. The Secretary of State evidently hoped these harsh tactics would force the Communists to return to the negotiating table. Morrison reluctantly agreed that additional measures might have to be taken to put pressure on the Communists but opposed a blockade since this would push China into Moscow's hands while risking conflict with the Soviet Union if its ships were prevented from reaching its ports in East Asia.[37]

Sixth Session of the General Assembly

With the armistice negotiations in turmoil it appeared that another bitter debate on Korea would inevitably take place at the Sixth

Session of the General Assembly, opening in Paris in mid-November 1951. But events in October prevented this eventuality. The Communist delegation had agreed to resume talks, the atmosphere at Panmunjom was much improved and gradual progress was being made on the demarcation line question. At the same time, after its abortive offensive in October 1951 the UNC had accepted that a military breakthrough was impossible and assumed defensive positions with a ceasefire in mind. The much-feared Communist counteroffensive also never materialized. The Truman administration, therefore, abandoned any plans to have the UN impose further sanctions against the PRC and concluded that the General Assembly should not consider any aspect of the Korean item so long as the armistice talks were moving forward and the risk of military disaster remained at a minimum.[38]

These events also coincided with the election of the Churchill government. Eden, eager to demonstrate that Britain supported US policy at the UN, at Panmunjom and on the battlefield, told Acheson when they met for a NATO conference in Paris prior to the Sixth Session that he fully concurred with the US position and would support this course during the General Assembly.[39] With Anglo-American views aligned none of the other Commonwealth members raised any objections to this strategy. Interestingly, even the Soviet bloc members were opposed to discussing the Korean item at the General Assembly for the time being, suggesting that the Communists were also determined to find a solution at Panmunjom. As a result, when the Sixth Session commenced a Brazilian proposal was overwhelmingly adopted to place the Korean item fourth on the agenda to allow time for the armistice negotiations to succeed before the UN became involved.[40]

Be that as it may, the Commonwealth delegations sought to coordinate their approach to the Korean question well in advance of the debate. A clear sense of optimism prevailed in the discussions that took place between the Commonwealth representatives in Paris that the Korean crisis was abating since they focused on possible courses the General Assembly could pursue after an armistice was signed. Rajeshwar Dayal of the Indian delegation opened proceedings by suggesting that a UN 'study group', composed of individuals and not government representatives, be established to meet with all the interested parties and produce a report on how the various problems connected with a Korean settlement could best be solved. The other Commonwealth representatives, however, predicted difficulties in finding candidates acceptable to all members for such a group. As a compromise, therefore, British Minister of State Selwyn Lloyd— granted much autonomy by Eden regarding the Korean item since the Foreign Secretary spent little time in Paris during the Sixth Session—suggested the formation of an informal Commonwealth study group that could submit a report for consideration by the General Assembly later if this course was deemed desirable. This proposal was then accepted by all the Commonwealth representatives, including Dayal.[41]

Nonetheless, when this informal Commonwealth study group met, Rau and Panikkar, now a member of the Indian delegation, continued to promote the UN study group plan. They stated that the Indian government envisaged a three-man body composed of impartial figures, such as the President of the International Court of Justice or the President of the International Red Cross, which would take soundings of both the UN and Communist sides on political issues relating to Korea in preparation for a conference of all the 'real parties of interest'. Notwithstanding this more detailed explanation, the Old Commonwealth members had little enthusiasm for the Indian proposal and Jebb suggested that a single impartial 'rapporteur' could better fulfil this function. The Commonwealth members had much sympathy for this proposal but they were not prepared to commit to any course until they had heard Washington's views on this matter.[42]

The US delegation, however, was being cagey on the Korean item. Even when Austin eventually agreed to talk to Pearson before the latter left Paris for Ottawa, so as not to snub the Canadian Foreign Minister, he gave no indication of US thinking.[43] Evidently, the Truman administration was wary of engaging in negotiations with its Commonwealth allies, given the tensions that had emerged during the previous session of the General Assembly. The US government instead preferred to remain silent and present the Commonwealth with a fait accompli once an armistice had been signed. The policy the Americans had in mind was the creation of a small UN commission composed of four members contributing forces to the Korean action—preferably the United States, Australia, Thailand and Turkey—and the Soviet Union to discuss terms for a political settlement with the two Koreas and the PRC. The State Department considered this method preferable to the British suggestion for a rapporteur since selection of a suitable individual was fraught with political difficulties and would not adequately represent UN interests.[44]

At last, in mid-December 1951 after numerous calls for consultation, Austin revealed these views to the Australian Deputy Permanent Representative Sir Keith Officer, creating immediate rifts within the Commonwealth.[45] The Australian and New Zealand delegations came out strongly in favour of the US proposal, arguing that they must support procedures acceptable to Washington since the Americans had borne the brunt of the fighting.[46] In stark contrast, Pearson, drawing on his experience with the Cease-fire Committee a year before, argued that it would be impossible for a UN commission to establish a meeting to discuss a political settlement since the Chinese, North Koreans and Russians would refuse to have any dealing with such a body.[47] This position was vociferously supported by the Indian delegation. But in between these polarized positions the British delegation attempted to find a compromise by marrying the US proposal to the rapporteur concept. Jebb suggested that if a UN commission was established then it could appoint an individual to act as a 'dove from the ark' and get in touch with the other parties to lay the groundwork for a meeting.[48]

As the General Assembly adjourned over the Christmas period it thus appeared that tension between the United States and the Commonwealth members was a very real possibility in the upcoming Korean debate. But two developments prevented these fissures developing into a schism. Firstly, hopes of an early armistice faded in January 1952 as negotiations at Panmunjom became deadlocked over, first, the reconstruction of airfields and then the prisoners of war questions. In consequence, the need to agree to a post-armistice policy during the remaining few weeks of the Sixth Session evaporated. And secondly, partly as a result of the first development, Soviet Foreign Minister Andrei Vyshinsky, present in Paris, launched an aggressive campaign to have the Korean question discussed immediately in the First Committee. Under this pressure the Old Commonwealth members thought it safest to support US policy at the UN and give no indication of divisions.

Vyshinsky's initial move was to table a broad draft resolution on collective measures including a provision calling for an immediate meeting of the Security Council to discuss the Korean ceasefire negotiations. The US delegation—now chaired by Eleanor Roosevelt, the widow of former president Franklin D. Roosevelt, after Acheson had departed Paris and while Austin recovered from severe respiratory problems[49]—feared that many UN members, including the Commonwealth countries, might accept this Soviet proposal on the grounds that the UN could not completely ignore the Korean question while the war continued.[50] Yet these concerns appeared to be largely misplaced since the Old Commonwealth delegations were in general agreement that debate at the UN should be avoided until a ceasefire had been signed.[51] The Indian and Pakistani delegations, however, did warn their Commonwealth colleagues that the Arab-Asian group was becoming anxious that the armistice negotiations were stalling and felt that the Security Council might be able to lend a hand in hastening an agreement.[52]

These differences were reflected in the First Committee debate when it finally got underway. The Old Commonwealth representatives joined with Mrs Roosevelt in protesting against the Soviet proposal while the New Commonwealth delegations remained silent. In the end, the United States, Britain, France and Brazil tabled an amendment to the Soviet draft resolution deleting the controversial provision regarding the Security Council meeting to discuss Korea. This amendment was adopted by an overwhelming majority, with all the Commonwealth delegations except India, who abstained, voting in favour. Even so, the Commonwealth members did all support a US proposal to place the Korean item last on the First Committee's agenda on the understanding that if an armistice was concluded, or if developments in Korea required discussion, the matter could be taken up at once.[53]

All the same, during the next item on the agenda looking at measures to combat the threat of a new world war and to strengthen peace, Vyshinsky tabled another draft resolution including a provision for immediate debate on Korea. In the subsequent discussion the US and Old Commonwealth representatives protested that the Soviet delegation had wilfully ignored the decision to postpone consideration of the Korean question. The vast majority of the other members agreed and the First Committee soon decided to refer the majority of the Soviet draft resolution to the Disarmament Commission, while the paragraph referring to Korea was rejected.[54]

Meanwhile, behind the scenes the Commonwealth delegations began to have doubts regarding US policy at the UN. Lloyd was especially concerned that British public opinion would not understand it if Korea was not discussed at all at the Sixth Session. He was also worried that the Soviet proposals were gaining sympathy among the neutral members, including India and Pakistan, while the West appeared to be taking an entirely negative attitude.[55] Acheson was quick to respond to these concerns by formulating a new draft resolution. This proposal would adjourn the General Assembly immediately but allowed for the Sixth Session to be resumed or a special session of the General Assembly to be held as soon as an armistice had been signed or when other developments in Korea made this desirable. The Secretary of State then left it to the US delegation to decide which of these two options was preferable based on its discussions with the other UN members.[56] Surprisingly, all the Commonwealth delegations, even India, supported the US proposal to defer the Korean question and the consensus view was that a special session of the General Assembly in New York was more practical than the resumption of the Sixth Session in Paris.[57]

Yet before this plan could be put into effect a decision had to be taken on what to do with the contentious reports of UNCURK and UNKRA.[58] The Australian and Pakistani delegations, as members of UNCURK, wanted the former report discussed and a decision to be taken on the future of the Commission.[59] The US and other Commonwealth delegations, however, were concerned that the Soviet bloc would take advantage of UNCURK's report to criticize Syngman Rhee's political record in the ROK. Australia and Pakistan thus grudgingly accepted US calls to close the General Assembly without consideration of this report.[60] The US delegation also opposed debating UNKRA's report, fearing Soviet criticism of the Agency's working arrangements with the UNC and its very limited relief and rehabilitation work. The Commonwealth members supported this course and agreed that the UN Negotiation Committee for Extra-Budgetary Funds should simply be requested to undertake negotiations regarding voluntary contributions to UNKRA.

With all other items on the First Committee's agenda dealt with, the debate on Korea finally got underway on 2 February 1952. Gross took the lead tabling a joint US-British-French draft resolution postponing the item until either the armistice was signed or developments made it necessary to reconsider the Korean problem and stressing that premature debate at the UN could delay or complicate the ceasefire negotiations.[61] In the brief deliberations that followed, the Old Commonwealth delegations backed the US position against Soviet calls for immediate consideration of the reports of UNCURK and UNKRA. The New Commonwealth members, moreover, remained silent indicating their passive compliance with the draft resolution. In this atmosphere the Three-Power proposal was adopted with only the five Soviet bloc members voting against it.[62] This voting pattern was then repeated in the Plenary, the draft became General Assembly Resolution 507 (VI) (see Appendix 10, p. 268–9), and the Sixth Session was closed.[63]

More premature post-armistice planning

The adoption of this resolution demonstrated the faith of the UN members, including all the Commonwealth countries, in the ability of the UN negotiators to bring the Korean conflict to an end. These views initially appeared well founded in early 1952 since hopes of an armistice were rekindled by advances made at Panmunjom over the questions of supervision, the reconstruction of airfields and the recommendation to hold a post-armistice political conference on Korea. The US and Commonwealth governments then demonstrated their optimism by setting about forming policies for the special session of the General Assembly to be called if and when an armistice was signed. In these circumstances, it was generally felt in Washington and the Commonwealth capitals, the first task to be settled by the UN would be the establishment of the post-armistice political conference on Korea agreed to by the negotiators at Panmunjom. But little common ground existed between these countries concerning the nature of this conference.

The Truman administration favoured a UN resolution calling for a two-sided conference composed of the belligerents. This resolution would appoint a 'UN delegation', selected strictly from members who had contributed forces, while China and North Korea would make up the 'Communist Delegation'. Washington vehemently opposed the participation of neutrals, especially India, and would only accept the Soviet Union's presence at the conference if they were invited to join the Communist delegation.[64] Still, when this proposal was discussed with the Old Commonwealth members a range of positions was expressed. Eden was opposed to a two-sided conference replicating the hostile atmosphere at Panmunjom, preferring a round-table conference with the Soviet Union and India being invited as 'parties of interest'.[65] Pearson agreed with Eden that India should be invited as an important Asian state and due to its contribution of a field medical unit. But he would not commit to a position on Soviet participation until Moscow's views were known.[66] On the contrary, the New Zealand government did not think it necessary to include India since the Commonwealth would be amply represented.[67] Australia also opposed Indian participation on the grounds that Nehru would try to broaden discussions to include other Asian issues.[68]

Before these differences could be resolved, however, discussions on the nature of the post-armistice political conference petered out as a result of the deadlock at Panmunjom. With both sides showing no intention of making concessions on the prisoner of war question it became apparent to the US and Commonwealth governments that a ceasefire was a very distant reality. These views were further compounded on 4 March 1952 when Malik in the UN Disarmament Commission accused the UNC of conducting bacteriological warfare in North Korea and Manchuria. The US delegation vehemently denied these charges and called for the Communists to accept the offer already made by the International Committee of the Red Cross (ICRC) to investigate them.[69] Additionally, the Commonwealth members represented on the Disarmament Commission quickly demonstrated their loyalty to Washington and vociferously supported US calls for an impartial investigation.[70] Unsurprisingly, Malik rejected this proposal arguing that the ICRC was not competent to deal with such issues and could not act objectively.[71]

No further action was taken on this matter in the Disarmament Commission but in June 1952 Malik, as President of the Security Council, tabled a draft resolution appealing to all states to accede to and ratify the Geneva Protocol of 1925 for the prohibition of the use of bacteriological weapons. This proposal was clearly aimed directly at the US government, which had not ratified the Geneva Protocol, and was intimately connected to Moscow's germ warfare campaign. Yet the US delegation refused to take the bait and simply called for the matter to be referred back to the Disarmament Commission.[72] The British and Pakistani delegations, expressing the views of the other Commonwealth members not represented on the Security Council, emphatically agreed to this course.[73] In the end, the Soviet draft resolution received just one affirmative vote while the other ten Council members supported the US proposal.[74] Evidently, Soviet actions had served to strengthen relations between the United States and the Commonwealth members at the UN.

Acheson, nevertheless, was not prepared to let the matter rest there since he was concerned that the Communist germ warfare propaganda campaign had made gains in the Third World. Consequently, he instructed the US delegation to table a draft resolution in the Security Council requesting the ICRC to investigate the charges and calling upon all governments to give this body full cooperation such as the freedom of movement in any areas the committee deemed necessary in performance of its task. If this proposal was vetoed by the Soviets, as Acheson predicted, the US delegation was then to table a second draft resolution concluding from the refusal of those governments making the charges to permit the impartial investigation that their accusations were without substance and should be dismissed as false propaganda. These governments would also be condemned for disseminating false charges, seeking to prevent the UN from achieving its objectives in Korea, and increasing tensions between nations.[75]

When debate on the first US draft resolution got underway Malik retaliated by calling for representatives of China and North Korea to take part since they were the victims of bacteriological warfare. But Gross insisted that the Security Council was not the best place to give a verdict on the charges laid against the UNC until they had been thoroughly investigated. An impartial body thus had first to be established that would have full opportunity to discuss its mission with any authorities or individuals concerned, including the Chinese and North Koreans.[76] Ten members of the Security Council, including Britain and Pakistan, then voted against the Soviet proposal.[77] Furthermore, Jebb, now President of the Security Council, played a crucial role in resisting Malik's repeated calls to have this decision reconsidered. After much heated debate, in which the British and Pakistani delegations voiced support for an impartial investigation, the US draft resolution received ten affirmative votes but was vetoed by the Soviet Union.

Nevertheless, US-Commonwealth harmony was not to last long as the US delegation immediately tabled its much more controversial second draft resolution condemning the Communists.[78] A number of Commonwealth members, notably Britain, Canada, India and Pakistan, had privately criticized this proposal for the implicit assumption contained that the Communist accusations were false despite the fact no impartial investigation had taken place. Still, the Old Commonwealth members were unwilling to make this a breaking point with the United States. As such, in the Security Council Jebb supported the US draft resolution and launched a scathing attack on Moscow's underhand methods. Pakistan's Foreign Minister, Muhammad Zafrullah Khan, in contrast, claiming to express the views of the Arab-Asian bloc, voiced his government's concerns with the proposal.[79] The US draft resolution thus received nine affirmative votes, with Pakistan abstaining, but was again defeated by the Soviet veto.[80]

Conclusion

Relations between the United States and the Commonwealth members at the UN during the middle 12 months of the Korean War were the most harmonious they had been since the outbreak of the conflict. The Commonwealth coalition that had emerged during the winter of 1950–51 to challenge US hegemony in the world organization had fragmented long before July 1951 and did not rematerialize throughout this period. While a number of minor issues did arise, at no time did the Commonwealth members feel the need to unite to try to constrain US policy. Behind this trend was the fact that the conditions necessary to bring about a united Commonwealth in opposition to US policy were completely absent.

To begin with, a military stalemate at the 38th parallel had existed since late May 1951 and the resulting war of attrition had convinced both sides that a breakthrough was very unlikely. At the same time, armistice negotiations were being held in Korea and some progress was made, even if the talks were often exceedingly slow and almost broke down over a range of issues. In consequence, there were few immediate concerns that the conflict would escalate beyond Korea. The key personalities within the Commonwealth were also content to allow Washington to exercise sole responsibility for the UN negotiating position and to dominate UN proceedings, especially as they all had more pressing domestic and international concerns and were in general agreement that the UN could do little to precipitate the armistice negotiations. Moreover, during these 12 months the only time a number of important Commonwealth figures, such as Eden and Pearson, were in the same location was during the opening weeks of the Sixth Session of the General Assembly. Very few of them waited around in Paris until the Korean debate finally got underway at the end of the session. As a result, no serious effort was made to discuss Korea or coordinate a Commonwealth position. Finally, the US government made it clear that it was unwilling to alter its policy at the UN even if the Commonwealth members had attempted to constrain it. The Truman administration's popularity never recovered after the MacArthur controversy but the President was determined to present himself as a tough leader who was not unduly influenced by external pressures. Partly for this reason, the United States adopted an uncompromising attitude at the UN. Evidently, domestic pressures now strongly outweighed international ones as the President's position became increasingly untenable.

CHAPTER 5

THE INDIAN RESOLUTION, JUNE–DECEMBER 1952

After the relative tranquillity at the UN throughout the previous 12 months, during the second half of 1952 the Commonwealth conducted its most sustained challenge to US dominance at the world organization since Chinese intervention. With the armistice negotiations effectively transferred from Panmunjom to New York, the General Assembly once again provided a forum in which the Commonwealth members could directly influence the Korean question. Yet the Truman administration was adamant that the UN should do little more than legitimize the position of its negotiators. What was most significant in the autumn of 1952 compared to the winter crisis of 1950–51, however, was that the Truman administration, rather than the Commonwealth governments, made the ultimate concessions. This episode more than any other during the Korean War demonstrated that when united, the Commonwealth could act as an agent of constraint upon US policy at the UN due to the moral authority it drew from its multiethnic composition and liberal democratic traditions.

Crucially, during this six-month period all the conditions necessary for Commonwealth unity converged. At the heart of this challenge to US dominance were two concerns shared by the Commonwealth capitals. The first concern, born from the breakdown of the armistice negotiations, was that the Korean War might be prolonged indefinitely thus draining resources away from more vital Cold War theatres. The second and greater fear was that General Dwight D. Eisenhower, the US president-elect after his election victory in November, would adopt an aggressive strategy that might risk a global conflict. By fortunate coincidence the Seventh Session of the General Assembly opened at this critical moment, allowing numerous key Commonwealth personalities to gather in New York. Eden, Pearson and Nehru's personal representatives demonstrated great determination in undertaking intense diplomatic activity to formulate a united position to resist the will of the Americans. But most important to the success of the Commonwealth was the unprecedentedly weak position, domestically and internationally, of the US government during the interregnum period. The Truman administration now lacked the strength to bring its Commonwealth allies into line and US hegemony at the UN was momentarily lost. But the blow to US prestige was softened by the actions of the Communists.

The Commonwealth's united front at the UN in late 1952 did not, however, occur in a vacuum. It emerged within a complex web of military, domestic and international events as well as the armistice negotiations. These contextual factors must be explained before detailed analysis can commence.

The military situation

The military stalemate in Korea at the 38th parallel endured throughout the second half of 1952.[1] Nevertheless, both the UNC and the Communist High Command stepped up the war of attrition in an effort to force the pace of negotiations at Panmunjom. In June 1952 Ridgway was replaced as Commander-in-Chief of the UNC by General Mark Clark, whose first move was to intensify the UN aerial bombing campaign in North Korea. Civilian centres, especially Pyongyang, and communication and supply lines were the main targets. But, more controversially, Clark ordered the bombing of the Suiho power station on the Yalu river bordering the PRC and supplying Manchuria with much of its electricity. This action had limited military impact but infuriated those countries who had contributed forces to the UN action but had not been consulted in advance. The British government was particularly upset since Washington had previously promised to give London prior warning before taking such action. Under scrutiny in the House of Commons, Eden pleaded with Acheson, who was currently in London, for 'no more surprises'. The Secretary of State thus publicly apologized for this 'snafu'. In addition, a British officer was appointed deputy chief of staff on the UNC in Tokyo so that Britain would be fully informed of such decisions in the future.[2]

Shortly thereafter Clark sought to make strategic territorial advances. On 26 June Operation Counter was launched to capture a series of Communist outposts located in west-central Korea on 'Old Baldy' hill that provided a view over UN positions. The ensuing battle was bitter as the defending Communist forces held strong defensive positions. As a result, it took five weeks for the UNC to achieve its objectives and that only after receiving considerable losses. More serious fighting then erupted in early October 1952 when massive Communist forces attacked 'White Horse' hill in the strategic Iron Triangle area in central Korea. Ten days of brutal fighting followed as the Communists threw forward wave after wave of soldiers while the UNC used its superior fire power to defend its positions. Approximately 3,000 UN and 7,000 Communist casualties were inflicted before the attackers withdrew to their former positions. In retaliation to this assault, and to try to force the Communist negotiators at Panmunjom to make concessions, Van Fleet was then authorized to launch his long-planned Operation Showdown, designed to capture the nearby 'Triangle Hill'. The UNC committed a large number of ground and air forces to this mission, but the well dug-in Communist defenders refused to budge. Following six weeks of intense fighting Van Fleet ordered his forces to withdraw. In consequence, Clark concluded, as his predecessor had done a year earlier, that large-scale offensive operations for limited gains were futile. But Clark maintained that the conflict could be won if his superiors in Washington gave him authorization to extend the fighting to China and to use atomic weapons.

Domestic developments

The domestic dimension in each of the Commonwealth countries was relatively stable between June and December 1952. In Britain, the Churchill government was now firmly ensconced in power, the elderly Prime Minister appeared to be coping with the rigours of leadership and his Cabinet was firmly behind him. The only noteworthy change within the Churchill government at this time was the replacement of Lord Salisbury as Secretary of State for Commonwealth Relations, due in large part to his imperialist views which aggravated relations with the New Commonwealth members, with the more liberal-minded Lord Swinton.[3] Similarly, in Canada, Australia, New Zealand and South Africa the position of each government appeared stable. In India, Nehru was supremely confident after his recent landslide victory in the first Indian general elections and as his country recovered from the famine of the previous year. Only in Pakistan was the political situation troubled as the unelected Prime Minister Khwaja Nazimuddin struggled to get to grips with the tensions between East and West Pakistan.[4] With domestic stability prevailing in the Commonwealth countries, foreign affairs, especially the Korean War, could once again take centre stage.

In the United States, in stark contrast, the presidential election set for 4 November 1952 created much upheaval. In July the Democrat and Republican conventions took place with Governor Adlai Stevenson of Illinois and General Dwight Eisenhower being nominated respectively. Stevenson was an articulate intellectual who held moderate political views and was from a rich political dynasty. But despite being Truman's hand-picked successor, Stevenson had been reluctant to run for the nomination until no other Democrat could win enough support. Similarly, Eisenhower was selected to bridge divisions within the Republican Party. Moderate, internationalist Republicans had convinced the General to run to prevent Senator Robert Taft being nominated. Taft remained popular within his Party but Eisenhower's standing with the US public eventually convinced the majority of Republicans, desperate for power after 20 years out of office, that he was far more electable.[5]

The presidential election itself was hotly contested on a number of issues. On the domestic front, Eisenhower's 'I Like Ike' campaign was designed to appease the Taftist Republican Right by promoting conservative policies and fiscal prudence, criticizing the corruption of the Truman administration and even reiterating some of McCarthy's allegations. Eisenhower's foreign policy, on the other hand, was aimed at the internationalists since he promised to step up Truman's interventionist policy of containment. In contrast, Stevenson's campaign defended the Democrats' long strong economic record and interventionism, and denounced McCarthyism. In addition to policy, the personality of the two candidates played a major part in the campaign. On one hand, Eisenhower was a war hero whose down-to-earth and warm nature made him instantly popular nationwide. Stevenson, on the other hand, was a great orator but his intellectual style, liberal views and privileged background alienated him from many core Democrat voters.[6]

Yet in the autumn of 1952 one issue concerned US voters above all else: how to end the Korean War. The Truman administration's limited war strategy had disillusioned the public since it offered no hope of a decisive victory and appeared to be failing to wear down the will of the enemy. Stevenson, however, defended the existing course, believing that the alternatives were a humiliating withdrawal or escalation. Eisenhower, in contrast, adopted a partisan position, heavily criticizing Truman's record in Korea and calling for an end to the fighting. Even so, he gave no clear indication of how he planned to achieve this goal and only very late in the campaign did he famously promise that if elected, 'I shall go to Korea'. Although this announcement was incredibly vague, Eisenhower's popularity and military credentials convinced large sections of the US electorate that he would bring the Korean conflict to a conclusion. The divergence of policies on Korea was thus crucial to Eisenhower's landslide victory, taking over 55 per cent of the popular vote, 39 of the 48 states, and 442 of 531 Electoral College votes.[7]

International relations

For the US and Commonwealth governments the second half of 1952 was noticeably quiet on the international front considering the escalation of Cold War tensions over the previous years. In Europe, NATO continued to develop, with its members becoming more closely bound and rearmament continuing despite the economic strain this was having on a number of countries, especially Britain. The ANZUS members were also drawn together in military talks although Australia was becoming increasingly frustrated at Washington's refusal to form a joint command structure and expand the scope of the treaty to southeast Asia. Moreover, in Indochina, the French position steadily deteriorated, whereas in Malaya Templar's 'hearts and minds' campaign continued to bear much fruit.

Nevertheless, a number of new international developments did serve to distract attention away from Korea. The outbreak of the Mau Mau uprising in Kenya concerned the British but this problem did not threaten international stability.[8] Likewise, London viewed with much apprehension the revolution in Egypt that saw King Farouk I overthrown by General Mohammed Neguib and his deputy Colonel Gamal Abdul Nasser. The Churchill government feared that Neguib would press Britain to withdraw from its massive Suez military base. The Truman administration, however, largely supported the Egyptian Revolution.[9]

The most relevant international development for the US and Commonwealth governments, however, was the political crisis in the ROK between May and July 1952. With elections forthcoming, Rhee used various coercive methods to amend the ROK Constitution so that the presidency was chosen directly by the electorate and not by the National Assembly. The US government, UNCURK and those Commonwealth countries contributing forces to the UN action protested at Rhee's methods as they did not want to appear to be defending an undemocratic regime. In Tokyo, moreover, Clark held grave worries that the political crisis might jeopardize the UNC's position in Korea. As a result, the UN Commander formulated Operation Everready to remove Rhee if the situation deteriorated further. But this eventuality never occurred and the US and Commonwealth governments accepted Rhee's actions in order to end the crisis as quickly as possible.[10]

One significant contributing factor to this relative inactivity was the US presidential election. The departing Truman administration realized that it lacked the authority to take any radical new departures in foreign policy since it would not be present to oversee their implementation. The President was also wary not to take any controversial decisions that might damage Stevenson's election campaign. International stability rather than adventurism was, accordingly, seen as essential in these critical months. Among Commonwealth members there also existed a general feeling that they should not pursue any new courses until the next occupant of the White House was known.

The election of Eisenhower, therefore, received a mixed response. The Old Commonwealth governments were generally positive since the General had vast international prestige and was recognized as a man of strong character, determination and action. Eisenhower had also enjoyed close personal relations with many leading Commonwealth figures, notably Churchill, Eden and Pearson, through his Second World War and NATO experiences. Churchill and Eden, in particular, were hopeful that the Anglo-American 'special relationship' would blossom under Eisenhower due to these shared experiences. Furthermore, Churchill hoped that Eisenhower would be more receptive than Truman to his calls to hold a summit with Stalin to resolve all outstanding Cold War issues. These desires were made clear shortly after the election when Eden visited Eisenhower in New York to congratulate him and discuss policy even before he had taken office.

In spite of this optimism, all the Commonwealth governments, especially India, also had grave misgivings regarding Eisenhower. Serious worries were commonplace that the new and inexperienced President, and his appointed Secretary of State, Republican foreign affairs guru John Foster Dulles, would try to placate the Republican Right by adopting either an isolationist or an aggressive Cold War strategy. Both of these courses could ultimately threaten

Commonwealth security by either leaving them undefended or by dragging them into a global conflict they did not desire. In addition, despite the restraint and diplomatic panache he had demonstrated as Supreme Allied Commander in Europe during the Second World War and at NATO, many of Eisenhower's Commonwealth friends still considered him principally a soldier who would seek to use US military might to resolve crises.

Korea lay at the forefront of these concerns. All the Commonwealth members had, for over 18 months, desired an early termination of this conflict and were greatly worried that the prolongation of hostilities had increased Cold War tensions and drawn vital resources away from higher priority areas. Now, with the election of Eisenhower, Commonwealth fears were once again raised that fighting might spread beyond Korea and escalate into a global conflict. The General's promise to end the war had, by and large, been interpreted in the Commonwealth capitals as meaning that he would seek to force the Communists to accept an armistice through military means rather than through concessions. Furthermore, the Commonwealth governments were worried that Eisenhower would succumb to pressures to extend the fighting to China. Many of his close associates at the Pentagon, as well as his old West Point classmate Mark Clark, supported this course. For the Commonwealth members, then, time was of the essence and a genuine effort to solve the prisoners of war question had to be made at the General Assembly before Eisenhower took office.[11]

The armistice negotiations

As discussed in Chapter 4, by June 1952 the UN and Communist negotiators at Panmunjom had agreed to all aspects of an armistice agreement except one issue: the post-war fate of prisoners of war. The talks continued throughout the summer but had become little more than slanging matches between the UN and Communist delegations designed more for propaganda purposes than to make progress. While the UN team continued to champion the principle of non-forcible repatriation, the Communists insisted that all prisoners should be returned to their homelands. Few efforts were made to find a compromise and tensions rapidly escalated. Under these conditions the Commonwealth governments began to raise questions, both privately and publicly, over the Truman administration's handling of the negotiations. Their thoughts then turned to finding a solution to the prisoner of war question through bilateral channels beyond Panmunjom.[12]

Following a conversation between Mrs Pandit—while in Beijing leading an Indian cultural delegation—and Zhou En-lai in which the latter indicated that the PRC would accept the return of 100,000 prisoners of war, the British and Indian governments believed that a direct approach should be made to the Chinese. Eden first wanted US endorsement of this action so as not to suggest a lack of faith in the UN negotiators. But, without warning, Nehru instructed Panikkar to go ahead and discuss 'principles' for resolution of the prisoner of war question. As a result, on 14 June 1952 the Indian Ambassador met with Zhou En-lai, who made two proposals. Plan A involved 90,000 North Korean and all 20,000 Chinese prisoners being returned. Alternatively, Plan B suggested that any prisoner showing a disinclination to repatriation could be brought to a neutral place where they would be interviewed by the representatives of four neutral nations and the ICRC. Nehru thought that Plan B in particular represented a genuine opening that should be pursued, but Eden and Acheson doubted Panikkar's reliability and Beijing's sincerity.

Meanwhile, the Soviet government appeared to be sending out its own peace feelers. In June Soviet UN Assistant Secretary-General Konstantin Zinchenko had indicated to the Israeli delegation that an armistice could be signed without any article on prisoners of war at all. More significantly, later that month Zinchenko informally approached Gross and while the Russian merely reiterated the Communist position at Panmunjom, Gross interpreted this move as an attempt to indicate Moscow's willingness to talk. For that reason Acheson instructed Gross to inform Zinchenko that the US government favoured Plan B mentioned by Zhou En-lai to Panikkar. All the same, Zinchenko snubbed Gross' approaches before leaving New York for Moscow.[13]

At Panmunjom, moreover, US hopes that the Communists were seeking a compromise were quickly dashed. Nam Il was as intransigent as ever and denied the proposals made by Zhou En-lai when they were brought up by the new chief UN negotiator, General William Harrison. The UN team's breaking point was finally reached on 28 September 1952 when, on Truman's instructions, Harrison tabled three final proposals based on the principle of non-forcible repatriation and the talks were adjourned for ten days to give the Communists ample time for consideration. When this deadline expired the Communist negotiators, as predicted, rejected all three proposals and reiterated their demands that all prisoners of war be returned home at the war's end. With its ultimatum ignored, the UNC took the unilateral decision to recess the negotiations until the Communist delegation either accepted one of the UN proposals already tabled or made a constructive contribution of its own. As neither of these eventualities took place, no further meetings were held at Panmunjom during 1952.

Early preparations for the Seventh Session of the General Assembly

In the summer of 1952 US and Commonwealth attention inevitably shifted to the UN. The armistice negotiations were truly deadlocked, normal diplomatic channels of communication were closed, and tensions were rapidly mounting with the intensified military situation, the political crisis in the ROK and the US presidential election campaign getting underway. Hence the vast majority of UN members, including all the Commonwealth countries, came to the early conclusion that it would be necessary to discuss the Korean question at the Seventh Session of the General Assembly due to open in mid-October 1952. The US government was less eager to take this course since it did not wish to share responsibility for negotiating the armistice, but it bowed to the collective will of the UN. Still, there existed a general sense of pessimism in Washington that the world organization would not be able to find an acceptable solution to the prisoner of war problem and debate in New York would only further complicate the matter.

In this anxious climate, therefore, US and Commonwealth planning gradually got underway for the forthcoming session. The State Department got the ball rolling by drawing up a working paper envisaging a two-step action. The first step involved the adoption of a draft resolution calling for the Communist negotiators to accept the principle of non-forcible repatriation so that an armistice could be signed. Predicting a negative Communist response to this proposal, the second step entailed a draft resolution imposing additional measures against the PRC, including a total trade embargo and a call for all members to sever, limit or refuse diplomatic relations with Beijing.[14] The Old Commonwealth governments all expressed support for the first step but the second step proved much more controversial. Churchill initially believed that since the United States was bearing practically all the military burden in Korea, Britain should not take too stiff a line on additional measures. He also felt the Chinese should be made to feel as uncomfortable as possible and played down the risk of escalation, writing of the PRC, 'They cannot swim, they are not too much good at flying and the Trans-Siberian railway is already overloaded.'[15] Yet Eden convinced Churchill that a total embargo would require a naval blockade of all East Asian ports including Port Arthur, Dairen and Vladivostok—risking conflict with the Soviet Union—and Hong Kong, threatening the British colony with economic ruin. Eden also did not want to remove Britain's valuable 'listening-post' in Beijing. And, anyway, the Foreign Secretary doubted that the US proposal would win the support of the Arab-Asian bloc at the UN.[16]

A very similar conclusion was drawn by the Canadian,[17] New Zealand[18] and South African[19] governments. The Australian government, however, was divided on the second step. On one hand, Spender, ever eager to promote relations with Washington, had 'little objection' to additional measures.[20] Casey, on the other hand, was more concerned with the 'cool' reaction of the British and preferred to adopt a wait-and-see policy.[21] At this point neither India nor Pakistan were consulted as regards to American thinking.

Another contentious issue between the United States and the Old Commonwealth members was whether the UN debate on Korea should be postponed until after the US presidential election. Eden promoted this course, arguing that any comment on Korea at the UN would be dragged into the campaign. The Foreign Secretary made it clear that he at least would not be attending the Seventh Session until after the election to avoid saying something that might potentially damage Anglo-American relations.[22] Interestingly, the US government officially adopted a position of 'neutrality' on this question since Truman was confident that the election would not impact upon the deliberations on Korea or threaten US dominance at the UN. In addition, Acheson suspected that Eden wanted postponement so he could disassociate himself from the Truman administration's policy, assuming Eisenhower would be elected.[23] Even so, Eden received very little support from his Commonwealth colleagues. Pearson felt very few members would favour postponement given the importance of the Korea item.[24] Casey also did not like the idea of subordinating the UN programme to US domestic events.[25] Finally, the New Zealand government thought the Soviet Union would use postponement to its propaganda advantage.[26] In light of these arguments, Eden let the matter drop.

In the meantime, an informal proposal made by the Mexican government to resolve the prisoner of war question further complicated US and Commonwealth planning. The Mexican scheme involved an immediate ceasefire and then the reclassifying of all non-repatriate prisoners as political refugees so that they could be granted asylum in any country that was willing to accept them. Unsurprisingly, Acheson was annoyed with the Mexican government for meddling in what he considered US business without prior consultation, especially as the proposal lacked any reference to the principle of non-forcible repatriation. The Secretary of State also believed that the Mexican President, Miguel Aleman Valdes, was interfering in this matter in an attempt to win the Nobel Peace Prize before he left office. Still, Acheson was not totally dismissive of the plan and told the Mexicans that he would keep it under consideration.[27]

The Commonwealth response to the Mexican proposal was also mixed. Eden believed that it should be pursued as long as it was directed solely at those members who had not contributed forces to the UN action; that neither Communist members nor the Chinese Nationalists would be permitted to grant asylum; and that the proposal be put forward through normal diplomatic channels rather than as a UN draft resolution.[28] Pearson[29] and the South African[30] government concurred with this analysis. The Australian[31] and New Zealand[32] governments, in contrast, thought that the Mexican proposal did not overcome the fundamental disagreement between the two sides on non-forcible repatriation. Nehru went one step further, stating he would oppose the Mexican proposal if tabled since Beijing would not accept any solution that did not see its soldiers repatriated to China.[33]

The 21-Power draft resolution

By mid-September 1952 little progress had been made by the US and Commonwealth governments on the course they would pursue at the forthcoming General Assembly. With preparation time running out, the Truman administration decided to take the initiative. Acheson accepted the wishes of the Old Commonwealth members and reluctantly dropped the second phase of his plan for the imposition of additional measures. He then formulated a draft resolution simply calling for the Communists to accept one of the three proposals recently put forward by the UN negotiators at Panmunjom. Acheson was eager to have this proposal co-sponsored by all the members contributing to the Korean action, including all the Commonwealth countries.[34]

Initially the Commonwealth members were divided over this US draft resolution. Casey quickly expressed Australia's willingness to co-sponsor it but the British and Canadian governments were more wary.[35] Eden worried that the proposal sounded too much like an ultimatum implying that if the Communists did not accept non-forcible repatriation further UN action would be taken.[36] Pearson agreed that any provocative language needed to be removed.[37] Yet over the first half of October 1952 the US and Old Commonwealth governments became fully galvanized into action. The outbreak of large-scale ground operations in Korea, the Communist negotiators' rejection of the UN proposals and the subsequent breakdown of the armistice negotiations convinced these countries that a united position had to be found before the Korean debate commenced.

This goal was achieved at a meeting chaired by Acheson of the 21 member states contributing forces, goods or services to the UN action, excluding India, which refused to participate in these meetings in an effort to retain its neutrality. In these circumstances, all 21 delegations endorsed the US draft resolution without question, except the British who continued to argue that the proposal sounded too much like an ultimatum. Importantly, Acheson, determined above all to present a united Western front and conscious of the moral authority of the Commonwealth at the UN, agreed to amend his draft resolution so that the President of the General Assembly would transmit the resolution to Beijing and Pyongyang and would report on its progress. This concession meant that if the Communists rejected the proposal there was no implication that the UN would automatically take further action.[38] Consequently, the British agreed to join with the other 20 sponsors of the US draft resolution.[39]

The following day the Korean item came up in the First Committee. Acheson tabled the 21-Power draft resolution and over the next few days the Old Commonwealth delegations publicly expressed their support for this proposal. They also argued against a Soviet draft resolution calling for an immediate ceasefire and a post-armistice conference composed of both interested and neutral countries to discuss all outstanding issues, including the prisoners of war.[40] Buoyed by this united Western front, Acheson reported to Truman that, 'After the first ten days of this session of the General Assembly, I think it is fair to report that things are moving for us perhaps better than we might have expected.'[41] Acheson's optimism, however, was ill founded. The British and Canadian governments had already concluded that the 21-Power draft resolution would be rejected by the Communists and would not contribute towards a peaceful settlement. More significantly, Nehru, with strong domestic support, was once again determined to play a significant role in international affairs and strongly believed that a compromise formula could be found to resolve the prisoners of war question. The Indian delegation, now headed by Mrs Pandit, had thus set its mind on playing a leading role at the Seventh Session.[42] She realized that India was in a unique position because of its relationships with Beijing, the neutral bloc and the West through the Commonwealth, and she thought that, 'We alone can help in negotiations [regarding Korea] of a diplomatic character when they arise.'[43]

The Indian position was developed at the UN by V.K. Krishna Menon, a member of the Indian delegation and close friend of Nehru who had been hand-picked to represent the Prime Minister's views on Korea.[44] Menon had formerly been the Indian High Commissioner to Britain where he had enjoyed ambiguous relations with the host government. Regardless of his British education, mannerisms and respect for British liberal democratic traditions, Menon was a staunch Indian nationalist and had been reluctant to coordinate policy too closely with either the Attlee or Churchill governments.[45] As a consequence, Menon's appointment to the Indian delegation led to some initial concerns by the other Commonwealth delegations. Still, Menon remained someone that the other Commonwealth represen-tatives at the UN could deal with. As Jebb wrote of him in his memoirs, 'It was best, in spite of his grim fakir-like appearance, not to think of him as an Indian at all. And indeed he was a completely *New Statesman*, London School of Economics type, who could not, I believe, talk any Indian language.'[46] In addition, Mrs Pandit saw Menon as a rival and as a source of disharmony within the Indian delegation, regularly complaining to her brother regarding Menon's behaviour even though she did appreciate his zeal.[47]

Nonetheless, Menon was unperturbed and at a meeting of Commonwealth delegations he took the lead by tentatively stating that an opportunity had arisen to make a compromise proposal.[48] When the Commonwealth delegations next met Menon went much further stating that the Indian government could not support the 21-Power draft resolution because the Chinese would perceive it as an ultimatum and would reject it. He then informally suggested as an alternative that a repatriation commission be established to take custody of all non-repatriate prisoners after an armistice and to decide upon their final disposition. Menon hoped that this would be acceptable to the Chinese and that the two superpowers would at least abstain on such a proposal to allow its passage at the UN.[49]

The Indian proposal was greeted with sympathy by the other Commonwealth delegations, particularly the British and Canadians, who were now extremely apprehensive about the US election and were worried by the intensified fighting at Triangle Hill. But none of the Commonwealth representatives were willing to give Menon's suggestion explicit support until the views of the Americans were made known. Selwyn Lloyd, leading the British delegation until Eden arrived in New York after the US presidential election, thus took it upon himself to raise the matter with Acheson. The Secretary of State, though, immediately denounced Menon's plan for leaving unresolved the ultimate fate of non-repatriate prisoners of war. He argued that unless this problem was answered in advance the Communists would have a ready-made pretext for breaching the armistice.[50] Two days later Lloyd met with Acheson again and added that Menon was 'trying to be helpful' and 'full of ideas'. Acheson, however, dismissed Lloyd's arguments as reflecting the 'traditional difference' between the United States and Britain on the need to mobilize the fullest Arab-Asian support in the General Assembly.[51] Indeed, Acheson later wrote in his memoirs that Menon's proposal was a 'nebulous idea, which had every vice and was an about-face'.[52]

Even so, Nehru was encouraged in his mission by reports coming from the new Indian Ambassador to the PRC, Nedyam Raghavan, that Zhou En-lai was willing to make concessions on the prisoners of war question.[53] Strengthened by this news, Menon further elaborated his proposal for his Commonwealth colleagues. He highlighted that the Geneva Convention on Prisoners of War allowed for prisoners to be handed to a 'protecting power' after hostilities. Menon suggested that this role could be assumed by a body consisting of representatives from Sweden, Switzerland, Czechoslovakia and Poland—the four nations already accepted by both sides at Panmunjom to serve on the NNSC—plus an umpire appointed by the Commission to cast the deciding vote.[54] This proposal had the blessing of Nehru, who explained to the British High Commissioner that it was designed to reconcile without loss of face the two contradictory but 'right' positions on repatriation adopted at Panmunjom.[55]

Meanwhile, it had become clear in the First Committee debate that it was not only India who doubted the utility of the 21-Power draft resolution. A number of Arab-Asian members, notably Indonesia, India's biggest rival within this group, informally made suggestions for a compromise solution. This fact alarmed Mrs Pandit, who wrote to her brother that Menon was ignoring the wishes of India's Arab-Asian partners 'of which he has supreme contempt'.[56] Mrs Pandit thought it essential to consult with other friendly nations, not just the Commonwealth, if the Indian initiative was to be successful.[57] Moreover, the Latin American group got involved in the matter. Against the express wishes of the Truman administration, the Mexican delegation formally tabled its earlier proposal to reclassify non-repatriate prisoners as asylum seekers. Within days the Peruvian delegation also tabled a draft resolution calling for an end to the fighting and for all non-repatriate prisoners to be sent to a neutral nation where they would remain in custody until a solution could be found. The situation in New York, therefore, had suddenly become very complicated with Soviet, Mexican and Peruvian proposals now on the table alongside the 21-Power draft resolution and the Commonwealth on the verge of making a contribution of its own.

The impact of the US presidential election on the Korean debate

Despite their anxieties towards the 21-Power draft resolution, prior to the US presidential election the Old Commonwealth members remained disunited and felt obliged to remain loyal to the position they had publicly endorsed. But Eisenhower's victory on 4 November 1952 emboldened the Commonwealth members to unite and mount their most successful challenge to US policy at the UN during the entire Korean conflict. At the heart of this Commonwealth unity was the shared fear that if a quick solution to the prisoner of war question could not be found the new US government would likely pursue a more aggressive military policy in Korea. Rather than bringing an end to the conflict as they desperately desired, the Commonwealth governments believed this course would at least prolong the conflict and might even lead to its escalation into a global war. Consequently, the Commonwealth members were determined to use the moral authority they had at the UN, drawn from the organization's multiethnic composition and liberal democratic traditions, to find a solution to the prisoners of war question and bring the war to a speedy end.

What made this Commonwealth attempt to constrain US policy more potent than the one outlined in Chapter 2 was that the Truman administration now lacked the strength to resist Commonwealth pressure indefinitely. During the interregnum period Truman was a lame duck president of the weakest kind, especially when it came to the Korean conflict. His limited war strategy, championed by Stevenson during the election, had been resoundingly rejected by the US voters. Acheson, as the chief architect of Truman's foreign policy, had also fared particularly badly throughout the campaign, being vilified by the Republican press and McCarthy. Much of his personal prestige had vanished and he could no longer dominate his colleagues in New York as he had done in the past. In these circumstances, the departing Truman administration's policy bore little weight at the UN without the endorsement of the President-Elect.[58] Truman tried to address this problem by first sending a letter to Eisenhower asking for him to publicly support the US position in the Korean debate.[59] The General, however, replied that he had no decision-making authority.[60] Truman then invited Eisenhower to the White House and Acheson outlined the difficulties faced in New York. All the same, Eisenhower only vaguely promised to consider issuing a statement clarifying his views on Korea.[61] This statement never materialized as he did not want to jeopardize his election promise to end the war before even taking office.

Also of major importance to Commonwealth unity was the leading role played by key Commonwealth personalities in shaping the UN debate on Korea. As already mentioned, Nehru was determined to bring about a compromise solution and, although he was not personally present in New York, his views were ably represented by Menon and Mrs Pandit. For Britain, Lloyd and, even more so, Eden after his arrival on 8 November 1952, passionately set about trying to find common ground between the Indian and US positions. A similar line was pursued by Pearson who had been elected President of the General Assembly for the Seventh Session. Officially this post is purely administrative but Pearson believed it his duty as President of the General Assembly to try to bring together delegations to find a consensus position.[62] The other Commonwealth representatives present in New York also lent their support to their Commonwealth partners even though they were more wary of upsetting Washington, especially the Australian delegation led by Casey and Spender. Nevertheless, the fact that all these Commonwealth personalities were gathered together resulted in a united front against US policy.

The rallying point for Commonwealth unity appeared on 6 November 1952. After Lloyd had given considerable technical advice on its drafting, Menon formally presented his proposal as a draft resolution, consisting of two distinct sections, at a meeting of Commonwealth delegations. The first section was a lengthy preamble supporting the UN negotiators at Panmunjom and the principle of non-forcible repatriation. The second more important substantive section listed 17 'proposals', with the most important being the establishment of the repatriation commission outlined previously by Menon to take custody of all prisoners after the fighting had ceased. Those prisoners who were willing to be repatriated would be expeditiously returned to their homelands. Over the following 90 days representatives of the belligerents would then be able to explain to non-repatriate prisoners matters relating to their return home. If after this process there remained non-repatriate prisoners, their fate would be discussed at the political conference on Korea for a further 90 days. If no decision could be reached there the final disposition of non-repatriate prisoners would be transferred to the UN. The Commonwealth representatives present all immediately voiced their support for this draft resolution over that of the 21-Powers.[63]

Given the strength of the Commonwealth's convictions, the widespread calls at the General Assembly for a compromise solution, and further reports from Raghavan that Zhou En-lai was considering making concessions,[64] Acheson did briefly consider how the Indian draft resolution could be incorporated into the 21-Power draft resolution.[65] But any faint hope of the US government relaxing its position soon evaporated when Soviet Foreign Minister Andrei Vyshinsky launched a scathing attack in the First Committee on the 21-Power, Mexican and Peruvian draft resolutions.[66] For Acheson this statement had 'slammed the door shut' to finding a compromise solution.[67] The Secretary of State now campaigned to have the 21-Power draft resolution adopted and set about convincing the Commonwealth members to support this course, using all the diplomatic weapons at his disposal.

To begin with, on meeting Menon for the first time Acheson unequivocally stated that the Indian draft resolution was unacceptable since it did not make sufficiently clear its support for non-forcible repatriation or whether non-repatriate prisoners would be released at the end of the process.[68] Acheson explained this last point further when he spoke to the Old Commonwealth delegations, stating that the Indian draft resolution gave prisoners a choice between repatriation and remaining in custody for an indefinite period which amounted to no choice at all. Yet the majority of the Old Commonwealth representatives, led by Pearson and Eden, made their support for the Indian proposal clear, only agreeing that it needed to be redrafted. Only Spender, always eager to please the Americans, agreed with Acheson that the 21-Power draft resolution should take priority even though this ran contrary to his instructions from Canberra to support the Indian proposal.[69] Acheson was greatly concerned by this insubordination but remained confident that the majority of the 21 sponsoring members would continue to back their own draft resolution, forcing the Old Commonwealth countries to follow suit. Still, at a meeting of the group of 21, to the Secretary of State's horror, only a handful of these members backed the US position. The majority called for an effort to try to accommodate the two draft resolutions. This development clearly demonstrated the moral authority wielded by the Commonwealth at the UN.[70]

Acheson, nonetheless, was not about to roll over. Staying on at the General Assembly far longer than he had planned and was his habit, he adopted an increasingly aggressive stance towards his uncooperative Commonwealth colleagues. To start with, Acheson had Lovett and Chairman of the Joint Chiefs of Staff General Omar Bradley meet with the British and Canadian delegations in New York. Lovett and Bradley argued that if the final disposition of prisoners of war was not settled before an armistice then the Communists could later use this as a pretext for resuming hostilities. But Lloyd and Pearson argued that many other excuses could be given by the Communists to restart the conflict if they wished to and so it was better to bring about a ceasefire immediately.[71] Next, in discussions with Eden and Pearson, Acheson issued the vague warning that the 'British and Canadians, in encouraging Menon, were themselves running very great risks'.[72] He also launched a personal attack upon Lloyd, accusing him of meddling in issues that he did not understand. Despite their vindictiveness, Eden did not take these criticisms too seriously, realizing that Acheson's hostility was a result of the intense domestic pressure he was under.[73] In spite of this acknowledgement, relations between Acheson and Eden reached a nadir since the former seriously questioned the latter's loyalty, given his late arrival at the General Assembly and his meeting with Eisenhower in New York to discuss future policy, including Acheson's successor.

Up until this point disagreements between the US and Commonwealth delegations had been kept private. This situation changed dramatically on 19 November 1952 when Menon tabled the Indian draft resolution in the First Committee without prior consultation with Acheson. Two days later the Indian representative then gave a statement claiming that his proposal simply wove all the existing points of agreement into a pattern without sacrificing principles and expressing hope that all parties would find it acceptable.[74] The Indian delegation had decided to take this action since Nehru was unwilling to bend any further to the will of the Americans. He wrote to Mrs Pandit, 'Let us try to follow the right path. That is more important than getting a resolution passed in the UN.'[75] Furthermore, in the debate in the First Committee that followed Eden expressed sympathy for the Indian draft resolution although he was still careful not to dismiss the 21-Power draft resolution.[76]

The US delegation made no comment in the First Committee regarding the Indian draft resolution, but privately Acheson was furious. He wrote to Truman complaining that the British and Canadians were soft on 'our principles' and they had 'grave apprehensions' about Eisenhower's future policy on Korea.[77] In his growing state of desperation, Acheson warned the group of 21 in no uncertain terms that if they were willing to compromise principles to gain Asian support the United States could not vote along with them. Even so, while Spender supported Acheson, once more ignoring his instructions, the other Old Commonwealth members claimed that the Indian draft resolution met their fundamental views and they only wished to revise its text. The vast majority of the other members present backed this position and the group decided to establish a sub-committee—chaired by Spender but also including the US, British and Canadian delegations—to consider amendments to the draft resolution.[78] But when this body met no progress was made.[79]

In spite of these growing fissures the Commonwealth members wanted to avoid a split with Washington and to make the Indian draft resolution acceptable to the Truman administration. As a result, in close cooperation with Eden and Pearson, Menon revised his proposal so that the final disposition of prisoners of war would be discussed for 60 rather than 90 days at the post-armistice political conference before being transferred to the UN. But these efforts to find a compromise were completely ignored by the US delegation, which retaliated by leaking to the press its opposition to the Indian draft resolution and emphasizing Anglo-American differences.[80] Evidently Acheson hoped to bludgeon his allies into backing down, but the Commonwealth members were not to be bullied as was demonstrated at the next meeting of the group of 21. Acheson

stressed that he could not accept the Indian draft resolution unless it
specifically stated a time limit for the detention of prisoners before
they would be released. All the same, a clear majority of the
delegations present, including all the Commonwealth representatives, even Spender, supported Lloyd's argument that the Indian draft
resolution should be supported as it stood.[81] At this point Truman
reluctantly granted the Secretary of State permission to break with
the Commonwealth.[82]

Adopting the Indian Resolution

Crucially, however, Acheson did not find it necessary to exercise these
powers. The irreconcilable differences of opinion between Washington and the Commonwealth capitals on what course the UN should
adopt were never fully resolved but their positions were effectively
aligned by the actions of the Soviet Union. On 24 November
Vyshinsky made a scathing statement in the First Committee
denouncing the Indian draft resolution, claiming that the proposal
was based on the US principle of forced detention and ran counter to
the Geneva Convention on Prisoners of War. He also warned that
such a resolution could only lead to the continuation of the conflict.
Acheson immediately leapt at this opportunity to express publicly
that the differences between the Indian proposal and the 21-Power
draft resolution were linguistic rather than substantive, indicating
that the former would be acceptable if the final disposition of
prisoners was clarified.[83] Why was the Secretary of State so willing to
make this concession after resisting the Indian proposal so
vehemently for so long? In short, Vyshinsky's statement allowed
the US government to support the Indian draft resolution in the
belief it would never be accepted by the Communists. Acheson
remained confident that US national interests would thus not be
jeopardized by accepting the Indian draft resolution since it would
come to nothing. In contrast, he firmly held that great harm would
have been done to the United States' global position if it had broken
with its closest Commonwealth allies.[84]

The Old Commonwealth members shared this sense of relief. Eden felt that differences between the US and Indian viewpoints had now narrowed to 'manageable proportions' and was thankful that a 'head-on collision had been avoided'.[85] He left New York the following day, therefore, confident that Anglo-American relations had not been permanently damaged but convinced that the Indian draft resolution would bear no fruit. Pearson was also pleased that Vyshinsky's statement had allowed the United States to concede but still hoped that the Indian initiative was making an impression in Beijing.[86] For the Australian, New Zealand and South African delegations, who had felt much more uncomfortable challenging US policy all along, Washington's acceptance of the Indian draft resolution averted the catastrophe of voting against the Western superpower. Unity between the United States and the Old Commonwealth members was then fully restored at a meeting the next day of the group of 21. The representatives present unanimously agreed that voting priority should be given to the Indian draft resolution but clarification would be sought on the final disposition of prisoners.[87]

Needless to say the Indian reaction to Vyshinsky's statement was far more negative. Nehru concluded that the Indian attempt at finding a solution had failed and wrote to his sister that 'the world is determined to commit suicide' and 'there is really no common ground between the American position and the Chinese'. Nehru added that while the Indian draft resolution was an ingenious attempt to get around the basic difficulties, the proposal was too inclined towards the 'UK point of view' and was critical of Menon for negotiating so closely with the Commonwealth.[88] Nehru's views were compounded the next day when the Chinese government indicated to Raghavan that it could not accept the Indian draft resolution for exactly the same reasons given by Vyshinsky.[89] This news still came as something to a shock to the Indians since Raghavan's previous reports had all indicated that the Chinese would accept the Indian proposal. The Indian Secretary-General of the Ministry of External Affairs and Nehru's cousin, R.K. Nehru, later attributed blame for China's reversal to Stalin's desire to prolong the Korean conflict and Mao's determination to toe the Soviet line.[90]

In light of the Indian government's reaction, the US and Old Commonwealth governments were gravely concerned that Menon would withdraw his draft resolution now their views had been aligned. To prevent this happening they put pressure on India to stand firm. Eden sent a personal message to Nehru praising the work of Menon and revealing that at his private meeting with Eisenhower the president-elect had welcomed the Indian initiative.[91] Similarly, Pearson wrote to Nehru praising Menon's 'skill, integrity and patience' and stating that the Indian draft resolution represented a real advance toward a peaceful settlement even if the reaction of the Chinese and Soviets was unsatisfactory.[92] But the United States adopted more aggressive tactics. Acheson told Menon that it would be disastrous if the Indian draft resolution were withdrawn now that it had been given priority.[93] Acheson also warned that if India did withdraw its draft resolution then the United States might consider sponsoring it.[94]

In addition, Acheson continued to press Menon to revise his draft resolution further to safeguard the principle of non-forcible repatriation just in case the Communists later did a U-turn.[95] The Secretary of State's key demand was that the length of time the final disposition of prisoners should be discussed at the post-armistice conference be reduced to 30 days. The British and Canadian delegations attempted to defend the Indian draft resolution as it stood but were becoming increasingly annoyed by Menon's uncompromising position now that the Americans were onside.[96] Eventually, the Indian representative agreed that if another member tabled the US amendment he would not oppose it.[97] This concession reflected Nehru's view that the Indian resolution had to be voted upon after everything that had gone before.[98]

With the US and Commonwealth positions finally aligned the Korean debate moved inexorably towards its conclusion despite Soviet attempts to derail the Indian draft resolution by tabling a series of amendments that would have essentially transformed it into the Soviet proposal.[99] When the debate came to a head on 1 December 1952 these were overwhelmingly rejected, while a Danish amendment reducing the period of consideration by the political conference to 30 days was adopted by a large majority. Immediately thereafter the Indian draft resolution received unanimous non-Communist support. Two days later in the Plenary the proposal was adopted, becoming General Assembly Resolution 610 (VII) (see Appendix 11, p. 269–73). Meanwhile, the Soviet draft resolution was rejected by the same margin and the 21-Power, Mexican and Peruvian draft resolutions were withdrawn.[100]

Implementing the Indian Resolution

The adoption of the Indian Resolution was generally welcomed by the US and Commonwealth governments. Conscious that it had backed down under Commonwealth pressure, the Truman administration remained confident that US control over the armistice negotiations

Figure 5.1 Acheson addresses the General Assembly during the autumn of 1952.
Source: Casey: *Selling the Korean War*, p. 317.

would be unaffected since the Communists would reject the resolution. Washington was also relieved that no permanent rift had emerged between itself and its key allies. Eden shared these sentiments but praised the 'Commonwealth front' which had shown great determination in standing up to 'tough' and 'inept' US tactics. Eden also reserved special congratulations for India and Menon. More significantly, Eden believed that the Indian Resolution represented 'the beginning of an alignment of the Asian position in a more positive sense on the side of the free world'. His only regrets were the prolonged and highly publicized spat with the US delegation and Spender's hesitancy in supporting the Indian proposal.[101] In addition, Pearson wrote in his diary that the resolution was an important step even though it was unlikely to bring about an immediate armistice. Pearson thought it provided a 'United Nations basis in the best sense of the word' for a future settlement.[102]

The Indian government, on the other hand, was far from positive. Mrs Pandit was concerned that the Indian Resolution had been watered down too much and she told Nehru that she had almost felt like voting against it.[103] The Indian Permanent Representative thus predicted that the resolution would not lead to an end to the conflict and India would have to take a leading role at the UN once again when the incoming Eisenhower administration pushed to extend the fighting. Mrs Pandit believed 'our present popularity will then suffer!!'.[104] Nehru also had little hope that the Indian Resolution would be successful, given the Soviet and latent US opposition. Yet he was pleased with the Indian stand at the General Assembly and was convinced that the resolution would play a role in limiting Eisenhower's end-the-war strategy. For that reason Nehru believed that Indian diplomacy had achieved its principal goal of mediating between the two superpowers. He was more hopeful, therefore, that India would be able to play a similar future role at the UN.[105]

Before this question arose, however, the Indian Resolution had to run its course. Its final provision requested the President of the General Assembly to transmit the document to the Chinese government and the North Korean authorities, invite their acceptance of the proposals and make a report during the present session. Controversially, Pearson decided it would be necessary to include alongside the text of the resolution an 'explanatory and objective communication' to remove any misunderstandings on the part of the Communists.[106] The US delegation was annoyed by Pearson's interpretation of his mission and complained that the note was an unwarranted attempt to weight the resolution in favour of universal repatriation. But Pearson was determined to go through with his plan.[107] In addition, Pearson hoped the Indian Embassy in Beijing would deliver these documents to the Chinese, allowing Raghavan to explain his government's views.[108] Still, Nehru was opposed to this course, fearing the Chinese government might perceive it as unwanted Indian interference on behalf of the UN. As a result, he urged Pearson to convey the resolution directly to the PRC government to prevent giving the impression to the Chinese that he thought he was 'too big a man' to deal with them. The Indian Ambassador would then be able to explain the intentions of the proposal if asked.[109] Pearson grudgingly accepted this course.

On 15 December 1952, as widely predicted, the PRC unequivocally rejected the Indian Resolution. Pearson decided against an immediate report to the General Assembly since he did not want to precipitate controversial discussion before the winter recess. For that reason he was dismayed when the Soviet delegation decided to introduce a last-minute agenda item condemning the 'massacre' of prisoners of war at the UNC camps at Pongnam.[110] Evidently, Vyshinsky hoped to divide the UN members, united by the Indian Resolution, but this ploy proved ineffective. In spite of Soviet efforts to prolong the debate their draft resolution was rejected by 45 votes to five, with ten Arab-Asian members abstaining.[111] Finally, two days before Christmas the General Assembly went into recess without any protest since all the members were content to let the Korean issue drop after the last two tumultuous months.

Conclusion

Relations between the United States and the Commonwealth at the UN during the Korean conflict reached a nadir in the autumn of

1952. Since the beginning of the armistice talks the Commonwealth members had largely allowed the US free rein in deciding policy. Even so, Commonwealth confidence in the United States to bring the Korean conflict to an end had diminished as the negotiations deadlocked and frustration grew at the prolongation of fighting. These feelings then came to the surface in a dramatic way when consideration of the Korean question resumed at the UN. The Commonwealth members seized upon this opportunity to use their moral authority within the world organization to try to end the deeply unpopular conflict by compromising with the Communists on the prisoner of war question. This course led them into direct conflict with the Truman administration, which wished to retain direct control over the negotiations and was unwilling to make concessions. However, unlike the diplomatic crisis following Chinese intervention, this time the Commonwealth remained united and Washington eventually backed down.

The reasons for the strength of Commonwealth unity during this period were manifold. To begin with, the breakdown of the armistice negotiations, the eruption of fierce fighting in Korea, tensions surrounding the political crisis in the ROK and, most importantly, the election of Eisenhower convinced the Commonwealth members that the conflict might escalate. Coincidentally, all these factors converged at the very moment the Seventh Session of the General Assembly got underway. This twist of fate meant that a number of key Commonwealth personalities were brought together in New York where they could personally oversee the formulation of a united position. Central to this process were the roles played by Pearson, Eden and Nehru, acting through Menon and Mrs Pandit. These figures all displayed firm resolve in trying to answer the prisoners of war question and to end the war even against US adversity. Nonetheless, the crucial difference between this challenge to US hegemony and the one in the winter of 1950–51 was the tenuous position of the Truman administration during the interregnum period. The US government was forced into unaccustomed negotiations with its Commonwealth allies. In the end, Washington very reluctantly agreed to drop its proposal, and then only when it was convinced that the Commonwealth-backed Indian Resolution would have no impact on the Korean question. These views were to prove ill-founded over the following seven months, since the Indian Resolution provided the means for bringing an end to the conflict.

CHAPTER 6

THE KOREAN WAR ENDGAME, JANUARY–JULY 1953

The final seven months of the Korean War were chaotic and events beyond the UN took centre stage in finally bringing the conflict to a close. It is unsurprising, therefore, that historians of this period have most commonly scrutinized the policies adopted in, and the interactions between, Washington, Moscow and Beijing. As will be discussed in more detail below, this body of literature has generally been divided between those who argue in favour of or against Eisenhower's atomic diplomacy being the principal cause of the termination of hostilities. Yet important decisions were also taken at the UN, where relations between the United States and the Commonwealth members gradually stabilized after the upheavals of the previous autumn. This process resulted from the analysis shared by the US and Commonwealth governments that the UN could or should do very little now that the Indian Resolution had been adopted, especially once other indicators increasingly pointed towards peace. Occasional arguments did break out between the United States and the Commonwealth members, particularly Britain and India, over the details of what course should be pursued at the UN. But at no time did the Commonwealth members feel the need to come together in an effort to constrain US policy as they had done just a couple of months before.

The Commonwealth remained disunited during the concluding phase of the Korean War because the conditions necessary to bind these countries were absent. First of all, while the General Assembly was in session there appeared to be little risk of the conflict escalating beyond the Korean peninsula. Earlier worries that the Eisenhower administration was going to employ more drastic military measures lessened as it became clear that the new president had no ready-made plans to end the war. Commonwealth fears diminished further once the armistice negotiations resumed and steady progress toward peace was being made. Even Eisenhower's much-heralded veiled threats to use atomic weapons against the PRC failed to unite the Commonwealth members since these were made only after the General Assembly had been adjourned. Furthermore, the US government adopted a moderate policy at the UN and did not call for retaliatory measures to be taken after the Communists rejected the Indian Resolution. In these positive circumstances the key Commonwealth personalities were unwilling to exert their influence to try to alter US policy. They were more concerned that if they attempted to seize the initiative they might inadvertently delay peace or jeopardize future relations with the Eisenhower administration. As a result, even when these central Commonwealth figures were brought together at the General Assembly and in London for a Prime Ministers' Conference, little effort was made to coordinate a united position. Finally, the immensely popular new US government, with a full four-year term ahead, quickly demonstrated its determination to dominate the UN and not to bow to Commonwealth pressure.

Once more, the overlapping military, domestic and international spheres in which the Korean debate at the UN took place will be laid out first, providing fuller understanding of the actions and motivations of the US and Commonwealth governments throughout the final phase of the conflict.

The military situation

When President Eisenhower took office in January 1953 the military situation in Korea remained stalemated at the 38th parallel. Over the

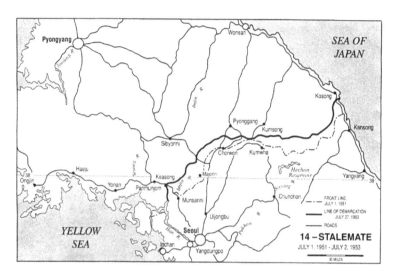

Figure 6.1 The military stalemate, July 1951–July 1953.
Source: Stueck: *The Korean War*, p. 226.

following months, while debates raged in Washington over how to bring the war to an end by military means, the UNC continued to employ the limited war strategy pursued by the Truman administration. Clark's only notable positive initiative was to further intensify the bombing campaign against North Korea in an attempt to break the will of the enemy. In May 1953 irrigation dams were targeted for the first time, resulting in the flooding of large swathes of farmland, as well as population centres and the transportation network. Still, this policy had minimal military success and both the United States' enemies and allies heavily criticized these bombings for being inhumane.[1]

The Communist High Command, in stark contrast, instigated a number of incidents to capture strategic territory and demonstrate its determination and ability to fight on. Between late March and May 1953 Communist forces attacked a number of targets in the Iron Triangle area. In each case, the objectives were small, the fighting was short and brutal, and the UNC was able to repel the numerically stronger Communist forces by utilizing its technological superiority.

But far more serious military activity took place between 13 and 20 July 1953 as the armistice negotiations were drawing to a conclusion. The Communists launched their largest offensive of the war since 1951 in an effort to recover the territory north of the 38th parallel occupied by UN forces before hostilities ceased. Initially, the Communist forces pushed deep into areas defended by the ROKA but the battlefront soon stabilized once UNC reinforcements arrived. These minor territorial gains helped save Communist face and demonstrated what might happen if President Rhee attempted to fulfil his promise to bring about the unification of Korea by force after the armistice. The guns were then finally silenced on 27 July 1953 with the signing of the Korean Armistice Agreement, as will be discussed below.

Domestic developments

By far the most dramatic domestic developments in the first half of 1953 took place in the United States. On 20 January 1953 Eisenhower took office with a strong popular mandate. Due to both his past military leadership in a time of national crisis and his personable character, the American people placed much trust in Eisenhower. They were also willing to give the new president a lengthy honeymoon period before subjecting him to the criticism levelled against Truman in his final years in office. Nonetheless, Eisenhower was still something of an unknown entity when it came to politics and it remained unclear what kind of leadership style he would adopt. Traditional accounts often describe Eisenhower as an aloof leader who delegated much responsibility to his subordinates and took decisions collegially. More recently a number of writers, notably Fred Greenstein, have questioned this view, claiming that Eisenhower was a shrewd behind-the-scenes operator who subtly retained close control over the decision-making process. This image is more accurate although it did take the new president a number of months in the post to develop his individual style.[2]

At the start of 1953 Eisenhower also kept his policy position purposefully vague to maintain his freedom of action. On the same day the President was elected, the Republican Party had for the first time in many years gained majorities, albeit slim, in both Houses of Congress. Moreover, in the Senate the Majority Leader was Eisenhower's greatest rival, Robert Taft. In an attempt to bring about the unity necessary to pass legislation, therefore, Eisenhower married conservative domestic with interventionist foreign policies. In terms of the latter, while his anti-Communist views and desire to put greater pressure on the Soviet Union were well known, he had given little indication of how he planned on achieving his goals. Due in large part to his past experiences, Eisenhower made the security of Europe his foreign policy priority and considered Britain and Canada to be the United States' closest friends. Learning from Truman's mistakes, though, the President was eager to look beyond Europe, particularly to Asia, where he felt Moscow had been given too much freedom. He was also determined to build closer relations with the United States other allies, especially those in the Commonwealth and Western Europe as well as the newly-independent countries that looked towards Washington for leadership.[3]

Secretary of State John Foster Dulles was crucial to the formulation of the new administration's foreign policy. Dulles was appointed not because of any close ties to Eisenhower but because of his high standing within the Republican Party and his vast experience in foreign affairs as an international lawyer and as a bipartisan figure serving in the State Department during the Truman years. Relations between Dulles and Eisenhower were, to begin with, overly formal, but they shared a very similar analysis of the global situation. Since resigning from the State Department soon after the signing of the Japanese Peace Treaty, Dulles had been highly critical of Truman's foreign policy, especially its limited war strategy in Korea. A devout Presbyterian and vehemently anti-Communist, Dulles argued that a more aggressive stance needed to be taken to curtail Soviet influence worldwide. He believed that this could only be achieved through tough talking, military strength and binding the United States and her allies in a tight network of security treaties.[4]

For both Eisenhower and Dulles the highest priority in early 1953 was finding a means to end the Korean War. But neither of these two men had a specific strategy in mind for achieving this elusive goal.

Eisenhower's much-hyped trip to Korea in early December 1952 provided no answers. The president-elect only spent three days in the country and, much to Clark's disappointment, held no detailed military talks.[5] Soon after his return, Eisenhower, under pressure from his own party, had then reluctantly met with MacArthur, whom he greatly disliked, to hear the retired general's views. However, Eisenhower had little sympathy for MacArthur's drastic plan to issue an ultimatum to Stalin to accept a political settlement. If this was ignored MacArthur proposed dropping atomic bombs along the Yalu river, creating a radioactive belt preventing the movement of troops and supplies, and the bombing of targets in China. In fact, the only significant action taken by Eisenhower during his early tenure in office was to announce on 30 January 1953 he would be reversing his predecessor's decision to station the US Seventh Fleet in the Taiwan Strait. The President stressed that, rather than protecting the Chinese Nationalists, this measure prevented Chiang Kai-shek from launching an invasion of the mainland, allowing Beijing to concentrate its forces in Korea.

Meanwhile, behind-the-scenes the Eisenhower administration considered how to militarily force an armistice. Dulles was most vocal in these early deliberations. He called for an advance to the narrow 'waist' of the peninsula between Pyongyang and Wonsan arguing that this strategy would create a shorter and more defensible line than the 38th parallel, a politically and economically viable ROK and would not risk Soviet intervention. Still, the new fiscally-minded Secretary of Defense, Charles Wilson, and the Joint Chiefs of Staff were opposed to this move due to the risk of failure and the considerable loss of manpower and treasure it would entail for minor territorial gains. Eisenhower concurred, fearing that even a limited offensive would create rifts between the United States and its allies. The President thus asked the Joint Chiefs to consider other ways to force the Communists to sue for peace. As a result, in April 1953 NSC-147 was drawn up listing six possible courses of military action of increasing intensity, culminating in the use of nuclear weapons against China. Importantly, unlike his predecessor, Eisenhower did not distinguish atomic from conventional weapons and was willing to explore the possibility of their tactical use to end the war in Korea.

Even so, NSC-147 was not formally endorsed by the President until late May 1953. This decision was then conveyed to the Communists through three channels in an effort to pressure them to accept peace. To start with, while in New Delhi Dulles, on the assumption that the Indian Prime Minister would relay this message to Beijing, hinted to Nehru that the UNC would escalate the conflict if the Communists did not accept an armistice. Next, Clark transmitted a letter to the Communist High Command emphasizing that the truce talks had entered their final stage, indicating that they would be broken off and hostilities intensified if no solution was found. Finally, Charles Bohlen, the US Ambassador in Moscow, highlighted to the new Soviet Foreign Minister, Vyacheslav Molotov, that the UN negotiators at Panmunjom would make no further concessions.[6]

Historians of the Korean War have extensively scrutinized the impact of these threats and a number of divergent arguments have been presented. On one hand, the traditional view posited most prominently by David Rees, Edward Keefer and Edward Friedman argues that Eisenhower's policy of nuclear coercion effectively forced the Communists to sue for peace and accept an armistice or face an extension of the fighting. This viewpoint reflects the statements made by the Eisenhower administration, most prominently by Dulles in an article in *Life* magazine, in the aftermath of the conflict, and these authors lavish much praise on the President for his execution of this plan.

Revisionist historians such as Rosemary Foot and Roger Dingman, on the other hand, question the importance of Eisenhower's use of nuclear coercion. They argue effectively that these threats were at most implicit; that the Indian government later denied it had ever passed Dulles' message on to the PRC; and that Mao had very publicly described atomic weapons as a 'paper tiger' that would have limited effect on China given its massive population and lack of urban and industrial centres to act as targets. These historians also stress that at the armistice negotiations, as will be outlined below, both sides had made all the necessary concessions before these threats were even made. Moreover, they emphasize that the Eisenhower administration only publicly claimed this use of atomic diplomacy much later when they were outlining their 'New Look' strategy. Matthew Jones takes a more nuanced approach. He argues that while the US threats may not have been the crucial factor in convincing the Communists to sue for peace, he does believe they were made sincerely and if they had been ignored then Eisenhower would have been forced to take action.

In comparison, domestic politics within each of the Commonwealth countries in the first half of 1953 was relatively stable, although some notable developments did take place. For instance, the British government was destabilized by the ill-health of some of its key personalities. At the start of April 1953 Eden suffered a serious problem with his bilary tract and underwent a series of operations. During his long recuperation Churchill assumed control of foreign affairs. This development was important for Anglo-American relations in particular. Due to the Prime Minister's old age and his expected retirement, Eden had come to dominate British foreign policy and had increasingly shown a willingness to adopt a position independent of the United States. In addition, poor relations existed between Eden and Dulles. In the winter of 1951–52 the two men had clashed over the 'Yoshida Letter', a letter written by Dulles and signed by the Japanese Prime Minister Yoshida Shigeru offering a peace treaty to the Chinese Nationalist government of Chiang Kai-shek. Eden had protested against this move on the grounds that it went against earlier Anglo-American agreements. He also believed that Japan should seek close ties with the PRC to form a bulwark against the Soviet Union in East Asia and to prevent Japan competing with Britain for trade in southeast Asia. He was then greatly angered when the Yoshida Letter was made public in mid-January 1952 shortly after he had ended discussions with Acheson and Dulles in New York, giving the impression he endorsed this move.[7] This episode largely provided the basis for Eden's advice to Eisenhower in December 1952 not to appoint Dulles, a discussion of which Dulles was aware. To cap it off, there was a distinct personality clash between the extrovert Foreign Secretary and the dour Secretary of State.

Eden's illness thus presented an opportunity for Churchill to smooth Anglo-American relations. Nevertheless, in late June 1953 the Prime Minister suffered a serious stroke that incapacitated him for almost four months. During this uncertain period, therefore, the Lord President of the Council, Lord Salisbury, was appointed Acting Foreign Secretary. Salisbury lacked experience in foreign affairs and had little international reputation, especially in Washington. Accordingly, Salisbury was tentative in his dealings with the Eisenhower administration and was very wary of damaging the special relationship. Salisbury was also a staunch imperialist and had little respect for Britain's non-white Commonwealth partners.[8]

Considerable domestic developments also occurred in two other Commonwealth countries. In South Africa in April 1953 the National Party government of Prime Minister Daniel Malan was re-elected, gaining an outright majority of seats for the first time. This vote reflected the growing republican sentiment in South Africa as many former United Party supporters realized that the 1949 London Declaration allowed South Africa to become a republic but still retain its ties to Britain through the Commonwealth. Malan's re-election also demonstrated that his *apartheid* policies had now won widespread appeal among the white electorate.[9] In the same month Pakistani Prime Minister Khawaja Nazimuddin was dismissed by Governor-General Malik Ghulam Mohammed. This was the result of mass rioting that had erupted after demands for the removal of the Ahmadi religious minority from positions of power, including Foreign Minister Muhammad Zafrullah Khan, were refused by the Prime Minister. The Governor-General then selected the relatively unknown Pakistan Ambassador to the United States, Mohammed Ali Bogra, to become Prime Minister. Bogra's main priority for the remainder of this period was bringing about domestic stability and building closer relations with Washington. These efforts soon bore fruit as Dulles visited Karachi in May 1953 and Pakistan agreed to join with a group of states to form a 'northern tier' to contain Soviet expansion in the Middle East.[10]

International relations

The first six months of 1953 represented a key turning point in the Cold War. Two events were of particular importance. The first was the announcement made by the departing President Truman in early January that two months earlier the United States had successfully tested its first hydrogen bomb. This achievement was the result of Truman's decision taken three years earlier to create a crash programme into nuclear fusion in response to the Soviet Union's testing of its first atomic bomb. The awesome power of this new weapon—up to 1,000 times that of the bomb dropped on Nagasaki—was to have a radical impact on the grand strategies of the two superpowers for decades to come.[11] But in the short term the most significant international development of this period was Stalin's death on 5 March 1953. Stalin had been the undisputed leader of the Soviet Union for almost 30 years and had kept a tight control over all aspects of domestic and foreign policy. No immediate successor to Stalin existed but a group of prominent Presidium members wrestled for leadership over the following months. Even so, at Stalin's funeral Premier Georgii Malenkov publicly called for peaceful co-existence between the superpowers and announced a 'peace offensive', starting with Korea, to lessen Cold War tensions.

The reasons why the new Soviet leadership launched this campaign remain unclear. A number of historians, most notably William Stueck, have argued convincingly that the new Soviet leaders realized that their position was far from secure, given Stalin's dominance of politics for such a long period. They thus desired a stable international climate to consolidate their position at home. The Soviet leadership also believed that by ending the Korean conflict they could alleviate the Soviet economy which had been overstretched by the provision of assistance to the Communist combatants and by meeting Western rearmament triggered by the conflict. This problem became more pronounced in June and July 1953, when strikes and anti-Soviet riots broke out in east central Europe, most notably in East Germany, as a result of economic hardship.[12] At the same time, the Soviet Union's allies fighting in

Korea welcomed the peace offensive. Kim Il-sung desperately desired an end to the fighting to allow for reconstruction following the devastation inflicted upon North Korea, particularly during the recent UNC airpower offensive. More significantly, Mao was now concerned that China had spent considerable manpower and resources that could have been used for rapid industrialization while failing to gain either Taiwan or UN membership.[13]

The reactions of the US and Commonwealth governments to Stalin's death and the subsequent Soviet peace offensive covered a broad spectrum of emotions. All were privately, and often publicly, pleased that they would no longer have to deal with the unpredictable generalissimo who had, in their eyes, been the root cause of the Cold War. Simultaneously, these governments were divided on how to approach the new Soviet leadership. Eisenhower and Dulles were wary of developments in the Soviet Union, fearing that Stalin's successors might adopt an even more aggressive foreign policy to secure their grip on power. The US government, therefore, doubted the sincerity of the Soviet peace feelers and was wary of engaging with Moscow. Eisenhower's suspicions were made apparent in his 'Chance for Peace' speech delivered on 16 April 1953 when he demanded that the new Soviet leadership's peaceful 'words' be attested by 'deeds', starting with peace in Korea.

The majority of the Commonwealth countries agreed that the Soviet peace offensive had to be treated with caution and supported the US position. Nevertheless, the British, Indian and Canadian governments desired to open channels of communication with Moscow. Churchill, in particular, was convinced that the time was ripe to hold a three-power summit composed of the United States, the Soviet Union and Britain to try to resolve all the outstanding Cold War issues. He wrote a number of letters to Eisenhower urging him to agree to this course or else he threatened to visit Moscow himself. The US President, in contrast, doubted the utility of summitry, especially while the situation was in such a delicate state of flux. In addition, Nehru took the Soviet moves at face value and thought that the United States should reciprocate with its own peace gestures.[14]

Armistice negotiations

At the start of 1953 the armistice negotiations at Panmunjom remained in recess since the Communists continued to refuse to accept the principle of non-forcible repatriation of prisoners of war. Indeed, no progress was made until the Soviet peace offensive first manifested itself in a letter sent by the Communist High Command to the UNC agreeing to the latter's earlier suggestion for the exchange of sick and wounded prisoners. More importantly, on 30 March Zhou En-lai broadcast a radio statement expressing his hope that this exchange would lead to the resumption of full armistice negotiations. He then proposed that all non-repatriate prisoners be taken to a neutral country for six months while representatives from their homelands would try to persuade them to return home. If there remained non-repatriate prisoners at the end of this period their final disposition would be determined by the post-armistice political conference already accepted by the negotiators. This proposal was evidently based on the Indian Resolution and represented the first instance in which the Chinese had recognized non-forcible repatriation.[15]

Still, Eisenhower and Dulles gave a mixed response to this initiative. They remained wary of a Soviet trap but they did agree to the holding of negotiations on the exchange of sick and wounded prisoners as a test of good faith. To their surprise, the resulting talks at Panmunjom in early April 1953 went remarkably smoothly and the exchange, codenamed Operation Little Switch, was completed by the end of the month. Following on from this success, the US government agreed to resume full armistice negotiations. All the same, hopes of an early settlement based on Zhou En-lai's proposal were soon dashed as the UN negotiators argued against the removal of prisoners from Korea and claimed that 60 days was ample time for persuasion. In early May 1953 the Communist negotiators then revealed their willingness to move further towards the Indian Resolution with Nam Il proposing the establishment of a Neutral Nations Repatriation Commission (NNRC) composed of Sweden, Switzerland, Czechoslovakia, Poland, and umpired by India.

Furthermore, the Communists conceded that non-repatriate prisoners should remain in custody in Korea and shortened the persuasion period to four months.

In comparison, the position of the UN negotiators moved further away from the Indian Resolution since Eisenhower was under great pressure from the Republican Right not to make concessions. While accepting the NNRC concept, on 13 May Harrison tabled a proposal calling for all Korean non-repatriate prisoners to be immediately released to civilian status and for only Chinese non-repatriate prisoners to be held for just 60 days of persuasion before being automatically released. The Communist delegation gave this proposal the expected vitriolic treatment but the Commonwealth members, particularly the British, Canadians and Indians, were also deeply critical of Washington's tough stance.[16] Under the weight of external pressure and after much deliberation within the National Security Council, Eisenhower accepted that the provisions of the Indian Resolution had to be adhered to even if this meant upsetting his own party.

In consequence, the UN negotiators tabled a new proposal conceding that all non-repatriate prisoners would be held in custody for 90 days before the final disposition of any remaining prisoners would be considered by the political conference for another 30 days. After this time the prisoners would either be released or handed over to the General Assembly. The Communists could choose. With the UN and Communists positions almost identical Nam Il accepted this proposal and somewhat surprisingly agreed that prisoners should be released at the end of the persuasion period. The terms of reference of the repatriation commission were then established and the negotiators agreed that India should provide the custodial forces during the detention period.

On 8 June 1953 Harrison and Nam Il signed the prisoners of war agreement and it appeared that the armistice would soon be concluded. But the conflict was to continue for another seven weeks due to the actions of Syngman Rhee. Since negotiations re-opened Rhee had stepped up his protests against the signing of any agreement that left Korea divided. His efforts to scupper the ceasefire then came to a head when he secretly masterminded the release of 27,000 Korean non-repatriate prisoners from the UNC camps. In response, the Communist negotiators immediately denounced this action, unilaterally recessed the armistice talks, called for the prisoners to be recaptured and demanded that Rhee make a commitment to abide by an armistice. Additionally, the Soviet and Chinese governments accused the United States of using their 'puppet' to prolong the conflict. Even so, the Communist reaction was less severe than could be expected since they gave no suggestion that they wished to terminate the negotiations.[17]

The US and Commonwealth governments were equally angered by Rhee's devious behaviour and sent letters of protest to the ROK President. Eisenhower even considered pulling US forces out of Korea and having Rhee removed. Nonetheless, the US President quickly realized that the only course available to him was to have Rhee accept the armistice, and so sent Assistant Secretary of State for Far Eastern Affairs Walter Robertson to Seoul to negotiate with the South Korean leader.[18] After lengthy and difficult talks, Rhee finally agreed to accept an armistice, although he refused to sign the document. In return, Robertson promised: a US-ROK mutual security treaty; an aid package of $200 million; an expansion of the ROKA; that the ROK and the United States would pull out of the post-armistice political conference if it did not find a solution within 90 days; and that prisoners of war would be moved to the demilitarized zone so that the Indian custodial force would not have to enter ROK territory.

Once Rhee's commitment was made known the Communist negotiators dropped their demand for the recapture of prisoners and negotiations resumed at Panmunjom. Despite the final Chinese offensive launched to recapture territory north of the 38th parallel at this time, the final military agreements were reached quickly and arrangements were made for the signing ceremony. After some difficulty on this last point, the Korean Armistice Agreement was signed on 27 July 1953, first by the negotiators at Panmunjom and then by the respective military commanders at their headquarters at Kaesong and Munsan-ni.

Planning during the winter recess of the Seventh Session

In the early months of 1953 the world's attention was fixed first on Washington, then Moscow, and finally on Panmunjom. While these developments were vital for bringing the Korean War to a close, events in New York also played an important part. The Seventh Session of the General Assembly was due to resume in mid-February 1953 and shortly after the winter break US and Commonwealth planning for the Korean debate commenced. Yet the Eisenhower administration's views toward the UN remained unclear. The new president had not had any previous dealings with the world organization and in his election campaign he had paid no more than lip service to it. Privately, however, Eisenhower had expressed the importance he attached to the UN and his disappointment with the way in which the US case had been presented in New York by his predecessor. He was now determined to build up the US public's

Figure 6.2   The signing of the Korean Armistice Agreement, 27 July 1953.
Source: Rees, David, *Korea: The Limited War* (London, 1964).

confidence in the organization by transforming it into an effective instrument of peace.[19]

Dulles had an even more ambiguous relationship with the UN. On one hand, he was an expert in international law, had been one of the original promoters of the organization, was partly responsible for drafting the UN Charter and had on numerous occasions been a member of the US delegation to the General Assembly. As a result, the new Secretary of State had an intimate knowledge of the UN that those around him found formidable.[20] On the other hand, Dulles had become disillusioned with the organization since the breakdown of the wartime grand alliance had rendered its collective security function impotent. He thus believed that the UN could achieve very little in the Cold War climate.[21] Dulles' views are encapsulated in a comment he made to Eisenhower a few months later when he said, 'The UN was a good propaganda forum but that it was useless to submit things to it about which it could do nothing, it only builds up the idea of futility.'[22] Consequently, compared to other areas of foreign affairs that he micromanaged, Dulles took a relatively hands-off approach to UN policy. Still, Dulles' idealistic faith in the UN endured on some level and he hoped that once Cold War tensions had subsided, the organization could play a crucial function in maintaining peace.[23]

Also of importance to the Eisenhower administration's policy was the appointment of Henry Cabot Lodge Junior as US Permanent Representative to the UN.[24] Lodge was a young high-flier in the Republican Party and a close friend of Eisenhower who had managed the General's election campaign. In devoting his energies to this task Lodge had lost his own position as Senator of Massachusetts to John F. Kennedy. In return, according to Lodge, Eisenhower had offered him any position in the government, including that of Secretary of State. But he had chosen US Permanent Representative to the UN on the condition this position was raised to Cabinet status. The highly ambitious Lodge was drawn to this post by the opportunities it presented to be seen to be taking the fight to the Soviet Union. Furthermore, Lodge wanted to cast off the shadow of his grandfather, Henry Cabot Lodge Senior, who had led the successful campaign against the ratification of the League of Nations in the Senate in 1919.

Unlike his predecessor Warren Austin, who adhered strictly to the instructions sent to him by the State Department, Lodge believed that he was responsible for the new administration's UN policy and took instruction only from the President. Lodge came to this conclusion since: he enjoyed much closer personal relations with Eisenhower than Dulles did; Eisenhower raised the post of US Permanent Representative to the UN to a Cabinet position specifically for him; and Dulles paid relatively little attention to day-to-day goings-on in New York.[25] Nonetheless, Dulles firmly held that as Secretary of State he maintained overall policy at the UN, leading to some friction between these two men. The extent to which Dulles and Lodge clashed, though, is still an unresolved issue. Many eye-witnesses suggest that Lodge viewed Dulles with respect due to his vast experience while the latter was impressed by the younger man's vigour and zeal. These contemporaries claim that while the two men did not always see eye-to-eye, they dealt with their differences formally and with Dulles always having the final say.[26] Other observers claim, however, that the personalities of the sombre Dulles and Lodge the showman were incompatible and they were in constant competition for the President's ear.[27]

One aspect of UN policy that definitely did unite the Eisenhower administration was the belief that the United States should regain a tight grip on the General Assembly after the events of the previous autumn. The US government's biggest concern with the resumed Seventh Session was that India would seek to find a compromise solution to the prisoners of war question even more favourable to the Communists, especially since its previous endeavours had led to deteriorating Sino-Indian relations. Eisenhower and Dulles were especially fearful that such an initiative might interfere with their planning to find a military solution to the Korean conflict. With their minds focused firmly on this task, the US delegation was instructed to pursue a policy at the UN that would not tie Washington's hands and Lodge was given free rein in formulating the precise tactics during the Korean debate.[28]

The US Permanent Representative firmly believed that the United States had to retain harmonious relations with its allies, particularly the Commonwealth members. He concluded, therefore, that the best course was to stand by the Indian Resolution, which had been adopted with near-unanimous support, and oppose any new proposals that might jeopardize the UN's negotiating position at Panmunjom or restrict condemnatory action in the future.[29] Lodge was also opposed to tabling a draft resolution imposing additional economic, political or military measures upon the Chinese since this would neither lessen Beijing's intransigence nor weaken its capacity to fight. It would, moreover, struggle to win widespread support at the UN. Even so, Lodge realized that some positive action might have to be taken at the General Assembly since a number of Arab-Asian members, particularly India, were uncomfortable being aligned with the West behind the Indian Resolution. He predicted that these members might table proposals making too many concessions to the Soviet position in an effort to reclaim a neutral position. If this occurred, Lodge was willing to support a simple draft resolution reaffirming the Indian Resolution and appealing to members for additional military contributions.[30]

The Commonwealth members were generally relieved when they were informed of US thinking on UN policy. Ever since Eisenhower's statement regarding the withdrawal of the US Seventh Fleet from the Taiwan Strait they had feared that the new administration would try to have the General Assembly impose additional measures against the PRC. The Commonwealth capitals had worried that such action would risk escalating the conflict beyond Korea's borders. But on hearing of Lodge's draft resolution, the Australian[31] and New Zealand[32] representatives in Washington immediately expressed their concurrence. The Canadian Cabinet also approved this course.[33] What is more, when Dulles held discussions with Eden while visiting London, the two men agreed that no political initiatives should be taken at the General Assembly and all efforts should be made to maintain the unity of opinion achieved over the Indian Resolution.[34]

Despite the fact Commonwealth fears of escalation had been quelled they did still hold concerns that the US proposed course of action did not go far enough in trying to end the conflict. Eden in particular thought Lodge's draft resolution would not secure the support of the Arab-Asian members since the Indian Resolution had already been rejected and no enthusiasm existed for providing additional forces. So he suggested an alternative proposal noting the Chinese and North Korean rejection of the Indian Resolution, making a humanitarian appeal for the exchange of sick and wounded prisoners of war and reaffirming the desire for an early armistice.[35] This concept proved instantly popular with the other Commonwealth members. To start with, the Indian government expressed its sympathy for the British draft resolution and insisted that it had no plans of its own to take the initiative.[36] Pearson, still acting as President of the General Assembly, also agreed that a humanitarian resolution was the only type of proposal that might win unanimous support.[37] Casey, as well, supported a humanitarian resolution but thought an appeal for additional pledges to UNKRA was a more appropriate action for the General Assembly to take given the complications regarding the prisoners of war issue.[38] And the New Zealand government held similar views.[39]

The State Department, nevertheless, thought that the British proposal went too far and worried that a call for the exchange of sick and wounded prisoners might encourage other delegations to table more extensive draft resolutions aimed at appeasing the Communists.[40] To nip the emerging Commonwealth unity in the bud before the General Assembly resumed, therefore, the UNC sent a message to their Communist counterparts calling for just such an exchange.[41] This clearly demonstrated that the new US government was prepared to take action without consulting its Commonwealth allies and was not overly concerned with upsetting them. At the same time, the Commonwealth members accepted this fait accompli since they were unwilling to challenge the strong and popular Eisenhower administration whom they all wished to court. As a result, when the General Assembly resumed on 25 February 1953 no decision had been taken on whether a draft resolution should be tabled and, if so, what form it should take.

The resumed Seventh Session of the General Assembly

As the delegations gathered in New York it soon became apparent that neither the United States nor the Commonwealth members wished to utilize the General Assembly to seek a solution to the prisoners of war question. At a meeting of the Heads of the Commonwealth delegations no new proposals were put forward and the Indian and Pakistani representatives assured their colleagues that the Arab-Asian group had no plans to take the initiative.[42] The Eisenhower administration also made it apparent that it did not see any breakthrough occurring at the General Assembly since Dulles only planned on attending the first few days of the session. Lodge was thus given personal responsibility to deal with the Korean question unless dramatic developments occurred.[43] His first move was to speak to Mrs Pandit to reassure her of US support for the Indian Resolution, to emphasize that no useful purpose could be served by a new proposal, and to express his hope for close US-Indian relations on Korea.[44] Importantly, Mrs Pandit concurred that there was no point in trying to push forward with another resolution on Korea unless it might lead to the end of hostilities.[45]

The lack of desire to discuss Korea was then quickly felt in the First Committee. Lodge, in his first statement as US Permanent Representative and the Eisenhower administration's first official comment on the Korean question at the General Assembly, defended the Indian Resolution as a representation of 'the conscience of the world and the striving of suffering humanity for peace'. He went on to stress that its proposals provided the only means for answering the prisoners of war question and that the UN members should remain loyal to them. He also criticized the Communist aggressors for rejecting the Indian Resolution, claiming that this showed they desired the prolongation of the conflict.[46] At the next meeting it became clear that very few delegations wished to speak. Of the Commonwealth members, only Australia made a statement supporting Lodge's views while the British and Canadian delegations, demonstrating the Commonwealth's desire to bypass the Korean question completely, called for the First Committee to discuss other items on its agenda. This motion did not pass but the majority of members did agree to adjourn the Korean debate for almost a week.[47]

Although this inactivity pleased the Eisenhower administration, the US public increasingly demanded that some form of positive action be taken in light of the Communists' rejection of the Indian Resolution. In consequence, during this brief recess the US delegation formulated a draft resolution requesting all members to make good their existing pledges to UNKRA and recommending that all governments, specialized agencies and non-governmental organizations make additional pledges. This suggestion was very similar to the one already made by the Australian government and was welcomed by the Old Commonwealth members since it fulfilled their desire for a humanitarian appeal while not risking an escalation of the conflict. Subsequently, Britain and Canada—as well as France, Denmark, the Philippines and Thailand—agreed to co-sponsor this draft resolution.[48]

In an attempt to prevent the West seizing the initiative, the Soviet delegation then tabled a proposal calling for the discontinuance of UNCURK. The Soviet bloc members argued that this organ had become a subsidiary of the UNC and was being used to prolong the conflict. They also stressed that there was no point taking any decisions on UNKRA for the moment since that body could do very little until the conflict had been concluded. Still, after a very limited debate the Soviet proposal was rejected with only the Soviet bloc voting in its favour while the 7-Power draft resolution was approved with the support of all non-Soviet members.[49] The proposal was formally adopted in the Plenary on 11 March 1953 becoming General Assembly Resolution 701 (VII) (see Appendix 12, p. 273–4).[50]

For the next two weeks the Korean item was left on ice and the appointment of Secretary-General Trygve Lie's successor dominated proceedings in New York. After much bitter debate between the two superpowers Dag Hammarskjöld, a relatively unknown bureaucrat in the Swedish Ministry of Foreign Affairs, was eventually found as a compromise candidate and elected unanimously on 31 March 1953.

In the meantime, much to the alarm of the Eisenhower administration, the mood of expectation in New York grew exponentially following Stalin's death. Toward the end of March the US delegation tried to dampen this atmosphere by resurrecting the US proposal for an impartial investigation of the charges made by the Communists regarding the use by UN forces of bacteriological weapons. Washington hoped that renewed debate on this issue would finally quash the continuing Communist propaganda campaign against the UNC while providing an opportunity to test the new Soviet leadership's professed intentions. The Old Commonwealth members deeply regretted the timing of this item seeing as the new Soviet leadership appeared to be moving in the direction of peace. But they sympathized with the US position and agreed to co-sponsor, along with all 16 members contributing forces to the Korean action, the US draft resolution establishing an impartial investigation commission.[51]

In the debate that followed the Old Commonwealth's loyalty to Washington was further demonstrated. They joined with the US delegation in opposing the Soviet proposal to invite Chinese or North Korean representatives to take part in discussions, arguing that they simply wished to establish an impartial investigation commission and that Beijing and Pyongyang would have ample opportunity to present their cases to this body. The Indian delegation, however, argued and voted in favour of the Soviet draft resolution along with a number of other Arab-Asian members who stated that all interested parties should be represented at the UN. Even so, this was not enough to prevent the Soviet proposal being resoundingly rejected. Next, the Old Commonwealth members followed Lodge's lead by denouncing the Soviet claims that an impartial investigation was unnecessary given that the evidence was so overwhelming. On 8 April 1953 the First Committee then approved a revised version of the 16-Power draft resolution, naming Brazil, Egypt, Pakistan, Sweden and Uruguay as the members of its investigation commission. Only the Soviet bloc delegations voted against this proposal and three members, including India, abstained.[52]

This proposal later became General Assembly Resolution 706 (VII) (see Appendix 13, p. 274–6).[53]

In spite of this show of support for the UNC, the Korean question was complicated considerably by the first tangible evidence of the Communist peace offensive. The Communist High Command's belated acceptance of the UNC's call for the exchange of sick and wounded prisoners and Zhou En-lai's new proposal on the prisoners of war question created a flurry of activity at the General Assembly. In the resulting atmosphere of anticipation many members clamoured to take advantage of this opportunity for peace. Leading the way in this drive for action was Nehru's personal spokesman on Korea, V.K. Krishna Menon. Immediately upon hearing the news of Zhou En-lai's statement, Menon requested a special meeting of the Plenary at which he praised the Chinese initiative and stressed that it could not be ignored by the UN.[54] Privately, Menon went even further, stressing to Lodge that the UN could only maintain its prestige by acting upon the Chinese overtures and bringing about peace in Korea.[55]

While Menon received much support from the Arab-Asian group, the response of the United States and the Old Commonwealth members was far less enthusiastic. In Washington, suspicions lingered regarding the sincerity of the Communist peace offensive and Dulles warned Eisenhower that an out-of-hand debate at the General Assembly could jeopardize the chances of rekindling direct negotiations at Panmunjom.[56] Dulles then instructed Lodge to argue that the exchange of sick and wounded prisoners was a necessary first step before any broader discussions in New York.[57] Lodge concurred but warned Dulles that the United States should not appear 'lukewarm' if demands arose for action at the UN. He thought in these circumstances it would be necessary for the US delegation to take the initiative to prevent the adoption of proposals put forward by other members, particularly India, making too many concessions to the Communists.[58]

With the risk of escalation now seemingly much reduced and peace within sight, the Old Commonwealth governments generally shared Washington's fears regarding renewed debate on the Korean question at the General Assembly. Churchill, assuming control over foreign policy during Eden's illness, was unwilling to challenge the Eisenhower administration at the UN and preferred to wholeheartedly back the UN negotiators at Panmunjom in an attempt to win favour with the Americans.[59] Pearson was also eager to please Washington and attempted to use his position as President of the General Assembly to stymie debate. For example, when he received a cablegram from Zhou En-lai containing the Chinese proposed solution to the prisoners of war problem he simply transmitted this document to the UNC rather than distributing it to the members.[60] He only stated in the General Assembly, moreover, that he had received Zhou En-lai's message and that it contained 'certain new proposals for solving the prisoner of war problem in Korea'.[61] Additionally, when Menon requested a special meeting of the Plenary to highlight Zhou En-lai's proposal he had tried to dissuade the Indian representative from this course.[62]

Nonetheless, it proved impossible to prevent discussion on Korea in the First Committee. The Polish delegation, acting on behalf of the Soviet Union, tabled a draft resolution calling for an immediate ceasefire in Korea and the implementation of the Chinese proposal.[63] The US and Commonwealth delegations were united in their opposition to this proposal but they did not entirely agree over what action should be taken in response. On one side, the Indian and British delegations favoured a moderate positive proposal that would win the unanimous support of all the UN members, including the Soviet bloc. To achieve this goal, Menon suggested a draft resolution approving the present negotiations at Panmunjom and urging the negotiators to conclude an armistice as quickly as possible. With Eden back in Britain, Lloyd welcomed this proposal but added a provision urging 'wider political settlements' after peace had been restored.[64] The US delegation, on the other side, continued to argue that no further action should be taken unless this became necessary to block undesirable proposals. If this eventuality did arise, Lodge proposed a draft resolution noting the recent agreement on the exchange of sick and wounded prisoners, expressing support for an early armistice and adjourning the General Assembly until an armistice had been signed or developments required discussion.[65]

The Commonwealth reaction to Lodge's proposal was somewhat mixed. Churchill feared that that the British public would not accept such a wholly negative draft resolution but was hopeful that it could be merged with the Anglo-Indian text. If this proved impossible he would reluctantly support the US proposal until another state put forward a more constructive counter-proposal.[66] But the other Old Commonwealth members showed little desire to try to merge the two proposals or to constrain US policy at the UN now that the Eisenhower administration had accepted negotiations for the exchange of sick and wounded prisoners. Furthermore, the Indian and Pakistani delegations were unhappy with Lloyd's amendment to the Indian draft resolution calling for a broader political settlement, fearing that the Communists might reject such a far-reaching proposal at this juncture.[67]

Yet the US delegation demonstrated some willingness to meet the views of its closest ally. With Operation Little Switch underway and widespread optimism in evidence in New York that full armistice negotiations would soon commence, the US delegation invited the Commonwealth, French, Brazilian and Chilean delegations to discuss a solution acceptable to all. As a result of this meeting, a procedural draft resolution was formulated that combined elements of the US, British and Indian proposals. This proposal: noted deep satisfaction over agreement on the exchange of sick and wounded; expressed hope that the renewed negotiations at Panmunjom would lead to an early armistice; and decided to recess the UN debate immediately, giving the President of the General Assembly the power to reconvene the session either when the unified command had notified the Security Council of the signing of the armistice or when the majority of members thought that other developments in Korea required consideration. This ad hoc group also agreed that Brazil should sponsor this draft resolution so that the Soviet bloc would be less likely to vote against it.[68]

This plan was put in motion the next day. During the subsequent debate the US and Commonwealth delegations all expressed their support for this proposal and stressed that the armistice negotiations at Panmunjom should be left to take their course. Initially, the Soviet bloc argued against this procedural draft resolution and continued to promote the Polish proposal. But on 16 April 1953 the Polish delegation unexpectedly withdrew its draft resolution without any explanation. This action allowed for an immediate vote on the Brazilian draft resolution, which received unanimous approval.[69] Two days later the Plenary then formally adopted General Assembly Resolution 705 (VII) (see Appendix 14, p. 276–7) and the Seventh Session went into recess.[70] This vote was significant in a number of ways. To start with, this was the first time all the UN members had voted in favour of a resolution on Korea. Furthermore, it clearly indicated that all the UN members agreed that the armistice would best be decided by the negotiators at Panmunjom. And most importantly, the adoption of this strictly procedural resolution implied that all the member states accepted that the solution to the prisoners of war question was to be found in the outstanding Indian Resolution. This resolution thus set the acceptable parameters for the full armistice negotiations when they got underway a couple of weeks later.

The General Assembly in recess

The vast majority of UN members now wanted to allow the negotiations at Panmunjom to run their course. The provision in the Brazilian Resolution allowing for the resumption of the General Assembly, however, was to prove controversial. No significant calls for further debate emerged while the full armistice negotiations made progress, even when the UN negotiators drifted away from the terms of the Indian Resolution, putting the talks in jeopardy. But in early June 1953, with growing expectation that the fighting would soon end, the Commonwealth Prime Ministers—meeting for the first time since January 1951 and assembled in London for the coronation of Queen Elizabeth II—held tentative discussions concerning what course should be taken at the General Assembly after the armistice had been signed. Lloyd, speaking on behalf of Churchill, opened discussions stating that the General Assembly would have to establish the political conference on Korea designed to bring about a final settlement. The British government's view was that, as well as a UN team, it would be necessary to invite the Soviet Union, the PRC, and North and South Korea if any progress was to be made. Nehru agreed with this analysis but the other Prime Ministers were reluctant to commit to any course until Washington had been consulted.[71] As a result, the London talks quickly petered out following the signing of the prisoners of war agreement on 8 June 1953. With the risk of escalation now at its lowest ebb since the outbreak of the conflict, the Prime Ministers clearly did not see any urgent need to coordinate a united Commonwealth position.[72]

Ten days later, though, Rhee's release of 27,000 non-repatriate Korean prisoners from the UNC camps triggered a flurry of activity in New York. Pearson suddenly came under intense pressure to have the Seventh Session resumed to discuss this development. Leading these calls was Nehru, who sent a letter to the President of the General Assembly stating that the situation was so fraught with dangers that it needed immediate consideration.[73] The US government, in contrast, placed even greater pressure on Pearson to hold firm. Dulles was convinced that the only way to achieve an armistice was to keep the UN in the background while Rhee was made to accept the armistice, fearing that the Arab-Asian members might push for action that would jeopardize Rhee's acquiescence.[74] Significantly, the Old Commonwealth governments, determined to have the armistice signed without delay, sided with the United States on this matter. Lloyd was convinced that a General Assembly meeting would likely degenerate into a slanging match between the US and Soviet delegations over whether the UNC was responsible for the release of the prisoners.[75] The Australian[76] and the New Zealand[77] governments agreed with this analysis. Subsequently, Pearson, who also personally shared these views, explained to Nehru that time was needed to convince Rhee to adhere to the armistice. He would therefore only poll the members if the Indian Prime Minister made a formal request for him to do so.[78]

Nehru initially accepted this reasoning but was increasingly concerned with the length of the Rhee-Robertson talks and sent another message to Pearson expressing his anxiety that the situation might deteriorate if the General Assembly did not become involved. Even so, Pearson held firm and told Nehru that the armistice would likely be signed in the forthcoming days, but if not he would circulate Nehru's message to all the members to ascertain whether the majority desired to meet. If they did, the General Assembly could resume within ten days.[79] But by mid-July 1953, following the major offensive launched by the Communist forces in Korea, even Pearson's patience was beginning to wear thin. He was concerned that he was unnecessarily antagonizing Nehru and warned the United States that he could not resist forever the mounting pressure to resume the Seventh Session.[80]

It was lucky for Pearson, consequently, that Rhee finally conceded and the Communist offensive was brought to an end after making only limited gains. With these hurdles overcome it was only a matter of time before hostilities in Korea ceased. In New York, all that had to be decided now was how long after the armistice was signed should the General Assembly reconvene. To resolve this issue Pearson held a meeting of the 16 contributing members, the Indian delegation and Secretary-General Hammarskjöld, and suggested that the session be resumed on 12 August 1953. But Lodge revealed that Dulles would be in Seoul at this time to finalize the agreements made between Robertson and Rhee and suggested 17 August. This date was readily accepted by everyone present, including all the Commonwealth members.[81] As a result, when the Korean Armistice Agreement was signed on 27 July 1953 the UN was set to take centre stage in answering the Korean question one more time.

Conclusion

Compared to the period of turbulent relations between the United States and the Commonwealth members during the initial phase of the Seventh Session of the General Assembly, the second phase in early 1953 witnessed a gradual return to the normal state of affairs at the UN. The Commonwealth remained largely disunited and no serious attempts were made to constrain US policy due principally to the fact the United States adopted a relatively moderate course in an effort to maintain the unity created by the adoption of the Indian Resolution. The Commonwealth had at first feared that the incoming Eisenhower administration would try to use the UN to heap pressure on the Communists and risk escalating the conflict. Once Washington had shown it had no such plans and Stalin's death had resulted in the resumption of the armistice negotiations, the Commonwealth members gained confidence that the fighting would not extend beyond Korea. Accordingly, they were largely content to have the UN do the bare minimum until the armistice had been concluded.

These views were held most strongly by the key Commonwealth personalities who remained comparatively quiet throughout this period. Churchill, Pearson and even Nehru generally supported the course proposed by the US government and, even though they had some reservations, were prepared to concede in an effort to maintain good relations with Washington and facilitate the armistice negotiations. Not even when the Commonwealth delegations met in New York or the Commonwealth Prime Ministers gathered in London did any concerted effort to coordinate a united position take place. And even if they had tried to constrain US policy at the UN, the evidence clearly suggests that the Eisenhower administration, confident in its domestic and international position, would not have bent to the will of the Commonwealth. The President and his chief aides, notably Dulles and Lodge, were determined to restore US hegemony at the UN and were adamant that the armistice was to be found at Panmunjom. They would not permit the Commonwealth to use its moral authority at the UN to interfere with their plans.

CHAPTER 7

THE ROAD TO GENEVA, AUGUST 1953-JUNE 1954

With the signing of the Korean Armistice Agreement the UN was no longer preoccupied with finding a means to end the fighting in Korea. The organization could at long last seek to fulfil the political objectives it had held since 1947: to facilitate the emergence of a unified, independent and democratic Korea. In the months following the armistice it attempted to achieve these goals by focusing on the establishment of a Korean political conference designed to bring about a peaceful settlement. Yet despite the fact hostilities were over, relations between the United States and the Commonwealth members at the UN continued to be fraught with controversy. At the heart of this tension was whether India should be invited to attend the post-armistice conference. India's Commonwealth allies loyally championed its membership even though the Eisenhower administration remained adamantly opposed to the presence of any neutral countries, specifically India, at the conference table. Washington did eventually get its way but only after nine difficult months of negotiations that went far beyond the UN.

Throughout this period, however, the Commonwealth never seriously threatened US dominance of the UN since its members largely remained disunited. The most important factor limiting Commonwealth influence at the world organization was the absence of fighting. After three long years of war both sides were relieved that a ceasefire had been reached. While fears remained that the conflict could be rekindled and contingency plans for this eventuality were discussed, neither side took any action that seriously risked the resumption of hostilities. Under these conditions, and with Indochina now a greater threat than Korea to international peace and stability, the Commonwealth members, and particularly the key personalities within each government, were much more willing to defer decisions to Washington. Also, no occasions arose in which these Commonwealth figures were brought together to coordinate a united position.

Furthermore, the domestic and international standing of the Eisenhower administration was at its zenith during this period. Rightly or wrongly, the President was seen to have achieved in six months what Truman had failed to do in over two years; he had brought the Korean War to an end. Riding this crest of popularity the US government now sought to take the Cold War fight to the Soviet Union and paid far less attention to the views of its Commonwealth allies. At the same time, the majority of the Commonwealth members placed ever-increasing priority in developing close bilateral relations with Washington over their Commonwealth allegiances. As a result, the Commonwealth gradually ceased to operate as an agent of constraint over US policy and returned to being the informal collection of states it had been at the UN before the outbreak of the Korean conflict.

During the 11 months between the signing of the Korean Armistice Agreement and the closing of the Geneva Conference on Korea a whole host of issues emerged that impacted on the UN debate. These factors will be covered in brief below before the detailed analysis of discussions in New York gets underway.

Military situation

Although the fighting in Korea had ceased, the Korean Armistice Agreement covered a range of military articles that needed to be implemented. Article I, 'Military Demarcation Line and Demilitarized Zone', proved unproblematic since it had already been agreed that the demarcation line would be the line of contact when the fighting stopped with both sides immediately retiring 2 km from this line to form a demilitarized zone. Equally easy to execute was Article V, 'Miscellaneous', whose only significant provision was that the armistice would remain in effect until another mutually acceptable military agreement superseded it.[1]

But there were numerous problems implementing Article II, 'Concrete Arrangements for Cease-fire and Armistice', which created two organs to ensure the stability of the armistice. First, the Military Armistice Commission (MAC) was composed of senior officers appointed by the UNC and the Communist High Command. Its general mission was to provide a forum so that violations of the armistice could be settled by negotiation. The work of the MAC proved relatively uncontroversial, however, since the rest of the supervisory mechanism broke down and it was left with little to do. The root cause of this problem was the inability of the Neutral Nations Supervisory Commission (NNSC), the second organ, to fulfil its mission. The NNSC was composed of representatives from Sweden, Switzerland, Czechoslovakia and Poland and carried out the broad function of supervising, observing, inspecting and investigating the armistice. To achieve these aims the NNSC appointed inspection teams to make sure reinforcements did not enter Korea and to investigate any alleged violations. Such allegations soon commenced and tensions quickly mounted as North Korea restricted the movement of the NNSC inspection teams in its territory while the ROK protested against the presence of Czech and Polish representatives within its borders. The NNSC members, moreover, could not unanimously report allegations to the MAC. The Czech and Polish representatives invariably supported the claims made by the Communists whereas the Swedish and Swiss members backed the UNC's accusations. Frustrations soon boiled over, and in April 1954 the Swedish and Swiss members called for the abolition of the NNSC. Even so, the Czech and Polish representatives refused to agree and the body muddled on.

The implementation of Article III 'Arrangement Relating to Prisoners of War' proved even more problematic. Few difficulties were encountered over the exchange of willing repatriate prisoners. By late September 1953 Operation Big Switch had seen more than 75,000 Chinese and North Korean prisoners and almost 13,000 ROK and UN prisoners returned to their homelands. Nevertheless, after 60 days approximately 23,000 non-repatriate prisoners, of which over 22,000 were Chinese and North Korean, were transferred to the custody of the Neutral Nations Repatriation Commission (NNRC), composed of representatives from Sweden, Switzerland, Czechoslovakia, Poland and umpired by India, in the demilitarized zone. Problems with these arrangements soon arose since only a small portion of the 6,000-strong Indian Custodial Force (ICF) had arrived. Behind this delay was the ROK government's refusal to permit Indian troops to enter its territory. These soldiers had thus been transferred to a US aircraft carrier and flown by helicopter to the demilitarized zone. In addition, once it had formed, Rhee tried to intimidate the ICF by threatening to have the ROKA release the prisoners.[2]

Yet the NNRC experienced much more serious problems during the 90 days allocated for representatives from the prisoners' homelands to try and persuade them to return home. The central problem was having the prisoners attend these explanation meetings and making sure they did not end in violence. Before the UNC handed over the prisoners in its custody it had, along with ROK representatives, done its utmost to convince them not to agree to the explanations by organizing intimidation gangs and using propaganda. These methods proved successful as the prisoners refused to attend interviews in groups of fewer than 25. This demand placed the Indian chairman of the NNRC, General K.S. Thimayya, in an impossible situation. The Czech and Polish representatives called for the use of force to compel the prisoners to listen to the explanations but the Swedish and Swiss representatives threatened to withdraw from the NNRC if coercion was employed. The UNC supported this latter position and Thimayya reluctantly complied.

The situation grew increasingly tense as the Korean political conference failed to materialize before the NNRC was due to refer the final disposition of any remaining prisoners to this body when the explanations ceased on 22 January 1954. By this date only 15 per cent of prisoners had received explanations and over 22,000 prisoners remained in custody. In consequence, the UNC and the ROK government demanded that these prisoners be released in accordance with the Armistice Agreement. The Swedish and Swiss representatives agreed but the Indian, Czech and Polish representatives were against releasing prisoners on the grounds that disruptions had prevented the required 90 days of explanations. As no breakthrough could be found the ICF, against protests from all sides, simply returned the non-repatriate prisoners to the former detaining powers two days before the deadline. The UNC then swiftly released its prisoners, with Koreans settling in the ROK and Chinese going to Taiwan. The Communists protested at this action but could do nothing to prevent it.

The NNRC's problems did not end there. The body was not due to dissolve until 22 February 1954 since the Korean political conference

Figure 7.1   The release of non-repatriate prisoners of war, January 1954. Source: MacDonald: *Korea*, Plate 31.

was meant to consider the final disposition of prisoners until that date. During this period the body came under further criticism from the ROK government for transporting to India until a permanent host could be found 88 prisoners who had opted to go to a neutral country. In addition, the NNRC clashed with the UNC over the fate of 17 prisoners the ICF continued to hold who had committed murders in the prison camps. The NNRC wished to hand these prisoners over to the UNC on the condition they would be tried but the UNC refused to make this commitment. Friction mounted and the NNRC eventually conceded when the ICF had to return home. Finally, the NNRC's members could not agree to the content of the body's report to the General Assembly. In the end, two reports were written. The majority report signed by the Indian, Czech and Polish members claimed that no freedom of choice was present in the camps and was critical of the UNC's use of intimidation and propaganda. The Swedish-Swiss minority report stated the exact opposite.

Domestic developments

In the United States the domestic situation remained stable as the standing of the Eisenhower administration was further boosted by the end of the fighting in Korea, for which it claimed credit. The President also felt less constrained, especially in the realm of foreign policy, following the death of Taft just three days after the armistice was signed. From its position of strength the US government thus sought to find a new strategy to gain the initiative in the Cold War. After long and often fraught discussions between various departments, the 'New Look' was formed to meet the US ever-increasing global military commitments without overburdening the domestic economy.

Dulles first made this policy public on 12 January 1954 at the Council on Foreign Relations in New York when he stated that the United States would respond to any military challenge with all weapons at its disposal, including nuclear weapons, at whatever location it chose, implying a direct attack on the Soviet Union. This policy, which was later dubbed 'massive retaliation', had two aims: to deter Moscow from military adventurism and to redress the perceived imbalance of power in conventional forces, particularly in Europe, favouring the Soviet Union. Crucially for the fiscally-minded Eisenhower administration and the Republican Party, the cost of building up a sizable nuclear arsenal and delivery system was much less than maintaining massive conventional forces. The slogan 'more bang for the buck', therefore, came to characterize the New Look. Nonetheless, for this strategy to be effective it relied upon the US government constantly raising the ante through what Dulles termed 'brinkmanship'. This apparently more aggressive policy gained many critics at home and abroad who felt that the Eisenhower administration was increasing Cold War tensions at a time when Stalin's death and the end of the Korean War had created an opening for *rapprochement*.[3]

The majority of the Commonwealth governments also enjoyed relative domestic stability at this time. No significant developments took place in New Zealand or South Africa and in Canada on 10 August 1953 the Liberal Party was re-elected for a fifth time by a record majority demonstrating the Canadian public's continued support for St Laurent's domestic and foreign policies.[4] Even in Pakistan, after its recent tumultuous past, Prime Minister Mohammad Ali Bogra was enjoying considerable support as he tried to shepherd the country towards a republican future and to heal the growing rifts between East and West Pakistan. Bogra's prestige was also boosted by signing a mutual defence treaty with the United States in May 1954, a move that greatly concerned Nehru.[5]

Nevertheless, there were considerable anxieties in the other Commonwealth countries. In Britain, the Conservative government remained destabilized by the illnesses of both Churchill and Eden. During much of this period, therefore, foreign affairs remained in the hands of the relatively unknown and controversial Lord Salisbury. The government was thus boosted by the return to duty of the Prime Minister and his Foreign Secretary in October 1953. Still, Churchill's Cabinet colleagues quickly realized that the Prime Minister, now 78, had been seriously weakened by his ordeal and would struggle to cope with the burden of leadership.[6] Eden, consequently, increasingly dominated all aspects of foreign policy-making and Churchill began to slip into the background.[7]

Even more dramatic events took place elsewhere in the Commonwealth. In Australia, Menzies called a snap election in the midst of an economic crisis and the Labor Party, headed by Dr Herbert Evatt, was confident of victory. However, just weeks before the voters went to the polls on 24 May 1954, Vladimir Petrov, an attaché at the Soviet Embassy in Canberra, defected, claiming that a Soviet spy ring including two members of Evatt's staff, was operating in Australia. As a result, Menzies' Liberal/Country Party coalition won a narrow majority despite receiving fewer votes than Labor.[8] Nehru also courted much controversy at this time. First, he refused to hold the plebiscite in the State of Jammu and Kashmir called for by the UN Security Council to determine its status. And then in August 1953 he engineered the dismissal and arrest of the Prime Minister of this state, Sheikh Mohammed Abdullah, on the grounds that he held separatist ambitions.[9]

International relations

The signing of the Korean Armistice Agreement failed to significantly reduce Cold War tensions since both sides claimed victory and showed little enthusiasm for follow-up discussions on other outstanding issues. Even so, the Soviet government publicly maintained its 'peace offensive' as the Soviet leaders struggled to get to grips with the country's many problems and retain power while warring with each other over who would succeed Stalin.[10] Despite these pacific claims, however, the Soviet Union did raise fears in the West by announcing that it had tested its first hydrogen bomb, less than a year after the United States had done so.[11] As a result, Eisenhower tried to regain the propaganda initiative in December 1953, by delivering his famous 'Atoms for Peace' speech at the General Assembly. The President called for the two superpowers to abandon their atomic arsenals and to share their nuclear technology with other nations who could use it for peaceful purposes. These calls did have some impact in the West and the Third World in demonstrating Washington's flexibility, but they were completely ignored by Moscow.[12]

Hopes of the Korean armistice leading to a more general *rapprochement* then suffered an even greater setback due to events in Indochina. The Viet Minh, with much-increased Chinese financial and military assistance as well as the arrival of many more Chinese advisors since the end of the Korean War, had continued to gain control of large areas of Vietnam and had spread the fighting to Laos. In retaliation, the French had established a strong military base of approximately 20,000 troops at Dien Bien Phu, a valley in the remote northwest of the country, in an attempt to block the Viet Minh's route to Laos while drawing the enemy into a pitched battle beyond its supply lines. The French military believed that they would then be able to take advantage of their air and artillery superiority to win a decisive victory. But within a matter of weeks the Viet Minh had moved approximately 100,000 troops and heavy artillery through the jungle into the hills surrounding Dien Bien Phu. The Viet Minh attacked in overwhelming numbers on 12 March 1954 and after 55 days of bloody fighting the French forces declared a ceasefire. Although unknown at the time this battle effectively marked the end of the French Indochina War.[13]

The US government found these events deeply distressing. Since the end of the Korean War Washington had greatly increased its economic assistance to the State of Vietnam so it was funding 80 per cent of the French military effort. Dulles had also identified Indochina as the United States' highest Cold War priority. Before the collapse of the French position, however, the Eisenhower administration had publicly and privately opposed direct US military intervention in the conflict due principally to fears of becoming embroiled in another costly war on the Asian mainland. Yet between March and April 1954, as the Battle of Dien Bien Phu raged, serious consideration took place in the National Security Council regarding possible direct intervention in Indochina and, more specifically, the use of atomic weapons. Eisenhower also for the first time hinted at the concept that would become known as the 'domino theory': that if Indochina fell to Communism then each of its neighbours in southeast Asia and beyond would do so in turn. It was with much regret, therefore, that the US government eventually decided to supply the French with additional aircraft and pilots only.[14]

The reaction of the Commonwealth members was crucial to this decision not to intervene in Indochina. The British government shared US concerns regarding the implications of a Viet Minh victory, especially since it was continuing its counter-insurgency in Malaya. Still, when consulted by Dulles regarding intervention, Eden showed no desire to become militarily involved in Indochina, much to the Secretary of State's chagrin. Eden was convinced that the French would be militarily defeated and believed that the best course was to find an acceptable political solution at the negotiating table. The Canadian government supported this position. In addition, the Australian and New Zealand governments, even though they supported intervention in Indochina to prevent the spread of communism in southeast Asia, stressed that they did not have the resources to provide any assistance. Furthermore, the Indian and Pakistani governments sympathized with the Viet Minh's anti-colonial cause and were opposed to the West intervening militarily to prop up the clearly defunct French regime in Indochina. This negative Commonwealth response proved crucial since Dulles was only prepared to deploy US troops on the Asian mainland as part of a coalition.[15]

Another international development during this period that was particularly significant for the United States and Britain and further distracted attention away from Korea was the Iranian coup d'état that took place on 19 August 1953. Relations between Iran and Britain had seriously soured following Prime Minister Mohammad Mossadegh's decision in early 1951 to nationalize the massive Anglo-Iranian Oil Company refinery at Abadan. London had reacted angrily by using the Royal Navy to blockade Iran and by boycotting its oil. The Churchill government, though, had resisted trying to overthrow Mossadegh due to the Truman administration's reluctance to support such undemocratic colonial measures. The Eisenhower administration, in contrast, proved much more amenable to such plans and the CIA, at the request of MI6, planned Operation Ajax to topple the Iranian Prime Minister. This action had the compliance of Shah Mohammed Reza Pahlavi and the military under General Fazlollah Zahedi, who had both been heavily bribed by Washington. The coup proved successful despite public outcries and in its aftermath the Shah returned from exile, Zahedi was made Prime Minister and oil rights were shared between the Anglo-Iranian Oil Company and a number of US, Dutch and French companies.[16]

The Special Session of the General Assembly on Korea

Almost a year earlier, after the signing of the Korean Armistice Agreement, thoughts in Washington and the Commonwealth capitals had automatically turned to the Special Session of the General Assembly on Korea scheduled to open on 17 August 1953. With the demarcation line and demilitarized zone created, Operation Big Switch underway and the supervisory mechanism appearing robust, the US and Commonwealth governments were in agreement that the only issue the General Assembly had to deal with was Article IV of the Armistice Agreement, 'Recommendations to the Governments Concerned on Both Sides'. This article called for the commanders on both sides to recommend to their governments that within three months of the armistice becoming effective, a political conference should be held to bring about through negotiations a peaceful settlement to the Korean question. The General Assembly would decide on this conference's composition.

The Commonwealth members were eager to coordinate a position with the United States on this issue. Yet the US delegation refused to discuss its views in the absence of Dulles and Lodge, who were in Seoul concluding the US-ROK mutual defence pact promised to Rhee a month earlier. To make matters more difficult, ten days before the Special Session commenced, the UNC issued its report on the armistice to the Security Council containing a 'warning statement', signed by the 16 UN member states contributing forces, stating that if the Communists resumed hostilities in Korea or elsewhere— implying Indochina—the resulting conflict would not be limited.[17]

The Commonwealth members, particularly Britain and South Africa, had been reluctant to issue this ill-timed statement, originally agreed to 18 months earlier, given the upcoming talks on Korea. But the Eisenhower administration insisted on taking a tough stance.

Discussions on the Korean political conference, therefore, got underway only days before the Special Session of the General Assembly opened. After arriving back from Seoul, Lodge first met with Lloyd, present in New York while Eden was still incapacitated. The American stated that the Korean Armistice Agreement clearly envisaged a two-sided conference of belligerents with the General Assembly appointing the UN side and the Communists deciding their side. He also outlined a draft resolution, written with Dulles on the flight back from Korea, consisting of a long preamble referring to the history and success of the UN action in Korea and paying tribute to the soldiers who had fought there. The substantive section of the proposal then stated that the UN side should be composed of an undisclosed number of the members who had contributed forces and that the conference would take place at a time and place to be arranged in discussions between the US government, acting on behalf of the UN side, and the Communists.

The response of the Old Commonwealth members to this proposal was generally unenthusiastic. Lloyd took the lead on behalf of the Commonwealth and argued that the Soviet Union would reject the preamble because it had consistently opposed the UN action in Korea. He hence thought it best that this section be tabled as a separate proposal so as not to confuse this issue with the political conference on Korea. More importantly, he argued that the conference should be round-table in nature and should include interested non-belligerents, particularly the Soviet Union and India. Lloyd then revealed to Lodge that Britain had already promised a seat to India and stressed that the Commonwealth felt that such a conference stood a much better chance of success than resurrecting the tense cross-table talks at Panmunjom.[18] This position was strongly supported by the Canadian government,[19] but the Australian, New Zealand and South African governments only tentatively backed the British since they did not wish to upset

Washington now the fighting had ceased. India and Pakistan were not consulted at this stage.

Dulles was in no mood to compromise, however, and instructed Lodge to refuse membership to neutral countries such as India and only to accept Soviet participation as part of the Communist 'aggressor' side.[20] At a meeting of the 16 contributing states, therefore, the US delegation tabled a revised draft resolution specifying that the ROK as well as Australia, Britain, Canada, Columbia, France, the Philippines, Thailand, Turkey and the United States should participate at the conference as the UN side. Still, the US delegation did make one concession to the British by removing their original preamble and instead circulating a separate proposal paying tribute to the UN forces. All 16 members instantly agreed to co-sponsor this latter draft resolution, but the former proposal caused more problems since those contributing members not included in the list or participants raised objections.[21] As he was under instructions to have the draft resolution sponsored by all 16 members, Lodge agreed to remove the enumeration of states, replacing it with a general clause giving all states with armed forces in Korea the right to participate if they so wished. This concession proved successful with all the contributing members agreeing to co-sponsor the proposal except South Africa, which claimed a lack of interest in the Korean problem now that the fighting had ceased.[22]

Despite this progress, relations between the United States and the Commonwealth members deteriorated over the issue of Soviet participation. Asserting himself for the first time, Salisbury insisted on a separate draft resolution inviting the Soviet Union as an interested party. He argued convincingly that if it were left to the Communist side to take this action it would imply that Moscow was an aggressor.[23] To prevent this problem arising the British delegation produced a draft resolution recommending Soviet participation 'if the other side desires it'. The Canadian and Indian delegations gave this proposal strong support while the other Commonwealth members gave it quiet consent.

Nevertheless, Dulles remained adamantly opposed to the presence of non-belligerents and argued that the US public would not tolerate

Soviet participation.[24] With tensions mounting Salisbury, fearing for Anglo-American relations, instructed Lloyd to accept any procedure acceptable to Washington to bring about Soviet membership.[25] Before the Commonwealth had to concede, though, Dulles grudgingly accepted the need to invite the Soviet Union if the conference was to stand any chance of success. He agreed to the British proposal on the condition that it had 'respectable' sponsorship but not including Britain since this would stir the mounting anti-British sentiment in the United States.[26] In consequence, the draft resolution was co-sponsored by two Commonwealth countries, Australia and New Zealand, as well as Denmark and Norway.[27]

The problems encountered over the question of Soviet participation paled into insignificance compared to the friction produced between the United States and the Commonwealth members concerning Indian membership. Salisbury had given the British delegation firm instructions to sponsor a draft resolution inviting India to participate at the conference.[28] Crucially, all the Old Commonwealth members firmly supported this proposal. This unity was demonstrated at a meeting of the 16 contributing members. The Australian and New Zealand delegations tabled the British proposal and the other Old Commonwealth delegations stated that their governments would co-sponsor the draft resolution. They argued that India had played a crucial role in bringing the Korean conflict to an end and was directly interested in a peaceful settlement as chairman of the NNRC and provider of the custodial force. Only the South African delegation remained silent, due to its traditional enmity towards India. In contrast, Lodge warned that the US government would do all it could to exclude India from the conference. He argued that India's presence would jeopardize the participation of the ROK, which was essential to any Korean settlement.[29]

Immediately after this meeting, rather than trying to convince the Old Commonwealth members to change their views, Lodge decided directly to approach Menon, who was again in New York as Nehru's special representative. Lodge told Menon that while his government had the 'greatest respect and admiration' for India, its participation at the conference would cause 'great embarrassment' between the United States and the ROK. He added that it would also lead to other 'interested' governments, such as Japan and the Chinese Nationalists, demanding membership. The US delegation hoped that, instead, India would announce it would not pursue a place at the conference. In response, Menon cryptically stated that India would only participate if requested by both sides but stressed that India had a right to be present at the conference since it had contributed a field hospital unit to the UN action.[30] Adding to the confusion, Menon then told Lloyd that India definitely did wish to participate and criticized the 15-Power draft resolution for inviting only belligerents.[31]

The Special Session of the General Assembly got underway with the US and Commonwealth governments thoroughly divided. These differences of opinion were soon made public in the debate. While Lodge argued against the participation of non-belligerents, the Commonwealth representatives argued that the General Assembly had the authority to recommend the membership of any nation, such as the Soviet Union and India, as long as it was agreed by both sides.[32] Yet the US and Old Commonwealth delegations did rally against a Soviet draft resolution proposing the establishment of a round-table conference composed of the two Koreas plus the Soviet Union, China, the United States, Britain, France, Czechoslovakia, Poland, India and Burma. They criticized this proposal on the grounds that the resulting conference would be dominated by Soviet bloc members and countries sympathetic to communism while 13 contributing members and two members of the NNRC would not be included. In response, the Soviet delegation simply added four additional members—Mexico, Indonesia, Syria and Egypt—which were considered equally unacceptable by the United States and Commonwealth members.[33]

Interestingly, during the early debate at the Special Session the Indian delegation remained silent due in part to the fact Nehru was preoccupied with the domestic controversy caused by his dismissal of the Prime Minister of the State of Jammu and Kashmir. But behind the scenes Menon was in close discussion with India's Arab-Asian allies. These members were deeply unsatisfied with the 15-Power draft resolution but were wary of challenging US policy. As a result, India, Burma, Indonesia and Liberia tabled a procedural draft resolution stating that any resolution adopted by the General Assembly should be communicated to the other side as a 'proposal', not a final decision, and requesting the Secretary-General to report its progress.[34] This proposal helped to widen the growing schism between the US and Commonwealth delegations. On one hand, Lodge claimed that its purpose was to ensure that a Communist counter-proposal would have to be discussed at the Eighth Session of the General Assembly.[35] The Commonwealth members, on the other hand, offered immediate support to the Arab-Asian proposal in the First Committee. This pressure forced Lodge to concede and he expressed US support for the Arab-Asian draft resolution if it was amended so that the Secretary-General would simply 'inform' members of the Communist response.[36] Menon accepted this revision.[37]

Still, the US and Commonwealth positions over the question of Indian participation remained as far apart as ever. The Eisenhower administration had become increasingly concerned that the Commonwealth draft resolution would win widespread support. Dulles thus instructed Lodge to make it abundantly clear to the Commonwealth delegations that the US government would vote against Indian participation. The Secretary of State hoped that this would be enough to secure the number of votes necessary to block the passage of the proposal.[38] However, in talks in Washington held between Dulles, Salisbury and Spender, the British Acting Foreign Secretary stated that while it was 'silly' for a split to occur on this question, his government had made a firm commitment to India to support its membership of the conference. Spender added that Australia was reluctantly supporting Indian participation since if it was the only Commonwealth country not doing so they would 'stick out like a sore thumb'.[39] Even so, privately Salisbury was becoming increasingly concerned at the damage being done to Anglo-American relations. Consequently, he instructed the British delegation not to canvass other members to support the Commonwealth draft resolution.[40]

A split between the United States and the Commonwealth on Indian participation seemed inevitable until, at the eleventh hour, Menon intervened to spare both Indian and Commonwealth blushes. He told Lloyd that while he was practically certain that the draft resolution would obtain a simple majority, he doubted it would receive the two-thirds majority necessary to be formally adopted. In these circumstances, he revealed that India would withdraw its candidacy.[41] Menon stated in the First Committee, moreover, that India would not seek a place at the conference unless it was clear that all the major parties desired its assistance. Seizing on this point, Lodge publicly announced that the US government opposed Indian membership on the grounds that India's presence would prevent the ROK from attending the conference.[42] In connection to these developments, Salisbury decided that if the Commonwealth draft resolution did not receive overwhelming support in the First Committee Britain would seek the agreement of the other Commonwealth co-sponsors to withdraw their proposal.[43]

After ten days of deliberation, therefore, the Special Session concluded in chaotic scenes. At the last minute, the Soviet delegation introduced a number of amendments to the various draft resolutions. After each of these amendments was decisively rejected, the 15-Power draft resolution was voted upon and was overwhelmingly approved, with the United States and Old Commonwealth members voting in its favour and India and Pakistan abstaining. Next, the 4-Power draft resolution recommending Soviet participation was taken up and approved with all members, excluding the Chinese Nationalists, voting for it. The Commonwealth draft resolution proposing Indian membership was then approved narrowly by 27 votes to 21, with 11 abstentions. Significantly, all the Commonwealth members supported this proposal but the US delegation voted against it, representing the first time such a split had occurred during the debate on Korea. In addition, the 4-Power Arab-Asian procedural draft resolution was approved unanimously. Finally, the Soviet draft resolution was rejected, with the US and Old Commonwealth members voting against it and India abstaining.[44]

Immediately after this voting had taken place the Commonwealth delegations met. The Old Commonwealth representatives placed intense pressure on Menon to withdraw India's candidacy now it was clear that their draft resolution would not gain the necessary two-thirds majority to be formally adopted by the General Assembly. The Indian representative grudgingly accepted this course and the four co-sponsors agreed that their proposal should not be put to the vote even though they were upset that it appeared they were bowing to US pressure.[45] This plan was put into action when the Plenary met the following day. Menon announced that India 'declined to participate' in the conference and urged that the draft proposing her participation not be voted upon. The New Zealand delegation then called for the Commonwealth draft resolution not to proceed to the vote and the other members agreed. The subsequent voting on the other draft resolutions repeated the pattern in the First Committee. The 15-Power and two 4-Power proposals were then combined to form General Assembly Resolution 711 (VII) (see Appendix 15, p. 277–9).[46] Finally, the 15-Power draft resolution paying tribute to the UNC soldiers was adopted with non-Soviet unanimity, becoming General Assembly Resolution 712 (VII) (see Appendix 16, p. 279–80).[47] Publicly the US and Commonwealth positions had been aligned but privately none of these governments was entirely happy with the outcome of the Special Session of the General Assembly on Korea.

The Eighth Session of the General Assembly

In this climate it was hardly surprising that tensions soon erupted again between the United States and the Commonwealth members, with the Eighth Session of the General Assembly set to open less than three weeks later. Re-examination of the composition question seemed inevitable to the Commonwealth delegations once Beijing rejected General Assembly Resolution 711 (VII) and called for a conference along the lines proposed by the Soviet Union.[48] Even so, the US delegation told the British that it would oppose discussing the Chinese reply in the General Assembly since the UN had already made its decision on this matter and it should not be held to ransom by the aggressors.[49] Dulles was thus taken aback by the Commonwealth reaction since he believed it 'unthinkable' that Washington's allies desired another 'tiff' over Indian participation.[50] With the Eisenhower administration so adamantly against reopening the Korean debate it was agreed at a tense meeting of the US and Commonwealth delegations that the Korean item should be placed late on the First Committee's agenda. This move would give them time to overcome in private their differences on the composition question.[51]

As a result of this agreement, the United States and the Commonwealth members appeared united when the Eighth Session commenced in mid-September 1953. To begin with, they all supported the election of Mrs Pandit as President of the General Assembly. This decision was to prove a significant since, like Pearson, Mrs Pandit believed that she should use this appointment to play an active role in trying to find a compromise solution to the Korean question and was willing to meet with anyone towards the achievement of this goal.[52] Then in the general debate, the US and Commonwealth delegations all expressed their belief that the composition question should not be reopened, arguing that the Communists should accept the decision of the General Assembly.[53] Furthermore, in the General Committee the US and Commonwealth members joined together to vote down the Soviet proposal to have the Chinese reply discussed immediately.[54]

Behind the scenes, however, the US and Commonwealth members remained divided on the timing of the Korean debate. Menon was once again at the heart of this controversy. The Indian representative argued that the General Assembly would have to act in good time before 28 October 1953—the deadline for the commencement of the political conference stated in the Armistice Agreement—if no progress had been made on the composition question.[55] To meet this eventuality, the US and Old Commonwealth delegations agreed that the Korean item should be placed last on the agenda but that the Australian delegation would table a motion allowing this issue to be taken earlier if a majority of members concurred.[56] This course was approved in the First Committee by all the UN members except the Soviet bloc.[57]

Yet Menon almost immediately called for the Korean item to be taken up in light of the difficulties India was experiencing as chairman of the NNRC and provider of the custodial force with prisoners of war refusing to listen to explanations and Rhee's threats of using force to release them.[58] The other Commonwealth members were sympathetic to India's desire to discuss its delicate role in Korea.[59] But Dulles was adamantly opposed to such action, fearing that the UNC's activities would be criticized. He argued that the Armistice Agreement covered the question of prisoners of war and the General Assembly was in no position to get involved. He also formulated a draft resolution censoring Indian partiality on the NNRC for use if India tabled its item.[60] Initially, Nehru refused to succumb to this US pressure, claiming that the General Assembly had to meet to discuss the work of the NNRC or else India would be unable to fulfil its obligations.[61] Menon, though, convinced his Prime Minister that raising this matter now would only heighten tensions and further complicate the composition question.[62]

Behind Dulles' opposition to reopening the Korean debate was his desire to open bilateral negotiations between the United States and the PRC. He had become frustrated at having to deal with both Washington's Commonwealth allies and uninterested parties at the UN and wanted to exploit the provision in General Assembly Resolution 711 (VII) permitting the US government to discuss the time and place of the conference with the Communist side. In consequence, Dulles transmitted a communication to Beijing suggesting a meeting of emissaries at Panmunjom. Somewhat surprisingly, Zhou En-lai accepted this proposal and a meeting was set for 26 October 1953.[63] For this task Dulles appointed Arthur Dean, a trusted former colleague from the Sullivan and Cromwell international law firm who was now working at the State Department.[64]

The talks between Dean and his Chinese counterpart, Huang Hua, however, were doomed from the outset. The Communist representative refused to discuss technical details such as the date and location of the conference until the composition question had been resolved.[65] Dean, in contrast, was under strict instructions not to make any concessions on this matter.[66] Accordingly, these meetings quickly descended into bitter slanging matches as each side accused the other of trying to sabotage the conference. But, even though a breakthrough was not forthcoming, Dulles insisted that the talks be dragged out to head off debate at the UN.[67]

Meanwhile, at the General Assembly the US delegation tabled two items that placed additional barriers in the way of establishing the Korean conference and added to the growing friction with the Commonwealth. The first item was a rehashed version of the previous item concerning the Communist charges that the UNC had used bacterial warfare. Lodge argued that it was necessary to discuss this item again in light of statements made by US airmen repatriated under Operation Big Switch in which they claimed that the confessions to the use of bacterial weapons they had given while in Communist custody had been extracted using coercive methods. In response, the Soviet delegation denied these assertions and tabled another draft resolution inviting all members who had not already done so to sign or ratify the Geneva Protocol of 1925 forbidding the use of bacterial weapons.[68] These developments placed the Commonwealth members in a difficult position since they had serious misgivings regarding the timing of this debate and the effect it was having on the prospects of holding the Korean political conference. In spite of these concerns Britain, Canada, Australia and New Zealand agreed to co-sponsor a US draft resolution transferring the Soviet proposal to the Disarmament Commission. This 5-Power draft resolution was overwhelmingly approved while the Soviet proposal was rejected.[69] It became General Assembly Resolution 714 (VIII) (see Appendix 17, p. 280).[70]

The second US item was a new one accusing the Chinese and North Koreans of committing atrocities against the UNC prisoners of war held in Communist camps. These claims were based on a number of statements taken from repatriated US servicemen. However, neither the State Department[71] nor the Commonwealth members were consulted before Lodge announced to the press his intention of raising this matter at the General Assembly.[72] Lodge claimed that he had been left no choice but to take this action after the War Department published the soldiers' statements without warning, creating massive pressure in Congress to have the matter discussed at the UN. Still, the Commonwealth governments were suspicious that this was a US attempt to scupper the Korean political conference and considered making a formal protest to Washington.[73]

While this protest never came, the Commonwealth members were concerned that it would be difficult to resist calls to have Chinese and North Korean representatives invited to discuss these charges. They also feared that if an investigation commission were to examine the alleged atrocities committed by the Communists then this body would also have to investigate the claims made against the UNC at its camps on Goje Island.[74] Eden, who had recently returned to work, thus felt that the only draft resolution possible was one limited to deploring all atrocities.[75] Lodge agreed that no investigation commission could be formed but wanted to table a proposal more substantive than Eden's suggestion, expressing 'concern' at the reports of atrocities committed in the Communist prisoner of war camps.[76] This limited proposal was acceptable to the 16 contributing states, including the Old Commonwealth members, who agreed to co-sponsor it. The majority of members concurred and General Assembly Resolution 804 (VIII) (see Appendix 18, p. 280–1) was adopted with most Arab-Asian members, including India and Pakistan, abstaining and the Soviet bloc voting in opposition.[77]

In the meantime, the three-month limit for the opening of the Korean political conference passed relatively unnoticed at the UN. Evidently, the vast majority of members, including all the Commonwealth countries, were content not to interfere now that talks between Dean and Huang Hua were underway at Panmunjom. But with the agenda of the General Assembly progressing at a rapid rate, discussions between the US and Commonwealth delegations on how the Korean item should be handled got underway in late November 1953. Dulles remained vehemently opposed to making any concessions on the composition question and instructed Lodge to move to adjourn the session for an indefinite period on the grounds that the Korean question was under active discussion at Panmunjom.[78] Consequently, Lodge penned a procedural draft resolution noting the negotiations and recessing the session but allowing for it to be reconvened if the majority of members agreed.[79] The Indian delegation, however, was not prepared to go this far. Menon agreed there was little point in holding a UN debate on Korea while bilateral talks were progressing, but he insisted that a date be set to reconvene the General Assembly to discuss the NNRC before it completed its work on 22 February 1954.[80] These polarized views placed Britain in a difficult position. Eden did not want the UN debate interfering with Dean's efforts but was sympathetic towards India's position concerning the NNRC. To bridge these positions he sought to persuade Lodge to agree to amend his draft resolution so that a special session of the General Assembly could be called if the Panmunjom talks broke down or if any 'unforeseen circumstances' arose.[81] Yet Lodge refused to accept any provision that would allow General Assembly discussion of the prisoners of war question since the Armistice Agreement clearly stated that all remaining non-repatriate prisoners should be released on 23 January 1954.[82] As this was a point of procedure rather than substance Eden was not prepared to test US patience and instructed the British delegation to support the US proposal.[83] The Old Commonwealth members concurred and agreed that the US draft resolution should be tabled by Brazil.[84]

Menon, all the same, was less willing to bow to US pressure. He formulated a rival proposal recessing the session but empowering the President of the General Assembly to reconvene the body on 9 February 1954 or at an earlier date if circumstances dictated. In addition, Menon warned his Commonwealth colleagues that Nehru regarded their support on this proposal as a 'question of confidence'. But the other Commonwealth representatives, while expressing sympathy for the Indian proposal, all stated that they had pledged their support to the Brazilian draft resolution and suggested that India seek to amend it.[85]

Dulles, however, firmly opposed fixing a specific date for reopening the session or any procedure giving Mrs Pandit power to reconvene the General Assembly without the consent of the majority of members.[86] As a consequence, Lodge met with Menon and proposed that India and

Brazil table a joint draft resolution immediately recessing the debate but giving the President of the General Assembly power to reconvene the session at any time with the concurrence of the majority of members. Menon agreed to this compromise but only on the condition that Lodge make a public statement expressing Washington's appreciation of India's role in Korea and promising that the United States would support the Indian government if it wished to reconvene the General Assembly 'for good reason'.[87] This plan was put into action the next day in the First Committee and, after a very short debate, the Indian-Brazilian draft resolution was approved with only the Soviet bloc abstaining.[88] It became General Assembly Resolution 716 (VIII) (see Appendix 19, p. 282).[89]

The General Assembly in recess

In spite of the near consensus view that the General Assembly should go into recess, pressure quickly mounted for the Korean debate to be reconvened. The reason for this shift in mood was the rapid realization that the talks at Panmunjom had become deadlocked. On the same day as the Indian-Brazilian Resolution was adopted, Dean had made a final effort to find a breakthrough on the composition question by conceding that some non-belligerent nations should be allowed to 'participate' at the conference but not be permitted to introduce items or vote. Huang Hua, nevertheless, dismissed this proposal as 'absurd, ridiculous and stale' and left the text received from Dean lying on the table at the end of the meeting.[90] Dean wished to break off the talks at this point but in light of the almost unanimous decision to recess the Korean debate in deference to these negotiations, Dulles instructed him to prolong the talks until 12 December 1953.[91] At a meeting that day, therefore, Dean recessed the negotiations on the pretext that Huang Hua had charged the United States with perfidy. And shortly thereafter Dean returned to the United States.[92]

On hearing this news Menon began canvassing the Common-wealth delegations to gain their support for having the Eighth Session reconvened. He suggested meeting on 12 January 1954, ten days before all remaining non-repatriate prisoners were to be released, claiming that India only wished the General Assembly to express its appreciation of India's handling of its difficult task. The British delegation thought that this demand was reasonable and believed that the US government could not object to an early debate, given the collapse of the negotiations at Panmunjom and the public commitments it had made to Menon.[93] Yet Dulles did oppose the Indian proposal, suspecting that Nehru wished to reopen the entire composition question.[94]

The Eisenhower administration, moreover, was now convinced that the Korean political conference could only be established through bilateral negotiations with the Soviet Union. The President had thus recently agreed with Churchill and French Premier Joseph Laniel when they met at Bermuda to accept a Soviet suggestion that the foreign ministers of these four states meet in Berlin in January 1954.[95] Dulles worried that further debate at the UN would jeopardize this conference and he tried to stymie Menon's campaign by instructing Kenneth Young, Dean's deputy at Panmunjom, to try to resume talks on the condition that the Communists retracted their charge of perfidy.[96] But Huang Hua refused to back down and these talks remained in a state of indefinite recess.

Consequently, the Indian government stepped up its calls to have the Eighth Session resumed but, in an effort to meet the United States half way, Menon now proposed that the General Assembly meet in early February 1954. He stressed this would allow the NNRC to submit its report before the commission ceased its activities.[97] Before the views of the United States or the other Commonwealth members towards this course could be ascertained, the Indian government then formally requested Mrs Pandit to canvass the members to see if there was sufficient support for reconvening the session on 9 February 1954. Mrs Pandit duly obliged and added in her communication to the members a provision stating that if a delegation had not replied by 22 January 1954 she would assume that an affirmative answer had been given.[98]

Predictably, Dulles opposed this course and argued against Mrs Pandit's unprecedented 'silence gives consent' procedure. He was especially wary of the fact the deadline date specified coincided with the date all remaining prisoners were due to be released, leading him to suspect that India wished to prolong the detention of these prisoners so that the General Assembly could make the final decision on their disposal.[99] Dulles then instructed Lodge to oppose Mrs Pandit's request and to urge other delegations not to reply until after the remaining prisoners had been released.[100] He also stressed to the British government that discussion of the report of the NNRC would be more productive much later when mutual recriminations over the release of the prisoners had died down.[101] What is more, the timing of Dulles' response was significant since he had just made public the New Look strategy. He realized that in this climate of increased anxieties debate at the General Assembly would be intensely acrimonious.

In response, Menon did try to allay US concerns by claiming that the deadline date for replies was selected simply due to its practicality. But he only served to confirm Dulles' fears when he revealed that he thought that the General Assembly should reconsider the composition question since the Americans were evidently stringing out the talks at Panmunjom on purpose.[102] Menon also highlighted that the General Assembly would have to consider the controversial question of the fate of the 88 prisoners remaining in the NNRC's custody who had expressed their wish to go to a neutral country.[103] These words placed the Old Commonwealth members in a difficult position. While they unanimously agreed with India that the General Assembly should be reconvened to let India report on the NNRC, they concurred with Dulles that silence-gives-consent procedure, as described above, was inappropriate. Resulting from this reaction, Mrs Pandit did make a partial concession by agreeing to extend the deadline for replies to 29 January 1954 and to drop the controversial procedure for replies. She refused, though, to postpone the proposed date for the resumption of the session.

The NNRC's decision to then return the remaining non-repatriate prisoners to their former captors ended any possibility that the Commonwealth might form a united front against US policy on this matter. Dulles now argued that since the NNRC had failed to complete its duty, the General Assembly was under no obligation to meet to hear its report.[104] Crucially, this argument resonated among the Old Commonwealth members. The Australian and New Zealand delegations felt least bound to India and were quickest to realign with the United States.[105] Next, Eden reluctantly decided to give a negative reply to Mrs Pandit's request but expressed his willingness to have the General Assembly reconvened when the situation had stabilized.[106] The Canadian delegation remained most faithful to India, continuing to indicate that Ottawa would give an affirmative answer to the request.[107] Yet within a matter of days Canada had bowed to pressure coming from its closest allies and gave a negative response.[108] With the US and Old Commonwealth positions aligned against the resumption of the Korean debate, very few members gave a positive answer to Mrs Pandit's request and the matter was dropped.

Important to this response was the fact that Dulles, Eden, Soviet Foreign Minister Vyacheslav Molotov and French Foreign Minister Georges Bidault were now holding discussions in Berlin and the vast majority of UN members were content to let these men find a way to break the deadlock on the composition question. The Berlin Conference was nominally held to discuss the German and Austrian questions but, given the gravity of both the Korean and Indochina situations, the first item on the agenda tabled by Molotov was a proposal for a conference consisting of the Big Four plus the PRC to tackle all outstanding East Asian issues.[109] Dulles refused to accept this proposal on the grounds that the US government could not recognize the PRC as the legitimate government of China or as an equal. He also remained opposed to discussing other East Asian issues until the Korean question had been resolved. Eden and Bidault, however, were more sympathetic to the Soviet suggestion. After lengthy and often rancorous debate, the four foreign ministers eventually agreed that a meeting of their nations would take place at Geneva on 26 April 1954 to resolve the Korean question. The United States would invite the ROK and the other UN contributing states to participate while the Soviet Union would invite the PRC and North Korea. If the discussions on Korea made satisfactory progress then a separate but contemporaneous conference on Indochina could be established, with its composition decided at the time.[110]

Despite the success of the Berlin Conference in finally establishing a political conference on Korea, there were a number of calls to have the General Assembly reconvened in the interim. For example, Menon told Secretary-General Dag Hammarskjöld that the UN should discuss the fate of the 17 prisoners who had committed murders in the prison camps and who remained in the custody of the ICF.[111] But Hammarskjöld gave Menon no encouragement and the 17 prisoners were returned to the UNC without much controversy. The Indian government then hinted that the General Assembly should consider the two reports published by the NNRC. In addition, with the breakdown of the NNSC the Swedish and Swiss delegations suggested that there might have to be some kind of UN debate on the armistice supervisory mechanism. However, there was no enthusiasm for controversial discussions in New York, especially among the US and Old Commonwealth governments, now that plans were in place for the Geneva Conference. The solution to the Korean question, therefore, passed out of the hands of the UN. Still, a peaceful settlement proved just as impossible to find through bilateral channels.

The Korean phase of the 1954 Geneva Conference

After months of logistical planning and a number of scares that the two Koreas or the PRC might not participate,[112] the Geneva Conference on Korea finally got underway.[113] Its first act was to appoint Eden, Molotov and Prince Wan Waithayakon of Thailand as its joint chairmen.[114] Nonetheless, from the outset it was clear that the non-Korean participants believed that Korea had been superseded by Indochina as the most dangerous international crisis and should be dealt with immediately. These states generally felt that a balance of power existed in Korea, the resumption of hostilities was unlikely and the peninsula could be allowed to remain divided for the time being since a solution acceptable to all would be impossible to attain. Dulles gave the clearest indication that he saw little likelihood of finding a breakthrough at Geneva by only attending the first week of the conference and controversially refusing to shake hands with Zhou En-lai. The early discussions, therefore, were dominated by ROK Foreign Minister Pyun Yung-tai and his North Korean counterpart,

General Nam Il. Pyun called for the 'aggressors' to withdraw from Korea and for UN-observed elections to take place in North Korea to fill the 100 empty seats of the ROK National Assembly. In stark contrast, Nam Il demanded that all foreign forces should be withdrawn within six months and that all-Korea elections arranged by an equal North–South committee should be held to establish a fully representative government.

In the debates that followed, the Soviet Union and China backed Nam Il's proposal while the United States supported Pyun's suggested solution. Importantly, very few of the other UN contributing states became involved because they wanted to table a compromise proposal. These delegations, especially those of the Old Commonwealth members, had little confidence that a settlement could be found. But they argued that if the Communists rejected a moderate formula then the Korean phase of the conference could be terminated with the UN side claiming it had shown flexibility while the Communists had been intransigent. This action would allow attention at Geneva to focus solely on the Indochina negotiations that had begun in early May following the fall of Dien Bien Phu. In spite of these arguments the ROK refused to make any concessions, placing the US delegation, now headed by Under Secretary of State Walter Bedell Smith, in a very difficult position. Smith did not wish to pressure Pyun unduly since he realized that any settlement depended on ROK concurrence. Still, he agreed with the Commonwealth delegations that all-Korea elections were preferable to elections only in North Korea.

As a way out of this deadlock Smith proposed that the UN side formulate a set of general unification 'principles' that would uphold the UN's authority to answer the Korean question. He thought this could best be achieved by calling for the world organization to supervise all-Korea elections. This point was eventually accepted by Pyun and the other UN representatives. Even so, the Communist side refused to accept the UN's authority in this matter, claiming that the world organization had no right to meddle in the domestic affairs of a sovereign state, and suggested that a neutral international commission be formed to supervise the elections. In consequence, on 15 June 1954 the UN side unilaterally recessed the Korean phase of the conference without any decisions on the fate of the peninsula being taken.[115]

Conclusion

Ultimately the UN failed in its efforts to establish a political conference to bring about a permanent settlement of the Korean question. No formula could be found regarding the composition of the conference acceptable to all the interested parties at either the Special Session on Korea or the subsequent Eighth Session of the General Assembly. In the end, negotiations beyond the UN proved necessary to bring about the Geneva Conference. However, what was also significant during this period was the level of tension between the United States and the Commonwealth members at the UN on the membership issue. While Washington was adamant that the conference should be restricted to belligerents, the Commonwealth members believed it essential to include certain neutral parties, specifically the Soviet Union and India. The second of these countries proved most contentious within the US–Commonwealth alliance. Nonetheless, despite this friction, at no time did the Commonwealth effectively unite to constrain US policy at the UN. This episode demonstrated that when push came to shove the Old Commonwealth members accepted US hegemony at the world organization at India's expense.

The reasons for this failure to unite were manifold. Most importantly, the Commonwealth members were no longer worried that the Korean situation might lead to a global conflict. The armistice appeared firm and Korea became much less of a priority while other international crises, particularly the Indochina situation, unfolded and domestic concerns gained precedence. The Commonwealth governments did desire a Korean settlement but shared the view with Washington that if one could not be found then the chances of the Korean War reigniting were minimal anyway. What was especially noticeable during this period, therefore, was the passivity of the key Commonwealth personalities. Eden, Salisbury and Lloyd did at different times raise some protests over Indian participation at the Korean political conference but eventually accepted US policy. And the other Old Commonwealth characters were almost obsolete. Only Nehru and his representatives in New York, Menon and Mrs Pandit, took a tough stance with the United States but even they reluctantly backed down on Indian membership. Even when some of these figures were gathered in New York for the Special Session and the Eighth Session of the General Assembly very few efforts were made to coordinate a united Commonwealth policy. Furthermore, the Eisenhower administration paid less and less attention to the views of its allies at the UN as it adopted a tougher Cold War stance. The Commonwealth members recognized this fact and in their efforts to retain US support accepted US hegemony at the world organization.

EPILOGUE

The Geneva Conference represented the one and only serious international effort to bring about the unification of Korea after the war ended. However, to finish the analysis abruptly at this point would suggest that this fact was known at the time. In reality, the failure to find a solution to the Korean question at Geneva simply meant this responsibility passed once again to the UN. Brief consideration of the fate of the Korean item at the world organization subsequent to the summer of 1954 is therefore important to this study.

Yet what became immediately apparent after the Korean phase of the Geneva Conference had been terminated was that little enthusiasm existed, especially among the United States and Old Commonwealth members, to discuss Korea at the UN. These states felt that the status quo was generally acceptable, there was no pressing emergency to deal with, and that time was needed to let tempers cool. Consequently, the UN side, before leaving Geneva, agreed to postpone submission of its report to the General Assembly until shortly before its Ninth Session was due to open in September 1954.[1] In the meantime, nevertheless, a series of other crises overtook Korea in terms of international importance, pushing this issue further to the sidelines.

Top of this list of developments was the pressing matter of Indochina, which was already under discussion at Geneva. But these talks became quickly embittered and a solution appeared impossible before the June appointment of Pierre Mendes-France, the anti-colonial leader of the Radical Party, as the new French Premier. Realizing his country's desperate position, Mendes-France now pressed for a complete French withdrawal and paid little attention to US pressure to stand firm. In addition, Eden and Molotov, the co-chairmen of the Indochina phase of the Geneva Conference, played a key role in calling for compromise. As a result, on 21 July 1954 the Geneva Accords were signed. French sovereignty in Indochina thus ended; Laos and Cambodia were 'neutralized'; and Vietnam was temporarily divided at the 17th parallel. The pro-Communist Democratic Republic of Vietnam would govern the north while the pro-American State of Vietnam would control the south until nationwide elections were held two years later. Significantly though, the United States and the State of Vietnam refused to sign this agreement, although they did recognize it.[2]

Despite this apparent easing of Cold War tensions, relations between the United States and the PRC soon reached a nadir. To begin with, in August, Beijing announced that it had found 15 US airmen guilty of espionage. The Chinese claimed that the planes these individuals had been travelling in had been shot down over the PRC during the Korean War. The US government, in contrast, claimed these planes had been shot down over North Korea and so the airmen were prisoners of war who should have been returned under the terms of the Korean Armistice Agreement. Then a few weeks later the PRC began shelling a number of Nationalist-held islands in the Taiwan Strait sparking a diplomatic crisis with the Eisenhower administration.[3] Meanwhile, on 8 September 1954, the Manila Pact was signed, laying the foundations for the Southeast Asia Treaty Organisation (SEATO). Dulles' brainchild, this collective security organization was clearly designed to contain Chinese expansionism and was composed of the United States and a number of its Western and Asian allies, including four Commonwealth members: Britain, Australia, New Zealand and Pakistan.[4]

Cold War friction also mounted in other parts of the world. Just days after the Korean phase of the Geneva Conference had ended, the CIA launched a covert operation to depose Guatemalan President

Jacobo Arbenz Guzman. Washington had become increasingly concerned by Arbenz's radical land reform policy, fearing that the Soviet Union was controlling him and was trying to spread Communism to the Western Hemisphere. The CIA, therefore, recruited, trained, armed and supported an invasion force of right-wing exiles led by Colonel Carlos Castillo Armas. This action triggered the conservative Guatemalan Army to revolt and Arbenz was forced to resign, to be replaced by Castillo Armas.[5]

Attention also shifted back to Europe. Although Western European countries had agreed to establish the EDC over two years earlier, this initiative dramatically collapsed in August 1954 when the French parliament failed to ratify the treaty. Initially, the Western alliance appeared to be under threat. But major rifts were avoided as an alternative formula allowing for West German rearmament was found at the London and Paris Conferences of September and October. The Western European Union (WEU) was created by modifying the 1948 Treaty of Brussels to incorporate the FRG and Italy alongside the original five signatories. In addition, it was agreed that West Germany would be allowed to rearm but its forces would come under the direct control of NATO.[6]

With these numerous crises unfolding it is hardly surprising that the US and Commonwealth governments gave little thought as to how to handle the Korean question until a few days before the Ninth Session of the General Assembly opened. Even then, the United States adopted an entirely negative position, opposing any substantive debate on Korea until the Communist side accepted the 'principles' for unification put forward by the UN side at the Geneva Conference.[7] The Old Commonwealth delegations, realizing the Eisenhower administration's intransigence in light of its growing feud with Beijing and eager to maintain good relations with Washington now stability in Korea had been restored, accepted this policy without question.[8] India, however, was less compliant. Menon threatened that if the General Assembly adopted a resolution implying that fruitful negotiations were at an end he would demand discussion of the NNRC report that would potentially embarrass the UNC and Washington.[9]

Consequently, when the General Assembly got underway India was isolated from its Commonwealth partners. Indeed, India and many of the Arab-Asian group found themselves alongside the USSR calling for every effort to be made to achieve a political settlement. Still, the United States and Old Commonwealth members joined together and convinced the majority to place the Korean item last on the First Committee's agenda to allow the UN side time to submit its report on the Geneva Conference.[10]

Behind the scenes, therefore, the 15 contributing states worked feverishly to come to an agreement on the wording of their report. But this proved to be an unexpectedly difficult task. On the one hand, Lodge argued that the report should cover only what was publicly said at the conference. The Canadian delegation, on the other hand, wished to express its private position since it could no longer support the principle of holding elections in Korea only 'under UN supervision'. This issue proved so controversial since this principle was the precise sticking point on which the conference had been broken off. The reason for Ottawa's change of heart was that Canada had since been appointed a member of a non-UN commission to supervise future elections in Indochina.[11] A solution was finally found by Sir Pierson Dixon, the new British Permanent Representative to the UN. Dixon suggested that the report simply omit reference to the supervision procedure since the definition of free elections was covered earlier in the text. This proposal was gratefully accepted by all the contributing states and their report was submitted.[12]

India, however, made it clear that it could not approve the UN side's report since this implied supporting as final the 'principles' already rejected by the Communists. Nehru, who had recently returned from a trip to Beijing, revealed that the Chinese hoped that India would table a resolution calling for renewed negotiations. The Indian Prime Minister was sympathetic to this suggestion, agreeing that the negotiations at Geneva had only been suspended, not terminated.[13] In light of this news, Menon attempted to seize the initiative in New York by suggesting a draft resolution noting the 'progress' made at Geneva and calling on the conference's three chairmen to continue their efforts to bring about a solution. This proposal was designed to act as a compromise between US calls for no further action on Korea and Soviet insistence that another conference be established to re-examine the unification question. Importantly, Menon realized that in the current climate a new conference on Korea would only heighten tensions and so opposed the Soviet plan.[14]

While the other Commonwealth members remained wholly behind the United States and paid little attention to the Indian proposal, Britain once again sought to reconcile the positions of Washington and New Delhi. Eden was strongly opposed to Menon's three chairmen plan, believing that the UN should not delegate its responsibility to three individuals, one being himself. The Foreign Secretary thus suggested a procedural draft resolution ending the Korean debate, expressing hope that a solution would be found in due course and calling upon all nations to bring to the attention of the General Assembly any developments which might make this possible.[15] Lodge expressed general support for the British proposal but feared the last phrase would encourage the Indians to make future proposals. Instead, the US delegation preferred either a negative proposal blaming the Communists for the failure at Geneva, endorsing the UN report and calling on the Communists to cooperate, or one simply terminating the debate at the Ninth Session.[16]

Given this choice, Eden preferred the latter and he urged the Indians to back down.[17] But Menon refused to withdraw his draft resolution and insisted that it was necessary for the UN to take some action to encourage further negotiations.[18] Menon took this matter up with Nehru, stressing that his three chairmen proposal provided the necessary nexus with the Geneva Conference and offered some hope that a solution might still be found.[19] Nehru agreed with this analysis and stressed to the British High Commission that the Indian proposal was designed to put the Korean debate into 'cold storage', preventing the USSR from calling for a new conference or forcing India to bring up the NNRC report.[20]

Faced with the prospect of siding with either the United States or India, the new British Minister of State Anthony Nutting, now in New York, chose the former.[21] The British delegation thus produced a draft resolution approving the UN report, reaffirming the UN's objectives in Korea, expressing hope that a solution would soon be found and postponing the Korean debate until the Tenth Session.[22] Yet Eden remained eager to retain Commonwealth unity and urged Nehru to co-sponsor the British proposal.[23] But Menon—who had taken an instant disliking to Nutting, believing he did not show adequate regard for India's position—opposed the British draft resolution, claiming it was too close to the US position and offered no hope of finding a peaceful settlement.[24] Nehru concurred with this position but instructed Menon not to break with the British if a compromise could yet be found.[25]

Nonetheless, Lodge made it clear that his government would not make any concessions and, in fact, wanted the British draft resolution 'strengthened'.[26] Moreover, he revealed that Washington did not want India to act as a co-sponsor.[27] Menon, therefore, rejected the British proposal outright.[28] Lodge now wholeheartedly backed the British draft resolution and convinced the 14 other contributing states to co-sponsor it even though the other Commonwealth members expressed their regret that India had refused to join them.[29] With Washington and New Delhi's positions so far apart Eden decided it was time to close ranks with the United States since everything possible had been done to meet the Indians half way.[30]

The Korean debate in the First Committee finally got underway the following day with the United States and Old Commonwealth states adopting a clearly divergent position from India. Lodge took the lead, tabling the 15-Power draft resolution, while the Soviet Permanent Representative, Yakov Malik, tabled a rival draft resolution calling for a new conference to discuss the proposals made by North Korea at Geneva. Malik also tabled a second draft resolution disbanding UNCURK. But when Menon tabled his three chairmen proposal the Soviet delegation, sensing the divisions between the West and India, withdrew its first draft resolution in deference to this plan. In spite of this action the 15-Power draft resolution was approved by a large majority, endorsing the Geneva 'principles'. The Indian delegation thus reluctantly withdrew its proposal. The Soviet draft resolution calling for the dissolution of

UNCURK was then overwhelmingly rejected.[31] This pattern was then repeated in the Plenary where the 15-Power draft resolution became General Assembly Resolution 811 (IX) (see Appendix 20, p. 282–3).[32]

* * *

The significance of the decision taken at the Ninth Session of the General Assembly to endorse the Geneva 'principles' and not to hold further negotiations on Korean unification was difficult to judge at the time. Yet this decision shaped the UN debate on Korea for the next two decades. Perennially, the United States and its allies continued to call for the Communists to accept the UN side's report and the principles on unification it contained. In stark contrast, the Soviet bloc repeatedly argued in favour of the proposal put forward by North Korea at Geneva. In addition, each year the USSR unsuccessfully tabled its draft resolution calling for the dissolution of UNCURK.

Still, with no progress being made on the substantive issue of Korea's future, debate increasingly focused on the procedural question over whether North as well as South Korea should be invited to participate. As decolonization accelerated a proliferation of new members joined the UN and calls for the participation of both Koreas grew steadily. This process was symbolic of the shifting power dynamic within the UN. With the ever-growing number of neutral states, and the emergence of the Non-Aligned Movement, US dominance faded and successive US governments looked less and less to the UN to pursue their policy. At the same time, the Soviet Union's anti-imperialist propaganda received increased support, emboldening Moscow's activities at the world organization. Finally, in 1974, following the PRC's admission to the UN, enough support was raised and North Korea was invited to participate. Ironically though, that same year the Korean item was removed from the General Assembly's agenda and UNCURK was dissolved as bilateral negotiations between Seoul and Pyongyang appeared to be bearing fruit. Thereafter discussions on Korea focused on whether both the ROK and DPRK should be admitted as members. For the vast majority of UN members, including the United States and the Commonwealth states, this decision came as a relief since it ended the recurrent futile discussions on an unsolvable problem.[33]

What is more, the debates at the General Assembly in late 1954 clearly confirmed that the Commonwealth was again divided along its traditional Old–New axis and there was no longer any strong desire among its members to unite to constrain US policy at the UN. Evidently, the factors necessary to bring the Commonwealth together had disappeared by this time: the Korean crisis had ended without escalation; none of the key Commonwealth personalities, except Nehru, was willing to exercise his global influence even when gathered together; and the Eisenhower administration had made it abundantly clear it was unwilling to make concessions on Korea.

These developments were indicative of the Commonwealth's changing role in international affairs during the mid-1950s. As the world became increasingly polarized into two superpower blocs, and as Britain's Great Power status disappeared, especially after the Suez Crisis, the Commonwealth became increasingly obsolete as a third force. The majority of the Commonwealth members, including Britain, decided that its long-term interests were best served by developing its own 'special relationship' with Washington. Only India took an alternative route. Partly due to Nehru's disappointment at what he viewed as his Commonwealth partners' willingness to bow to US pressure at the UN during the Korean War, the Indian Prime Minister pursued his policy of neutrality with ever-more vigour. Nehru had already demonstrated these convictions in April 1954 when he had agreed with Mao to the 'Five Principles of Peaceful Coexistence' that he had promoted shortly thereafter at the Asian Prime Ministers Conference at Colombo. He subsequently demonstrated his convictions even further by playing an integral part at the Asian–African Conference held at Bandung in mid-1955 and in establishing the Non-Aligned Movement in Belgrade in 1961.[34]

Differences within the Commonwealth then became even more apparent during the late 1950s and 1960s as its membership increased dramatically and its nature radically altered as Britain relinquished its Empire. The original 'white' Commonwealth states increasingly felt outnumbered and alienated among the newly-independent 'non-white' members. As a result, less effort was made to coordinate policy on important issues, especially at the UN. The vast majority of the new members were small developing powers who were able to make their voices better heard by joining with the non-aligned states with whom they shared many problems. In contrast, they had little in common with the wealthier Old Commonwealth countries, whom they generally distrusted. Likewise, the Old Commonwealth members saw little point trying to build bridges with a hostile Third World, preferring to assume an anonymous supporting role within the Western bloc. Hence the Commonwealth's cooperative experience at the UN during the Korean War was a one-off not to be replicated. Even after the Singapore Declaration of 1971, in which the Commonwealth gained a formal structure and its members agreed to a framework of core political values and common goals, the organization became more of a symbol than a forum for pursuing a united policy.[35]

CONCLUSION

This book has demonstrated that on numerous occasions throughout the four years between the outbreak of the Korean War and the 1954 Geneva Conference the Commonwealth was able to constrain US policy at the UN and play a vital role in preventing the escalation of the conflict. At the heart of this study has been the examination of what exactly gave the Commonwealth its unique position and under what conditions the organization was able to exercise its influence.

To begin with, the Commonwealth mattered because of its unique nature and composition. The Commonwealth was an intergovernmental organization of states with a shared experience of being part of the British Empire. Unlike other contemporary international organizations such as the UN or NATO, it had no precise structure or function. Its members were not bound politically, economically or militarily and they only met formally on a sporadic basis. Yet in the early 1950s the organization represented a cornerstone of each of its members' foreign policy. Sentimentalism had some part to play but for each government the furtherance of national interests was at the forefront of the decision to remain part of, and to act through, the Commonwealth. Its members thus remained intimately connected through the High Commission network and through close personal relationships between diplomatic and military officials.

Yet the Commonwealth was not always a happy organization. Between 1945 and 1950, as shown in the Prologue, it had invariably failed to exercise any significant global influence. Its members had drifted apart since the close wartime alliance, especially as Britain's global position had been eclipsed by that of the United States. For that reason the foreign policy priority of virtually all the Commonwealth governments was building ever-closer ties with Washington even if this meant sacrificing Commonwealth loyalties. In addition, with the onset of decolonization the Commonwealth members had become increasingly divided along the Old–New axis due to their pursuit of different national interests, conflicting Cold War perspectives and security concerns, and racial prejudices.

During the Korean War the Commonwealth became important, however, precisely because of its unique position in international relations. Despite US global preponderance at this time, Washington desired close and reliable allies in regions it saw as important. For Washington, a friendly Commonwealth was imperative because its members represented key partners in Western Europe, North America and the Pacific, together with the leading voice in the emerging Third World. The United States was particularly sensitive to Commonwealth sentiment in UN debates, where it relied on the votes of allies to maintain its hegemonic position. The Commonwealth was thus significant itself as a voting bloc. But, more importantly, the Commonwealth wielded enormous moral authority at the UN because of both its multiethnic nature and the shared liberal democratic values of its members. Consequently, the Commonwealth was in a position to influence the voting behaviour of many other groups. The UN also provided a forum in which all the Commonwealth members were brought together and could cooperate. Even though they maintained strong bilateral relations, the Commonwealth members found it difficult to coordinate policy due to the physical distance between each capital.

This book has also emphasized that the unity of its members was essential to the success of the Commonwealth. Acting alone, none of the Commonwealth countries, not even Britain, had sufficient influence to force the US government to divert from its chosen course. Still, under certain conditions the usually incongruent Commonwealth members could be brought together to challenge US dominance at the UN as was seen between 1950 and 1954. Commonwealth unity occurred when the risk of a global conflict was at its greatest, when key Commonwealth personalities were prepared to exercise their influence, when coincidence brought the Commonwealth members together and when Washington was willing to bow to Commonwealth pressure. These conditions were in a constant state of flux and when they were removed Commonwealth cooperation broke down. Each chapter of this book has used this proposition to evaluate the level of constraint exercised by the Commonwealth upon US policy at the UN and to explain this pattern during successive phases of the Korean War.

The first chapter began by examining the establishment of the UN's first collective security action in response to the North Korean invasion of the ROK. It highlighted the nearly complete US control of this process, taking the lead in formulating the various resolutions adopted by the Security Council. US dominance was made possible partly due to the absence of the Soviet delegation—but also because the Commonwealth members failed to unite and attempt to constrain US policy since all the necessary conditions were absent. To start, the Commonwealth members were in agreement that the UN had to repel this act of aggression and did not think such limited action risked Soviet or Chinese intervention. The Old Commonwealth members were even willing to contribute forces to demonstrate their support. In addition, because the Korean question was taken in the Security Council only Britain and India were represented and none of the key Commonwealth personalities were present. Very little consultation, therefore, took place between the Commonwealth members. And even if they had tried to unite in opposition, the Truman administration had made clear its determination to use the UN to legitimize its position. Only India, despite supporting the intervention, raised any objections to the nature of the action and tried to mediate between the superpowers.

The second section of Chapter 1 was dedicated to the early discussions on Korea at the Fifth Session of the General Assembly. It stressed that the US government was again able to use its dominance of the UN to facilitate the adoption of a resolution permitting the unification of Korea by force. Despite the fact that all the Commonwealth countries were represented in the General Assembly and a large number of key personalities were in attendance, its members remained disunited and the Old Commonwealth actively supported the US position. Behind this stance was the massive improvement in the military situation following the Inchon landings and the belief that neither the Soviet Union nor China would intervene on North Korea's behalf. Furthermore, the US government made clear its unwillingness to alter its position now the opportunity to unite Korea had arisen even when India warned that Beijing would intervene if the 38th parallel was crossed.

The story told in Chapter 2 was very different. During the winter crisis following Chinese intervention in early November 1950 the Commonwealth united to an unprecedented level and was able to constrain US policy for a considerable period. Even so, this unity did not occur immediately. For a number of weeks the Chinese intervention appeared limited in size and scope. And so the Old Commonwealth members largely accepted US estimates that the risk of escalation was low. Also, just like in June, because this matter was taken up in the Security Council the Commonwealth struggled to form a cohesive bloc. All the same, Britain and India did begin to coordinate their policy as both governments sought to give China the opportunity to explain its actions and to reassure Beijing that the UN had no aggressive designs. These arguments did moderate US policy since Washington was prepared to wait for Beijing's response before pressing its draft resolution calling on Chinese forces to withdraw. Still, when the PRC refused to talk and launched its massive second phase offensive, forcing UN forces to retreat, the US delegation demanded immediate action. In these circumstances, Britain could do no more than support the US draft resolution while India quietly abstained.

Nevertheless, the Soviet delegation exercised its veto. The United States thus had the debate moved to the General Assembly where they wished to use their traditional dominance to have China branded an aggressor. What they had not counted on was the determination of the Commonwealth members to facilitate a ceasefire. For almost two months the united Commonwealth was able to constrain US policy, during which time the United States reluctantly accepted the establishment of the Cease-fire Group and the adoption of the ceasefire 'principles'. The presence of all the conditions necessary for Commonwealth unity made this possible. In the dire military situation grave fears existed in the Commonwealth capitals that if China was found to have committed aggression the United States would press the UN to impose drastic sanctions upon Beijing. This action would in turn lead China and its ally, the Soviet Union, to take retaliatory action entailing an extension of fighting beyond Korea. A number of key Commonwealth personalities, therefore, were determined to exercise their influence. These individuals seized upon the fact they were brought together at the General Assembly and at a Prime Ministers' Conference in London to coordinate policy. Facing this challenge, the Truman administration showed a great willingness to accommodate Commonwealth views despite domestic pressures. Acheson gambled that once Chinese intransigence had been demonstrated, the United States' allies would come to their senses and support the aggressor resolution.

This venture proved partially effective. In the final days of January 1951 the Commonwealth did become disjointed and its Old members gradually fell in line behind US policy as the conditions for unity were removed one by one. Firstly, the Communist offensive was halted, leading to renewed hope that a line could be held. The Commonwealth then forced the United States to amend their draft resolution so that consideration of sanctions would be postponed until after a further effort to bring about a ceasefire. Escalation of the conflict now appeared much less likely and the Commonwealth members were content that they had delayed US policy for long enough to prevent the more hawkish elements of the Truman administration gaining prominence. Secondly, the key Common-wealth personalities had begun to disperse and the majority of them, realizing that US patience had worn out, were no longer willing to challenge the US position. And finally, by this time Washington had made it clear that it would not stop until Beijing was punished. The

Old Commonwealth members thus supported the modified aggressor resolution while India found itself voting alongside the Soviet bloc.

Chapter 3 analyzed the continued disintegration of Commonwealth unity and the restoration of US hegemony at the UN during the spring of 1951. But the Commonwealth did play a moderating, rather than a constraining, role upon US policy. The Truman administration, under intense domestic pressures, pressed for the early termination of the Good Offices Committee so that sanctions could be considered. The Commonwealth governments, however, were opposed to precipitous action. With the UN forces now gradually moving north Washington was willing to accept some delay. Yet when it became obvious that the Chinese were not prepared to discuss a ceasefire without preconditions the US government demanded consideration of sanctions and the Commonwealth conceded. Even then, the United States did not get it all its own way in the Additional Measures Committee. The British and Australian delegations, for their own domestic reasons, cautioned against military sanctions and wished to slow discussions. Again, Truman and Acheson demonstrated some flexibility as they simply proposed stopping the export of strategic goods to the PRC. Once the Communists launched their Spring Offensive, though, US pressure for action mounted. In light of the moderate nature of the US proposal, the Commonwealth members backed down.

Clearly during this phase of the conflict few of the conditions necessary for Commonwealth unity were present. While some Commonwealth fears lingered regarding the Communist response to UN measures, the risk of escalation had greatly diminished for two reasons. The first reason was the steady improvement in the military situation. As a result, with the UN's position on the peninsula secured and MacArthur having been removed by Truman, the Commonwealth members held fewer concerns that the fighting would extend beyond Korea. The second reason was the recognition in the Commonwealth capitals that the limited economic sanctions proposed by Washington were unlikely to lead to any significant Communist retaliation. In addition, the key Commonwealth personalities made little effort to exercise their influence or coordinate policy now that the winter crisis had abated. The British, Canadians and even the Indians, for varying reasons, were particularly anxious to repair any damage done to their relations with Washington during the previous months. Finally, the Truman administration made it clear that it would only give so much ground before it expected the Commonwealth to fall into line.

The fourth chapter demonstrated that by July 1951 the Commonwealth members were thoroughly disunited and had little interest in constraining US policy at the UN. This situation continued and intensified during the next 12 months following the commencement of armistice negotiations as the Korean question was taken out of the hands of the world organization and placed in those of the UN and Communist commands. Although a number of crises were experienced, forcing the talks to move from Kaesong to Panmunjom, reasonable progress had been made before the Sixth Session of the General Assembly opened in Paris in November 1951. Washington and the Commonwealth capitals, including New Delhi, thus concluded that the UN could do little more to further the cause for peace. In fact, all were in agreement that separate talks in Paris would only complicate the work of the UN negotiators in whom they trusted. Consideration of the Korean item, therefore, was postponed until the outcome of the talks was known.

Evidently, none of the conditions necessary for Commonwealth unity were present during this period. Fighting in October 1951 had only reinforced the fact that a military stalemate existed and Commonwealth fears of escalation reached their lowest point in over a year. With the relative importance of Korea declining and other domestic and international issues to worry about, the Commonwealth personalities were also not prepared to exercise their influence or coordinate policy. Moreover, since Washington had sole control over the UN negotiating position it was determined to maintain its monopoly and was unwilling to discuss matters in the General Assembly. Yet in the spring of 1952 hopes of an early end to hostilities were dealt a severe blow. Serious disagreement emerged at Panmunjom over the fate of the prisoners of war. The Communist negotiators insisted that all prisoners should be repatriated at war's end while the UN team argued against forcibly returning to their homelands the large numbers of prisoners who would violently resist repatriation. The armistice negotiations became deadlocked on this matter for the next six months before completely breaking down. Meanwhile, tensions at the UN mounted as the Soviet delegation accused the UNC of maltreating prisoners of war and conducting bacteriological warfare in Korea.

Chapter 5 outlined how, in these dangerous circumstances, the Commonwealth was able to wage its most successful campaign of constraint upon US policy at the UN. The Truman administration grudgingly accepted Commonwealth arguments that the Korean item had to be discussed at the Seventh General Assembly. But with US presidential elections taking place in early November 1952 Washington simply wanted the UN to legitimize the position it had adopted at Panmunjom. In stark contrast, the Commonwealth members were determined to try to find a compromise solution. They rallied behind a lengthy proposal put forward by Nehru's personal representative Krishna Menon calling for the establishment of a repatriation commission to take custody of all prisoners after an armistice had been signed and outlined a detailed procedure dealing with the fate of non-repatriate prisoners. In spite of strident US protests against this proposal, the Commonwealth remained firm. Eventually Washington conceded and the Indian Resolution was adopted by a massive majority.

Behind the Commonwealth's successful attempt to constrain US policy was the convergence of all the conditions necessary for Commonwealth unity. With the breakdown of the armistice negotiations the Commonwealth members, desperate to terminate the costly conflict in Korea, were worried that fighting might be prolonged indefinitely and might even escalate if Washington took more drastic military measures. These latter concerns were brought into the open with the election of General Dwight D. Eisenhower who had criticized Truman's limited war strategy and promised to end the conflict. More significantly, Eisenhower's election placed the outgoing Truman administration in an exceptionally weak position. The key Commonwealth personalities gathered in New York, particularly Eden, Pearson and Menon, realized this fact and sought to use their influence to find a solution to the prisoner of war question before Eisenhower took office. Finally, the Truman administration, even though it did not want to bend to Commonwealth pressure, had few weapons at its disposal since it clearly did not represent the views of the incoming president. Even so, it only conceded once the Soviet Union made it clear that the Indian proposal was unacceptable. The United States thus incorrectly assumed that the resolution's adoption would have no long-standing impact. This should not, however, detract from the fact that the Commonwealth had for the first time forced Washington to abandon its preferred course.

Nonetheless, the Commonwealth's ability to constrain US policy at the UN was short-lived. As Chapter 6 showed, the Eisenhower administration soon reasserted US hegemony at the world organization. Although the new president assumed power in January 1953 without a clear idea of how he would end the conflict, he did decide early on that the United States would respect the Indian Resolution since this represented the will of the world community. As a consequence, when the General Assembly resumed discussions a month later the US delegation championed the resolution and called for no further action to be taken. The Old Commonwealth members agreed with this course and so made no real effort to constrain US policy. India did initially argue that the Korean problem needed to be reconsidered in light of the Communist rejection of the Indian Resolution. But even India backed down once the Communists had indicated their willingness to negotiate on the basis of the outstanding Indian Resolution and talks had been resumed. The Commonwealth members were then generally content to let Washington take the lead at Panmunjom. Only in May 1953, when the UN negotiators drifted away from the terms of the Indian Resolution, did the Commonwealth members complain, and then through bilateral channels rather than the UN. Also, when the talks were threatened by Rhee's decision to release 27,000 prisoners, the Old Commonwealth members joined with the United States in dismissing Indian calls to have the UN debate reopened.

The reasons for Commonwealth disunity in this instance were manifold. At the outset, it quickly emerged that the Eisenhower administration had no immediate plans to take more drastic military action that might risk escalation. Only after the UN discussions on Korea had ended did the President make his vague threats to use nuclear weapons against China. But by this time the armistice negotiations had been resumed following Stalin's death and significant concessions had been made towards the Indian Resolution. With an armistice now a real possibility none of the key Commonwealth personalities felt any need to meddle through the UN, especially as they all hoped to build close ties with the new US government. And, even if they had wished to exercise their influence, all the indications were that the popular and strong Eisenhower administration was not prepared to bow to allied pressure at the UN. Commonwealth faith in the UN negotiators eventually paid off as the Korean Armistice Agreement was signed on 27 July 1953.

The final chapter revealed that even after the termination of hostilities, relations between the United States and the Commonwealth members remained fraught. Within a matter of days, the attention of these states shifted to finding a way to establish a conference to bring about the peaceful settlement of the Korean question. The Eisenhower administration was resolute that this conference should be composed solely of belligerents whereas the Commonwealth argued that certain neutral countries, chiefly India, should also be represented. Commonwealth efforts to constrain US policy, though, were half-hearted and fruitless. The Commonwealth members did remain loyal to India and tabled a draft resolution proposing its membership. But once it became clear this proposal would not gain a majority in the General Assembly the Commonwealth members accepted, if somewhat grudgingly, the US position. Furthermore, when the Communists rejected the UN composition formula, only India pushed for reconsideration of neutral membership. The Old Commonwealth governments, on the contrary, acknowledged that a solution to this problem was to be found through bilateral means and they welcomed the establishment of the Geneva Conference by the Big Four at Berlin even though India was excluded.

While the Commonwealth members were all opposed to the US position regarding the composition of the political conference on Korea, their convictions were insufficiently strong to unite to constrain the United States at the UN. Crucially, the Commonwealth members soon realized that neither belligerent camp wished to resume fighting in Korea and so the threat of escalation reached its lowest ebb since the outbreak of the war. In this more placid environment the key Commonwealth personalities quickly shifted their attention away from Korea to other more pressing matters, such as Indochina, now that disaster had been averted. For these decision-makers, the idea of seriously challenging US policy now only risked damaging their own long-term national interests. The Commonwealth members realized the strength of the Eisenhower administration's convictions and that they could no longer wield sufficient influence in Washington to shift the US government away from its chosen course.

The Epilogue then briefly confirmed that these processes solidified in the months and years following the failure of the Geneva Conference. With the armistice holding and both Cold War camps content with the status quo in Korea a list of other international crises soon took precedence. By the time the UN next met to discuss Korean unification it was clear that the United States was opposed to any serious debate. Both Washington and Moscow were also unprepared to compromise the positions they had adopted at Geneva. In this climate, all the Commonwealth members except India sided with the Western superpower. Subsequently, the Korean question at the UN remained deadlocked along these lines for the next two decades. During this same period, the US gradually came to overlook the UN as its hegemonic position disappeared with the hastening of decolonization. Moreover, the Commonwealth became increasingly less important for its members and in global affairs. The divisions that had existed within the organization before 1950 returned and were exacerbated by Britain's waning great power status and the influx of newly-independent states. By the early 1960s the Commonwealth had become largely irrelevant with its Old 'white' members content to play a subservient role within the US camp while the rest joined with India as part of the Non-Aligned Movement.

In the final analysis, the preceding pages have demonstrated that during the Korean War—the first major Cold War crisis that came before the UN—the Commonwealth, when united, could constrain US policy at the world organization. While the necessary conditions for Commonwealth unity were never entirely replicated after this four-year crisis, this book is still of enormous significance. In the historiography of the Korean War, writers have for too long concentrated solely on the role of the superpowers and almost completely overlooked the important function played by the Commonwealth at the UN. This book has thus filled a major gap. It has provided an important dimension to our knowledge of the Korean War. It has added depth to our historical knowledge of the practical workings of the UN, revealing that the United States, even during its years of hegemony, could not completely dominate the organization. Most notably, it has shown that in the early post-war period the Commonwealth was more than a symbolic group of states bound by a common history. Its disparate members continued to see the organization as an important means for furthering their national interests and, as such, could work closely when necessary to achieve shared goals. At the height of the Cold War, therefore, the Commonwealth mattered in international relations. And the interaction of its members with each other and with external powers warrants greater academic study.

APPENDICES

1. Security Council Resolution 82 of 25 June 1950

82 (1950). Resolution of 25 June 1950
[S/1501]

The Security Council,

Recalling the finding of the General Assembly in its resolution 293 (IV) of 21 October 1949 that the Government of the Republic of Korea is a lawfully established government having effective control and jurisdiction over that part of Korea where the United Nations Temporary Commission on Korea was able to observe and consult and in which the great majority of the people of Korea reside; that this Government is based on elections which were a valid expression of the free will of the electorate of that part of Korea and which were observed by the Temporary Commission; and that this is the only such Government in Korea,

Mindful of the concern expressed by the General Assembly in its resolutions 195 (III) of 12 December 1948 and 293 (IV) of 21 October 1949 about the consequences which might follow unless Member States refrained from acts derogatory to the results sought to be achieved by the United Nations in bringing about the complete independence and unity of Korea; and the concern expressed that the situation described by the United Nations Commission on Korea in its report menaces the safety and well-being of the Republic of Korea and of the people of Korea and might lead to open military conflict there,

Noting with grave concern the armed attack on the Republic of Korea by forces from North Korea,

Determines that this action constitutes a breach of the peace; and

I

Calls for the immediate cessation of hostilities;

Calls upon the authorities in North Korea to withdraw forthwith their armed forces to the 38th parallel;

II

Requests the United Nations Commission on Korea:

(*a*) To communicate its fully considered recommendations on the situation with the least possible delay;

(*b*) To observe the withdrawal of North Korean forces to the 38th parallel;

(*c*) To keep the Security Council informed on the execution of this resolution:

III

Calls upon all Member States to render every assistance to the United Nations in the execution of this resolution and to refrain from giving assistance to the North Korean authorities.

Adopted at the 473rd meeting
by 9 votes to none, with 1
absetention (Yugoslavia).

2. Security Council Resolution 83 of 27 June 1950

83 (1950). Resolution of 27 June 1950

[S/1511]

The Security Council,

Having determined that the armed attack upon the Republic of Korea by forces from North Korea constitutes a breach of the peace,

Having called for an immediate cessation of hostilities,

Having called upon the authorities in North Korea to withdraw forthwith their armed forces to the 38th parallel,

Having noted from the report of the United Nations Commission on Korea that the authorities in North Korea have neither ceased hostilities nor withdrawn their armed forces to the 38th parallel, and that urgent military measures are required to restore international peace and security,

Having noted the appeal from the Republic of Korea to the United Nations for immediate and effective steps to secure peace and security.

Recommends that the Members of the United Nations furnish such assistance to the Republic of Korea as may be necessary to repel the armed attack and to restore international peace and security in the area.

Adopted at the 474th meeting
by 7 votes to 1 (Yugoslavia).

3. Security Council Resolution 84 of 7 July 1950

84 (1950). Resolution of 7 July 1950

[S/1588]

The Security Council,

Having determined that the armed attack upon the Republic of Korea by forces from North Korea constitutes a breach of the peace,

Having recommended that Members of the United Nations furnish such assistance to the Republic of Korea as may be necessary to repel the armed attack and to restore international peace and security in the area,

1. *Welcomes* the prompt and vigorous support which Governments and peoples of the United Nations have given to its resolutions 82 (1950) and 83 (1950) of 25 and 27 June 1950 to assist the Republic of Korea in defending itself against armed attack and thus to restore international peace and security in the area;
2. *Notes* that Members of the United Nations have transmitted to the United Nations offers of assistance for the Republic of Korea;
3. *Recommends* that all Members providing military forces and other assistance pursuant to the aforesaid Security Council resolutions make such forces and other assistance available to a unified command under the United States of America;
4. *Requests the* United States to designate the commander of such forces;
5. *Authorizes* the unified command at its discretion to use the United Nations flag in the course of operations against North Korean forces concurrently with the flags of the various nations participating;
6. *Requests* the United States to provide the Security Council with reports as appropriate on the course of action taken under the unified command.

Adopted at the 476th meeting
by 7 votes to none, with 3
abstentions (Egypt, India, Yugoslavia).

4. Security Council Resolution 85 of 31 July 1950

85 (1950). Resolution of 31 July 1950
[S/ 1657)
The Security Council,
Recognizing the hardships and privations to which the people of Korea are being subjected as a result of the continued prosecution by the North Korean forces of their unlawful attack,

Appreciating the spontaneous offers of assistance to the Korean people which have been made by Governments, specialized agencies, and non-governmental organizations,

1. *Requests* the Unified Command to exercise responsibility for determining the requirements for the relief and support of the civilian population of Korea and for establishing in the field the procedures for providing such relief and support;

2. *Requests* the Secretary-General to transmit all offers of assistance for relief and support to the Unified Command;

3. *Requests* the Unified Command to provide the Security Council with reports, as appropriate, on its relief activities;

4. *Requests* the Secretary-General, the Economic and Social Council in accordance with Article 65 of the Charter of the United Nations, other appropriate United Nations principal and subsidiary organ, the specialized agencies in accordance with the terms of their respective agreements with the United Nations, and appropriate non-governmental organizations to provide such assistance as the Unified Command may request for the relief and support of the civilian population of Korea and as appropriate in connexion with the responsibilities being carried out by the Unified Command on behalf of the Security Council.

Adopted at the 479th meeting
by 9 votes to none, with 1
abstention (Yugoslavia).

5. General Assembly Resolution 376 (V) of 7 October 1950

376 (V). The problem of the independence of Korea

The General Assembly,

Having regard to its resolutions of 14 November 1947 (112 (II)), of 12 December 1948 (195 (III)) and of 21 October 1949 (293 (IV)),

Having received and considered the report of the United Nations Commission on Korea,

Mindful of the fact that the objectives set forth in the resolutions referred to above have not been fully accomplished and, in particular, that the unification of Korea has not yet been achieved, and that an attempt has been made by an armed attack from North Korea to extinguish by force the Government of the Republic of Korea,

Recalling the General Assembly declaration of 12 December 1948 that there has been established a lawful government (the Government of the Republic of Korea) having effective control and jurisdiction over that part of Korea where the United Nations Temporary Commission on Korea was able to observe and consult and in which the great majority of the people of Korea reside; that this government is based on elections which were a valid expression of the free will of the electorate of that part of Korea and which were observed by the Temporary Commission; and that this is the only such government in Korea,

Having in mind that United Nations armed forces are at present operating in Korea in accordance with the recommendations of the Security Council of 27 June 1950, subsequent to its resolution of 25 June 1950, that Members of the United Nations furnish such assistance to the Republic of Korea as may be necessary to repel the armed attack and to restore international peace and security in the area,

Recalling that the essential objective of the resolutions of the General Assembly referred to above was the establishment of a unified, independent and democratic Government of Korea,

1. *Recommends* that:
    (a) All appropriate steps be taken to ensure conditions of stability throughout Korea;
    (b) All constituent acts be taken, including the holding of elections, under the auspices of the United Nations, for the establishment of a unified, independent and democratic government in the sovereign State of Korea;
    (c) All sections and representative bodies of the population of Korea, South and North, be invited to co-operate with the organs of the United Nations in the restoration of peace, in the holding of elections and in the establishment of a unified government;
    (d) United Nations forces should not remain in any part of Korea otherwise than so far as necessary for achieving the objectives specified in sub-paragraphs *(a)* and *(b)* above;

(*e*) All necessary measures be taken to accomplish the economic rehabilitation of Korea:

2. *Resolves* that:

(*a*) A Commission consisting of Australia, Chile, Netherlands, Pakistan, Philippines, Thailand and Turkey, to be known as the United Nations Commission for the Unification and Rehabilitation of Korea, be established to (i) assume the functions hitherto exercised by the present United Nations Commission on Korea; (ii) represent the United Nations in bringing about the establishment of a unified, independent and democratic government of all Korea; (iii) exercise such responsibilities in connexion with relief and rehabilitation in Korea as may be determined by the General Assembly after receiving the recommendations of the Economic and Social Council. The United Nations Commission for the Unification and Rehabilitation of Korea should proceed to Korea and begin to carry out its functions as soon as possible;

(*b*) Pending the arrival in Korea of the United Nations Commission for the Unification and Rehabilitation of Korea, the governments of the States represented on the Commission should form an Interim Committee composed of representatives meeting at the seat of the United Nations to consult with and advise the United Nations Unified Command in the light of the above recommendations; the Interim Committee should begin to function immediately upon the approval of the present resolution by the General Assembly;

(*c*) The Commission shall render a report to the next regular session of the General Assembly and to any prior special session which might be called to consider the subject-matter of the present resolution, and shall render such interim reports as it may deem appropriate to the Secretary-General for transmission to Members;

The General Assembly furthermore,

Mindful of the fact that at the end of the present hostilities the task of rehabilitating the Korean economy will be of great magnitude,

3. *Requests* the Economic and Social Council, in consultation with the specialized agencies, to develop plans for relief and rehabilitation on the termination of hostilities and to report to the General Assembly within three weeks of the adoption of the present resolution by the General Assembly;

4. *Also recommends* the Economic and Social Council to expedite the study of long-term measures to promote the economic development and social progress of Korea, and meanwhile to draw the attention of the authorities which decide requests for technical assistance to the urgent and special necessity of affording such assistance to Korea;

5. *Expresses* its appreciation of the services rendered by the members of the United Nations Commission on Korea in the performance of their important and difficult task;

6. *Requests* the Secretary-General to provide the United Nations Commission for the Unification and Rehabilitation of Korea with adequate staff and facilities, including technical advisers as required; and authorizes the Secretary-General to pay the expenses and *per diem* of a representative and alternate from each of the States members of the Commission.

294th plenary meeting.
7 October 1950.

6. Security Council Resolution 88 of 8 November 1950

88 (1950). Resolution of 8 November 1950
[S/1892]
The Security Council,

Decides to invite, in accordance with rule 39 of the provisional rules of procedure, a representative of the Central People's Government of the People's Republic of China to be present during discussion by the Council of the special report of the United Nations Command in Korea.

Adopted at the 520th meeting
by 8 votes to 2 (China, Cuba),
with 1 abstention (Egypt).

7. General Assembly Resolution 384 (V) of 14 December 1950

384 (V). Intervention of the Central People's Government of the People's Republic of China in Korea

The General Assembly,

Viewing with grave concern the situation in the Far East,

Anxious that immediate steps should be taken to prevent the conflict in Korea spreading to other areas and to put an end to the fighting in Korea itself, and that further steps should then be taken for a peaceful settlement of existing issues in accordance with the Purposes and Principles of the United Nations,

Requests the President of the General Assembly to constitute a group of three persons, including himself, to determine the basis on which a satisfactory cease-fire in Korea can be arranged and to make recommendations to the General Assembly as soon as possible.

324th plenary meeting,
14 December 1950.

*

* *

The President of the General Assembly, at the 325th plenary meeting on 14 December 1950, announced the constitution of a group consisting of the following persons: Mr. L. B. Pearson (Canada), Sir Benegal Rau (India) and Mr. N. Entesam (Iran).

8. General Assembly Resolution 498 (V) of 1 February 1951

498 (V). Intervention of the Central People's Government of the People's Republic of China in Korea

(Resolution adopted on the report of the First Committee)

The General Assembly,

Noting that the Security Council, because of lack of animity of the permanent members, has failed to exercise its primary responsibility for the maintenance of international peace and security in regard to Chinese communist intervention in Korea,

Noting that the Central People's Government of the People's Republic of China has not accepted United Nations proposals to bring about a cessation of hostilities in Korea with a view to peaceful settlement, and that its armed forces continue their invasion of Korea and their large-scale attacks upon United Nations forces there.

1. *Finds* that the Central People's Government of the People's Republic of China, by giving direct aid and assistance to those who were already committing aggression in Korea and by engaging in hostilities against United Nations forces there, has itself engaged in aggression in Korea;

2. *Calls upon* the Central People's Government of the People's Republic of China to cause its forces and nationals in Korea to cease hostilities against the United Nations forces and to withdraw from Korea;

3. *Affirms* the determination of the United Nations to continue its action in Korea to meet the aggression;

4. *Calls upon* all States and authorities to continue to lend every assistance to the United Nations action in Korea;

5. *Calls upon* all States and authorities to refrain from giving any assistance to the aggressors in Korea;

6. *Requests* a Committee composed of the members of the Collective Measures Committee as a matter of urgency to consider additional measures to be employed to meet this aggression and to report thereon to the General Assembly, it being understood that the Committee is authorized to defer its report if

the Good Offices Committee referred to in the following paragraph reports satisfactory progress in its efforts;

7. *Affirms* that it continues to be the policy of the United Nations to bring about a cessation of hostilities in Korea and the achievement of United Nations objectives in Korea by peaceful means, and requests the President of the General Assembly to designate forthwith two persons who would meet with him at any suitable opportunity to use their good offices to this end.

327th plenary meeting,
1 February 1951.

*

*   *

The President of the General Assembly, on 19 February 1951, informed (A/1779) the members of the General Assembly that Dr. Luis Padilla Nervo (Mexico) and Mr. Sven Grafstrom (Sweden) had accepted his invitation to form with him the Good Offices Commitee, as provided in the above resolution.

9. General Assembly Resolution 500 (V) of 18 May 1951

500 (V). Additional measures to be employed to meet the aggression in Korea

(Resolution adopted on the report of the First Committee)

The General Assembly,

Noting the report of the Additional Measures Committee dated 14 May 1951,

Recalling its resolution 498 (V) of 1 February 1951,

Noting that:

(*a*) The Additional Measures Committee established by that resolution has considered additional measures to be employed to meet the aggression in Korea,

(*b*) The Additional Measures Committee has reported that a number of States have already taken measures designed to deny contributions to the military strength of the forces opposing the United Nations in Korea,

(c) The Additional Measures Committee has also reported that certain economic measures designed further to deny such contributions would support and supplement the military action of the United Nations in Korea and would assist in putting an end to the aggression,

1. *Recommends* that every State:

(a) Apply an embargo on the shipment to areas under the control of the Central People's Government of the People's Republic of China and of the North Korean authorities of arms, ammunition and implements of war, atomic energy materials, petroleum, transportation materials of strategic value, and items useful in the production of arms, ammunition and implements of war;

(b) Determine which commodities exported from its territory fall within the embargo, and apply controls to give effect to the embargo;

(c) Prevent by all means within its jurisdiction the circumvention of controls on shipments applied by other States pursuant to the present resolution;

(d) Co-operate with other States in carrying out the purposes of this embargo;

(e) Report to the Additional Measures Committee, within thirty days and thereafter at the request of the Committee, on the measures taken in accordance with the present resolution;

2. *Requests* the Additional Measures Committee:

(a) To report to the General Assembly, with recommendations as appropriate, on the general effectiveness of the embargo and the desirability of continuing, extending or relaxing it;

(b) To continue its consideration of additional measures to be employed to meet the aggression in Korea, and to report thereon further to the General Assembly, it being understood that the Committee is authorized to defer its report if the Good Offices Committee reports satisfactory progress in its efforts;

3. *Reaffirms* that it continues to be the policy of the United Nations to bring about a cessation of hostilities in Korea, and the achievement of United Nations objectives in Korea by peaceful means, and requests the Good Offices Committee to continue its good offices.

10. General Assembly 507 (VI) of 5 February 1952

507 (VI). The problem of the independence of Korea: report of the United Nations Commission for the Unification and Rehabilitation of Korea

Relief and rehabilitation of Korea: report of the United Nations Agent General for Korean Reconstruction

The General Assembly,

Desiring to facilitate to the greatest possible extent the negotiations in Panmunjom and the conclusion of an armistice in Korea, and

Wishing to avoid premature consideration of items 17 and 27 of the agenda of the present session,

I

Decides that:

(*a*) Upon notification by the Unified Command to the Security Council of the conclusion of an armistice in Korea, the Secretary-General shall convene a special session of the General Assembly at the Headquarters of the United Nations to consider the above-mentioned items; or

(*b*) When other developments in Korea make desirable consideration of the above-mentioned items, the Secretary-General, acting in accordance with Article 20 of the Charter and with the rules of procedure of the General Assembly, shall convene a special session or an emergency special session of the General Assembly at the Headquarters of the United Nations;

II

Requests the Negotiating Committee for Extra-Budgetary Funds established by General Assembly resolution 571 B (VI) of 7 December 1951 to undertake negotiations regarding voluntary contributions to the programme of the United Nations Korean Reconstruction Agency for the relief and rehabilitation of Korea.

375th plenary meeting,
5 February 1952.

11. General Assembly Resolution 610 (VII) of 3 December 1952

610 (VII). Korea: reports of the United Nations Commission for the Unification and Rehabilitation of Korea

The General Assembly,

Having received the special report of the United Nations Command of 18 October 1952 on "the present status of the military action and the armistice negotiations in Korea" and other relevant reports relating to Korea,

Noting with approval the considerable progress towards an armistice made by negotiation at Panmunjom and the tentative agreements to end the fighting in Korea and to reach a settlement of the Korean question,

Noting further that disagreement between the parties on one remaining issue, alone, prevents the conclusion of an armistice and that a considerable measure of agreement already exists on the principles on which this remaining issue can be resolved,

Mindful of the continuing and vast loss of life, devastation and suffering resulting from and accompanying the continuance of the fighting,

Deeply conscious of the need to bring hostilities to a speedy end and of the need for a peaceful settlement of the Korean question,

Anxious to expedite and facilitate the convening of the political conference as provided in article 60 of the draft armistice agreement,

1. *Affirms* that the release and repatriation of prisoners of war shall be effected in accordance with the Geneva Convention relative to

the Treatment of Prisoners of War, dated 12 August 1949, the well-established principles and practice of international law and the relevant provisions of the draft armistice agreement;

2. *Affirms* that force shall not be used against prisoners of war to prevent or effect their return to their homelands, and that they shall at all time be treated humanely in accordance with the specific provisions of the Geneva Convention and with the general spirit of the Convention;

3. *Accordingly requests* the President of the General Assembly to communicate the following proposals to the Central People's Government of the People's Republic of China and to the North Korean authorities as forming a just and reasonable basis for an agreement so that an immediate cease-fire would result and be effected; to invite their acceptance of these proposals and to make a report to the General Assembly during its present session and as soon as appropriate:

PROPOSALS

I. In order to facilitate the return to their homelands of all prisoners of war, there shall be established a Repatriation Commission consisting of representatives of Czechoslovakia, Poland, Sweden and Switzerland, that is, the four States agreed to for the constitution of the Neutral Nations Supervisory Commission and referred to in paragraph 37 of the draft armistice agreement, or constituted, alternatively, of representatives of four States not participating in hostilities, two nominated by each side, but excluding representatives of States that are permanent members of the Security Council.

II. The release and repatriation of prisoners of war shall be effected in accordance with the Geneva Convention relative to the Treatment of Prisoners of War, dated 12 August 1949, the well-established principles and practice of International Law and the relevant provisions of the draft armistice agreement.

III. Force shall not be used against the prisoners of war to prevent or effect their return to their homelands and no violence to their persons or affront to their dignity or self-respect shall be permitted in any manner or for any purpose whatsoever. This duty is enjoined on and entrusted to the Repatriation Commission and each of its members. Prisoners of war shall at all times be treated humanely in accordance with the specific provisions of the Geneva Convention and with the general spirit of that Convention.

IV. All prisoners of war shall be released to the Repatriation Commission from military control and from the custody of the detaining side in agreed numbers and at agreed exchange points in agreed demilitarized zones.

V. Classification of prisoners of war according to nationality and domicile as proposed in the letter of 16 October 1952 from General Kim II Sung, Supreme Commander of the Korean People's Army, and General Peng Teh-huai, Commander of the Chinese People's Volunteers, to General Mark W. Clark, Commander-in-Chief, United Nations Command, shall then be carried out immediately.

VI. After classification, prisoners of war shall be free to return to their homelands forthwith, and their speedy return shall be facilitated by all parties concerned.

VII. In accordance with arrangements prescribed for the purpose by the Repatriation Commission, each party to the conflict shall have freedom and facilities to explain to the prisoners of war "depending upon them" their rights and to inform the prisoners of war on any matter relating to their return to their homelands and particularly their full freedom to return.

VIII. Red Cross teams of both sides shall assist the Repatriation Commission in its work and shall have access, in accordance with the terms of the draft armistice agreement, to prisoners of war while they are under the temporary jurisdiction of the Repatriation Commission.

IX. Prisoners of war shall have freedom and facilities to make representations and communications to the Repatriation Commission and to bodies and agencies working under the Repatriation Commission, and to inform any or all such bodies of their desires on any matter concerning themselves, in accordance with arrangements made for the purpose by the Commission.

X. Notwithstanding the provisions of paragraph III above, nothing in this Repatriation Agreement shall be construed as derogating from the authority of the Repatriation Commission (or its authorized representatives) to exercise its legitimate functions and responsibilities for the control of the prisoners under its temporary jurisdiction.

XI. The terms of this Repatriation Agreement and the arrangements arising therefrom shall be made known to all prisoners of war.

XII. The Repatriation Commission is entitled to call upon parties to the conflict, its own member governments, or the Member States of the United Nations for such legitimate assistance as it may require in the carrying out of its duties and tasks and in accordance with the decisions of the Commission in this respect.

XIII. When the two sides have made an agreement for repatriation based on these proposals, the interpretation of that agreement shall rest with the Repatriation Commission. In the event of disagreement in the Commission, majority decisions shall prevail. When no majority decision is possible, an umpire agreed upon in accordance with the succeeding paragraph and with article 132 of the Geneva Convention of 1949 shall have the deciding vote.

XIV. The Repatriation Commission shall at its first meeting and prior to an armistice proceed to agree upon and appoint the umpire who shall at all times be available to the Commission and shall act as its Chairman unless otherwise agreed. If agreement on the appointment of the umpire cannot be reached by the Commission within the period of three weeks after the date of the first meeting this matter should be referred to the General Assembly.

XV. The Repatriation Commission shall also arrange after the armistice for officials to function as umpires with inspecting teams or other bodies to which functions are delegated or assigned by the Commission or under the provisions of the draft armistice agreement, so that the completion of the return of prisoners of war to their homelands shall be expedited.

XVI. When the Repatriation Agreement is acceded to by the parties concerned and when an umpire has been appointed under paragraph 14 above, the draft armistice agreement, unless otherwise altered by agreement between the parties, shall be deemed to have been accepted by them. The provisions of the draft armistice agreement shall apply except in so far as they are modified by the Repatriation Agreement. Arrangements for repatriation under this agreement will begin when the armistice agreement is thus concluded.

XVII. At the end of ninety days, after the Armistice Agreement has been signed, the disposition of any prisoners of war whose return to their homelands may not have been effected in accordance with the procedure set out in these proposals or as otherwise agreed, shall be referred with recommendations for their disposition, including a target date for the termination of their detention to the political conference to be called as provided under article 60 of the draft armistice agreement. If at the end of a further thirty days there are any prisoners of war whose return to their homelands has not been effected under the above procedures or whose future has not been provided for by the political conference, the responsibility for their care and maintenance and for their subsequent disposition shall be transferred to the United Nations, which in all matters relating to them shall act strictly in accordance with international law.

399th plenary meeting,
3 December 1952.

12. General Assembly Resolution 701 (VII) of 11 March 1953

701 (VII). Korea: reports of the United Nations Agent General for Korean Reconstruction

The General Assembly,

1. Reaffirms the objective of the United Nations, adopted in General Assembly resolution 410 (V) of 1 December 1950, to provide relief and rehabilitation in assisting the Korean people to relieve their sufferings and to repair the great devastation and destruction in their country;

2. *Recognizes* that the need of such relief and rehabilitation continues to be most urgent;

3. *Takes* note of the reports of the Agent General on the work of the United Nations Korean Reconstruction Agency for the period February 1951 to 15 February 1953;

4. *Notes with approval* that the Agent General has now undertaken, in co-operation with the Government of the Republic of Korea and the United Nations Command, and in consultation with the United Nations Commission for the Unification and Rehabilitation of Korea, a programme of relief and rehabilitation projects for the period ending June 1953, which has received the approval of the United Nations Advisory Committee to the Agent General, and looks forward to its successful execution;

5. *Expresses its appreciation* of the contributions which have been made by governments, specialized agencies and non-governmental organizations;

6. *Requests* those governments which have made pledges to the United Nations Korean Reconstruction Agency to make prompt payment of such pledges;

7. *Further requests* all governments, specialized agencies and non-governmental organizations to assist, within the limits of their financial possibilities and in accordance with the provisions of their constitutions and statutes, in meeting the great and continuing need of the Korean people for relief and rehabilitation assistance.

414th plenary meeting,
11 March 1953.

13. General Assembly Resolution 706 (VII) of 23 April 1953

706 (VII). Question of impartial investigation of charges of use by United Nations Forces of bacteriological warfare

The General Assembly,

Noting that accusations have been made by certain governments and authorities charging the use of bacteriological warfare by United Nations Forces, and that the Unified Command has repeatedly denied such charges,

Recalling that when the charges were first made the Unified Command had requested that an impartial investigation be made of them,

Noting that the Central People's Government of the People's Republic of China and the North Korean authorities have so far refused to accept an offer by the International Committee of the Red Cross to carry out an investigation,

Noting that the draft resolution submitted in the Security Council by the Government of the United States of America proposing an investigation of these charges by the International Committee of the Red Cross failed to carry because of the negative vote of the Union of Soviet Socialist Republics,

Desiring to serve the interests of truth,

1. *Resolves* that, after the President of the General Assembly has received an indication from all the governments and authorities concerned of their acceptance of the investigation proposed in the present resolution, a Commission, composed of Brazil, Egypt, Pakistan, Sweden and Uruguay, shall be set up and shall carry out immediately an investigation of the charges that have been made;

2. *Calls upon* the governments and authorities concerned to enable the Commission to travel freely throughout such areas of North and South Korea, the Chinese mainland and Japan as the Commission may deem necessary in the performance of its task and to allow the Commission freedom of access to such persons, places and relevant documents as it considers necessary for the fulfilment of its task and to allow it to examine any witness, including prisoners of war, under such safeguards and conditions as the Commission shall determine: all prisoners of war who are alleged to have made confessions regarding the use of bacteriological warfare shall, prior to examination by the Commission, be taken to a neutral area and remain under the responsibility and custody of the Commission until the end of the Korean hostilities;

3. *Requests* the President of the General Assembly to transmit the present resolution immediately to the governments and authorities concerned, requesting them to indicate their acceptance of the investigation proposed in the present resolution;

4. *Requests* the President of the General Assembly to report to the General Assembly at the earliest practicable date on the results of his efforts;

5. *Directs* the Commission, when set up, to enlist the aid of such scientists of international reputation, especially epidemiologists, and such other experts as it may select;

6. *Directs* the Commission, after acceptance of the investigation proposed in the present resolution by all the governments and authorities concerned, to report to the Members of the General Assembly through the Secretary-General as soon possible and no later than 1 September 1953;

7. *Requests* the Secretary-General to furnish the Commission with the necessary staff and facilities.

428th plenary meeting,
23 April 1953.

14. General Assembly Resolution 705 (VII) of 18 April 1953

705 (VII). The Korean question

The General Assembly,

Reaffirming its unswerving determination to spare no efforts likely to create conditions favourable to the attainment of the purposes of peace and conciliation embodied in the Charter of the United Nations,

Noting, following the United Nations Command initiative for the exchange of sick and wounded prisoners of war, the communication by the Minister for Foreign Affairs of the Central People's Government of the People's Republic of China dated 31 March 1953 to the President of the General Assembly, and the exchange of communications between the United Nations Command and the Commanders of the Chinese People's Volunteers and the Korean People's Army in regard thereto,

Confident that a just and honourable armistice in Korea will powerfully contribute to alleviate the present international tension,

1. *Notes with deep satisfaction* that an agreement has been signed in Korea on the exchange of sick and wounded prisoners of war;

2. *Expresses the hope* that the exchange of sick and wounded prisoners of war will be speedily completed and that the further negotiations at Panmunjom will result in achieving an early armistice in Korea, consistent with the United Nations principles and objectives;

3. *Decides* to recess the present session upon completion of the current agenda items, and requests the President of the General Assembly to reconvene the present session to resume consideration of the Korean question (*a*) upon notification by the Unified Command to the Security Council of the signing of an armistice agreement in Korea; or (*b*) when, in the view of a majority of Members, other developments in Korea require consideration of this question.

427th plenary meeting,
18 April 1953.

15. General Assembly Resolution 711 (VII) of 28 August 1953

711 (VII). The Korean question

A

IMPLEMENTATATION OF PARAGRAPH 60 OF THE KOREAN ARMISTICE AGREEMENT

The General Assembly:

1. *Notes with approval* the Armistice Agreement concluded in Korea on 27 July 1953, the fact that the fighting has ceased, and that a major step has thus been taken towards the full restoration of international peace and security in the area;

2. *Reaffirms* that the objectives of the United Nations remain the achievement by peaceful means of a unified, independent and democratic Korea under a representative form of government and the full restoration of international peace and security in the area;

3. *Notes* the recommendation contained in the Armistice Agreement that "In Order to ensure the peaceful settlement of the Korean question, the military Commanders of both sides hereby recommend to the governments of the countries concerned on both sides that, within three (3) months after the Armistice Agreement is signed and becomes effective, a political conference of a higher level

of both sides be held by representatives appointed respectively to settle through negotiation the questions of the withdrawal of all foreign forces from Korea, the peaceful settlement of the Korean question, etc."

4. *Welcomes* the holding of such a conference:

5. *Recommends* that:

(*a*) The side contributing armed forces under the Unified Command in Korea shall have as participants of in the conference those among the Member States contributing armed forces pursuant to the call of the United Nations which desire to be represented, together with the Republic of Korea. The participating governments shall act independently at the conference with full freedom of action and shall be bound only by decision or agreements to which they adhere;

(*b*) The United States Government, after consultation with the other participating countries referred to in sub-paragraph (*a*) above, shall arrange with the other side for the political conference to be held as soon as possible, but not later than 28 October 1953, at a place and on a date satisfactory to both sides;

(*c*) The Secretary-General of the United Nations shall, if this is agreeable to both sides, provide the political conference with such services and facilities as may be feasible;

(*d*) The Member States participating pursuant to sub-paragraph (*a*) above shall inform the United Nations when agreement is reached at the conference and keep the United Nations informed at other appropriate times;

6. *Reaffirms* its intention to carry out its programme for relief and rehabilitation in Korea, and appeals to the governments of all Member States to contribute to this task.

430th plenary meeting,
28 August 1953.

B

The General Assembly,

Having adopted the resolution entitled "Implementation of paragraph 60 of the Korean Armistice Agreement",

Recommends that the Union of Soviet Socialist Republics participate in the Korean political conference provided the other side desires it.

430th plenary meeting,
28 August 1953.

C

The General Assembly,

Requests the Secretary-General to communicate the proposals on the Korean question submitted to the resumed meetings of the seventh session and recommended by the Assembly, together with the records of the relevant proceedings of the General Assembly, to the Central People's Government of the People's Republic of China and to the Government of the People's Democratic Republic of Korea and to report as appropriate.

430th plenary meeting,
28 August 1953.

16. General Assembly Resolution 712 (VII) of 28 August 1953

712 (VII). Tribute to the armed forces who have fought in Korea to resist aggression and uphold the cause of freedom and peace

The General Assembly,

Recalling the resolutions of the Security Council of 25 June, 27 June and 7 July 1950 and the resolution of the General Assembly of 7 October 1950, 1 December 1950, 1 February 1951, 18 May 1951 and 3 December 1952,

Having received the report of the Unified Command dated 7 August 1953,

Noting with profound satisfaction that fighting has now ceased in Korea on the basis of an honourable armistice,

1. *Salutes* the heroic soldiers of the Republic of Korea and of all those countries which sent armed forces to its assistance;
2. *Pays tribute* to all those who died in resisting aggression and thus in upholding the cause of freedom and peace;

3. *Expresses its satisfaction* that the first efforts pursuant to the call of the United Nations to repel armed aggression by collective military measures have been successful, and expresses its firm conviction that this proof of the effectiveness of collective security under the United Nations Charter will contribute to the maintenance of international peace and security.

431st plenary meeting,
28 August 1953.

17. General Assembly Resolution 714 (VIII) of 3 November 1953

714 (VIII). Question of impartial investigation of charges of use by United Nations forces of bacterial warfare

The General Assembly,

1. *Refers* to the Disarmament Commission the draft resolution of the Union of Soviet Socialist Republics contained in document A/C.1/L.67 for such consideration as deemed appropriate under its plan of work and pursuant to the terms of reference of that Commission as set forth in General Assembly resolutions 502 (VI) of 11 January 1952 and 704 (VII) of 8 April 1953;

2. *Decides* also to transmit to the Disarmament Commission for its information the records of the meetings of the First Committee at which this item was discussed.

456th plenary meeting,
3 November 1953.

18. General Assembly Resolution 804 (VIII) of 3 December 1953

804 (VIII). Question of atrocities committed by the North Korean and Chinese Communist forces against United Nations prisoners of war in Korea

The General Assembly,

Having considered the item "Question of atrocities committed by the North Korean and Chinese Communist forces against United Nations prisoners of war in Korea" proposed by the United States of America in documents A/2531 and A/2531/Add. 1 of 30 and 31 October 1953,

Recalling that basic legal requirements for humane treatment of prisoners of war and civilians in connexion with the conduct of hostilities are established by general international law and find authoritative reaffirmation in the Geneva Conventions of 1929 and 1949 relative to the treatment of prisoners of war and in the Geneva Convention of 1949 relative to the protection of civilian persons in time of war,

Recalling that these Conventions also embody precise and detailed provisions for giving effect to the basic legal requirements referred to above, and that these provisions, to the extent that they have not become binding as treaty law, have been accorded most general support by the international community,

Desiring to secure general and full observance of the requirements of international law and of universal standards of human decency,

1. *Expresses its grave concern* at reports and information that North Korean and Chinese Communist forces have, in a large number of instances, employed inhuman practices against the heroic soldiers of forces under the United Nations Command in Korea and against the civilian population of Korea;

2. *Condemns* the commission by any governments or authorities of murder, mutilation, torture, and other atrocious acts against captured military personnel or civilian populations, as a violation of rules of international law and basic standards of conduct and morality and as affronting human rights and the dignity and worth of the human person.

467th plenary meeting,
3 December 1953.

19. General Assembly Resolution 716 (VIII) of 8 December 1953

716 (VIII). The Korean question

The General Assembly

1. *Resolves* that the eighth session of the General Assembly stand recessed;

2. *Requests* the President of the General Assembly to reconvene the eighth session, with the concurrence of the majority of Member States, if (*a*) in the President's opinion developments in respect of the Korean question warrant such reconvening, or (*b*) one or more Member States make a request to the President for such reconvening by reason of developments in respect of the Korean question.

470th plenary meeting,
8 December 1953.

20. General Assembly Resolution 811 (IX) of 11 December 1954

811 (IX). The Korean question

The General Assembly,

Having noted the report of the United Nations Commission for the Unification and Rehabilitation of Korea signed at Seoul, Korea, on 17 August 1954,

Having received the report on the Korean Political Conference held in Geneva from 26 April to 15 June 1954, in pursuance of General Assembly resolution 711 (VII) of 28 August 1953,

Noting that the negotiations in Geneva have not resulted in agreement on a final settlement of the Korean question in accordance with the United Nations objectives in Korea,

Recognizing that these objectives should be achieved by peaceful methods and by constructive efforts on the part of the Governments concerned,

Noting that paragraph 62 of the Armistice Agreement of 27 July 1953 provides that the Agreement "shall remain in effect until expressly superseded either by mutually acceptable amendments and additions or by provision in an appropriate agreement for a peaceful settlement at a political level between both sides",

1. *Approves* the report on the Korean Political Conference;

2. *Reaffirms* that the objectives of the United Nations remain the achievement by peaceful means of a unified, independent and democratic Korea under a representative form of government and the full restoration of international peace and security in the area;

3. *Expresses the hope* that it will soon prove possible to make progress towards these objectives;

4. *Requests* the Secretary-General to place the item on the provisional agenda of its tenth, session.

510th plenary meeting,
11 December 1954.

NOTES

Introduction

1. The Commonwealth of Nations has been the official title of the former British Commonwealth of Nations since 1949 but will be referred to simply as the Commonwealth throughout this book.
2. Stueck, William, *The Korean War: An International History* (Princeton, 1995), pp. 54–61, 88–96, 138–42, 151–57, 162–66, 170–74 189–99, 253–58, 292–306; Stueck, William, *Rethinking the Korean War: A New Diplomatic and Strategic History* (Woodstock, 2002), pp. 62–65, 99–100, 125–29, 170–71.
3. Stueck: *The Korean War*, pp. 70–78, 83–84, 130–2, 136–38, 148–51, 184–87, 199–203, 210–16, 238–41, 283–92, 320–25; Stueck: *Rethinking the Korean War*, pp. 98–100, 124–27, 131–37, 216–30; Stueck, William, 'The limits of influence: British policy and American expansion of the war in Korea', *Pacific Historical Review* 55:1 (1986), pp. 69–95.
4. Foot, Rosemary, 'Anglo-American relations in the Korean crisis: the British effort to avert an expanded war, December 1950–January 1951', *Diplomatic History* 10:1 (1986), pp. 43–57; Foot, Rosemary, *A Substitute for Victory: The Politics of Peacemaking at the Korean Armistice Talks* (Ithaca, 1990), pp. 2–8, 20–33, 65–67, 79–80, 92–93, 132–35, 152–57, 171–75, 193–95, 201–04; Foot, Rosemary, 'Negotiating with friends and enemies: the politics of peacemaking in Korea', in C.B. Kim and J. Matray (eds), *Korea and the Cold War: Division, Destruction, and Disarmament* (Claremont, 1993), pp. 193–208; Foot, Rosemary, 'Nuclear coercion and the ending of the Korean conflict', *International Security* 13:3 (1988/9), pp. 92–112; Foot, Rosemary, *The Wrong War: American Policy and the Dimensions of the Korean Conflict, 1950–1953* (Ithaca, 1985), pp. 15–19, 53–61, 67–69, 84–85, 91–94, 110–17, 145–55, 166–75, 178–86, 198–201, 215–19.

5. Farrar-Hockley, Anthony, *The British Part in the Korean War*, vol. I, *A Distant Obligation* (London, 1990); Farrar-Hockley, Anthony, *The British Part in the Korean War*, vol. II, *An Honourable Discharge* (London, 1995).

6. MacDonald, Callum, *Britain and the Korean War* (Oxford, 1990).

7. Lowe, Peter, 'An ally and a recalcitrant general: Great Britain, Douglas MacArthur and the Korean War, 1950–1', *English Historical Review* 105:416 (1990), pp. 624–53; Lowe, Peter, *Containing the Cold War in East Asia: British policies towards Japan, China and Korea, 1948–1953* (Manchester, 1997), pp. 167–269; Lowe, Peter, 'Great Britain, Japan, and the Korean War, 1950–1951', *Proceedings of the British Association for Japanese Studies* 9 (1984), pp. 98–111; Lowe, Peter, 'Hopes frustrated: the impact of the Korean War upon Britain's relations with communist China, 1950–1953', in T.G. Fraser and K. Jeffery (eds), *Men, Women and War* (Dublin, 1993), pp. 211–26; Lowe, Peter, 'The frustrations of alliance: Britain, the United States, and the Korean War, 1950–1951', in J. Cotton and I. Neary (eds), *The Korean War in History* (Manchester, 1989), pp. 80–99; Lowe, Peter, 'The settlement of the Korean War', in J. Young (ed.), *The Foreign Policy of Churchill's Peacetime Administration, 1951–1955* (Leicester, 1988), pp. 207–31.

8. Dockrill, Michael, 'The Foreign Office, Anglo-American relations, and the Korean War, June 1950–June 1951', *International Affairs* 62:3 (1986), pp. 459–76; Dockrill, Michael, 'The Foreign Office, Anglo-American relations and the Korean truce negotiations, July 1951–July 1953', in J. Cotton and I. Neary (eds), *The Korean War in History* (Manchester, 1989), pp. 100–19.

9. Stairs, Denis, *The Diplomacy of Constraint: Canada, the Korean War, and the United States* (Toronto, 1974).

10. Melady, John, *Korea: Canada's Forgotten War* (Toronto, 1998).

11. O'Neill, Robert, *Australia in the Korean War, 1950–53*, vol. I, *Strategy and Diplomacy* (Canberra, 1991); O'Neill, Robert, *Australia in the Korean War, 1950–53*, vol. II, *Combat Operations* (Canberra, 1995).

12. McCormack, Gavan, *Cold War, Hot War: An Australian Perspective on the Korean War* (Sydney, 1983).

13. McGibbon, Ian, *New Zealand and the Korean War*, vol. I, *Politics and Diplomacy* (Auckland, 1992); McGibbon, Ian, *New Zealand and the Korean War*, vol. II, *Combat Operations* (Auckland, 1996).

14. Dayal, Shiv, *India's Role in the Korean Question: A Study in the Settlement of International Disputes under the United Nations* (Delhi, 1959).

15. Hall, H. Duncan, *Commonwealth: A History of the British Commonwealth of Nations* (London, 1971), pp. 604–05, 654–58, 763–879.

16. Walker, Patrick Gordon, *The Commonwealth* (London, 1962), pp. 45–56, 165–94, 197–252, 255–329.

17. Ovendale, Ritchie, *The English-Speaking Alliance: Britain, the United States, the Dominions and the Cold War, 1945–1951* (London, 1985), pp. 3–21, 211–38, 273–78.

18. Thornton, A.P., 'The transformation of the Commonwealth and the "special relationship"', in H. Bull and W.M.R. Louis (eds), *The Special Relationship: Anglo-American Relations since 1945* (Oxford, 1986), pp. 365–78.
19. Mount, Graeme, with Laferriere, Andre, *The Diplomacy of War: The Case for Korea* (Montreal, 2004).
20. Luard, Evan, *A History of the United Nations*, vol. I: *The Years of Western Domination, 1945–1955* (London, 1982), pp. 229–74.
21. Kennedy, Paul, *Parliament of Man: The United Nations and the Quest for World Government* (London, 2006), pp. 51–112.
22. Maurice, Bertrand, *The United Nations: Past, Present and Future* (The Hague, 1997), pp. 37–45, 60–64.
23. Yoo, Tae-Ho, *The Korean War and the United Nations: A Legal and Diplomatic Historical Study* (Louvain, 1965), pp. 23–81, 177–81.
24. Goodrich, Leland, *Korea: A Study of US Policy in the United Nations* (New York, 1956), pp. 102–213.

Prologue

1. For broad accounts of the international and peninsula origins of the Korean War see, for instance, Dobbs, Charles, *The Unwanted Symbol: American Foreign Policy, the Cold War, and Korea, 1945–1950* (Kent, 1981); Lowe, Peter, *The Origins of the Korean War* (London, 1986); Matray, James, 'Civil war of a sort: the international origins of the Korean conflict', in D. Meador and J. Monroe (eds), *The Korean War in Retrospect: Lessons for the Future* (Lanham, 1998), pp. 3–35; Matray, James, *Reluctant Crusade: American Foreign Policy in Korea, 1941–1950* (Honolulu, 1985); Merrill, John, *Korea: The Peninsular Origins of the War* (Newark, 1989); Millett, Allan, *The War for Korea, 1945–1950: A House Burning* (Lawrence, 2006); Stueck, William, 'Cold War revisionism and the origins of the Korean War: the Kolko thesis', *Pacific Historical Review* 42:4 (1973), pp. 537–60.
2. For more on wartime planning for Korea see, for instance, Matray, James, 'An end to indifference: America's Korean policy during World War II', *Diplomatic History* 2:2 (1979), pp. 181–96; Stueck, William, *The Road to Confrontation: American Policy Toward China and Korea, 1947–1950* (Chapel Hill, 1981), pp. 19–22; Stueck, William, 'The United States, the Soviet Union, and the division of Korea: a comparative approach', *Journal of American-East Asia Relations* 4:1 (1975), pp. 1–27.
3. For more on the US and Soviet occupations see, for instance, Armstrong, Charles, *The North Korean Revolution, 1945–1950* (Ithaca, 2003), pp. 35–214; Cumings, Bruce, *The Origins of the Korean War*, vol. I, *Liberation and the Emergence of Separate Regimes, 1945–1947* (Princeton, 1981), pp. 135–427; Matray, James, 'Hodge podge: American occupation policy in Korea, 1945–1948', *Korean Studies* 19 (1975), pp. 17–38; Stueck, William, and Yi, Boram, '"An alliance forged in blood": the American occupation of Korea, the Korean War,

and the US–South Korean alliance', *Journal of Strategic Studies* 33:2 (2010), pp. 177–209; Stueck: *The Road to Confrontation*, pp. 22–8.

4. For more on Korean developments between 1947–1950 see, for instance, Cumings, Bruce, *The Origins of the Korean War*, vol. II, *The Roaring of the Cataract, 1947–1950* (Princeton, 1990); McGlothlen, Ronald, 'Acheson, economics and the American commitment in Korea, 1947–1950', *Pacific Historical Review* 58:1 (1989), pp. 23–54; Stueck: *The Road to Confrontation*, pp. 75–110, 153–75.

5. For more on the creation of the PRC and its relations with the United States and the Soviet Union in 1949–50 see, for instance, Chen, Jian, 'The myth of America's "lost chance" in China: a Chinese perspective in light of new evidence', *Diplomatic History* 21:1 (1997), pp. 77–86; Heinzig, Dieter, *The Soviet Union and Communist China 1945–1950: The Arduous Road to the Alliance* (Armonk, NY, 2004), pp. 126–384; McLean, David, 'American nationalism, the China myth, and the Truman doctrine: the question of accommodation with Peking, 1949–1950', *Diplomatic History* 10:1 (1986), pp. 25–42; Niu, Jun, 'The birth of the People's Republic of China and the road to the Korean War', in M. Leffler and O. Westad (eds), *The Cambridge History of the Cold War*, vol. 1 (Cambridge, 2010), pp. 231–36; Niu, Jun, 'The origins of the Sino-Soviet alliance', in O. Westad (ed.), *Brothers in Arms: The Rise and Fall of the Sino-Soviet Alliance, 1945–1963* (Stanford, 1998), pp. 69–74; Westad, O., *Decisive Encounters: The Chinese Civil War, 1946–1950* (Stanford, 2003), pp. 297–315; Westad, O., 'Introduction', in O. Westad (ed.), *Brothers in Arms: The Rise and Fall of the Sino-Soviet Alliance, 1945–1963* (Stanford, 1998), pp. 7–12.

6. For more on this phase of the First Indochina War see, for instance, Dalloz, Jacques, *The War in Indochina, 1945–54* (Dublin, 1990), pp. 129–32; Chen, Jian, 'China and the First Indochina War', *China Quarterly* 133 (1993), pp. 86–91; Rotter, Andrew, *The Path to Vietnam: Origins of the American Commitment to Southeast Asia* (London, 1987), pp. 172–203; Short, Anthony, *The Origins of the Vietnam War* (London, 1989), pp. 75–84.

7. For more on this phase of the Malayan Emergency see, for instance, Jackson, Robert, *The Malayan Emergency: The Commonwealth's War, 1948–1966* (London, 1990), pp. 31–34; Ramakrishna, Kumar, *Emergency Propaganda: The Winning of Malayan Hearts and Minds, 1948–1958* (Richmond, 2001), pp. 87–89; Short, Anthony, *The Communist Insurrection in Malaya, 1948–1960* (London, 1975), pp. 206–41.

8. For more on the Communist decision to invade South Korea see, for instance, Bajanov, Evgueni, 'Assessing the politics of the Korean War, 1949–51', *Cold War International History Project Bulletin* 6–7 (1995/96), pp. 54, 87–91; Goncharov, Sergei, Lewis, John and Xue, Litai, *Uncertain Partners: Stalin, Mao, and the Korean War* (Stanford, 1993), pp. 130–54; Simmons, Robert, *The Strained Alliance: Peking, Pyongyang, Moscow, and the Politics of the Korean Civil War* (New York, 1975), pp. 102–30; Weathersby, Kathryn, 'Soviet aims in Korea and the origins of the Korean War, 1945–1950: new evidence from

Russian archives', *Cold War International History Project Working Paper* 8 (1993), pp. 5–37; Weathersby, Kathryn, 'The Soviet role in the early phase of the Korean War: new documentary evidence', *Journal of American-East Asian Relations* 2:4 (1993), pp. 425–58; Weathersby, Kathryn, 'To attack or not to attack? Stalin, Kim Il Sung, and the prelude to war', *Cold War International History Project Bulletin* 5 (1995), pp. 1–9; Shen, Zhihua, 'Sino-Soviet relations and the origins of the Korean War: Stalin's strategic goals in the Far East', *Journal of Cold War Studies* 2:2 (2000), pp. 44–68.

9. For more on the Truman administration's decision to intervene in the Korean War see, for instance, Bernstein, Barton, 'The week we went to war: American intervention in the Korean civil war', *Foreign Service Journal* 54:1 (1977), pp. 6–12; Gaddis, John, *The Long Peace: Inquiries into the History of the Cold War* (New York, 1987), pp. 72–103; James, D. Clayton with Wells, Anne, *Refighting the Last War: Command and Crisis in Korea, 1950–1953* (New York, 1993), pp. 11–16, 131–57; Kaufman, Burton, *The Korean War: Challenges in Crisis, Credibility, and Command*, 2nd edn (Westport, 1999), pp. 21–27; Paige, Glenn, *The Korean Decision, June 24–30, 1950* (New York, 1968); Stueck: *The Korean War*, pp. 41–44; Stueck: *Rethinking the Korean War*, pp. 81–82; Stueck: *The Road to Confrontation*, pp. 177–95.

10. For Truman's views of the UN see, for instance, Donovan, Robert, *Conflict and Crisis: The Presidency of Harry S. Truman, 1945–1948* (New York, 1977), pp. 13, 39, 49–50, 54–55; Donovan, Robert, *Tumultuous Years: The Presidency of Harry S. Truman, 1949–1953* (New York, 1982), pp. 199–203, 208, 218; Truman, Harry, *Memoirs*, vol. 1, *Year of Decisions, 1945* (New York, 1955), pp. 11, 98–99, 192–219; Truman, Harry, *Memoirs*, vol. 2, *Years of Trial and Hope, 1946–1953* (New York, 1956), pp. 167, 227–28, 241, 264, 380.

11. For Acheson's views of the UN see, for instance, Beisner, Robert, *Dean Acheson: A Life in the Cold War* (New York, 2006), pp. 51–52, 121, 128–34, 529–33, 625–26, 651; Chace, James, *Acheson: The Secretary of State Who Created the American World* (New York, 1998), pp. 107–08; McLellan, David, *Dean Acheson: The State Department Years* (New York, 1976), pp. 49–52, 65, 275, 306, 407.

12. *HST* Communication Artifacts, Bess Wallace Truman Estate, IX H3 Box 4, 85.219.1603.

13. For good accounts of the post-war evolution and nature of the Commonwealth see, Hall: *Commonwealth*, pp. 639–40, 649–54, 763–879; Thornton, A.P.: 'The transformation of the Commonwealth and the "special relationship"', pp. 365–78; Walker: *The Commonwealth*, pp. 128–41, 165–94, 197–329.

14. Ceylon was not a member of the UN until 1955 and so will not be considered in this thesis.

15. For more on the establishment of the Colombo Plan see, for instance, Adeleke, Ademola, '"Cocksparrow diplomacy": Percy Spender, the Colombo plan, and Commonwealth relations', *Australian Journal of Politics and History* 54:2 (2008), pp. 173–84; Lowe, David, *Australian Between Empires: The Life of Percy Spender*

(London, 2010), pp. 128–31; Lowe, David, 'Percy Spender and the Colombo plan', *Australian Journal of Politics and History* 40:2 (1994), pp. 162–76; Spender, Percy, *Exercises in Diplomacy: The ANZUS Treaty and the Colombo Plan* (Sydney, 1969), pp. 191–282; Tarling, Nicholas, 'The United Kingdom and the origins of the Colombo plan', *Journal of Commonwealth and Comparative Politics* 24:1 (1986), pp. 3–34.

16. For more on the 'Third Force' concept see, for instance, Gordon, Michael, *Conflict and Consensus in Labour's Foreign Policy* (Stanford, 1969), pp. 182–98, 211; Kent, John, *British Imperial Strategy and the Origins of the Cold War, 1944– 49* (London, 1993), pp. 161–66, 189–95, 199–202, 215–16; Schneer, Jonathan, 'Hopes deferred or shattered: the British Labour left and the third force movement, 1945–1949', *Journal of Modern History* 56:2 (1984), pp. 197–226

17. For more on the Attlee government's views of the Commonwealth and the UN see, for instance, Attlee, Clement, *As It Happened* (London, 1954), pp. 170–73, 177–92; Beckett, Francis, *Clem Attlee* (London, 2000), pp. 181–82, 219–21; Bullock, Alan, *The Life and Times of Ernest Bevin*, vol. III, *Foreign Secretary* (London, 1967), pp. 64–65, 110–15, 192–93, 219, 234, 450–51, 633, 782; Eatwell, Roger, *The 1945–51 Labour Governments* (London, 1975), pp. 78, 140, 158; Fitzsimons, Matthew, *The Foreign Policy of the British Labour Government, 1945–1951* (Notre Dame, 1953), pp. 39, 145–49; Morgan, Kenneth, *Labour in Power, 1945–1951* (Oxford, 1984), pp. 188–231, 237–38; Pearce, Robert, *Attlee* (London, 1997), pp. 162–4; Walker, Patrick Gordon, 'The British Labour Party and the Commonwealth: architect of the Commonwealth', *Round Table* 60:240 (1970), pp. 506–08.

18. For more on the Menzies and Holland governments' views of the Commonwealth and the UN see, for instance, Lowe, David, 'Australia at the United Nations in the 1950s: the paradox of empire', *Australian Journal of International Affairs* 51:2 (1997), pp. 171–81; Lowe: *Australian Between Empires*, pp. 101, 107, 115–17, 123–28, 131–34, 155–59, 181–83; Lowe, David, *Menzies and the 'Great World Struggle': Australia's Cold War, 1948–1954* (Sydney, 1999), pp. 2, 19–20, 25–26, 44–45, 52, 85–87; McGibbon: *New Zealand and the Korean War*, pp. 1, 21–44, 47–52; Martin, Allan, *Robert Menzies: A Life*, vol. II, *1944–1978* (Melbourne, 1993–99), pp. 152–68; Menzies, Robert, *Afternoon Light: Some Memory of Men and Events* (London, 1967), pp. 186–87; Menzies, Robert, *The Measure of Years* (London, 1970), pp. 216–17; Miller, J.D.B., 'The "special relationship" in the Pacific', in H. Bull and W.M.R. Louis (eds), *The Special Relationship: Anglo-American Relations since 1945* (Oxford, 1986), pp. 382–86.

19. For more on the St Laurent government's views of the Commonwealth and UN see, for instance, English, John, *The Life of Lester Pearson*, vol. 1:, *The Shadow of Heaven, 1897–1948* (Toronto, 1989), pp. 262, 284–89, 292–93, 324–29; English, John, *The Life of Lester Pearson*, vol. II, *The Worldly Years, 1949–1972* (Toronto, 1992), pp. 27–28, 47; Mount: *The Diplomacy of War*, pp. xx–xxvi;

Pearson, Lester, *Memoirs of the Right Honourable Lester B. Pearson*, vol. 1, *Through Diplomacy to Politics, 1897–1948* (London, 1973), pp. 244–45, 264–83; Pearson, Lester, *Memoirs of the Right Honourable Lester B. Pearson*, vol. 2, *The International Years, 1948–1957* (London, 1974), pp. 24–41, 98–134; Stairs: *The Diplomacy of Constraint*, pp. xi, 10, 28, 316, 324; Thomson, Dale, *Louis St Laurent: Canadian* (Toronto, 1967), pp. 160–64, 176, 203, 216, 243, 247–50, 266–67, 279.

20. For more on the Malan government's views of the Commonwealth and the UN see, for instance, Mayall, James, 'Africa in Anglo-American relations', in H. Bull and W.M.R. Louis (eds), *The Special Relationship: Anglo-American Relations since 1945* (Oxford, 1986), pp. 337–39.

21. For more on the Nehru and Liaquat Ali-Khan governments' views of the Commonwealth and the UN see, for instance, Brown, Judith, *Nehru* (London, 1999), pp. 127–28, 184–85; Brown, Judith, *Nehru: A Political Life* (New Haven, 2003), pp. 178–79, 248–49, 251–58; Brown, Judith, 'Nehru', in S. Casey and J. Wright (eds), *Mental Maps in the Cold War Era* (Basingstoke, 2011), pp. 201–02, 209–15; Dayal: *India's Role in the Korean Question*, pp. 5–30; Saint Brides, Lord, 'Britain, the United States, and South Asia', in H. Bull and W.M.R. Louis (eds), *The Special Relationship: Anglo-American Relations since 1945* (Oxford, 1986), pp. 295–98; Ramachandram, G., *Nehru and World Peace* (New Delhi, 1990), pp. 98–114; Singh, Anita Inder, *The Limits of British Influence: South Asia and the Anglo-American Relationship, 1947–56* (London, 1993), pp. 2–5, 24–25, 28–29, 38, 50–51, 196.

Chapter 1   The UN Collective Security Action, June–October 1950

1. Lie, Trygve, *In the Cause of Peace: Seven Years with the United Nations* (New York, 1954), pp. 327–29.

2. For good accounts of the military situation during this period see, for instance, Blair, Clay, *The Forgotten War: America in Korea, 1950–53* (New York, 1987), pp. 65–372; Crane, Conrad, *American Airpower Strategy in Korea* (Lawrence, 2000), pp. 23–46; James with Wells: *Refighting the Last War*, pp. 157–95; MacArthur, Douglas, *Reminiscences* (London, 1964), pp. 372–415; Millett, Allan, *The War for Korea, 1950–1951: They Came from the North* (Lawrence, 2010), pp. 85–290; Sandler, Stanley, *The Korean War: No Victors, No Vanquished* (Lexington, 1999), pp. 47–116; Schnabel, James, *The US Army in the Korean War. Policy and Direction: First Year* (Washington, 1992), pp. 80–232.

3. For more on the Truman administration's early efforts to sell the Korean War and the popularity of the conflict see, for instance, Casey, Steven, 'Casualty reporting and domestic support for war: the US experience during the Korean War', *Journal of Strategic Studies* 33:2 (2010), pp. 291–94, 297–304; Casey,

Steven, *Selling the Korean War: Propaganda, Politics and Public Opinion* (Oxford, 2008), pp. 19–40, 67–123; Casey, Steven, 'White House publicity operations during the Korean War, June 1950–June 1951', *Presidential Studies Quarterly* 35:4 (2005), pp. 691–711; Wiltz, John, 'The Korean War and American society', in F. Heller (ed.), *The Korean War: A 25-Year Perspective* (Lawrence, 1977), pp. 112–30.

4. The Republican Party is commonly given this epithet.

5. For more on the outbreak of the Korean War's impact on the Truman administration see Bernstein, Barton, 'The Truman administration and the Korean War', in M. Lacey (ed.), *The Truman Presidency* (Cambridge, 1989), pp. 410–44.

6. For more on US civil–military relations see, for instance, Donovan: *Tumultuous Years*, pp. 248–67, 283–88; Higgins, Trumbell, *Korea and the Fall of MacArthur: A Précis in Limited War* (New York, 1960), pp. 33–60; Kaufman: *The Korean War*, pp. 45–48, 60–61; Pearlman, Michael, *Truman and MacArthur: Policy, Politics and the Hunger for Honor and Renown* (Bloomington, 2008), pp. 56–133; Schaller, Michael, 'Douglas MacArthur: the China issue, policy conflict, and the Korean War', in C.B. Kim and J. Matray (eds), *Korea and the Cold War: Division, Destruction, and Disarmament* (Claremont, 1993), pp. 167–83; Spanier, John, *The Truman-MacArthur Controversy and the Korean War* (New York, 1959), pp. 15–113; Weintraub, Stanley, *MacArthur's War: Korea and the Undoing of an American Hero* (New York, 2000), pp. 122–27, 175–96; Wiltz, John, 'Truman and MacArthur: the Wake Island meeting', *Military Affairs* 42:4 (1978), pp. 169–76.

7. For more on Commonwealth public opinion during the early stages of the Korean War see, for instance, MacDonald: *Britain and the Korean War*, pp. 23–27; McCormack: *Cold War, Hot War*, pp. 105–06; McGibbon: *New Zealand and the Korean War*, vol. I, pp. 72–74, 81–85, 92–95, 101; Melady: *Korea*, pp. 28–29, 35–37; O'Neill: *Australia in the Korean War, 1950–53*, vol. I, pp. 55–61, 69–70, 104–06; Stairs: *The Diplomacy of Constraint*, pp. 45–48, 55–61, 80–83, 90–1, 94, 110–16, 327–28.

8. For more on the impact of the Korean War on the Attlee government see, for instance, Eatwell: *The 1945–51 Labour Governments*, pp. 136–37; Fitzsimons: *The Foreign Policy of the British Labour Government, 1945–1951*, pp. 136–40; Jefferys, Kevin, *The Attlee Governments* (London, 1992), pp. 52–33; Lowe: 'The frustrations of alliance: Britain', pp. 80–86; Meehan, Eugene, *The British Left Wing and Foreign Policy* (New Brunswick, 1960), pp. 156–67; Morgan: *Labour in Power, 1945–1951*, pp. 422–26.

9. For more on the development of the early *apartheid* system see, for instance, Clark, Nancy and Worger, William, *South Africa: The Rise and Fall of Apartheid* (Harlow, 2004), pp. 35–61; Louw, P. Eric, *The Rise, Fall and Legacy of Apartheid* (Westport, 2004), pp. 55–62; Meredith, Martin, *In the Name of Apartheid: South Africa in the Post-war Period* (New York, 1994), pp. 52–69.

10. For more on this phase of the First Indochina War see, for instance, Dalloz: *The War in Indochina, 1945–54*, pp. 132–37; Chen: 'China and the First Indochina War', pp. 91–94; Rotter: *The Path to Vietnam*, pp. 204–11; Short: *The Origins of the Vietnam War*, pp. 84–92.

11. For more on the Chinese invasion of Tibet see Weiss, Julian, 'The PRC occupation of Tibet', *Journal of Social, Political and Economic Studies* 12:4 (1987), pp. 387–88.

12. *FRUS 1950 Vol. VII* Memorandum of Conversation (Charles Noyes), New York, 25 June 1950, pp. 144–47.

13. *NAI MEA* (CJK Branch), 52-CJK/50, Memorandum Foreign Secretary (K.P.S. Menon), New Delhi, 13 July 1950.

14. *UNSC Fifth Year No. 15*, 473rd Meeting, New York, 25 June 1950, pp. 1–13.

15. YUL Group No. 1703, UN Oral History Project Interview Transcripts and Tapes, Box 5, Folder 69 Gross, Ernest, 12 April 1990, pp. 4–8.

16. *UNSC Fifth Year No. 15*, 473rd Meeting, New York, 25 June 1950, pp. 14–15.

17. *FRUS 1950 Vol. VII* Memorandum of Conversation, Ambassador-at-Large (Phillip Jessup), Washington, 25 June 1950, pp. 157–61.

18. *FRUS 1950 Vol. VII* Memorandum of Conversation (Jessup), Washington, 26 June 1950, pp. 178–83.

19. *UKNA* FO371/84056, Bevin-Shone, London, 26 June 1950.

20. *UKNA* CAB128/17, CM(50) 39th Conclusions, London, 27 June 1950.

21. *FRUS 1950 Vol. VII* Statement (Truman), Washington, 27 June 1950, pp. 202–03.

22. *UNSC Fifth Year No.16*, 474th Meeting, New York, 27 June 1950, pp. 3–16.

23. *FRUS 1950 Vol. VII* Henderson-Acheson, New Delhi, 29 June 1950, pp. 234–37.

24. *FRUS 1950 Vol. VII* Acheson-Henderson, Washington, 27 June 1950, pp. 230–31.

25. *UKNA* FO371/84041, Nye-Walker, New Delhi, 28 June 1950.

26. *NMML* Papers of Vijaya Lakshmi Pandit (1st Part), Subject File No. 59, Pandit-Nehru, Washington, 29 June 1950.

27. *NAI MEA* (CJK Branch), 67-CJK/50, Secretary-General (Girja Bajpai)-Rau, New Delhi, 29 June 1950.

28. *FRUS 1950 Vol. VII* Memorandum of Conversation, Deputy US Representative on the UN Security Council (John Ross), New York, 28 June 1950, pp. 221–22.

29. *NARA* RG84-350-82-4-2 E.1030-F, Box 24, Tel-Out 551d-572d 6.28.50-7.1.50, Austin-Acheson, New York, 29 June 1950.

30. *UKNA* FO371/84080, Bevin-Jebb, London, 30 June 1950.

31. *FRUS 1950 Vol. VII* Acheson-Austin, Washington, 4 July 1950, pp. 299–301.

32. *FRUS 1950 Vol. VII* Austin-Acheson, New York, 5 July 1950, pp. 306–07.

33. *UKNA* FO371/88512, Bevin-Jebb, London, 6 July 1950.

34. *FRUS 1950 Vol. VII* Austin-Acheson, New York, 6 July 1950, p. 321.
35. *FRUS 1950 Vol. VII* Henderson-Acheson, New Delhi, 7 July 1950, pp. 324–25.
36. For more on the Indian peace feelers in early July 1950 see, for instance, Acheson, Dean, *Present at the Creation: My Years in the State Department* (London, 1969), pp. 416–20; Stueck: *The Korean War*, pp. 50–54.
37. *NMML* Papers of Vijaya Lakshmi Pandit (1st Part), Correspondence–Nehru, Jawaharlal, Nehru–Pandit, New Delhi, 8 July 1950.
38. *UNSC Fifth Year No. 18*, 476th Meeting, New York, 7 July 1950, pp. 3–11.
39. *HST* Papers of Harry S. Truman, Personal Secretary File, Korean War File, Box 206, United Nations Data Statement, Statement (Truman), Washington, 8 July 1950.
40. *UKNA* PREM8/1405 (Part 1), DO(50)11th Meeting, London, 28 June 1950.
41. *UNSC Fifth Year Supplement for June, July and August 1950* S/1522, New Zealand Permanent Representative to the UN (Carl Berendsen)-Lie, New York, 29 June 1950, p. 34.
42. *UNSC Fifth Year Supplement for June, July and August 1950* S/1524, Acting Australia Permanent Representative to the UN (K.C.O. Shann)-Lie, New York, 29 June 1950, p. 34.
43. *UNSC Fifth Year Supplement for June, July and August 1950* S/1530, Spender-Lie, Canberra, 30 June 1950, p. 38.
44. *LAC* Microfilm T-2366, Cabinet Meeting, Ottawa, 28 June 1950.
45. *LAC* Microfilm T-2366, Cabinet Meeting, Ottawa, 12 July 1950.
46. *UKNA* PREM8/1405 (Part 1), British High Commission in South Africa-Walker, Pretoria, 1 July 1950.
47. *UKNA* CAB128/18, CM(50)43rd, London, 6 July 1950.
48. *FRUS 1950 Vol. VII* US Ambassador in Britain (Lewis Douglas)-Acheson, London, 25 July 1950, p. 468.
49. *UNSC Fifth Year Supplement for June, July and August 1950* S/1637, Shann-Lie, New York, 26 July 1950, p. 106; S/1636, Berendsen-Lie, New York, 26 July 1950, p. 105.
50. NAA A1838, 88/1/10 PART 2, Spender-Certain Diplomatic Missions, Canberra, 26 July 1950.
51. *FRUS 1950 Vol. VII* Memorandum of Conversation (Acheson), Washington, 28 July 1950, pp. 489–90.
52. *LAC* RG25/4738/50069-A-40 Pt 7, Canadian High Commission in New Zealand-Pearson, Wellington, 4 August 1950.
53. *LAC* Microfilm T-2366, Cabinet Meeting, Ottawa, 19 July 1950.
54. *LAC* Microfilm T-2366, Cabinet Meeting, Ottawa, 28 July 1950.
55. *LAC* RG25/4738/50069-A-40 Pt 7, Memorandum (Pearson), Ottawa, 1 August 1950.
56. *LAC* Microfilm T-2367, Cabinet Meetings, Ottawa, 2, 3 and 7 August 1950.

57. *HST* Dean Acheson Papers, Secretary of State File 1945–1972, Memorandum of Conversations File 1949–1953, Box 67, July 1950, Memorandum of Conversation (David Satterthwaite), Washington, 24 July 1950.

58. *UNSC Fifth Year Supplement for June, July and August 1950* S/1669, South Africa Permanent Representative to the UN (J. Jordaan)-Lie, New York, 4 August 1950, p. 117.

59. *LAC* RG25/4738/50069-A-40 Pt 4, Canadian High Commission in Pakistan-Pearson, Karachi, 16 July 1950.

60. *HST*, Papers of Harry S. Truman, Personal Secretary's File, Subject File, Box 187, Memoranda for the President, Meeting Discussions 1950, Memorandum (James Lay), Washington, 11 August 1950.

61. *FRUS 1950 Vol. VII* Acheson-Douglas, Washington, 1 August 1950, pp. 513–14.

62. For more on British security concerns in Hong Kong at this time see Mark, Chi-Kwan, *Hong Kong and the Cold War: Anglo-American Relations, 1949–1957* (Oxford, 2004), pp. 40–82.

63. *UKNA* PREM8/1405, Walker-all High Commissions, London, 19 August 1950.

64. *UKNA* PREM8/1405, Walker-High Commissions Canberra/Wellington/Ottawa, London, 19 August 1950.

65. *UKNA* PREM8/1405, High Commission-Walker, Canberra, 23 August 1950.

66. *UKNA* PREM8/1405, High Commission-Walker, Wellington, 20 August 1950.

67. *LAC* Microfilm T-2366, Cabinet Meeting, Ottawa, 15 August 1950.

68. *HST* Papers of Harry S. Truman, Korean War File 1947–1952, Box 6, 16. Relief and rehabilitation (1 of 2 July–November 1950), Austin-Acheson, New York, 24 July 1950.

69. *HST* Papers of Harry S. Truman, Korean War File 1947–1952, Box 6, 16. Relief and rehabilitation (1 of 2 July–November 1950), Acheson-Austin, Washington, 25 July 1950.

70. *UKNA* FO371/88729, Bevin-Jebb, London, 22 July 1950.

71. *FRUS 1950 Vol. VII* Acheson-Austin, Washington, 28 July 1950, pp. 490–91.

72. *UKNA* FO371/88505, Bevin-Jebb, London, 28 July 1950.

73. *FRUS 1950 Vol. VII* Gross-Acheson, New York, 29 July 1950, pp. 496–98.

74. *UNSC* Fifth Year No. 21, 479th Meeting, New York, 31 July 1950, pp. 3–7.

75. *FRUS 1950 Vol. VII* Acheson-Austin, Washington, 29 July 1950, pp. 491–92.

76. *FRUS 1950 Vol. VII* Gross-Acheson, New York, 29 July 1950, pp. 495–96.

77. *UKNA* FO371/88515, Bevin-Jebb, London, 31 July 1950.

78. *NARA* RG84/350/82/4/2 E.1030-F, Box 24, Tel Out 126e-250e (26 July 1950–10 August 1950), US Delegation to the UN Daily Classified Summary No. 21, New York, 1 August 1950.

79. *UNSC* Fifth Year No. 22, 480th Meeting, New York, 1 August 1950, pp. 12–22.

80. *UNSC* Fifth Year No. 23, 481st Meeting, New York, 2 August 1950, pp. 1–19; No. 24 482nd Meeting, New York, 3 August 1950, pp. 1–23.

81. *UNSC* Fifth Year No. 25, 483rd Meeting, New York, 4 August 1950, pp. 1–16.

82. *FRUS 1950 Vol. VII* Acheson-Austin, Washington, 7 August 1950, pp. 536–37.

83. *UKNA* FO371/88516, Bevin-Jebb, London, 5 August 1950.

84. *UNSC* Fifth Year No. 26, 484th Meeting, New York, 8 August 1950, pp. 1–21.

85. *FRUS 1950 Vol. VII* Acheson-Austin, Washington, 9 August 1950, pp. 549–51.

86. *UKNA* FO371/88516, Bevin-Jebb, London, 10 August 1950.

87. *NMML* Papers of Vijaya Lakshmi Pandit (1st Part), Correspondence- Nehru, Jawaharlal, Nehru-Pandit, New Delhi, 10 August 1950.

88. *FRUS 1950 Vol. VII* Austin-Acheson, New York, 9 August 1950, pp. 548–49.

89. *FRUS 1950 Vol. VII* Acheson-Austin, Washington, 15 August 1950, pp. 585–86.

90. *UKNA* FO371/88516, Bevin-Jebb, London, 15 August 1950.

91. *UKNA* FO371/88517, Jebb-Bevin, New York, 16 August 1950.

92. *UKNA* FO371/88517, Bevin-Jebb, London, 17 August 1950.

93. *FRUS 1950 Vol. VII* Henderson-Acheson, New Delhi, 18 August 1950, pp. 607–08.

94. *FRUS 1950 Vol. VII* Gross-Acheson, New York, 18 August 1950, pp. 609–11.

95. *FRUS 1950 Vol. VII* Austin-Acheson, New York, 23 August 1950, pp. 639–40.

96. *UNSC Fifth Year No. 30*, 488th Meeting, New York, 17 August 1950, pp. 3–8.

97. *UNSC Fifth Year Nos 34–35*, 492nd–493rd Meeting, New York, 29–31 August 1950.

98. *UNSC Fifth Year No. 36*, 494th Meeting, New York, 1 September 1950, pp. 2–27.

99. *UNSC Fifth Year No. 37*, 495th Meeting, New York, 6 September 1950, pp. 2–21.

100. *UNSC Fifth Year No. 39*, 497th Meeting, New York, 7 September 1950, pp. 1–26.

101. *UNSC Fifth Year No. 44*, 502nd Meeting, New York, 18 September 1950, pp. 27–35.

102. *UNSC Fifth Year No. 50*, 508th Meeting, New York, 30 September 1950, pp. 3–11.

103. Lie: *In the Cause of Peace*, p. 341.

104. Mazunan, George, *Warren R. Austin at the UN, 1946–1953* (Kent, 1977), p. 158.

105. *YUL* Group No. 1703, UN Oral History Project Interview Transcripts and Tapes, Box 5, Folder 82 Jebb, Gladwyn, London, 21 June 1983, pp. 10–10a–z; Jebb, Gladwyn, *The Memoirs of Lord Gladwyn* (London, 1972), pp. 231–41, 249.

106. *NARA* RG84/350/82/3/4 E.1030-E, Box 24, IO: GA: Sessions 5th, Minutes Joint US-Britain-Canada Pre-General Assembly Discussion, New York, 24 August 1950.

107. *FRUS 1950 Vol. VII* US Delegation Minutes: SFM Min-4, New York, 14 September 1950, p. 728.

108. For more on the US decision to cross the 38th parallel see, for instance, Bernstein, Barton, 'The policy of risk: crossing the 38th parallel and marching to the Yalu', *Foreign Service Journal* 54:3 (1977), pp. 16–23; Matray, James, 'Truman's plan for victory: national self-determination and the thirty-eighth parallel decision in Korea', *Journal of American History* 66:2 (1979), pp. 314–33.

109. *FRUS 1950 Vol. VII* Position Paper Prepared for US Delegation to the UN General Assembly, New York, 19 September 1950, pp. 736–41.

110. *FRUS 1950 Vol. VII* Minutes 4th Meeting US Delegation to the UN General Assembly, New York, 21 September 1950, pp. 743–47.

111. For more on British views on a political settlement for Korea see Ra, Jong-yil, 'Political settlement in Korea: British views and policies, autumn 1950', in J. Cotton and I. Neary (eds), *The Korean War in History* (Manchester, 1989), pp. 51–65.

112. *FRUS 1950 Vol. VII* Minutes 6th Meeting US Delegation to the UN General Assembly, New York, 25 September 1950, pp. 768–73.

113. *LAC* RG25/4739/50069-A-40 Pt 10, MEA-Pearson, Ottawa, 28 September 1950.

114. *LAC* RG25/6443/5475-DW-4-40 [Pt 3.1], Pearson-MEA, New York, 2 October 1950.

115. *NAA* A1383, 88/1/10 PART 3, Spender-Shann, London, 28 September 1950.

116. *UKNA* DO35/2838, Walker-Nye, London, 26 September 1950.

117. *UKNA* DO35/2383, Nye-Walker, London, 28 September 1950.

118. *FRUS 1950 Vol. VII* Henderson-Acheson, New Delhi, 28 September 1950, pp. 808–10.

119. *UKNA* FO371/84109, Bevin-Nehru, New York, 29 September 1950.

120. *UKNA* FO371/84110, Bevin-FO, On Board the Queen Mary, 4 October 1950.

121. *LAC* RG25/6443/5475-DW-4-40 [Pt 3.1], Pearson-MEA, New York, 2 October 1950.

122. *NARA* RG84/350/82/2/4 Box 45 Korea (September to December 1950), Memorandum of Conversation (John Allison), New York, 4 October 1950.

123. *FRUS 1950 Vol. VII* Minutes 13th Meeting, US Delegation to the UN General Assembly, New York, 4 October 1950, pp. 862–63.

124. *UKNA* FO371/84099, Bevin-Younger, New York, 2 October 1950.
125. *LAC* Microfilm T-2367, Cabinet Meeting, 4 October 1950.
126. *UKNA* FO371/84110, Nye-Walker, New Delhi, 7 October 1950.
127. *NAA* A1838, 88/1/10 PART 3, Spender-MEA, New York, 3 October 1950.
128. *UNGA* Fifth Session First Committee 347th Meeting, New York, 30 September 1950, pp. 11–14.
129. *UNGA* Fifth Session First Committee 348th–351st Meetings, New York, 2–3 October 1950, pp. 17–43.
130. *UNGA* Fifth Session First Committee 352nd–353rd Meetings, New York, 4 October 1950, pp. 45–56.
131. *UNGA* Fifth Session Plenary 294th Meeting, New York, 7 October 1950, p. 232.
132. *UNGA* Fifth Session Plenary 314th Meeting, New York, 1 December 1950, pp. 521–25.

Chapter 2   Branding an Aggressor, October 1950–January 1951

1. For the best accounts of the winter crisis of 1950–51 see, for instance, Dockrill: 'The Foreign Office, Anglo-American relations, and the Korean War'; Foot: *The Wrong War*, pp. 88–130; Foot: 'Anglo-American relations in the Korean crisis'; Lowe: 'The frustrations of alliance'; Stueck: *The Korean War*, pp. 111–66; Stueck: *Rethinking the Korean War*, pp. 110–29; Stueck: 'The limits of influence'.
2. For more on the Chinese decision to enter the conflict see, for instance, Christensen, Thomas, 'Threats, assurances, and the last chance for peace: the lessons of Mao's Korean War telegrams', *International Security* 17:1 (1992), pp. 122–54; Hunt, Michael, 'Beijing and the Korean crisis, June 1950–June 1951', *Political Science Quarterly* 107:3 (1992), pp. 459–65; Chen, Jian, *China's Road to the Korean War: The Making of the Sino-American Confrontation* (New York, 1994), pp. 125–209; Goncharov, Lewis and Xue: *Uncertain Partners*, pp. 159–99; Mansourov, Alexandre, 'Stalin, Mao, Kim, and China's decision to enter the Korean War, Sept. 16–Oct. 15, 1950: new evidence from Russian archives', *Cold War International History Project Bulletin* 6/7 (1995/96), pp. 94–119; Ryan, Mark, *Chinese Attitudes Toward Nuclear Weapons: China and the United States during the Korean War* (Armonk, 1989), pp. 24–46; Shen, Zhihua, 'China and the dispatch of the Soviet Air Force: the formation of the Chinese-Soviet-Korean alliance in the early stages of the Korean War', *Journal of Strategic Studies* 33:2 (2010), pp. 211–30; Simmons: *The Strained Alliance*, pp. 137–68; Whiting, Allen, *China Crosses the Yalu: The Decision to Enter the Korean War* (Stanford, 1960); Hao, Yufan and Zhai, Zihai, 'China's decision to enter the Korean War: history revisited', *China Quarterly* 121 (1990),

pp. 94–115; Zhang, Shuguang, *Mao's Military Romanticism: China and the Korean War, 1950–1953* (Lawrence, 1995), pp. 55–94.

3. For more on the military situation in Korea between November 1950 and February 1951 see, for instance, Appleman, Roy, *Disaster in Korea: The Chinese Confront MacArthur* (College Station, 1989); Appleman, Roy, *East of Chosin: Entrapment and Breakout, 1950* (College Station, 1987); Appleman, Roy, *Escaping the Trap: US Army X Corps in Northeast Korea* (College Station, 1990); Appleman, Roy, *Ridgway Duels for Korea* (College Station, 1990), pp. 3–217; Blair: *The Forgotten War*, pp. 374–668; Crane: *American Airpower Strategy in Korea*, pp. 46–64; James with Wells: *Refighting the Last War*, pp. 53–63; MacArthur: *Reminiscences*, pp. 415–37; Millett: *The War for Korea, 1950–1951*, pp. 290–398; Ridgway, Matthew, *The War in Korea* (London, 1968), pp. 47–106; Sandler: *The Korean War*, pp. 117–96; Schnabel: *The US Army in the Korean War*, pp. 233–348; Zhang: *Mao's Military Romanticism*, pp. 95–138; Zhang, Xiaoming, *Red Wings over the Yalu: China, the Soviet Union, and the Air War in Korea* (College Station, 2002), pp. 78–113.

4. *FRUS 1950 Vol. VII* MacArthur-Joint Chiefs of Staff, Tokyo, 28 November 1950, p. 1237.

5. For more on consideration of the use of atomic weapons following Chinese intervention see, for instance, Dingman, Roger, 'Atomic diplomacy during the Korean War', *International Security* 13:3 (1988–89), pp. 65–69; Jones, Matthew, *After Hiroshima: The United States, Race and Nuclear Weapons in Asia, 1945–1965* (Cambridge, 2010), pp. 77–99.

6. For more on the Truman administration's efforts to sell the Korean War and NSC-68 during the winter crisis see, for instance, Casey: 'Casualty reporting and domestic support for war', pp. 304–07; Casey, Steven, 'Selling NSC-68: the Truman administration, public opinion, and the politics of mobilization, 1950–51', *Diplomatic History* 29:4 (2005), pp. 655–90; Casey: *Selling the Korean War*, pp. 127–43, 173–232; Casey: 'White House publicity operations', pp. 699–711; Gaddis, John Lewis, *Strategies of Containment: A Critical Appraisal of Postwar American National Security Policy* (Oxford, 1982), pp. 87–124; Wells, Samuel, 'Sounding the tocsin: NSC-68 and the Soviet threat', *International Security* 4:2 (1979), pp. 140–45; Wiltz: 'The Korean War and American society', pp. 130–42.

7. For accounts of the 'Great Debate' see, for instance, Caridi, Ronald, *The Korean War and American Politics: The Republican Party as a Case Study* (Philadelphia, 1969), pp. 126–37; Casey: *Selling the Korean War*, pp. 192–98; Ivie, Robert, 'Declaring a national emergency: Truman's rhetorical crisis and the Great Debate of 1951', in A. Kiewe (ed.), *The Modern Presidency and Crisis Rhetoric* (London, 1994), pp. 1–18; Kepley, David, *Collapse of the Middle Way: Senate Republicans and the Bipartisanship Foreign Policy, 1948–1952* (London, 1988), pp. 101–16.

8. For more on US civil-military relations during this phase of the Korean War see, for instance, Donovan: *Tumultuous Years*, pp. 289–320; Higgins: *Korea and*

the Fall of MacArthur, pp. 63–99; Kaufman: *The Korean War*, pp. 63–69, 73–75; Pearlman: *Truman and MacArthur*, pp. 134–61; Schaller: 'Douglas MacArthur', pp. 183–86; Spanier: *The Truman-MacArthur Controversy and the Korean War*, pp. 114–64, 187–97; Weintraub: *MacArthur's War*, pp. 301–07.

9. In this book all place names are given as they are commonly known today.

10. For more on Commonwealth public opinion following Chinese intervention see, for instance, MacDonald: *Britain and the Korean War*, pp. 42–43, 45–51; McGibbon: *New Zealand and the Korean War*, vol. I, p. 185; O'Neill: *Australia in the Korean War, 1950–53*, vol. I, p. 157.

11. For more on the impact of the Chinese intervention on the Attlee government see, for instance, Fitzsimons: *The Foreign Policy of the British Labour Government, 1945–1951*, pp. 147–9; Meehan: *The British Left Wing and Foreign Policy*, pp. 167–71; Morgan: *Labour in Power, 1945–1951*, pp. 426–31.

12. For more details on the evolution of NATO during this period see, for instance, Duignan, Peter, *NATO: Its Past, Present and Future* (Stanford, 2000), pp. 6–18; Kaplan, Lawrence, *The Long Entanglement: NATO's First Fifty Years* (Westport, 1999), pp. 60–62; Kaplan, Lawrence, *NATO Divided, NATO United: The Evolution of an Alliance* (Westport, 2004), pp. 9–27; Milloy, John, *North Atlantic Treaty Organisation, 1948–1957: Community or Alliance?* (Montreal, 2006), pp. 52–66; Powaski, Ronald, *The Entangling Alliance: The United States and European Security, 1950–1993* (Westport, 1994), pp. 1–17; Weber, Steve, *Multilateralism in NATO: Shaping the Post-war Balance of Power, 1945–1961* (Berkeley, 1991), pp. 33–37.

13. For more on this phase of the First Indochina War see, for instance, Dalloz: *The War in Indochina, 1945–54*, pp. 137–39; Chen: 'China and the First Indochina War', pp. 94–95; Rotter: *The Path to Vietnam*, pp. 211–13; Short: *The Origins of the Vietnam War*, pp. 87–92.

14. For more on this phase of the Malayan Emergency see, for instance, Barber, Noel, *The War of the Running Dogs: How Malaya Defeated the Communist Guerrillas, 1948–1960* (London, 1971), pp. 93–111; Clutterbuck, Richard, *The Long Long War: The Emergency in Malaya, 1948–1960* (London, 1967), pp. 55–64; Coates, John, *Suppressing Insurgency: An Analysis of the Malayan Emergency, 1948–1954* (Boulder, 1992), pp. 82–101; Jackson: *The Malayan Emergency*, pp. 35–39; O'Ballance, Edgar, *Malaya: The Communist Insurgent War* (London, 1966), pp. 97–114; Ramakrishna: *Emergency Propaganda*, pp. 89–119; Short: *The Communist Insurrection in Malaya, 1948–1960*, pp. 241–53; Stockwell, A.J., 'British imperial policy and decolonization in Malaya, 1945–1952', *Journal of Imperial and Commonwealth History* 13:1 (1984), pp. 72–83; Stubbs, Richard, *Hearts and Minds in Guerrilla Warfare: The Malayan Emergency, 1948–1960* (Singapore, 1989), pp. 98–132.

15. *UNSC Fifth Year Supplement for September through December* S/1885, UNC Special Report, 6 November 1950, pp. 104–12.

16. *FRUS 1950 Vol. VII* Acheson-Austin, Washington, 5 November 1950, pp. 1049–50.

17. *FRUS 1950 Vol. VII* Acheson-US Ambassador in Britain (Walter Gifford), Washington, 6 November 1950, pp. 1050–53.

18. *UNSC Fifth Year* No. 62, 520th Meeting, New York, 8 November 1950, pp. 3–10.

19. *UNSC Fifth Year Supplement for September–December 1950* S/1898, Zhou En-lai-Lie, 11 November 1950.

20. *NAI MEA* 52-CJK/50, Foreign Secretary (K.P.S. Menon)-Indian Delegation to the UN (Gopala Menon), New Delhi, 13 November 1950, pp. 113–14.

21. For more on Bevin's buffer zone plan see, for instance, Farrar, Peter, 'A pause for peace negotiations: the British buffer zone plan of November 1950', in J. Cotton and I. Neary (eds), *The Korean War in History* (Manchester, 1989), pp. 66–79.

22. *UKNA* CAB128/18, CM(50)73rd Conclusions, 13 November 1950.

23. *FRUS 1950 Vol. VII* Acheson-Gifford, Washington, 21 November 1950, pp. 1212–13.

24. *UKNA* CAB128/18, CM(50)76th Conclusions, 20 November 1950.

25. *FRUS 1950 Vol. VII* Memorandum of Conversation (Jessup), Washington, 28 November 1950, pp. 1242–49.

26. *UNSC Fifth Year* No. 70, 528th Meeting, New York, 29 November 1950, pp. 12–15.

27. *UKNA* CAB128/18, CM(50)79th Conclusions, London, 30 November 1950.

28. *UNSC Fifth Year* No. 72, 530th Meeting, New York, 30 November 1950, pp. 22–24.

29. *NARA* RG84/350/82/5/7 E.1030-H, Box 4, 1950 Tel Incs US-December, Acheson-Austin, Washington, 4 December 1950.

30. *UNGA Fifth Session Plenary* 302nd Meeting, New York, 3 November 1950, p. 347.

31. *UNSC Fifth Year* No. 69, 527th Meeting, New York, 28 November 1950, pp. 2–26.

32. *UKNA* FO371/84105, Jebb-Bevin, New York, 5 December 1950.

33. *UKNA* FO371/84106, Nye-Walker, New Delhi, 5 December 1950.

34. *YUL* Group No.1703 UN Oral History Project, Box 5, Folder 69, Gross, Ernest, New York, 12 April 1990, p. 34.

35. *UKNA* CAB128/18, CM(50)80th Conclusions, London, 30 November 1950.

36. *UKNA* FO371/84105, Ambassador to the United States (Oliver Franks)-Bevin, Washington, 5 December 1950.

37. *UNGA Fifth Session First Committee* 409–410th Meeting, New York, 7–8 December 1950, pp. 402–06.

38. *UKNA* FO371/84124, Record of a Meeting of the Heads of the Commonwealth Delegations, New York, 6 December 1950.
39. *UKNA* FO371/84122, Bevin-Jebb, London, 10 December 1950.
40. *NAA* A1838, 88/1/10 PART 4, MEA-Spender, Canberra, 12 December 1950.
41. *UKNA* PREM8/1405 Part 4, Record of Conversation Walker and Indian High Commissioner to Britain (V.K. Krishna Menon), London, 11 December 1950.
42. *HST* Papers of Harry S. Truman, Personal Secretary's File, Subject File 1940–1953, Box 187, Memoranda for the President: Meeting Discussions: 1950, Memorandum for the President, Executive Secretary of the National Security Council (James Lay), Washington, 12 December 1950.
43. *UNGA Fifth Session First Committee* 415th Meeting, New York, 12 December 1950, pp. 433–34.
44. *LAC* RG25/6444/5475-DW-4-40 [Pt 5], Record of a Meeting of the Heads of the Commonwealth Delegations, New York, 13 December 1950.
45. *HST* Dean G. Acheson Papers, Secretary of State File 1945–1972, Memoranda of Conversations File 1949–1953, Box 67, December 1951, Memorandum of Conversation with the President (Acheson), Washington, 11 December 1950.
46. *UNGA Fifth Session Plenary* 324th Meeting, New York, 14 December 1950, p. 655.
47. *UKNA* FO371/84136, Bevin-Jebb, London, 15 December 1950.
48. *UNARMS* S-0018-0003-05, Entezam/Rau/Pearson-Wu, New York, 15 December 1950.
49. Pearson: *Memoirs of the Right Honourable Lester B. Pearson*, vol. 2: *The International Years, 1948–1957* (London, 1974), p. 282.
50. *UNARMS* S-0018-0003-05, Statement by Wu Hsiu-chuan, New York, 16 December 1950.
51. *NARA* Microfilm C0042 Reel 1, Acheson-Austin, Washington, 15 December 1950.
52. *UNARMS* S-0018-0003-05, Entezam/Rau/Pearson-Zhou En-lai, New York, 20 December 1950.
53. *NARA* RG84/350/82/4/2 E.1030-F, Box 29, Delga 384-471 (12/6/50-12/30/50), Austin-Acheson, New York, 24 December 1950.
54. *FRUS 1950 Vol. VII* Acheson-Austin, Washington, 28 December 1950, pp. 1619–20.
55. Pearson: *Memoirs*, vol. 2, pp. 287–88.
56. *UNGA Fifth Session First Committee* 419th Meeting, New York, 3 January 1951, p. 459.
57. *FRUS 1951 Vol. VII* Austin-Acheson, New York, 3 January 1951, pp. 9–12.
58. Acheson, Dean, *The Korean War* (New York, 1969), p. 94.

59. *UNGA Fifth Session First Committee* 419th Meeting, New York, 3 January 1951, pp. 461–62.

60. *LAC* MG26 N1/22/Commonwealth—Prime Minister's Meeting 1951, P.M.M.(51)3rd Meeting, London, 5 January 1951.

61. *UKNA* PREM8/1405 Part 4, P.M.M(51)7 Memorandum by the British Government, London, 5 January 1951.

62. *LAC* MG26 N1/22/Commonwealth—Prime Ministers' Meeting 1951, P.M.M.(51)4th Meeting, London, 5 January 1951.

63. *LAC* RG25/4741/50069-A-40 Part 17, Pearson–St Laurent, New York, 5 January 1951.

64. *UKNA* PREM8/1405 Part 4, P.M.M.(51)8, Memorandum by the Prime Minister of India (Nehru), London, 5 January 1951.

65. *UKNA* PREM8/1405 Part 4, P.M.M.(51)5th Meeting, Minute 2, London, 8 January 1951.

66. *FRUS 1951 Vol. VII* Acheson-Truman, Washington, 8 January 1951, pp. 37–39.

67. *FRUS 1951 Vol. VII* Acheson-Gifford, Washington, 9 January 1951, pp. 39–40.

68. *UKNA* PREM8/1405 Part 4, P.M.M.(51)7th Meeting, Minute 1, London, 9 January 1951.

69. *UKNA* PREM8/1405 Part 4, P.M.M/(51)9, Note by the Secretariat, London, 11 January 1951.

70. *UKNA* PREM8/1405 Part 4, Jebb-Bevin, New York, 10 January 1951.

71. *HST* Dean G. Acheson Papers, Secretary of State File 1945–1972, Memoranda of Conversations File 1949–1953, Box 67, January 1951, Memorandum Conversation with President (Acheson), Washington, 11 January 1950.

72. *UKNA* PREM8/1405 Part 4, P.M.M.(51)10th Meeting, London, 11 January 1951.

73. *UNGA Fifth Session First Committee* 422nd–425th Meeting, New York, 11–13 January 1951, pp. 475–96.

74. *FRUS 1951 Vol. VII* Acheson-Austin, Washington, 13 January 1951, pp. 74–76.

75. *HST* Papers of Harry S. Truman, Korean War File 1947–1952, Box 8, 26. US efforts to obtain UN action re Chinese intervention, White House Press and Radio Conference, Washington, 18 January 1951.

76. *UNGA Fifth Session First Committee* 426th Meeting, New York, 18 January 1951, pp. 501–03.

77. *NARA* RG59/250/46/3/5 E.394B, Box 1, Memoranda from S and U 1951, Memorandum of Telephone Conversation, Special Assistant to the Secretary of State (Lucius Battle), Washington, 18 January 1951.

78. *FRUS 1951 Vol. VII* Acheson-Austin, Washington, 19 January 1951, pp. 108–10.

79. *UVL* Austin papers, Box 49, UN: Korea, Telephone Conversation Austin-Hickerson, 17 January 1950.
80. *NAA* A1838, 88/1/10 PART 5, Spender-Shann, New York, 17 January 1951.
81. *UKNA* PREM8/1405 Part 4, Bevin-Franks, London, 15 January 1951.
82. *UKNA* CAB128/19, CM(51)4th Conclusions, London, 18 January 1951.
83. *LAC* Microfilm T-2367, Cabinet Meeting, 17 January 1951.
84. *UKNA* PREM8/1405 Part 4, Menon-Attlee, London, 18 January 1951.
85. *UKNA* PREM8/1405 Part 4, Attlee-Nehru, London, 20 January 1951.
86. *LAC* RG25/4741/50069-A-40 Pt 18, St Laurent-Nehru, Ottawa, 18 January 1951.
87. *LAC* RG25/4741/50069-A-40 Pt 18, Pearson-MEA, New York, 20 January 1951.
88. *FRUS 1951 Vol. VII* Austin-Acheson, New York, 20 January 1951, pp. 114–15.
89. *NAA* A1838, 88/1/10 PART 5, Shann-Spender, New York, 20 January 1951.
90. *NARA* RG59/250/49/5/3 E.1459, Box 3, India 1951–1952, Clarification of certain points included in the counter proposal made by the Chinese government to Political Committee of the United Nations General Assembly.
91. *NARA* RG59/250/49/5/3 E.1459, Box 3, India 1951–1952, Extract from a personal message sent on 23rd January, 1951, to the Chinese Foreign Minister, Chou En-lai by the Prime Minister of India.
92. *UNGA Fifth Session First Committee* 429th Meeting, New York, 22 January 1951, pp. 525–32.
93. *NAA* A1838, TS88/1/10, Spender-Shann, Canberra, 24 January 1951.
94. *UKNA* PREM8/1405 Part 4, Australian Office of the Prime Minister (E. Bunting)-Permanent Secretary Commonwealth Relations Office (Percivale Liesching), London, 23 January 1951.
95. *UKNA* PREM8/1405 Part 5, Record of Conversation (Liesching), London, 25 January 1951.
96. *LAC* RG25/4741/50069-A-40 Pt 19, Canadian High Commissioner to New Zealand (Alfred Rive)-Pearson, Wellington, 25 January 1951.
97. *Documents on British Policy Overseas, Series II, Volume IV: Korea June 1950–April 1951* No. 114 Bevin-Franks, London, 23 January 1951, pp. 322–25.
98. *UKNA* CAB128/19, CM(51)8th Conclusions, London, 25 January 1951.
99. *UKNA* PREM8/1405 Part 5, Walker-all High Commissions, London, 26 January 1951.
100. 100 *UNGA Fifth Session First Committee* 431st Meeting, New York, 25 January 1951, pp. 543–50.
101. 101 *NARA* RG84/350/82/5/2 E.1030-H, Box 7, 1951 Tel Incs US Jan–March, Acheson-Austin, Washington, 26 January 1951.
102. 102 *FRUS 1951 Vol. VII* Acheson-Austin, Washington, 27 January 1951, p. 137.

103. *UKNA* CAB128/19, CM(51)10th Conclusions, London, 29 January 1951.
104. *UKNA* PREM8/1405 Part 5, Nye-Walker, New Delhi, 27 January 1951.
105. *NMML* Papers of Vijaya Lakshmi Pandit (1st Part), Subject File No. 50, Pandit-Nehru, Washington, 29 January 1951.
106. *UNGA Fifth Session First Committee* 435th–438th Meetings, 29–30 January 1951, pp. 579–602.
107. *UNGA Fifth Session Plenary* 327th Meeting, New York, 1 February 1951, pp. 692–96.
108. Stueck: *The Korean War*, pp. 152, 163–64.

Chapter 3   Responding to Chinese Aggression, February–July 1951

1. For accounts of the course of military events during this period see, for instance, Appleman: *Ridgway Duels for Korea*, pp. 218–580; Blair: *The Forgotten War*, pp. 669–940; Crane: *American Airpower Strategy in Korea*, pp. 64–75; James, with Wells: *Refighting the Last War*, pp. 63–66; Millett: *The War for Korea, 1945–1950*, pp. 398–460; Ridgway: *The War in Korea*, pp. 106–23, 150–83; Schnabel: *The US Army in the Korean War*, pp. 349–406; Zhang: *Mao's Military Romanticism*, pp. 138–53; Zhang: *Red Wings over the Yalu*, pp. 113–30.
2. Jackson, Colin, 'Lost chance or lost horizon?: strategic opportunity and escalation risk in the Korean War, April–July 1951', *Journal of Strategic Studies* 33:2 (2010), pp. 255–89.
3. For more on the Battle of Imjin River see, for instance, Farrar-Hockley, Anthony, *The Edge of the Sword* (London, 1954), pp. 11–67; Farrar-Hockley: *The British Part in the Korean War*, vol. II, pp. 111–37; Green, David, *Captured at the Imjin River: The Korean War Memoirs of a Gloster* (Barnsley, 2003), pp. 93–107; Salmon, Andrew, *To the Last Round: The Epic British Stand on the Imjin River, Korea 1951* (London, 2009); Taylor, Barry, 'Open road barred (Battle of Imjin River, 1951)', *Military History* 7:6 (1991), pp. 46–52.
4. For accounts of MacArthur's dismissal see, for instance, Donovan: *Tumultuous Years*, pp. 340–62; Higgins: *Korea and the Fall of MacArthur*, pp. 103–29; Kaufman: *The Korean War*, pp. 97–104; Pearlman: *Truman and MacArthur*, pp. 169–98; Schaller: 'Douglas MacArthur', pp. 186–91; Spanier: *The Truman-MacArthur Controversy*, pp. 197–207; Weintraub: *MacArthur's War*, pp. 311–42.
5. Stueck: *Rethinking the Korean War*, pp. 129–31.
6. For more on deliberations in Washington regarding the use of nuclear weapons during this period see, for instance, Dingman: 'Atomic diplomacy during the Korean War', pp. 69–79; Jones: *After Hiroshima*, pp. 102–05.
7. For the British part in MacArthur's dismissal see Lowe: 'An ally and a recalcitrant general', pp. 636–53.

8. For more on the MacArthur hearings see, for instance, Kaufman: *The Korean War*, pp. 104–11; Pearlman: *Truman and* MacArthur, pp. 199–216; Spanier: *The Truman-MacArthur Controversy*, pp. 211–80; Wilz, John, 'The MacArthur hearings of 1951: the secret testimony,' *Military Affairs* 39:4 (1975), pp. 167–73.

9. For more on Morrison's foreign policy perspectives see, for instance, Donoughue, Bernard and Jones, G.W., *Herbert Morrison: Portrait of a Politician* (London, 1973), pp. 479–514; Eatwell: *The 1945–51 Labour Governments*, pp. 137–41; Morrison, Herbert, *Herbert Morrison: An Autobiography* (London, 1960), pp. 270–83.

10. For a full account of Bevan's resignation and splits within the Labour Party see, for instance, Foot, Michael, *Aneurin Bevan: A Biography*, vol. II, *1945–1960* (London, 1973), pp. 280–346; Eatwell: *The 1945–51 Labour Governments*, pp. 140–45; Gordon: *Conflict and Consensus*, pp. 242–60; Jefferys: *The Attlee Governments*, pp. 53–56; Meehan: *The British Left Wing and Foreign Policy*, pp. 169–71; Morgan: *Labour in Power, 1945–1951*, pp. 277–79, 424, 433–34, 453–59.

11. For more on Spender's resignation as Minister for External Affairs and appointment as Ambassador to the United States see, for instance, Lowe: *Australian Between Empires*, pp. 141–61; Lowe, David, 'Mr Spender goes to Washington: an ambassador's vision of Australian-American relations, 1951–1958', *Journal of Imperial and Commonwealth History* 24:2 (1996), pp. 278–85.

12. For more on the 1951 Australian general election see, for instance, Martin: *Robert Menzies*, pp. 184–86; Menzies: *The Measure of Years*, pp. 184–85.

13. For more information on the New Zealand waterfront dispute see, for instance, Bassett, Michael, *Confrontation '51: The 1951 Waterfront Dispute* (Wellington, 1972); Bramble, Tom (ed.), *Never a White Flag: The Memoirs of Jock Barnes, Waterfront Leader* (Wellington, 1998), pp. 156–240; Scott, Dick, *151 Days: Official History of the Great Waterfront Lockout and Supporting Strikes, February 15–July 15, 1951* (Reed, 2001).

14. For a good account of US-Indian relations regarding food aid to India see McMahon, Robert, 'Food as a diplomatic weapon: the India wheat loan of 1951', *Pacific Historical Review* 56:3 (1987), pp. 349–77.

15. For accounts of the ANZUS negotiations see, for instance, Barclay, Glen, and Siracusa, John, 'Australia, the United States, and the Cold War, 1945–1951: from V-J Day to ANZUS', *Diplomatic History* 5:1 (1981), pp. 47–52; Harry, Ralphy, 'Security treaty between Australia, New Zealand and the United States of America', *Australian Outlook* 35:2 (1981), pp. 201–12; Lowe: *Australian Between Empires*, pp. 133–38; Lowe, David, 'Percy Spender's quest', *Australian Journal of International Affairs* 55:2 (2001), pp. 187–98; McCormack: *Hot War, Cold War*, pp. 100–06, 164–66; McGibbon: *New Zealand and the Korean War*, vol. I, pp. 203–15, 223, 289; McIntyre, David, *Background to the ANZUS Pact: Policy-Making, Strategy and Diplomacy, 1945–1955* (New York, 1995), pp. 223–347; McLean, David, 'ANZUS origins: a reassessment', *Australian*

Historical Studies 24:94 (1990), pp. 64–82; Meaney, Neville, 'Look back in fear: Percy Spender, the Japanese peace treaty and the ANZUS pact', *Japan Forum* 15:3 (2003), pp. 399–410; O'Neill: *Australia in the Korean War, 1950–53*, vol. I, pp. 185–200; Spender: *Exercises in Diplomacy*, pp. 11–190; Starke, J.G., *The ANZUS Treaty Alliance* (Melbourne, 1985), pp. 36–61.

16. For more on the British reaction to the signing of the ANZUS Treaty see McGibbon: *New Zealand and the Korean War*, vol. I, pp. 214–15, 223, 284–89; O'Neill: *Australia in the Korean War, 1950–53*, vol. I, pp. 234–35; Williams, John, 'ANZUS: a blow to Britain's self-esteem', *Review of International Studies* 13:4 (1987), pp. 243–63.

17. *NARA* RG59/250/50/23/7 E.1574, Box 1, Miscellaneous, Memorandum of Conversation (Henderson), New Delhi, 21 February 1951.

18. *NMML* Papers of Vijaya Lakshmi Pandit (1st Part), Subject File No. 59, Pandit-Nehru, Washington, 5 February 1951.

19. *NMML* Papers of Vijaya Lakshmi Pandit (1st Part), Correspondence–Nehru, Jawaharlal, Nehru-Pandit, New Delhi, 13 February 1951.

20. *LAC* Microfilm T-2367, Cabinet Conclusions, Ottawa, 7 February 1951.

21. *NARA* RG59/250/49/5/3 E.1459, Box 3, Korea-General-January-1951 Folder No. 5, Memorandum of Conversation (Bancroft), Washington, 12 February 1951.

22. *UKNA* FO371/92774, Bevin-Jebb, London, 3 February 1951.

23. *NAA* A1838, 88/1/10 PART 5, Spender-Makin, Canberra, 2 February 1951.

24. *FRUS 1951 Vol. VII* Gross-Acheson, New York, 5 March 1951, pp. 207–09.

25. *FRUS 1951 Vol. VII* Acting Secretary of State (James Webb)-Austin, Washington, 5 March 1951, pp. 209–10.

26. *UKNA* CAB128/19, CM(51)22nd Conclusions, London, 22 March 1951.

27. *NAA* A1838, 88/1/10 PART 5, Spender-Shann, Canberra, 9 March 1951; *LAC* RG24/21067/CSC 1227:1 Pt 1, Pearson-Wrong, Ottawa, 21 March 1951.

28. *UKNA* CAB128/19, CM(51)22nd Conclusions, London, 22 March 1951.

29. *NARA* Microfilm C0044 Reel 1, Memorandum of Conversation (U. Alexis Johnson), Washington, 30 March 1951.

30. *FRUS 1951 Vol. VII* Acheson-Austin, Washington, 5 February 1951, pp. 153–54.

31. *UKNA* FO371/92773, Bevin-Jebb, London, 3 February 1951.

32. *NAA* A1838, 88/1/10 PART 5, Spender-Shann, Canberra, 13 February 1951.

33. *NAA* A1838, 88/1/10 PART 5, Shann-Spender, New York, 16 February 1951.

34. *FRUS 1951 Vol.VII* Memorandum of Conversation (Ward Allen), Washington, 21 February 1951, pp. 184–85.

35. *UKNA* DEFE4/40, Chiefs of Staff Committee Meeting No. 24, London, 5 February 1951.

36. For more on British economic concerns regarding Hong Kong see Mark: *Hong Kong and the Cold War*, pp. 130–76.

37. *UKNA* DEFE4/40, Chiefs of Staff Committee Meeting No. 28, London, 9 February 1951.

38. *FRUS 1951 Vol. VII* Gross-Acheson, New York, 28 February 1951, pp. 197–201.
39. *NARA* RG84/350/82/4/2 E.1030-F, Box 29, Tel Out 1200e–1275e 2/27/51–3/14/51, United States Delegation to the UN Daily Classified Summary No. 184, New York, 8 March 1951.
40. *FRUS 1951 Vol. VII* Memorandum of Conversations Held on March 16 and 19, Prepared in the US Mission to the UN, New York, 19 March 1951, pp. 247–48.
41. *FRUS 1951 Vol. VII* Acheson-Austin, Washington, 26 March 1951, pp. 268–69.
42. *HST* Papers of Harry S. Truman, Korean War File 1947–1952, Box 9, 32. Adoption by UN of economic sanctions, Memorandum of Conversation (J. Shallow), Washington, 16 April 1951.
43. *FRUS 1951 Vol. VII* Acheson-Austin, Washington, 14 April 1951, p. 346.
44. *FRUS 1951 Vol. VII* Acheson-Gifford, Washington, 30 April 1951, pp. 390–04.
45. *FRUS 1951 Vol. VII* Acheson-Austin, Washington, 1 May 1951, pp. 396–97.
46. *UKNA* CAB129/45, CP(51)100, Memorandum (Morrison), London, 3 April 1951.
47. *HST* Papers of Harry S. Truman, Korean War File 1947–1952, Box 9, 32. Adoption by UN of economic sanctions, Memorandum of Conversation (Durward Sandifer), Washington, 27 April 1951.
48. *UKNA* PREM8/1405 Part 6, Australia High Commission in Britain-Attlee, London, 15 May 1951.
49. McGibbon: *New Zealand and the Korean War*, vol. 1, p. 241.
50. *LAC* Microfilm T-2367, Cabinet Conclusions, Ottawa, 17 May 1951.
51. *NARA* RG84/350/82/1/4 E.1030-D, Box 46, Korea (January to December 1951), Memorandum of Conversation (Thomas Cory), New York, 14 May 1951.
52. *FRUS 1951 Vol. VII* Austin-Acheson, New York, 1 May 1951, pp. 397–98.
53. *NARA* RG84/350/82/4/2 E.1030-F, Box 30, Tel Out 1476e–1550e 5/2/51–5/18/51, US Delegation to the UN Daily Classified Summary No. 223, New York, 3 May 1951.
54. *UKNA* PREM8/1405 Part 6, Morrison-Franks, London, 2 May 1951.
55. *UKNA* PREM8/1405 Part 6, Morrison-Franks, London, 4 May 1951.
56. *FRUS 1951 Vol. VII* Acheson-Gifford, Washington, 5 May 1951, pp. 417–18.
57. *UKNA* CAB128/19, CM(51)34th Conclusions, 7 May 1951.
58. *NARA* RG84/350/82/4/2 E.1030-F, Box 30, Tel Out 1476e–1550e 5/2/51–5/18/51, US Delegation to the UN Daily Unclassified Summary No. 230, New York, 14 May 1951.
59. *UNGA Fifth Session First Committee* 444–445th Meetings, New York, 17 May 1951, pp. 629–38.
60. *UNGA Fifth Session Plenary* 330th Meeting, New York, 18 May 1951, p. 742.

61. *NARA* RG84/350/82/5/2 E.1030-H, Box 7, 1951 Inc Tels US April–July 1951, Acheson-Austin, Washington, 29 May 1951.
62. *HST* Papers of Harry S. Truman, Korean War File 1947–52, Box 9, 32. Adoption by UN of economic sanctions [2 of 2: May–Sept 1951], Gifford-Acheson, London, 28 May 1951.
63. *HST* Papers of Harry S. Truman, Korean War File 1947–52, Box 9, 32. Adoption by UN of economic sanctions [2 of 2: May–September 1951], Gifford-Acheson, London, 29 May 1951.
64. *HST* Papers of Harry S. Truman, Korean War File 1947–52, Box 9, 32. Adoption by UN of economic sanctions [2 of 2: May–September 1951], Gifford-Acheson, London, 14 June 1951.
65. *UKNA* FO371/95648, Jebb-Morrison, New York, 23 May 1951.
66. *FRUS 1951 Vol. VII* Acheson-Austin, Washington, 5 June 1951, pp. 513–16.
67. *FRUS 1951 Vol. VII* Austin-Acheson, New York, 25 May 1951, pp. 457–60.
68. *FRUS 1951 Vol. VII* Acheson-Austin, Washington, 25 May 1951, pp. 472–73.
69. *UKNA* CAB128/19, CM(51)37th Conclusions, London, 28 May 1951.
70. *UKNA* FO371/92782, Morrison-Franks, London, 5 June 1951.
71. *NARA* RG84/350/82/4/2 E.1030-F, Box 30, Tel Out 1476e–1550e 5/2/51–5/18/51, US Delegation to the UN Daily Classified Summary No. 224, New York, 5 May 1951.
72. *FRUS 1951 Vol. VII* Kennan-Malik, Washington, 25 May 1951, p. 462.
73. *FRUS 1951 Vol. VII* Kennan-Deputy Under-Secretary of State (Matthews), Washington, 25 May 1951, pp. 507–11.
74. *FRUS 1951 Vol. VII* Editorial Note, 23 June 1951, pp. 546–47.
75. *NARA* RG59/250/49/14/7 E.1265, Box 17, Korea: Memoranda of Conversations 1951, Memorandum of Conversation (Hickerson), Washington, 28 June 1951.
76. *HST* Papers of Harry S. Truman, Korean War File 1947–52, Box 9, 31. Negotiations for an armistice December 1950–June 1951 [3 of 3: April to June 1951], Department of State Press Release No. 579, Washington, 29 June 1951.

Chapter 4   From Panmunjom to Paris and Back Again, July 1951–June 1952

1. For more on US consideration of the use of atomic weapons during this period see Jones: *After Hiroshima*, pp. 106–08, 133–35.
2. For accounts of the military situation in Korea during this phase of the conflict see, for instance, Crane: *American Airpower Strategy in Korea*, pp. 76–92; Hermes, Walter, *Truce Tent and Fighting Front: The United States Army in the Korean War* (Honolulu, 1992), pp. 73–111, 175–205; James, with Wells: *Refighting the Last War*, pp. 66–78; Ridgway: *The War in Korea*, pp. 185–96; Zhang: *Mao's Military Romanticism*, pp. 154–87, 216–24; Zhang: *Red Wings over the Yalu*, pp. 130–71.

3. For more detailed descriptions of the domestic political situation in the United States during this period see, for instance, Donovan: *Tumultuous Years*, pp. 365–71; Fried, Richard, *Nightmare in Red: The McCarthy Era in Perspective* (New York, 1990), pp. 113–70; Griffith, Robert, *The Politics of Fear: Joseph McCarthy and the Senate* (Amherst, 1987), pp. 115–52; Kaufman: *The Korean War*, pp. 150–53; Kepley: *Collapse of the Middle Way*, pp. 117–50.

4. For more on Truman's decision not to stand for re-election see, for instance, Donovan: *Tumultuous Years*, pp. 392–96; Truman: *Memoirs*, vol. 2, pp. 517–22.

5. For an account of the 1951 British General Election see, for instance, Butler, David, *The British General Election of 1951* (London, 1952).

6. For more information on Winston Churchill's Cold War perspectives when he took office see, for instance, Lambakis, Stephen, *Winston Churchill, Architect of Peace: A Study of Statesmanship and the Cold War* (Westport, 1993), pp. 85–137; Larres, Klaus, *Churchill's Cold War: The Politics of Personal Diplomacy* (New Haven, 2002), pp. 100–54; Young, John, *Winston Churchill's Last Campaign: Britain and the Cold War* (Oxford, 1995), pp. 19–40.

7. For accounts of Anthony Eden's Cold War views when he became Foreign Secretary in 1951 see, for instance, Dutton, David, *Anthony Eden: A Life and Reputation* (London, 1997), pp. 314–63; Eden, Anthony, *The Memoirs of Sir Anthony Eden: Full Circle* (London, 1960), pp. 3–12; Wilby, Peter, *Eden* (London, 2006), pp. 68–86.

8. *UKNA* PREM11/112, Churchill-Eden, London, 16 November 1951.

9. Reynolds, David, *In Command of History: Churchill Fighting and Writing the Second World War* (London, 2004), pp. 2–3, 41–47, 400–1, 474–86

10. For Truman's views of Churchill see Truman: *Memoirs*, vol. 1, pp. 265–66; Truman: *Memoirs*, vol. 2, pp. 274–75.

11. Lowe, Peter, *The Korean War* (Basingstoke, 2000), p. 84.

12. For Acheson and Eden's views of each other see, Acheson: *Present at the Creation*, pp. 511, 578–79, 603–06, 615–16, 643–44, 656–57, 680–85, 700–05; Beisner: *Dean Acheson*, pp. 462, 482; Chace: *Acheson*, p. 333; Dutton: *Anthony Eden*, pp. 329–35, 352–53; Eden: *The Memoirs of Sir Anthony Eden*, pp. 16–25; Wilby: *Eden*, p. 75.

13. For more on the Lord Ismay's spell as Secretary of State for Commonwealth Relations see Ismay, Lionel Hastings, *The Memoirs of General the Lord Ismay* (London, 1960), pp. 453–62.

14. For the Australian view on Churchill's election see, for instance, Martin: *Robert Menzies: A Life*, vol. II, p. 203.

15. *LAC* MG-26 N1/1/Pearson L. B.—Acheson, Dean—USA 1946–1955, Pearson-Acheson, Ottawa, 15 January 1952.

16. *LAC* MG26 N1/19/Britain-Canada Rels. 1950–1957, Discussion with Mr Eden (Pearson), London, 7 December 1951.

17. For more on Nehru's views of Churchill's election see Brown: *Nehru: A Political Life*, p. 249.

18. For accounts of the Indian 1951–52 General Election see, for instance, Brown: *Nehru*, pp. 98, 100–01, 105, 119, 121–22, 142–43; Brown: *Nehru: A Political Life*, pp. 197–98, 286, 346–48; Kogekar, Sadanand and Price, Richard, *Reports of the Indian General Elections, 1951–1952* (Bombay, 1956).

19. For more on the Pakistani domestic situation see Afzal, M. Rafique, 'Nazimuddin ministry: reasons for its dismissal', *Pakistan Journal of History and Culture* 15:2 (1994), pp. 47–49; Syed, M.M., 'Pakistan: struggle for power, 1947–58', *Pakistan Journal of History and Culture* 15:2 (1994), pp. 87–88.

20. For more on the 1951 New Zealand general election and the appointment of Webb see McGibbon: *New Zealand and the Korean War*, vol. I, p. 260.

21. For the role played by Dulles in concluding the Japanese peace treaty see Miyasoto, Seigen, 'John Foster Dulles and the peace settlement with Japan', in R. Immerman (ed.), *John Foster Dulles and the Diplomacy of the Cold War* (Princeton, 1989), pp. 189–212.

22. For Commonwealth perspectives of the Japanese peace treaty see, for instance, Lowe, Peter, 'Great Britain and the Japanese Peace Treaty, 1951', in P. Lowe and H. Moeshart (eds), *Western Interactions with Japan: Expansion, the Armed Forces, and Readjustments, 1859–1956* (Folkestone, 1990), pp. 91–104; Trotter, Ann, *New Zealand and Japan, 1945–1952: The Occupation and the Peace Treaty* (London, 1990), pp. 166–73.

23. For more on Acheson's role in the negotiations for the Japanese peace treaty see Igarashi, Takeshi, 'Dean Acheson and the Japanese peace treaty', in D. Brinkley (ed.), *Dean Acheson and the Making of US Foreign Policy* (Basingstoke, 1993), pp. 133–58.

24. For more details on the evolution of NATO during this period see, for instance, Duignan: *NATO*, pp. 6–18; Kaplan: *The Long Entanglement*, p. 62; Kaplan: *NATO Divided, NATO United*, pp. 9–27; Milloy: *North Atlantic Treaty Organisation, 1948–1957*, pp. 67–87, 97–103; Powaski: *The Entangling Alliance*, pp. 17–28.

25. For more on the negotiations for the EDC see, for instance, Dockrill, Saki, 'The evolution of Britain's policy towards a European army, 1950–1954', *Journal of Strategic Studies* 12:1 (1989), pp. 38–62; Fursdon, Edward, *The European Defence Community: A History* (London, 1980), pp. 105–49; Gavin, Victor, 'Power through Europe? The case of the European Defence Community in France (1950–1954)', *French History* 23:1 (2009), pp. 69–78; Mawby, Spencer, 'From distrust to despair: Britain and the European army, 1950–1954', *European History Quarterly* 28:4 (1998), pp. 487–502; Ruane, Kevin, *The Rise and Fall of the European Defence Community: Anglo-American Relations and the Crisis of European Defence, 1950–55* (Basingstoke, 2000), pp. 15–30.

26. For more on this phase of the Malayan Emergency see, for instance, Barber: *The War of the Running Dogs*, pp. 139–61, 177–84; Clutterbuck: *The Long Long War*, pp. 79–94; Coates: *Suppressing Insurgency*, pp. 109–36; Jackson: *The Malayan Emergency*, pp. 39–47; O'Ballance: *Malaya*, pp. 114–36; Ramakrishna: *Emergency Propaganda*, pp. 120–59; Short: *The Communist Insurrection in Malaya*,

1948–1960, pp. 323–87, 391–438; Stubbs: *Hearts and Minds in Guerrilla Warfare*, pp. 133–200.

27. For accounts of the course of the armistice talks during this period see, for instance, Bacchus, Wilfrid, 'The relationship between combat and peace negotiations: fighting while talking in Korea, 1951–53', *Orbis* 17:2 (1973), pp. 558–62; Bailey, Sydney, *The Korean Armistice* (Basingstoke, 1992), pp. 70–109; Foot: 'Negotiating with friends and enemies', pp. 193–208; Foot: *A Substitute for Victory*, pp. 42–107; Hermes: *Truce Tent and Fighting Front*, pp. 15–51, 112–74; Joy, C. Turner, *Negotiating While Fighting: The Diary of Admiral C. Turner Joy at the Korean Armistice Conference* (Stanford, 1978), pp. 11–437; Vatcher, William, *Panmunjom: The Story of the Korean Military Armistice Negotiations* (Westport, 1958), pp. 20–148.

28. For more on the prisoner of war question during this period see Bernstein, Barton, 'The struggle over the Korean armistice: prisoners of repatriation?' in B. Cumings (ed.), *Child of Conflict: The Korean-American Relationship, 1943–1953* (Seattle, 1983), pp. 261–96; Young, Charles, 'POWs: the hidden reason for forgetting Korea', *Journal of Strategic Studies* 33:2 (2010), pp. 317–32.

29. For more on the Truman administration's decision to support the principle of non-forcible repatriation see Acheson: *Present at the Creation*, pp. 652–54.

30. For more on the Goje Island Incident see Clark, Mark, *From the Danube to the Yalu* (London, 1954), pp. 39–54; Stueck: *The Korean War*, pp. 261–71, 276–84.

31. *FRUS 1951 Vol. VII* Acheson-Austin, Washington, 14 July 1951, pp. 678–81.

32. *UKNA* FO371/92788, Morrison-Franks, London, 28 July 1951.

33. *UKNA* FO371/92789, Jebb-Morrison, New York, 22 July 1951.

34. *FRUS 1951 Vol. VII* Acheson-Austin, Washington, 4 August 1951, pp. 783–74.

35. *FRUS 1951 Vol. VII* Hickerson/Merchant-Acheson, Washington, 3 August 1951, pp. 771–74.

36. *UKNA* FO371/92789, Jebb-Morrison, New York, 22 July 1951.

37. *FRUS 1951 Vol. VII* US Delegation Minutes of Second Meeting of US-British Foreign Ministers, Washington, 11 September 1951, pp. 893–99.

38. *FRUS 1951 Vol. VII* Webb-Acheson, Washington, 4 November 1951, p. 1087.

39. *UKNA* FO371/92796, Eden-Jebb, London, 9 November 1951.

40. *UNGA Sixth Session First Committee* 446th Meeting, New York, 17 November 1951, pp. 3–5.

41. *UKNA* FO371/92799, Record of the Meeting of the Heads of the Commonwealth Delegations, Paris, 30 November 1951.

42. *UKNA* FO371/92799, Summary Record of the Meeting of the Informal Commonwealth Study Group on Korea, Paris, 5 December 1951.

43. *NARA* RG84/350/82/4/2 E.1030-F, Box 32, Tel Outs–Delga–473–562 2 December–8 December 1951, Austin-Acheson, Paris, 6 December 1951.

44. *FRUS 1951 Vol. VII* Webb-Acheson, Washington, 8 December 1951, pp. 1282–85.

45. *FRUS 1951 Vol. VII* Austin-Acheson, Paris, 11 December 1951, pp. 1302–05.
46. *UKNA* FO371/92800, Record of the Meeting of the Heads of the Commonwealth Delegations, Paris, 14 December 1951.
47. *LAC* RG25/6446/5475-DW-14-40 [Pt 4], Pearson-MEA, Paris, 13 December 1951.
48. *UKNA* FO371/92800, Summary Record of the Meeting of the Informal Commonwealth Study Group on Korea, Paris, 12 December 1951.
49. Mazunan: *Warren R. Austin at the UN*, p. 178.
50. *NARA* RG84/350/82/4/2 E.1030-F, Box 36, Tel Outs–Delgas 810–9651 1 January–9 January 1952, Roosevelt-Acheson, Paris, 5 January 1952.
51. *UKNA* FO371/99596, Record of the Meeting of the Heads of the Commonwealth Delegations, Paris 4 January 1952.
52. *UKNA* FO371/99596, Record of the Meeting of the Heads of the Commonwealth Delegations, Paris, 5 January 1952.
53. *UNGA Sixth Session First Committee* 486th Meeting, New York, 9 January 1952, pp. 174–77.
54. *UNGA Sixth Session First Committee* 493rd Meeting, New York, 17 January 1952, pp. 209–13.
55. *UKNA* FO371/99596, Lloyd-Eden, Paris, 14 January 1952.
56. *FRUS 1952–54 Vol. XV* Acheson-Roosevelt, Washington, 21 January 1952, pp. 27–28.
57. *UKNA* FO371/99596, Record of the Meeting of the Heads of the Commonwealth Delegations, Paris, 23 January 1952.
58. *UNGA Sixth Session Supplements* A/1881, Supplement No. 12, Report of UNCURK, pp. 1–69; *UNGA Sixth Session Annexes* Agenda Items 17 and 27, A/1935, Report of UNKRA, New York, 3 November 1951, pp. 1–2.
59. *UKNA* FO371/99596, Record of the Meeting of the Heads of the Commonwealth Delegations, Paris, 18 January 1952.
60. *UKNA* FO371/99596, Record of the Meeting of the Heads of the Commonwealth Delegations, Paris, 23 January 1952.
61. *UNGA Sixth Session First Committee* 507th Meeting, New York, 2 February 1952, pp. 287–91
62. *UNGA Sixth Session First Committee* 508th Meeting, New York, 2 February 1952, pp. 293–301.
63. *UNGA Sixth Session Plenary* 375th Meeting, New York, 5 February 1952, p. 523.
64. *NARA* Microfilm C0042 Reel 4, Memorandum of Conversation (Hickerson), Washington, 5 March 1952.
65. *UKNA* PREM11/112, Ismay-All High Commissions, London, 21 February 1952.
66. *LAC* RG24/21067/CSC 1227:1 Pt 2, Pearson-Wrong, Ottawa, 27 March 1952.
67. *LAC* RG24/21067/CSC 1227:1 Pt 2, Rive-Pearson, Wellington, 4 April 1952.
68. *NARA* Microfilm C0042 Reel 4, Memorandum of Conversation (Hickerson), Washington, 7 April 1952.

69. *NARA* RG84/350/82/4/2 E.1030-F, Box 34, Tel Out 537f–625 1/3/52–3/19/52, US Delegation to the UN Daily Unclassified Summary No. 86, New York, 14 March 1952.

70. *NARA* RG84/350/82/4/2 E.1030-F, Box 34, Tel Out 626f–700 3/20/52–4/12/52, US Delegation to the UN Daily Unclassified Summary No. 91, New York, 20 March 1952.

71. *NARA* RG84/350/82/4/2 E.1030-F, Box 34, Tel Out 626f–700 3/20/52–4/12/52, US Delegation to the UN Daily Unclassified Summary No. 94, New York, 26 March 1952.

72. *UNSC Seventh Year* 577th Meeting, New York, 18 June 1952, pp. 15–30.

73. *UNSC Seventh Year* 578th Meeting, New York, 20 June 1952, pp. 1–19.

74. *UNSC Seventh Year* 583rd Meeting, New York, 26 June 1952, pp. 1–28.

75. *NARA* RG84/350/82/5/2 E.1030-H, Box 10, 1952 Inc Tels US (Jan–August), Acheson-Austin, Washington, 16 June 1952.

76. *UNSC Seventh Year* 580th Meeting, New York, 23 June 1952, pp. 1–23.

77. *UNSC Seventh Year* 581st Meeting, New York, 25 June 1952, pp. 1–22.

78. *UNSC Seventh Year* 587th Meeting, New York, 3 July 1952, pp. 1–15.

79. *UNSC Seventh Year* 589th Meeting, New York, 9 July 1952, pp. 1–20.

80. *UNSC Seventh Year* 590th Meeting, New York, 9 July 1952, pp. 1–7.

Chapter 5   The Indian Resolution, June–December 1952

1. For more on the military situation in Korea during these months see, for instance, Crane: *American Airpower Strategy in Korea*, pp. 110–54; Hermes: *Truce Tent and Fighting Front*, pp. 283–329, 366–400; James, with Wells: *Refighting the Last War*, pp. 102–25; Zhang: *Mao's Military Romanticism*, pp. 224–37; Zhang: *Red Wings over the Yalu*, pp. 172–91.

2. For more on the British response to the bombing of the Suiho power station see, for instance, Dockrill: 'The Foreign Office, Anglo-American relations and the Korean truce negotiations, July 1951–July 1953', pp. 107–08; Farrar-Hockley: *The British Part in the Korean War*, vol. II, pp. 320–22; Stueck: *The Korean War*, pp. 283–85.

3. For more on the appointment of Lord Swinton as Secretary of State for Commonwealth Relations see Cross, John, *Lord Swinton* (Oxford, 1982), pp. 273–74.

4. For more on the growing political crisis in Pakistan see, for instance, Afzal: 'Nazimuddin ministry', pp. 47–62; Syed: 'Pakistan', pp. 87–88.

5. For more on the Republican Party perspective on the 1952 US Presidential election see Caridi: *The Korean War and American Politics*, pp. 209–45; Kepley: *Collapse of the Middle Way*, pp. 139–50.

6. For fuller accounts of the 1952 US Presidential election see, for instance, Bernstein, Barton, 'Election of 1952', in A. Schlesinger (ed.), *History of American Presidential Elections, 1789–1968*, vol. 8 (New York, 1971),

pp. 3215–337; Greene, John, *The Crusade: The Presidential Election of 1952* (Lanham, 1985).

7. For accounts of the role of the Korean War in Eisenhower's campaign see, for instance, Divine, Robert, *Foreign Policy and US Presidential Elections, 1952–1960* (New York, 1974), pp. 10, 19–41, 45–46, 66–83; Medhurst, Martin, 'Text and context in the 1952 presidential campaign: Eisenhower's "I shall go to Korea" speech', *Presidential Studies Quarterly* 30:3 (2000), pp. 464–84.

8. For more on the Mau Mau uprising see, for instance, Branch, Daniel, *Defeating Mau Mau, Creating Kenya: Counterinsurgency, Civil War, and Decolonisation* (Cambridge, 2009), pp. 21–93; Branch, Daniel, 'The enemy within: loyalists and the war against the Mau Mau in Kenya', *Journal of African History* 48:2 (2007), pp. 291–302; Clough, Marshall, *Mau Mau Memoirs: History, Memory and Politics* (London, 1998), pp. 106–75; Edgerton, Robert, *Mau Mau: An African Crucible* (London, 1990), pp. 65–106; Wunyabari, Molaba, *Mau Mau and Kenya: An Analysis of a Peasant Revolt* (Bloomington, 1993), pp. 65–133.

9. For more on the Anglo-American perspective of the Egyptian Revolution see, for instance, Botman, Selma, 'Egyptian communists and the Free Officers, 1950–54', *Middle Eastern Studies* 22:3 (1986), pp. 350–66; McNamara, Robert, *Britain, Nasser and the Balance of Power in the Middle East, 1952–1967: From the Egyptian Revolution to the Six-Day War* (Portland, 2003), pp. 23–39; Morsy, Laila, 'American support for the 1952 Egyptian coup: why?', *Middle Eastern Studies* 31:5 (1995), pp. 307–16; Rubin, Barry, 'America and the Egyptian Revolution, 1950–1957', *Political Science Quarterly* 97:1 (1982), pp. 73–78; Thornhill, Michael, 'Britain, the United States and the rise of an Egyptian leader: the politics and diplomacy of Nasser's consolidation of power, 1952–4', *English Historical Review* 119:483 (2004), pp. 892–904.

10. For good accounts of the ROK political crisis see Keefer, Edward, 'The Truman administration and the South Korean political crisis of 1952: democracy's failure?', *Pacific Historical Review* 60:2 (1991), pp. 145–68; Ra, Jong-Yil, 'Political crisis in Korea, 1952', *Journal of Contemporary History* (1992) 27:2, pp. 301–18.

11. For the various reactions of the Commonwealth countries to Eisenhower's election see, for instance, Dutton: *Anthony Eden*, pp. 240, 333–40, 353–55, 359–60; Eden: *The Memoirs of Sir Anthony Eden*, pp. 49–51; Farrar-Hockley: *The British Part in the Korean War*, vol. II, pp. 387–88; Larres: *Churchill's Cold*, pp. 182–88; MacDonald: *Britain and the Korean War*, pp. 83–85; McGibbon: *New Zealand and the Korean War*, vol. I, pp. 321–21; O'Neill: *Australia in the Korean War, 1950–53*, vol. I, pp. 323–24; Young: *Winston Churchill's Last Campaign*, pp. 88–130.

12. For accounts of the course of the armistice talks during this period see, for instance, Bacchus: 'The relationship between combat and peace negotiations', pp. 562–65; Bailey: *The Korean Armistice*, pp. 109–26; Bernstein: 'The struggle over the Korean armistice', pp. 296–307; Foot: *A Substitute for*

Victory, pp. 130–52; Hermes: *Truce Tent and Fighting Front*, pp. 263–82; Vatcher: *Panmunjom*, pp. 148–77.

13. For more on these bilateral attempts to find a solution to the prisoner of war question see, for instance, Dayal: *India's Role in the Korean Question*, pp. 179–81; Dockrill: 'The Foreign Office, Anglo-American relations and the Korean truce negotiations', p. 107; Lowe: 'The settlement of the Korean War', pp. 212–19; Stueck: *The Korean War*, pp. 278–80.

14. *FRUS 1952–54 Vol. XV* Memorandum of Conversation (Hickerson), 14 August 1952, pp. 453–56.

15. *UKNA* PREM11/119, Churchill-Lloyd, London, 23 August 1952.

16. *UKNA* PREM11/119, Eden-Churchill, London, 1 September 1952.

17. *LAC* MG26 N1/64/UN General Assembly–1948–1952, Visit of the Secretary of State for External Affairs to Washington 4–5 September 1952, 8 September 1952.

18. *NAA* A1838 3123/5/14/1, Spender-Casey, Washington, 5 September 1952.

19. *UKNA* DO35/5829, South African Secretary for External Affairs (Forsyth)-South Africa High Commissioner to Britain (Rumbold), Pretoria, 23 September 1952.

20. *NAA* A1838 3123/5/14/1, Spender-Casey, Washington, 15 August 1952.

21. *NAA* A1838 3123/5/14/1, Casey-Spender, Canberra, 26 August 1952.

22. *UKNA* DO35/5829, Eden-Jebb, London, 16 September 1952.

23. *HST*, Dean G. Acheson Papers, Secretary of State File 1945–1972, Memoranda of Conversations File 1949–1953, Box 67, September 1952, Meeting with President (Acheson), Washington, 25 September 1952.

24. *LAC* MG26 N1/64/UN General Assembly–1948–1952, Visit of the Secretary of State for External Affairs to Washington 4–5 September 1952, 8 September 1952.

25. *NAA* A1838 3123/5/14/1, Casey-Spender, Canberra, 26 August 1952.

26. *NAA* A1838 3123/5/14/1, Australian High Commission in New Zealand-Casey, Wellington, 28 August 1952.

27. *NARA* RG84/350/82/5/2 E.1030-H, Box 11, 1952 Inc Tels US (September–December), Acheson-Austin, Washington, 17 September 1952.

28. *UKNA* DO35/5829, Eden-Franks, London, 18 September 1952.

29. *LAC* RG25/5984/50267-40 [Pt. 1.2], Cabinet Memorandum (Pearson), Ottawa, 6 October 1952.

30. *UKNA* DO35/5829, British High Commission in South Africa-Salisbury, Pretoria, 18 September 1952.

31. *NAA* A1838 3123/5/14/1, Casey-Australian High Commission in Britain, Canberra, 18 September 1952.

32. *UKNA* DO35/5829, British High Commission in New Zealand-Salisbury, Wellington, 26 September 1952.

33. *UKNA* DO35/5829, Nye-Salisbury, New Delhi, 24 September 1952.

34. *FRUS 1952–54 Vol. XV* Acheson-Austin, Washington, 19 September 1952, pp. 525–27.

35. *NAA* A1838 3123/5/14/1, Casey-Spender, Canberra, 2 October 1952.
36. *UKNA* DO35/5829, Eden-Franks, London, 27 September 1952.
37. *LAC* RG25/5984/50267-40 [Pt. 1.2], Cabinet Memorandum (Pearson), Ottawa, 6 October 1952.
38. *UKNA* DO35/5830, Jebb-Eden, New York, 17 October 1952.
39. *UKNA* DO35/5830, Lloyd-Eden, New York, 23 October 1952.
40. *UNGA Seventh Session First Committee* 512–514th Meetings, 24–29 October 1952, pp. 19–38.
41. *HST*, Dean G. Acheson Papers, Secretary of State File 1945–1972, Memoranda of Conversations File 1949–1953, Box 67, October 1952, Acheson-Truman, New York, 25 October 1952.
42. *NMML* Papers of Vijaya Lakshmi Pandit (1st Part), Subject File No. 47, Pandit-Nehru, New York, 15 October 1952.
43. *NMML* Papers of Vijaya Lakshmi Pandit (1st Part), Subject File No. 48, Pandit-Nehru, New York, 26 October 1952.
44. *NMML* Papers of Vijaya Lakshmi Pandit (1st Part), Subject File No. 47, Nehru-Pandit, New Delhi, 12 October 1952.
45. For more on Menon's past experiences and opinions see, for instance, Brecher, Michael, *Indian and World Politics: Krishna Menon's View of the World* (London, 1968), pp. 3–43, 107–20, 180–94, 289–333; George, T.J.S., *Krishna Menon: A Biography* (London, 1964), pp. 155–77.
46. Jebb: *The Memoirs of Lord Gladwyn*, p. 259.
47. *NMML* Papers of Vijaya Lakshmi Pandit (1st Part), Subject File No. 47, Pandit-Nehru, New York, 4 November 1952.
48. *UKNA* DO35/5830, Record of the Meeting of the Heads of the Commonwealth Delegations, New York, 24 October 1952.
49. *UKNA* PREM11/111, Jebb-Eden, New York, 28 October 1952.
50. *FRUS 1952–1954 Vol. XV* Memorandum of Conversation (Acheson), 29 October 1952, pp. 566–68.
51. *FRUS 1952–1954 Vol. XV* Gross-State Department, New York, 1 November 1952, pp. 570–72.
52. Acheson: *Present at the Creation*, p. 700.
53. *UKNA* PREM11/111, Nye-Salisbury, New Delhi, 28 October 1952.
54. *LAC* RG25/5984/50267-40 [Pt 1.2], Johnson-MEA, New York, 30 October 1952.
55. *UKNA* DO35/5831, Nye-Salisbury, New Delhi, 4 November 1952.
56. *NMML* Papers of Vijaya Lakshmi Pandit (1st Part), Subject File No. 47, Pandit-Nehru, New York, 4 November 1952.
57. *NMML* Papers of Vijaya Lakshmi Pandit (1st Part), Subject File No. 47, Pandit-Nehru, New York, 5 November 1952.
58. *NARA* RG59/250/46/3/4 E.394, Box 2, Memoranda of Conversations with the President 1952, Meeting with the President (Acheson), Washington, 5 November 1952.

59. *DDE* Name Series, Box 33, Truman, Harry S. 8/12/52–1/15/53 (2), Truman-Eisenhower, Washington, 6 November 1952.

60. *DDE* Name Series, Box 33, Truman, Harry S. 8/12/52–1/15/53 (2), Eisenhower-Truman, Augusta, 7 November 1952.

61. *MHS* Henry Cabot Lodge (1902–1985) Papers, Carton 23, Truman-Eisenhower 1952/53, Journal (Lodge), 18 November 1952.

62. Pearson: *Memoirs*, vol. 2, p. 315.

63. *LAC* RG25/5984/50267-40 [Pt 2.1], Johnson-MEA, New York, 6 November 1952.

64. *NARA* LM 081, DF795, Reel 19, Bowles-Acheson, New Delhi, 8 November 1952.

65. *FRUS 1952–1954 Vol.* XV Acheson-State Department, 8 November 1952, pp. 586–88.

66. *UNGA Seventh Session First Committee* 521st Meeting, New York, 10 November 1952, pp. 85–91.

67. Acheson: *Present at the Creation*, p. 701.

68. *FRUS 1952–1954 Vol.* XV Acheson-State, New York, 12 November 1952, pp. 607–10.

69. *UKNA* DO35/5831, Eden-Foreign Office, New York, 14 November 1952.

70. *FRUS 1952–1954 Vol.* XV Acheson-State, New York, 13 November 1952, pp. 619–21.

71. *FRUS 1952–1954 Vol.* XV Draft Memorandum of Conversation Held in New York, 16 November 1952, pp. 637–45.

72. *FRUS 1952–1954 Vol.* XV Acheson-State, New York, 15 November 1952, pp. 628–33.

73. *UKNA* DO35/5831, Eden-Foreign Office, New York, 15 November 1952.

74. *UNGA Seventh Session First Committee* 525th Meeting, New York, 19 November 1952, pp. 111–15.

75. *NMML* Papers of Vijaya Lakshmi Pandit (1st Part), Subject File No. 47, Nehru-Pandit, New Delhi, 18 November 1952.

76. *UNGA Seventh Session First Committee* 526th Meeting, New York, 20 November 1952, pp. 117–18.

77. *FRUS 1952–1954 Vol.* XV Acheson-Truman, New York, 20 November 1952, pp. 622–23.

78. *FRUS 1952–1954 Vol.* XV Acheson-State Department, New York, 19 November 1952, pp. 659–62.

79. *UKNA* DO35/5832, Eden-Foreign Office, New York, 21 November 1952.

80. Acheson: *Present at the Creation*, p. 705.

81. *LAC* RG25/5984/50267-40 [Pt 2.1], Johnson-MEA, New York, 24 November 1952.

82. Acheson: *Present at the Creation*, p. 705.

83. *UNGA Seventh Session First Committee* 529th Meeting, New York, 24 November 1952, pp. 135–41.

84. *FRUS 1952–1954 Vol.* XV Acheson-State Department, New York, 24 November 1952, pp. 669–74.
85. *UKNA* DO35/5832, Eden-Foreign Office, New York, 24 November 1952.
86. Pearson: *Memoirs*, vol. 2, p. 329.
87. *FRUS 1952–1954 Vol.* XV Acheson-State Department, New York, 25 November 1952, p. 676.
88. *NMML* Papers of Vijaya Lakshmi Pandit (1st Part), Subject File No. 47, Nehru-Pandit, New Delhi, 25 November 1952.
89. *LAC* MG31 E46/7/17 1952, Reid-Pearson, New Delhi, 28 November 1952.
90. *NMML* Oral History Transcripts, Oral History with R.K. Nehru (B.R. Nanda), New Delhi, 1 July 1971.
91. *UKNA* DO35/5832, Eden-Foreign Office, New York, 25 November 1952.
92. *LAC* RG25/6235/8254-K-40 [Pt 1.1], Pearson-Reid, New York, 27 November 1952.
93. *FRUS 1952–1954 Vol.* XV Acheson-State, New York, 26 November 1952, pp. 689–91.
94. *FRUS 1952–1954 Vol.* XV Acheson-State, New York, 28 November 1952, pp. 698–99.
95. *FRUS 1952–1954 Vol.* XV Acheson-Truman, New York, 26 November 1952, p. 686.
96. Pearson: *Memoirs*, vol. 2, pp. 330–31.
97. *LAC* RG25/6235/8254-K-40 [Pt 1.1], Pearson-MEA, New York, 27 November 1952.
98. *LAC* RG25/6235/8254-K-40 [Pt 1.1], Reid-Pearson, New Delhi, 28 November 1952.
99. *UNGA Seventh Session First Committee* 531st Meeting, New York, 26 November 1952, pp. 149–51.
100. *UNGA Seventh Session First Committee* 535–6th Meeting, New York, 1–2 December 1952, pp. 173–85; *UNGA Seventh Session Plenary* 399th Meeting, New York, 3 December 1952, pp. 295–308.
101. *UKNA* CAB129/57, CP(52)441, Memorandum (Eden), London, 15 December 1952.
102. Pearson: *Memoirs*, vol. 2, p. 332.
103. *NMML* Papers of Vijaya Lakshmi Pandit (1st Part), Subject File No. 48, Pandit-Nehru, New York, 4 December 1952.
104. *NMML* Papers of Vijaya Lakshmi Pandit (1st Part), Subject File No. 48, Pandit-Nehru, New York, 11 December 1952.
105. *NMML* Papers of Vijaya Lakshmi Pandit (1st Part), Subject File No. 50, Nehru-Pandit, New Delhi, 7 December 1952.
106. *LAC* RG25/6235/8254-K-40 [Pt 1.1], Pearson-Reid, Ottawa, 3 December 1952.
107. *FRUS 1952–1954 Vol.* XV Austin-Acheson, New York, 6 December 1952, p. 706.

108. *LAC* RG25/6235/8254-K-40 [Pt 1.1], Pearson-Reid, Ottawa, 3 December 1952.
109. *LAC* MG31 E46/7/17 1952, Reid-Pearson, New Delhi, 5 December 1952.
110. Pearson: *Memoirs*, vol. 2, p. 333.
111. *UNGA Seventh Session Plenary* 411th Meeting, New York, 21 December 1952, p. 530.

Chapter 6   The Korean War Endgame, January–July 1953

1. For more on the military situation in Korea during these months see, for instance, Crane: *American Airpower Strategy in Korea*, pp. 155–70; Hermes: *Truce Tent and Fighting Front*, pp. 459–78; James, with Wells: *Refighting the Last War*, pp. 125–27; Zhang: *Mao's Military Romanticism*, pp. 237–46; Zhang: *Red Wings over the Yalu*, pp. 191–200.
2. For more on Eisenhower's leadership style see, for instance, Ambrose, Stephen, *Eisenhower*, vol. 2, *The President* (London, 1984), pp. 9–10, 15–16, 19–20, 37, 44, 53, 71, 85, 114, 164–65, 327, 435, 549, 562, 579, 620–27; Divine, Robert, *Eisenhower and the Cold War* (New York, 1981), pp. 3–31; Greenstein, Fred, *The Hidden-Hand Presidency: Eisenhower as President* (New York, 1982); McAuliffe, Mary, 'Eisenhower, the President', *Journal of American History* 68:3 (1981), pp. 625–32.
3. For more on Eisenhower's Cold War perspective when he took office see, for instance, Bowie, Robert and Immerman, Richard, *Waging Peace: How Eisenhower Shaped An Enduring Cold War Strategy* (New York, 1998), pp. 41–80; Eisenhower, Dwight, *The White House Years: Mandate for Change, 1953–1956* (London, 1963), pp. 3–103; Pickett, William, *Dwight David Eisenhower and American Power* (Wheeling, 1995), pp. 98–138.
4. For good accounts of Dulles' Cold War views when appointed Secretary of State see, for instance, Hoopes, Townsend, *The Devil and John Foster Dulles* (Boston, 1973), pp. 124–60; Immerman, Richard, *John Foster Dulles: Piety, Pragmatism and Power in US Foreign Policy* (Wilimington, 1999), pp. 17–57; Marks, Frederick, *Power and Peace: The Diplomacy of John Foster Dulles* (Westport, 1993), pp. 97–118.
5. Clark: *From the Danube to the Yalu*, pp. 218–26.
6. For scholarship on the Eisenhower administration's strategy for ending the Korean War see, for instance, Dingman: 'Atomic diplomacy during the Korean War', pp. 79–91; Eisenhower: *The White House Years*, pp. 171–91; Foot: 'Nuclear coercion', pp. 92–112; Foot: *The Wrong War*, pp. 204–31; Friedman, Edward, 'Nuclear blackmail and the end of the Korean War', *Modern China* 1:1 (1975), pp. 75–91; Jones: *After Hiroshima*, pp. 144–61; Keefer, Edward, 'President Eisenhower and the end of the Korean War', *Diplomatic History* 10 (1986), pp. 267–89; Rees: *Korea*, pp. 402–20.
7. For more on Dulles-Eden relations concerning the Yoshida Letter see, for instance, Hosoya, Chihiro, 'Japan, China, the United States and the United

Kingdom, 1951–52: the case of the "Yoshida letter"', *International Affairs* 60:2 (1984), pp. 255–59; Schonberger, Howard, 'Peacemaking in Asia: the United States, Great Britain, and the Japanese decision to recognize Nationalist China, 1951–1952', *Diplomatic History* 10:1 (1986), pp. 67–73.

8. For more on the illnesses of Churchill and Eden and their impact on British policy see, for instance, Brain, Russell, 'Encounters with Winston Churchill', *Medical History* 44:1 (2000), pp. 12–14; Braasch, John, 'Anthony Eden's (Lord Avon) bilary tract saga', *Annals of Surgery* 238:5 (2003), pp. 772–75; Dutton: *Anthony Eden*, pp. 5–6, 13, 217, 240–43, 246, 326, 337–38, 358–60, 463–64; Eden: *The Memoirs*, pp. 51–52; Larres: *Churchill's Cold War*, pp. 263–65; Wilby: *Eden*, pp. 73–74; Young: *Winston Churchill's Last Campaign*, pp. 183–209.

9. For an account of the 1953 South African General Election see Price, T., 'The South African general election, 1953', *Parliamentary Affairs* 6:3 (1953), pp. 258–68.

10. For more on the dismissal of Nazimuddin see, for instance, Afzal: 'Nazimuddin ministry'; Syed: 'Pakistan', pp. 88–89.

11. For more on the origins, testing and impact of the first hydrogen bomb see, for instance, Holloway, David, 'Nuclear weapons and the escalation of the Cold War, 1945–1962', in Leffler, P., Westad, O. (eds), *The Cambridge History of the Cold War*, vol. 1 (Cambridge, 2010), pp. 382–97; Mandelbaum, Michael, *The Nuclear Question: The United States and Nuclear Weapons, 1946–1976* (Cambridge, 1979), pp. 46–68; Rhodes, Richard, *Dark Sun: The Making of the Hydrogen Bomb* (London, 1995); Rosenberg, David, 'American atomic strategy and the hydrogen bomb decision', *Journal of American History* 66:1 (1979), pp. 62–87; Rosenberg, David, 'The origins of overkill: nuclear weapons and American strategy, 1945–1960', *International Security* 7:4 (1983), pp. 27–71; Trachtenberg, Marc, 'A "wasting asset"? American strategy and the shifting nuclear balance, 1949–1954', *International Security* 13:3 (1988/89), pp. 33–49.

12. For more on the unrest in East Central Europe at this time see, for instance, Bekes, Csaba, 'East Central Europe, 1953–1962', in M. Leffler and O. Westad (eds), *The Cambridge History of the Cold War*, vol. 1 (Cambridge, 2010), pp. 335–38; Crampton, Richard, *Eastern Europe in the Twentieth Century and After* (London, 1997), pp. 275–80; Ostermann, Christian, 'New documents on the East German uprising in 1953', *Cold War International History Project Bulletin* 5 (1995), pp. 10–17, 57.

13. For more on the impact of Stalin's death on Communist policy regarding Korea see, for instance, Stueck: *The Korean War*, pp. 307–13, 326–27, 341; Stueck: *Rethinking the Korean War*, pp. 173–74.

14. For more on the US and Commonwealth reactions to Stalin's death see, for instance, Bowie and Immerman: *Waging Peace*, pp. 109–22, 149–57, 224–27; Brown: *Nehru: A Political*, pp. 259–60; Dutton: *Anthony Eden*, pp. 336–40; Eden: *Memoirs*, pp. 49–51; Eisenhower: *The White House Years*, pp. 143–49; Foot: *A Substitute for Victory*, pp. 182–83; Hoopes: *The Devil and John Foster Dulles*, pp. 170–75; Immerman: *John Foster Dulles*, pp. 52–55, 59–61, 70;

Keefer: 'President Eisenhower and the end of the Korean War'; Lambakis: *Winston Churchill, Architect of Peace*, pp. 137–61; Larres: *Churchill's Cold War*, pp. 189–240; Williamson, Daniel, *Separate Agendas: Churchill, Eisenhower, and Anglo-American Relations, 1953–1955* (Lanham, 2006), pp. 13–29; Young: *Winston Churchill's Last Campaign*, pp. 131–82.

15. For accounts of the course of the armistice talks during this period see, for instance, Bacchus: 'The relationship between combat and peace negotiations', pp. 565–68; Bailey: *The Korean Armistice*, pp. 126–38; Foot: *A Substitute for Victory*, pp. 159–89; Hermes: *Truce Tent and Fighting Front*, pp. 408–58, 479–97; Vatcher: *Panmunjom*, pp. 178–203.

16. For more on the Commonwealth reaction to the UN negotiation position see, for instance, Farrar-Hockley: *The British Part in the Korean War*, vol. II, pp. 387–92; Lowe: 'The settlement of the Korean War', pp. 224–26; MacDonald: *Britain and the Korean War*, pp. 86–93; McGibbon: *New Zealand and the Korean War*, vol. I, pp. 321–39; Mount, with Laferriere: *The Diplomacy of War*, pp. 137–49; O'Neill: *Australia in the Korean War, 1950–53*, vol. I, pp. 349–73.

17. For more on Rhee's decision to release 27,000 Korean prisoners of war see Stueck: *The Korean War*, pp. 330–42.

18. For more on the Robertson mission see *PUL* John Foster Dulles Oral History Project, Interview with Walter Robertson (Philip Crowl), Richmond, 23–24 July 1965, pp. 20–28.

19. *MHS* Henry Cabot Lodge (1902–1985) Papers, Carton 23, Truman-Eisenhower 1952/53, Journal Entry (Lodge), 21 November 1952.

20. *PUL* John Foster Dulles Oral History Project, Interview Joseph Sisco (Philip Crowl), Washington, 12 August 1966, pp. 17–20.

21. *PUL* John Foster Dulles Oral History Project, Interview Robert Murphy (Richard Challener), New York, 19 May and 8 June 1965, pp. 27–29.

22. *DDE* Papers of John Foster Dulles: Telephone Calls Series, Box 1, Telephone Memoranda (Excepting to and from White House), May–June 1953 (1), Memorandum of Telephone Conversation (Dulles), Washington, 25 June 1953.

23. *PUL* John Foster Dulles Oral History Project, Interview Ambassador John Hickerson (Philip Crowl), Washington, 11 October 1965, pp. 24–25; Interview Ambassador Henry Cabot Lodge (Richard Challener), Washington, 16 February 1965, pp. 14–15; Interview Ambassador Joseph Satterthwaite (Philip Crowl), Washington, 15 February 1966, pp. 2–3; Interview David Wainhouse (Philip Crowl), Washington, 24 August 1965, pp. 4–7.

24. For more on Lodge's appointment and views on the UN see Lodge, Henry Cabot, *As It Was: An Inside View of Politics and Power in the '50s and '60s* (New York, 1976), pp. 46–47, 53–63.

25. *PUL* John Foster Dulles Oral History Project, Interview Ambassador Joseph Satterthwaite (Philip Crowl), Washington, 15 February 1966, p. 2.

26. *PUL* John Foster Dulles Oral History Project, Interview Joseph Sisco (Philip Crowl), Washington, 12 August 1966, pp. 8–10; Interview James Wadsworth (Philip Crowl), Washington, 21 June 1965, pp. 8–10.

27. *PUL* John Foster Dulles Oral History Project, Interview David Wainhouse (Philip Crowl), Washington, 24 August 1965, pp. 34–36; Interview Robert Murphy (Richard Challener), New York, 19 May and 8 June 1965, pp. 29–33.

28. *NARA* RG59/250/49/26/07 Entry 1380, Box 1: File—Ambassador Gross, Hickerson-Gross, 23 January 1953.

29. *FRUS 1952–1954 Vol.* XV Lodge-Dulles, New York, 5 February 1953, pp. 733–35.

30. *FRUS 1952–1954 Vol.* XV Position Paper Prepared by the US Delegation to the UN, New York, 13 February 1953, pp. 779–83.

31. *NARA* RG84/350/82/1/4 Entry 1030-D, Box 47, File: Korea (January to June 1953), Memorandum of Conversation (Ward Allen), Washington, 11 February 1953.

32. *NARA* RG84/350/82/1/4 Entry 1030-D, Box 47, File: Korea (January to June 1953), Memorandum of Conversation (Allen), Washington, 13 February 1953.

33. *LAC* Microfilm T-2368, Cabinet Conclusions, Ottawa, 12 February 1953.

34. *UKNA* DO35/5833, Eden-British Ambassador to the United States (Roger Makins), London, 14 February 1953.

35. *UKNA* DO35/5833, Eden-Makins, London, 14 February 1953.

36. *UKNA* DO35/5834, High Commissioner to India (Alexander Clutterbuck)-Swinton, New Delhi, 17 February 1953.

37. *UKNA* DO35/5834, High Commissioner to Canada (Archibald Nye)-Swinton, Ottawa, 18 February 1953.

38. *UKNA* DO35/5834, Casey-Australian High Commission in Britain, Canberra, 19 February 1953.

39. *UKNA* DO35/5834, High Commission in New Zealand-Swinton, Wellington, 27 February 1953.

40. *FRUS 1952–54 Vol.* XV Memorandum of Conversation (Allen), Washington, 18 February 1953, pp. 787–88.

41. *FRUS 1952–54 Vol.* XV Clark-Department of the Army, Tokyo, 19 February 1953, pp. 788–90.

42. *NAA* A5954 1839/2, Spender-Casey, New York, 20 February 1953.

43. *DDE* Papers of John Foster Dulles, Telephone Calls Series, Box 1, File: Telephone Memoranda (Excepting to or from White House) January 1953–April 1953 (3), Telephone Conversation with Lodge, 16 February 1953.

44. *NMML* Papers of Vijaya Lakshmi Pandit (II Instalment), Subject File No. 4, Interview with Ambassador Henry Cabot Lodge, Leader of the US Delegation to the UN, New York, 25 February 1953.

45. *NMML* Papers of Vijaya Lakshmi Pandit (II Instalment), Subject File No. 4, Interview with Mr Lester Pearson, President of the UN General Assembly, New York, 25 February 1953.

46. *UNGA Seventh Session First Committee* 557th Meeting, 25 February 1953, pp. 349–50.
47. *UNGA Seventh Session First Committee* 559th Meeting, 26 February 1953, pp. 355–57.
48. *LAC* RG25/6497/8254-G-40 [Pt 11.2], Pearson-Johnson, Ottawa, 28 February 1953.
49. *UNGA Seventh Session First Committee* 560–569th Meetings, New York, 2–9 March 1953, pp. 362–423.
50. *UNGA Seventh Session Plenary* 414th Meeting, New York, 11 March 1953, p. 550.
51. *NAA* A1838 3123/5/13 PART 3, Spender-Casey, New York, 25 March 1953.
52. *UNGA Seventh Session First Committee* 590th–593rd Meetings, New York, 27 March–8 April 1953, pp. 553–77.
53. *UNGA Seventh Session Plenary* 428th Meeting, New York, 23 April 1953, p. 717.
54. *UNGA Seventh Session Plenary* 423rd Meeting, New York, 7 April 1953, p. 679.
55. *FRUS 1952–1954 Vol.* XV Lodge-Dulles, New York, 2 April 1953, pp. 836–37.
56. *FRUS 1952–1954 Vol.* XV Dulles-Eisenhower, Washington, 2 April 1953, p. 835.
57. *FRUS 1952–1954 Vol.* XV Dulles-Lodge, Washington, 2 April 1953, pp. 837–38.
58. *DDE* Papers of John Foster Dulles: Telephone Calls Series, Box 1, Telephone Memoranda (Excepting to or from White House) January 1953–April 1953 (1), Memorandum of Telephone Conversation (Dulles), Washington, 28 March 1953.
59. *UKNA* DO35/5835, Churchill-Makins, London, 3 April 1953.
60. *LAC* Microfilm T-2369, Cabinet Conclusions, Ottawa, 2 April 1953.
61. *UNGA Seventh Session Plenary* 420th Meeting, New York, 31 March 1953, p. 633.
62. *LAC* RG25/6338/619-J-40 Pt 1, Johnson-MEA, New York, 1 April 1953.
63. *UNGA Seventh Session First Committee* 594th Meeting, New York, 9 April 1953, p. 582.
64. *UKNA* DO35/5835, Lloyd-Churchill, New York, 9 April 1953.
65. *UKNA* DO35/5835, Jebb-Churchill, New York, 10 April 1953.
66. *UKNA* DO35/5835, Churchill-Jebb, London, 13 April 1953.
67. *UKNA* DO35/5835, Jebb-Churchill, New York, 14 April 1953.
68. *FRUS 1952–1954 Vol.* XV Lodge-Dulles, New York, 12 April 1953, p. 907.
69. *UNGA Seventh Session First Committee* 602nd–603rd Meetings, New York, 15–16 April 1953, pp. 637–48.
70. *UNGA Seventh Session Plenary* 427th Meeting, 18 April 1953, p. 710.
71. *LAC* MG26 L/85/C-10-21 1953 Conferences–Commonwealth Prime Ministers–London, England, 1953–Vol. 5–Secret, Meeting of Commonwealth Prime Ministers, London, 4 June 1953.

72. *LAC* MG26 L/85/C-10-21 1953 Conferences–Commonwealth Prime Ministers–London, England, 1953–Vol. 5–Secret, Meeting of Commonwealth Prime Ministers, London, 8 June 1953.

73. *UKNA* DO35/5839, Swinton-All High Commissioners, London, 27 June 1953.

74. *DDE* Papers of John Foster Dulles: Telephone Calls Series, Box 1, Telephone Memoranda (Excepting to and from White House), May–June 1953 (1), Memorandum of Telephone Conversation (Dulles), Washington, 25 June 1953.

75. *UKNA* DO35/5839, Lloyd-Jebb, London, 26 June 1953.

76. *NAA* A5954 1696/4, Casey-Embassy in Japan, Canberra, 27 June 1953.

77. *NAA* A5954 1696/4, High Commission in New Zealand-Casey, Wellington, 25 June 1953.

78. *UKNA* DO35/5839, Pearson-Canadian High Commission in Britain, Ottawa, 27 June 1953.

79. *UKNA* DO35/5840, Pearson-Canadian High Commission in Britain, Ottawa, 10 July 1953.

80. *LAC* RG25/21068/CSC 1227:1 Pt 5, Pearson-Wrong, Ottawa, 14 July 1953.

81. *LAC* RG25/21068/CSC 1227:1 Pt 6, Pearson-External, New York, 25 July 1953.

Chapter 7   The Road to Geneva, August 1953–June 1954

1. For more on the implementation of the Korean Armistice Agreement see, for instance, Bailey: *The Korean Armistice*, pp. 141–49, 171–77; Foot: *A Substitute for Victory*, pp. 190–205.

2. For more on the work of the NNRC see Bailey: *The Korean Armistice*, pp. 142–49; Dayal: *India's Role in the Korean Question*, pp. 192–259.

3. For more information on Eisenhower's New Look strategy see, for instance, Bowie and Immerman: *Waging Peace*, pp. 83–241; Divine: *Eisenhower and the Cold War*, pp. 33–39; Dockrill, Saki, *Eisenhower's New-Look National Security Policy, 1953–1961* (Basingstoke, 1996), pp. 15–101; Eisenhower: *The White House Years*, pp. 445–58; Hoopes: *The Devil and John Foster Dulles*, pp. 191–201; Immerman: *John Foster Dulles*, pp. 59–86; Jones, Matthew, 'Targeting China: US nuclear planning and "massive retaliation" in East Asia, 1953–1955', *Journal of Cold War Studies* 10:4 (2008), pp. 37–65; Wells, Samuel, 'The origins of massive retaliation', *Political Science Quarterly* 96:1 (1981), pp. 31–52.

4. For more on St Laurent's victory in the 1953 Canadian general election see Thomson: *Louis St Laurent*, pp. 349–55.

5. For more on Ali-Bogra's premiership see Syed: 'Pakistan: struggle for power, 1947–58', pp. 89–94.

6. For more on Churchill's declining health and ability to lead see, for instance, Brain: 'Encounters with Winston Churchill', pp. 14–15; Larres: *Churchill's Cold War*, pp. 288–340; Young: *Winston Churchill's Last Campaign*, pp. 183–265.

7. For more on Eden's dominance of British foreign policy during this period see, for instance, Dutton: *Anthony Eden*, pp. 337–63; Wilby: *Eden*, pp. 71–75.

8. For more on the Petrov affair see, for instance, Manne, Robert, *The Petrov Affair: Politics and Espionage* (Sydney, 1987); Thwaites, Michael, *The Truth Will Out: ASIO and the Petrovs* (Sydney, 1980); Whitlam, Nicholas, and Stubbs, John, *Nest of Traitors: The Petrov Affair* (Brisbane, 1974).

9. For more on Nehru's controversial policy regarding Jammu and Kashmir see Brown: *Nehru: A Political Life*, pp. 212–14, 266–67.

10. For more on the power struggle within the Soviet Union see Zubok, Vladislav and Pleshakov, Konstantin, *Inside the Kremlin's Cold War: from Stalin to Khrushchev* (Cambridge, 1996), pp. 154–73.

11. For more on the first Soviet hydrogen bomb see, for instance, Holloway, David, *Stalin and the Bomb: The Soviet Union and Atomic Energy, 1939–1956* (New Haven, 1994), pp. 294–345; Holloway, David, *The Soviet Union and the Arms Race* (New Haven, 1983), pp. 23–27; Zaloga, Steve, *The Kremlin's Nuclear Sword: The Rise and Fall of Russia's Strategic Nuclear Forces, 1945–2000* (Washington, DC, 2002), pp. 31–35.

12. For more on Eisenhower's 'Atoms for Peace' speech see, for instance, Chernus, Ira, *Eisenhower's Atoms for Peace* (College Station, 2002), pp. 79–131; Eisenhower: *The White House Years*, pp. 251–45; Hewlett, Richard and Holl, Jack, *Atoms for Peace and War, 1953–1961: Eisenhower and the Atomic Energy Commission* (Berkeley, 1989), pp. 209–37.

13. For more on the Battle of Dien Bien Phu see, for instance, Morgan, Ted, *Valley of Death: The Tragedy at Dien Bien Phu that Led America into the Vietnam War* (New York, 2010); Murray, Williamson, 'Dien Bien Phu', *Quarterly Journal of Military History* 9:3 (1997), pp. 40–51; Nordell, John, *Undetected Enemy: French and American Miscalculations at Dien Bien Phu* (College Station, 1995); Simpson, Howard, *Dien Bien Phu: The Epic Battle America Forgot* (Washington, 1994); Stone, David, *Dien Bien Phu* (London, 2004); Walker, John, 'Five hills at Dien Bien Phu', *Military Heritage* 8:3 (2006), pp. 32–39; Windrow, Martin, *The Last Valley: Dien Bien Phu and the French Defeat in Vietnam* (London, 2004); Worth, Richard, *Dien Bien Phu* (Philadelphia, 2002).

14. For more on the US reactions to the Indochina crisis see, for instance, Anderson, David, *Trapped by Success: The Eisenhower Administration and Vietnam* (New York, 1991), pp. 17–39; Arnold, James, *The First Domino: Eisenhower, the Military and America's Intervention in Vietnam* (New York, 1991), pp. 113–95; Herring, George and Immerman, Richard, 'Eisenhower, Dulles, and Dienbienphu: "the day we didn't go to war" revisited', *Journal of American History* 71:2 (1984), pp. 343–63.

15. For more on Commonwealth reactions to the Indochina situation see, for instance, Boquerat, Gilles, 'India's commitment to peaceful coexistence and the settlement of the Indochina War', *Cold War History* 5:2 (2005), pp. 211–20; Hughes, Philip, 'Division and discord: British policy, Indochina, and the origins of the Vietnam War, 1954–56', *Journal of Imperial and Commonwealth*

History 28:3 (2000), pp. 94–96; Ruane, Kevin, 'Refusing to pay the price: British foreign policy and the pursuit of victory in Indochina, 1952–54', *English Historical Review* 110:435 (1995), pp. 84–88; Trood, Russell, 'Alliance diplomacy: Australia, the United States and the 1954 Indochina crisis', *Australian Journal of Politics and History* 38:3 (1992), pp. 334–53; Umetsu, Uroyuki, 'Australia's response to the Indochina crisis of 1954 amidst Anglo–American confrontation', *Australian Journal of Politics and History* 52:3 (2006), pp. 398–416.

16. For good accounts of the Iranian coup see, for instance, Gasiorowski, Mark, 'The 1953 coup d'etat in Iran', *International Journal of Middle East Studies* 10:3 (1987), pp. 261–86; Heiss, Mary, *Empire and Nationhood: The United States, Great Britain, and Iranian Oil, 1950–1954* (Columbia, 1997).

17. *RLS* L179:186, Dag Hammarskjold's sambling, Korea 1953–57, 1953, Special Report of the Unified Command on the Armistice in Korea, August 1953.

18. *UKNA* FO371/105524, Lloyd-Salisbury, New York, 13 August 1953.

19. *LAC* Microfilm T-2369, Cabinet Meeting, Ottawa, 13 August 1953.

20. *DDE* Papers of JFD—Telephone Calls Series, Box 1, File: Telephone Memos (Except to and from White House) July–October 31, 1953 (3), Telephone Conversation (Lodge), 12 August 1953.

21. *UKNA* FO371/105525, Salisbury-Eden, New York, 15 August 1953.

22. *DDE* Papers of JFD—Telephone Calls Series, Box 1, File: Telephone Memos (Except to and from White House) July–October 31, 1953 (3), Telephone Conversation (Lodge), 14 August 1953.

23. *UKNA* FO371/105525, Salisbury-Lloyd, London, 14 August 1953.

24. *DDE* Papers of JFD—Telephone Calls Series, Box 1, File: Telephone Memos (Except to and from White House) July–October 31, 1953 (3), Telephone Conversation (Lodge), 14 August 1953.

25. *UKNA* FO371/105525, Salisbury-Lloyd, London, 15 August 1953.

26. *UKNA* FO371/105525, Lloyd-Salisbury, New York, 15 August 1953.

27. *UKNA* FO371/105525, Lloyd-Salisbury, New York, 16 August 1953.

28. *UKNA* FO371/105524, Salisbury-Lloyd, London, 13 August 1953.

29. *UKNA* FO371/105525, Lloyd-Salisbury, New York, 15 August 1953.

30. *FRUS 1952–54 Vol. XV* Memorandum of Conversation (Lodge), New York, 14 August 1953, pp. 1494–95.

31. *UKNA* FO371/105526, Lloyd-Salisbury, New York, 18 August 1953.

32. *UNGA Seventh Session First Committee* 613–618th Meetings, New York, 18–21 August 1953, pp. 699–730.

33. *UNGA Seventh Session First Committee* 615–624th Meetings, New York, 19–26 August 1953, pp. 709–64.

34. *UNGA Seventh Session First Committee* 621st Meeting, New York, 24 August 1953, pp. 737–41.

35. *UKNA* FO371/105526, Lloyd-Salisbury, New York, 21 August 1953.

36. *UKNA* FO371/105527, Lloyd-Salisbury, New York, 25 August 1953.

37. *UNGA Seventh Session First Committee* 624th Meeting, New York, 26 August 1953, pp. 757–64.

38. *NARA* RG59/250/49/26/07 Entry 1380, Box 2, File: 7th General Assembly, Assistant Secretary of State for UN Affairs (Robert Murphy)-Dulles, Washington, 19 August 1953.

39. *DDE* Papers of JFD—Telephone Calls Series, Box 1, File: Telephone Memos (Except to and from White House) July–October 31, 1953 (3), Telephone Conversation (Lodge), 24 August 1953.

40. *UKNA* FO371/105526, Salisbury-Lloyd, London, 24 August 1953.

41. *UKNA* FO371/105526, Lloyd-Salisbury, New York, 23 August 1953.

42. *UNGA Seventh Session First Committee* 623rd Meeting, New York, 25 August 1953, pp. 749–55.

43. *UKNA* FO371/105527, Salisbury-Lloyd, London, 27 August 1953.

44. *UNGA Seventh Session First Committee* 625th Meeting, New York, 27 August 1953, pp. 765–70.

45. *UKNA* FO371/105527, Lloyd-Salisbury, New York, 27 August 1953.

46. *UNGA Seventh Session Plenary* 430th Meeting, New York, 28 August 1953, pp. 724–34.

47. *UNGA Seventh Session Plenary* 431st Meeting, New York, 28 August 1953, p. 749.

48. *UKNA* FO371/105530, Jebb-Salisbury, New York, 14 September 1953.

49. *UKNA* FO371/105530, Jebb-Salisbury, New York, 14 September 1953.

50. *DDE* Papers of JFD—Telephone Calls Series, Box 1, File: Telephone Memos (Except to and from White House) July–October 31, 1953 (3), Telephone Conversation (Smith), 14 September 1953.

51. *NARA* RG84/350/63/05/04 Entry 2846, Box 2, File: 310—Political Conferences January–October 1953 Vol. I, Dulles-Department of State, Washington, 17 September 1953.

52. *NMML* Papers of Vijaya Lakshmi Pandit (1st Part), Subject File No. 50, Pandit-Nehru, New York, 23 September 1953.

53. *UNGA Eighth Session Plenary* 434th–440th Meetings, New York, 17–22 September 1953, pp. 17–83.

54. *UNGA Eighth Session General Committee* 88th Meeting, New York, 22 September 1953, p. 12.

55. *UKNA* FO371/105532, Foreign Office Minute (Lloyd), New York, 19 September 1953.

56. *LAC* RG24/21068/CSC 1227:1 Pt 6, Pearson-MEA, New York, 1 October 1953.

57. *UNGA Eighth Session First Committee* 627th–628th Meetings, New York, 30 September 1953, pp. 3–16.

58. *UKNA* FO371/105592, Jebb-Salisbury, New York, 5 October 1953.

59. *LAC* RG24/21068/CSC 1227:1 Pt 7, Johnson-Pearson, New York, 23 October 1953.

60. *DDE* Papers JFD—Telephone Calls Series, Box 1, File: Telephone Memoranda (Except to and from White House), July–October 31, 1953 (1), Telephone Conversation (Lodge), 2 October 1953.

61. *LAC* MG31 E46/7/19–Sept. 1/53–Dec. 3/53, Canadian High Commissioner to India (Escott Reid)-Pearson, New Delhi, 22 October 1953.

62. *NMML* Papers of Vijaya Lakshmi Pandit (1st Part), Subject File No. 51, Nehru-Pandit, New Delhi, 28 October 1953.

63. *NARA* RG59/250/49/06/03 Entry 1198, Box 2, File: Korean Political Conference October 1953 (1), Zhou En-lai-Hammarskjold, Beijing, 19 October 1953.

64. For a detailed analysis of Dean's mission to Panmunjom see *PUL* John Foster Dulles Oral History Project, Interview with Arthur Dean (Philip Crowl), New York, 21 May and 13 July 1964, pp. 77–87.

65. *FRUS 1952–54 Vol.* XV Dean-Dulles, Munsan-Ni, 1 November 1953, pp. 1578–79.

66. *FRUS 1952–54 Vol.* XV Dulles-Dean, Washington, 4 November 1953, pp. 1587–88.

67. *NARA* RG84/350/63/05/04 Entry 2846, Box 2, File: 310—Political Conference November 1953 Vol. II, Dulles-Dean, Washington, 18 November 1953.

68. *UNGA Eighth Session First Committee* 648th Meeting, New York, 26 October 1953, pp. 113–18.

69. *UNGA Eighth Session First Committee* 652nd–653rd Meetings, New York, 30–31 October 1953, pp. 135–45.

70. *UNGA Eighth Session Plenary* 456th Meeting, New York, 3 November 1953, p. 279.

71. *NARA* RG59/250/49/26/07 Entry 1380, Box 3, File: Memoranda to Secretary and Under Secretary (General Subjects—1953), Murphy-Dulles, Washington, 29 October 1953.

72. *UKNA* FO371/105585, Jebb-Eden, New York, 30 October 1953.

73. *UKNA* DO35/5848, Lloyd-Eden, New York, 31 October 1953.

74. *UKNA* DO35/5848, Lloyd-Eden, New York, 31 October 1953.

75. *UKNA* DO35/5848, Eden-Lloyd, London, 12 November 1953.

76. *MHS* Henry Cabot Lodge Papers II, Microfilm P-373, Reel 28, Lodge-Eisenhower, New York, 4 December 1953.

77. *UNGA Eighth Session Plenary* 463rd–466th Meetings, New York, 1–2 December 1953, pp. 361–418.

78. *NARA* RG84/350/63/05/04 Entry 2846, Box 4, File: 312—United Nations (UN) 1953–1954–1955, Dulles-Lodge, Washington, 20 November 1953.

79. *NARA* RG84/350/63/05/04 Entry 2846, Box 4, File: 312—United Nations (UN) 1953–1954–1955, Dulles-Lodge, Washington, 24 November 1953.

80. *UKNA* FO371/105596, Foreign Office Minute (Lloyd), New York, 25 November 1953.

81. *UKNA* FO371/105596, Eden-Jebb, London, 1 December 1953.

82. *UKNA* FO371/105596, Jebb-Eden, New York, 2 December 1953.
83. *UKNA* FO371/105596, Eden-Jebb, London, 3 December 1953.
84. *NARA* RG84/350/82/01/01, Entry 1030-D, Box48, File: Korea (September–December 1953), Assistant Secretary of State for UN Affairs (David Wainhouse)-Lodge, New York, 3 December 1953.
85. *UKNA* FO371/105596, Jebb-Eden, New York, 4 December 1953.
86. *FRUS 1952–54 Vol. XV* Smith-Lodge, Washington, 6 December 1953, pp. 1646–47.
87. *FRUS 1952–54 Vol. XV* Lodge-Dulles, New York, 6 December 1953, p. 1648.
88. *UNGA Eighth Session First Committee* 681st–682nd Meetings, New York, 7 December 1953, pp. 295–305.
89. *UNGA Eighth Session Plenary* 470th Meeting, New York, 8 December 1953, p. 446.
90. *FRUS 1952–54 Vol. XV* Dean-Dulles, Munsan-Ni, 8 December 1953, pp. 1651–52.
91. *NARA* RG84/350/63/05/04 Entry 2846, Box 4, File: 312—United Nations (UN) 1953–1954–1955, Dulles-Dean, Washington, 9 December 1953.
92. *FRUS 1952–54 Vol. XV* Dean-Dulles, Munsan-Ni, 12 December 1953, pp. 1655–57.
93. *UKNA* FO371/105597, Jebb-Lloyd, New York, 14 December 1953.
94. *NARA*, RG84/350/63/05/04 Entry 2846, Box 4, File: 312—United Nations (UN) 1953–1954–1955, Dulles-Ambassador in India (George Allen), Washington, 17 December 1953.
95. *FRUS 1952–54 Vol. V* Communiqué of the Bermuda Conference of the Heads of Government of the United States, United Kingdom, and France, Bermuda, 7 December 1953, pp. 1838–39.
96. *FRUS 1952–54 Vol. XV* Dulles-Young, Washington, 29 December 1953, pp. 1675–77.
97. *LAC* RG24/21068/CSC 1227:1 Pt 7, Reid-Pearson, New Delhi, 28 December 1953.
98. *RLS* L179:186, Dag Hammarskjold's sambling, Korea 1953–57, 1954, Menon-Pandit, New York, 10 January 1954; Pandit-Hammarskjold, New York, 10 January 1954.
99. *FRUS 1952–54 Vol. XV* Dulles-Allen, Washington, 11 January 1954, p. 1715.
100. *FRUS 1952–54 Vol. XV* Dulles-Lodge, Washington, 12 January 1954, pp. 1719–21.
101. *FRUS 1952–54 Vol. XV* Dulles-Ambassador in Britain (Winthrop Aldrich), Washington, 14 January 1954, pp. 1723–24.
102. *LAC* RG25/21038/CSC 1227:1 Pt 8, Reid-Pearson, New Delhi, 15 January 1954.
103. *LAC* RG25/21038/CSC 1227:1 Pt 8, Reid-Pearson, New Delhi, 19 January 1954.

104. *NARA* RG84/350/63/05/04 Entry 2846, Box 4, File: 312—United Nations (UN) 1953–1954–1955, Dulles-Lodge, Washington, 20 January 1954.

105. *NARA* RG RG84/350/82/01/01 Entry 1030-D, Box 48, File: Korea (1954), Memorandum (John Ross), New York, 21 January 1954.

106. *UKNA* FO371/110623, Eden-Churchill, Berlin, 26 January 1954.

107. *NARA* RG RG84/350/82/01/01 Entry 1030-D, Box 48, File: Korea (1954), Memorandum (Braggiotti), New York, 26 January 1954.

108. *NARA* RG RG84/350/82/01/01 Entry 1030-D, Box 48, File: Korea (1954), Memorandum (Ross), New York, 1 February 1954.

109. *FRUS 1952–54 Vol. VII* Dulles-State, Berlin, 25 January 1954, pp. 814–17.

110. *FRUS 1952–54 Vol. VII* Final Communiqué of the Berlin Conference, Berlin, 18 Februrary 1954, pp. 1205–06.

111. *RLS* L179:186, Dag Hammarskjold's sambling, Korea 1953–57, 1954, Menon-Hammarskjold, New York, 6 February 1954.

112. For detailed documentary evidence on the pre-Geneva Conference planning see *FRUS 1952–54 Vol. XVI*, pp. 14–142.

113. For more on the Korean phase of the 1954 Geneva Conference see, for instance, Bailey: *The Korean Armistice*, pp. 150–70; Brands, Henry, 'The Dwight D. Eisenhower administration, Syngman Rhee and the "other" Geneva conference of 1954', *Pacific Historical Review* 56:1 (1987), pp. 59–85; Dayal: *India's Role in the Korean Question*, pp. 260–87; Matsuda, Haruka, 'A clash of empires in East Asia: the Geneva conference on Korea, 1954', *Seoul Journal of Korean Studies* 20:2 (2007), pp. 193–211; Ra, Jong-Yil, 'The politics of conference: the political conference on Korea in Geneva, 16 April–25 June 1954', *Journal of Contemporary History* 34:3 (1999), pp. 399–416. For a detailed documentary account see *FRUS 1952–54 Vol. XVI*, pp. 143–387.

114. *FRUS 1952–54 Vol. XVI* First Plenary Session on Korea, Dulles-State, Geneva, 26 April 1954, pp. 144–45.

115. *FRUS 1952–54 Vol. XVI* Declaration by the Sixteen, Geneva, 15 June 1954, pp. 385–86.

Epilogue

1. *FRUS 1952–54 Vol. XVI* Smith-Dulles, Geneva, 16 June 1954, pp. 388–89.

2. For more on the Indochina phase of the Geneva conference see, for instance, Asselin, Pierre, 'The Democratic Republic of Vietnam and the 1954 Geneva conference: a revisionist critique', *Cold War History* 11:2 (2011), pp. 155–95; Cable, James, *The Geneva Conference of 1954 on Indochina* (Basingstoke, 1986); Chen, Jian and Shen, Zhihua, 'The Geneva conference of 1954: new evidence from the archives of the Ministry of Foreign Affairs of the People's Republic of China', *Cold War International History Project Bulletin* 16 (2007/8), pp. 7–84; Wingrove, Paul, 'Russian documents on the 1954 Geneva conference', *Cold War International History Project Bulletin* 16 (2007/8), pp. 85–104. For a detailed documentary account see *FRUS 1952–54 Vol. XVI*, pp. 395–1568.

3. For more on the First Taiwan Strait Crisis see, for instance, Brands, Henry, 'Testing massive retaliation: credibility and crisis management in the Taiwan strait', *International Security* 12:4 (1998), pp. 124–51; Chang, Gordon, 'To the nuclear brink: Eisenhower, Dulles, and the Quemoy-Matsu crisis', *International Security* 12:4 (1988), pp. 96–123.

4. For more on the establishment of SEATO see, for instance, Buszynski, Leszek, *SEATO: The Failure of an Alliance Strategy* (Singapore, 1983), pp. 1–46; Dingman, Roger, 'John Foster Dulles and the creation of the South-East Asian Treaty Organisation in 1954', *International History Review* 11:3 (1989), pp. 457–77; Ruane, Kevin, 'SEATO, MEDO, and the Baghdad Pact: Anthony Eden, British Foreign Policy and the collective defence of Southeast Asia and the Middle East, 1952–55', *Diplomacy and Statecraft* 16:1 (2005), pp. 169–80.

5. For more on the Guatemalan coup see, for instance, Fraser, Andrew, 'Architecture of a broken dream: the CIA and Guatemala, 1952–54', *Intelligence and National Security* 20:3 (2005), pp. 486–508; Gleijeses, Piero, *Shattered Hope: The Guatemalan Revolution and the United States, 1944–1954* (Princeton, 1991), pp. 319–60; Marks, Frederick and Rabe, Stephen, 'The CIA and Castillo Armas in Guatemala, 1954: new clues to an old puzzle', *Diplomatic History* 14:1 (1990), pp. 67–86; Schlesinger, Stephen and Kinzer, Stephen, *Bitter Fruit: The Story of the American Coup in Guatemala* (Garden City, 1982).

6. For more on the collapse of the EDC and its aftermath see, for instance, Deighton, Anne, 'The last piece of the jigsaw: Britain and the creation of the Western European Union, 1954', *Contemporary European History* 7:2 (1998), pp. 181–96; Dockrill: 'The evolution of Britain's policy towards a European army', pp. 38–62; Fursdon: *The European Defence Community*, pp. 191–339; Gavin: 'Power through Europe', pp. 78–87; Mawby: 'From distrust to despair', pp. 502–09; Ruane: *The Rise and Fall of the European Defence Community*, pp. 31–172.

7. *PRO*, FO371/110578, Dixon-Eden, New York, 13 September 1954.

8. *LAC* RG25/6447/5475-DW-33-40 [Pt 2.1], Johnson-Pearson, New York, 16 September 1954.

9. *LAC* RG25/6447/5475-DW-33-40 [Pt 2.1], Pearson-External, New York, 28 September 1954.

10. *UNGA Ninth Session Plenary* 475th–492nd Meeting, New York, 23 September–6 October 1954, pp. 17–236.

11. *PRO*, FO371/110578, Dixon-Eden, New York, 29 September 1954.

12. *PRO*, FO371/110578, Dixon-Eden, New York, 30 October 1954.

13. *PRO* DO35/5846, Clutterbuck-Swinton, New Delhi, 5 November 1954.

14. *PRO*, FO371/110578, Dixon-Eden, New York, 10 November 1954.

15. *PRO* DO35/5846, Eden-Dixon, London, 15 November 1954.

16. *PRO* DO35/5846, Dixon-Eden, New York, 16 November 1954.

17. *PRO*, FO371/110579, Eden-Dixon, London, 22 November 1954.

18. *PRO*, FO371/110579, Nutting-Eden, New York, 24 November 1954.

19. *NAI*, MEA 11(1)-FEA/55, Menon-Nehru, New York, 24 November 1954.

20. *NAI*, MEA 11(1)-FEA/55, Nehru-Menon, New Delhi, 27 November 1954.
21. *PRO*, FO371/110579, Nutting-Eden, New York, 26 November 1954.
22. *PRO*, FO371/110579, Nutting-Eden, New York, 26 November 1954.
23. *PRO* DO35/5846, Eden-Nutting, London, 28 November 1954.
24. *NAI*, MEA 11(1)-FEA/55, Menon-Nehru, New York, 28 November 1954.
25. *NAI*, MEA 11(1)-FEA/55, Nehru-Menon, New Delhi, 29 November 1954.
26. *PRO*, FO371/110579, Nutting-Eden, New York, 29 November 1954.
27. *PRO* DO35/5846, Nutting-Eden, New York, 30 November 1954.
28. *NAI*, MEA 11(1)-FEA/55, Menon-Nehru, New York, 30 November 1954.
29. *PRO*, FO371/110580, Nutting-Eden, New York, 30 November 1954.
30. *PRO*, FO371/110579, Eden-Nutting, London, 30 November 1954.
31. *UNGA Ninth Session First Committee* 736th–745th Meetings, New York, 1–9 December 1954, pp. 461–517.
32. *UNGA Ninth Session Plenary* 510th Meeting, New York, 11 December 1954, pp. 463–69.
33. For more on the Korean debate at the UN post-1954 see, for instance, Choi, Chong-Ki, 'The role of the United Nations and the Korean question', in T.H. Kwak, C. Kim and H.N. Kim (eds), *Korean Reunification: New Perspectives and Approaches* (Seoul, 1984), pp. 275–89; Clough, Ralph, *Embattled Korea: The Rivalry for International Support* (Boulder, 1987), pp. 275–82; Gills, Barry, *Korea versus Korea: A Case of Contested Legitimacy* (London, 1996), pp. 72–74, 95–96, 137–44, 174–89; Kim, Chonghan, 'Korean reunification: UN perspectives', in T.H. Kwak, C. Kim and H.N. Kim (eds), *Korean Reunification: New Perspectives and Approaches* (Seoul, 1984), pp. 406–23.
34. For more on the development of Nehru's foreign policy post-1954 see, for instance, Brown: *Nehru: A Political Life*, pp. 256–65, 299–337; Ramachandram: *Nehru and World Peace*, pp. 27–58, 73–97, 115–34; Zachariah, Benjamin, *Nehru* (London, 2004), pp. 215–52.
35. For more on the development of the Commonwealth in the late 1950s and 1960s see, for instance, Hamilton, W., Robinson, Kenneth and Goodwin, C. (eds), *A Decade of the Commonwealth, 1955–1964* (Durham, 1966); Walker: *The Commonwealth*, pp. 255–382.

BIBLIOGRAPHY

Unpublished primary sources

Churchill Archives Centre
Post-war Churchill Papers.
Papers of 1st Lord Gladwyn.
Papers of Selwyn Lloyd.

Columbia University Rare Book and Manuscript Library
Cordier Collection.

Dwight D. Eisenhower Library
Dulles, John Foster: Papers, 1951–59.
    General Correspondence and Memoranda Series.
    JFD Chronological Series.
    Subject Series.
    Telephone Calls Series.
    White House Memoranda Series.
Eisenhower, Dwight D.: Papers as President of the United States, 1953–61.
    Ann Whitman File.
    Administration Series.
    Cabinet Series.
    Campaign Series.
    Dulles-Herter Series.

International Series.
Legislative Meeting Series.
Name Series.
NSC Series.
Speech Series.
DDE Diary Series.
White House Central File.
Korean War Special Collection.
Jackson, C.D.: Papers, 1931–67.
Jackson, C.D.: Records, 1953–54.
White House Office, National Security Council Staff: Papers, 1948–61.
White House Office, Office of the Special Assistant for National Security Affairs: Records, 1952–61.

Harry S. Truman Library
Dean G. Acheson Papers, Secretary of State File, 1945–72.
　Memoranda of Conversations File, 1949–53.
　Press Conferences File, 1949–53.
Papers of Harry S. Truman.
　Korean War File, 1947–52.
　Official File.
　Official File 20: Department of State.
　Official File 85: United Nations.
　Official File 471, Korea.
　Official File 1392.
　Personal Secretary File.
　Chronological Name File.
　Diaries.
　Longhand Notes File, 1930–55.
Korean War File, 1946–53.
Subject File, 1940–53.
White House Central File.
Confidential File.
Official File.
The Korean War Collection.

The United Nations Collection.

Library and Archives Canada
Department of National Defence Fonds.
Department of External Affairs Fonds.
Arnold Danford Patrick Heeney Fonds.
Paul Martin Fonds.
Lester B. Pearson Fonds.
Escott Meredith Reed Fonds.
Rt Hon. L.S. St Laurent Fonds.
Microfilm T-2366—T-2369 Cabinet Conclusions.

Massachusetts Historical Society
Henry Cabot Lodge (1902–85) Papers.
Microfilm P-519 Henry Cabot Lodge Speeches, 1926–65.
Microfilm P-373 Henry Cabot Lodge Jr II Papers.
Lodge-Eisenhower Correspondence 1942–52.

National Archives and Records Administration (USA)
General Records of the Department of State.
Records of the Foreign Service Posts of the Department of State.
Microfilm C-0042 Reels 1–11.
Microfilm C-0044 Reels 1–11.
Microfilm LM 081 Reels 19–30.

National Archives of Australia
Department of External/Foreign Affairs—Correspondence Files,
    multiple numbers series, 1 January 1948–31 December 1989.
Department of Defence, History of Australian Defence Policy, 1
    January 1937–8 July 1971.

National Archives of India
    MEA Ministry of External Affairs Records, 1890–69.

National Archives of Norway
Trygve Lie Papers.

National Archives (UK)
Cabinet: Minutes (CM and CC Series).
Cabinet: Memoranda (CP and C Series).
Ministry of Defence: Chiefs of Staff Committee: Minutes 1947–73.
Ministry of Defence: Chiefs of Staff Committee: Memoranda 1947–45.
Dominions Office and Commonwealth Relations Office: Original
   Correspondence.
Foreign Office: Political Departments: General Correspondence from
   1906–66.
Prime Minister's Office: Correspondence and Papers, 1945–51.
Prime Minister's Office: Correspondence and Papers, 1951–64.

National Library of Sweden
Dag Hammarskjold sambling.

Nehru Memorial Museum and Library
Papers of Vijaya Lakshmi Pandit (1st Part).
Papers of Vijaya Lakshmi Pandit (2nd Instalement).
Papers of G. L. Mehta (3rd and 4th Instalement).

Princeton Seeley G. Mudd Manuscript Library
John Foster Dulles Papers.
John Foster Dulles Oral History Project.

United Nations Archives and Records Management Section
Secretary-General Dag Hammarskjold fonds.
Secretary-General Trygve Lie fonds, 1945–53.
Executive Assistant to the Secretary-General (1946–61: Cordier)
   fonds.
United Nations Reconstruction Agency (UNKRA) Records.
United Nations Commission for the Unification and Rehabilitation
   of Korea (UNCURK) Records.

University of Birmingham Library
Personal and Political Papers of Anthony Eden.

Avon Papers.
Papers of Lord Selwyn Lloyd of Wirral.

University of Vermont Library
Warren Austin Papers.

Yale University Library Manuscript Collections
UN Oral History Project Interview Transcripts and Tapes.

Published primary sources

Department of State Bulletin Volume 23 (1950).
Department of State Bulletin Volume 24 (1951).
Department of State Bulletin Volume 25 (1951).
Department of State Bulletin Volume 26 (1952).
Department of State Bulletin Volume 27 (1952).
Department of State Bulletin Volume 28 (1953).
Department of State Bulletin Volume 29 (1953).
Department of State Bulletin Volume 30 (1954).
Documents on British Policy Overseas, Series II, vol. IV, *Korea, June 1950–April 1951* (London, 1991).
Foreign Relations of the United States, 1950, vol. II, *The United Nations, The Western Hemisphere* (Washington, 1976).
Foreign Relations of the United States, 1950, vol. VII, *Korea* (Washington, 1976).
Foreign Relations of the United States, 1951, vol. II, *United Nations, Western Hemisphere* (Washington, 1979).
Foreign Relations of the United States, 1951, vol. VII: *Korea and China* (Washington, 1983).
Foreign Relations of the United States, 1952–1954, vol. III, *United Nations Affairs* (Washington, 1979).
Foreign Relations of the United States, 1952–1954, vol. V, *Western European Security* (Washington, 1983).
Foreign Relations of the United States, 1952–1954, vol. VII II, *Germany and Austria* (Washington, 1986).

Foreign Relations of the United States, 1952–1954, vol. XV II, *Korea* (Washington, 1984).

Foreign Relations of the United States, 1952–1954, vol. XVI II, *The Geneva Conference* (Washington, 1981).

United Nations Official Records of the General Assembly Fifth Session— Plenary Meetings vol. I, *19 September to 15 December 1950* (New York, 1950).

United Nations Official Records of the General Assembly Fifth Session— Plenary Meetings vol. II, *1 February to 5 November 1951* (New York, 1951).

United Nations Official Records of the General Assembly Seventh Session— Plenary Meetings, 14 October 1952 to 28 August 1953 (New York, 1953).

United Nations Official Records of the General Assembly Eighth Session— Plenary Meetings, 15 September to 9 December 1953 (New York, 1953).

United Nations Official Records of the General Assembly Fifth Session— First Committee vol. I, *20 September to 18 December 1950* (New York, 1950).

United Nations Official Records of the General Assembly Fifth Session— First Committee vol. II, *3 January to 17 May 1951* (New York, 1951).

United Nations Official Records of the General Assembly Seventh Session— First Committee, 14 October to 21 December 1952, 24 February to 23 April 1953 (New York, 1953).

United Nations Official Records of the General Assembly Eighth Session— First Committee, 16 September to 7 December 1953 (New York, 1953).

United Nations Official Records of the General Assembly Fifth Session— General Committee, 18 September to 15 December 1950 (New York, 1950).

United Nations Official Records of the General Assembly Eighth Session— General Committee, 15 September to 9 December 1953 (New York, 1953).

United Nations Official Records of the General Assembly Fifth Session— Annexes (New York, 1951).

United Nations Official Records of the General Assembly Fifth Session—Supplements (New York, 1951).

United Nations Official Records of the General Assembly Sixth Session—Annexes (New York, 1952).

United Nations Official Records of the General Assembly Sixth Session—Supplements (New York, 1952).

United Nations Official Records of the General Assembly Seventh Session—Annexes (New York, 1953).

United Nations Official Records of the General Assembly Seventh Session—Supplements (New York, 1953).

United Nations Official Records of the General Assembly Eighth Session—Annexes (New York, 1954).

United Nations Official Records of the General Assembly Eighth Session—Supplements (New York, 1954).

United Nations Security Council Official Records Fifth Year (New York, 1950).

United Nations Security Council Official Records Sixth Year (New York, 1951).

United Nations Security Council Official Records Seventh Year (New York, 1952).

Newspapers

Washington Evening Star.

Memoirs

Acheson, Dean, *Present at the Creation: My Years in the State Department* (London, 1969).

Attlee, Clement, *As It Happened* (London, 1954).

Casey, Richard, *Australian Foreign Minister: The Diaries of R.G. Casey, 1951–1960* (London, 1972).

Clark, Mark, *From the Danube to the Yalu* (London, 1954).

Eden, Anthony, *The Memoirs of Sir Anthony Eden: Full Circle* (London, 1960).

Eisenhower, Dwight, *The White House Years: Mandate for Change, 1953–1956* (London, 1963).

Ismay, Lionel Hastings, *The Memoirs of General the Lord Ismay* (London, 1960).

Jebb, Gladwyn, *The Memoirs of Lord Gladwyn* (London, 1972).

Lie, Trygve, *In the Cause of Peace: Seven Years with the United Nations* (New York, 1954).

Lodge, Henry Cabot, *As It Was: An Inside View of Politics and Power in the '50s and '60s* (New York, 1976).

MacArthur, Douglas, *Reminiscences* (London, 1964).

Menzies, Robert, *Afternoon Light: Some Memories of Men and Events* (London, 1967).

Menzies, Robert, *The Measure of Years* (London, 1970).

Morrison, Herbert, *Herbert Morrison: An Autobiography* (London, 1960).

Murphy, Robert, *Diplomat Among Warriors* (London, 1964).

Pandit, Vijaya Lakshmi, *The Scope of Happiness: A Personal Memoir* (London, 1979).

Pearson, Lester, *Memoirs of the Right Honourable Lester B. Pearson*, vol. 1, *Through Diplomacy to Politics, 1897–1948* (London, 1973).

Pearson, Lester, *Memoirs of the Right Honourable Lester B. Pearson*, vol. 2, *The International Years, 1948–1957* (London, 1974).

Reid, Escott, *Radical Mandarin: The Memoirs of Escott Reid* (Toronto, 1989).

Ridgway, Matthew, *The War in Korea* (London, 1968).

Rusk, Dean, *As I Saw It* (London, 1990).

Spender, Percy, *Exercises in Diplomacy: The ANZUS Treaty and the Colombo Plan* (Sydney, 1969).

Truman, Harry, *Memoirs*, vol. 1, *Year of Decisions, 1945* (New York, 1955).

Truman, Harry, *Memoirs*, vol. 2, *Years of Trial and Hope, 1946–1953* (New York, 1956).

Biographies

Ambrose, Stephen, *Eisenhower*, vol. 2, *The President* (London, 1984).

Aster, Sidney, *Anthony Eden* (London, 1976).

Ayre, W. Burton, *Mr. Pearson and Canada's Revolution by Diplomacy* (Montreal, 1966).

Barclay, Roderick, *Ernest Bevin and the Foreign Office, 1932–1969* (London, 1975).

Beal, John, *John Foster Dulles: 1888–1959* (Westport, 1974).

Beckett, Francis, *Clem Attlee* (London, 2000).

Beisner, Robert, *Dean Acheson: A Life in the Cold War* (New York, 2006).

Berding, Andrew, *Dulles on Diplomacy* (Princeton, 1965).

Bothwell, Robert, *Pearson: His Life and World* (Toronto, 1978).

Bowie, Robert and Immerman, Richard, *Waging Peace: How Eisenhower Shaped an Enduring Cold War Strategy* (New York, 1998).

Brecher, Michael, *Nehru: A Political Biography* (London, 1959).

Brecher, Michael, *Indian and World Politics: Krishna Menon's View of the World* (London, 1968).

Brittain, Vera, *Envoy Extraordinary: A Study of Vijaya Lakshmi Pandit and her Contribution to Modern India* (London, 1965).

Brookshire, Jerry, *Clement Attlee* (Manchester, 1996).

Brown, Judith, *Nehru* (New York, 1999).

Brown, Judith, *Nehru: A Political Life* (New Haven, 2003).

Bullock, Alan, *The Life and Times of Ernest Bevin*, vol. III, *Foreign Secretary* (London, 1967).

Bunting, John, *R.G. Menzies: A Political Life* (Sydney, 1988).

Burridge, Trevor, *Clement Attlee: A Political Biography* (London, 1985).

Byrnes, Mark, *The Truman Years, 1945–1953* (Harlow, 2000).

Capitanchik, David, *The Eisenhower Presidency and American Foreign Policy* (London, 1969).

Carlton, David, *Anthony Eden: A Biography* (London, 1981).

Carroll, Brian, *The Menzies Years* (Stanmore, 1977).

Chace, James, *Acheson: The Secretary of State who Created the American World* (New York, 1998).

Cross, John, *Lord Swinton* (Oxford, 1982).

Damms, Richard, *The Eisenhower Presidency, 1953–1961* (Harlow, 2002).

Danchev, Alex, *Oliver Franks: Founding Father* (Oxford, 1993).

Divine, Robert, *Eisenhower and the Cold War* (New York, 1981).

Donoughue, Bernard and Jones, G.W., *Herbert Morrison: Portrait of a Politician* (London, 1973).

Donovan, Robert, *Conflict and Crisis: The Presidency of Harry S. Truman, 1945–1948* (New York, 1977).

Donovan, Robert, *Tumultuous Years: The Presidency of Harry S. Truman, 1949–1953* (New York, 1982).

Drummond, Roscoe and Coblentz, Gaston, *Duel at the Brink: John Foster Dulles' Command of American Power* (London, 1961).

Dutton, David, *Anthony Eden: A Life and Reputation* (London, 1997).

Edwardes, Michael, *Nehru: A Political Life* (London, 1971).

English, John, *Shadow of Heaven: The Life of Lester Pearson*, vol. 1, *1897–1948* (Toronto, 1989).

English, John, *The Worldly Years: The Life of Lester Pearson*, vol. 2, *1949–1972* (Toronto, 1992).

Ewald, William, *Eisenhower the President: Crucial Days, 1951–1960* (Englewood Cliffs, 1981).

Foot, Michael, *Aneurin Bevan: A Biography*, vol. II, *1945–1960* (London, 1973).

George, T.J.S., *Krishna Menon: A Biography* (London, 1964).

Gerson, Louis, *John Foster Dulles* (New York, 1967).

Goold-Adams, Richard, *The Time of Power: A Reappraisal of John Foster Dulles* (London, 1962).

Gosnell, Harold, *Truman's Crises: A Political Biography of Harry S. Truman* (Westport, 1980).

Greenstein, Fred, *The Hidden-Hand Presidency: Eisenhower as President* (New York, 1982).

Greenwood, Sean, *Titan at the Foreign Office: Gladwyn Jebb and the Shaping of the Modern World* (Leiden, 2008).

Guhin, Michael, *John Foster Dulles: A Statesman and his Times* (London, 1972).

Hamby, Alonzo, *Man of the People: A Life of Harry S. Truman* (New York, 1995).

Harris, Kenneth, *Attlee* (London, 1995).

Hasluck, Paul, *Sir Robert Menzies* (Melbourne, 1980).

Hazlehurst, Cameron, *Menzies Observed* (Hornsby, 1979).

Hoopes, Townsend, *The Devil and John Foster Dulles* (Boston, 1973).

Hopkins, Michael, *Oliver Franks and the Truman Administration: Anglo-American Relations, 1948–1952* (London, 2003).

Howell, David, *Attlee* (London, 2006).

Hudson, W.J., *Casey* (Melbourne, 1986).

Immerman, Richard, *John Foster Dulles: Piety, Pragmatism, and Power in US Foreign Policy* (Wilmington, 1999).

James, Robert, *Anthony Eden* (London, 1986).

Jenkins, Roy, *Truman* (London, 1986).

Judd, Denis, *Jawaharlal Nehru* (Cardiff, 1993).

Lambakis, Steven, *Winston Churchill, Architect of Peace: A Study of Statesmanship and the Cold War* (Westport, 1993).

Larres, Klaus, *Churchill's Cold War: The Politics of Personal Diplomacy* (New Haven, 2002).

Lowe, David, *Menzies and the 'Great World Struggle': Australia's Cold War, 1948–1954* (Sydney, 1999).

Lowe, David, *Australian Between Empires: The Life of Percy Spender* (London, 2010).

McLellan, David, *Dean Acheson: The State Department Years* (New York, 1976).

McMahon, Robert, *Dean Acheson and the Creation of An American World Order* (Washington DC, 2009).

Marks, Frederick, *Power and Peace: The Diplomacy of John Foster Dulles* (Westport, 1993).

Marks, Stephen, *Ernest Bevin: Unskilled Labourer and World Statesman, 1881–1951* (London, 1983).

Martin, Allan, *Robert Menzies: A Life*, vol. II, *1944–1978* (Melbourne, 1993–99).

Mazunan, George, *Warren R. Austin at the UN, 1946–1953* (Kent, 1977).

Mishra, D.P., *The Nehru Epoch: From Democracy to Monocracy* (New Delhi, 2001).

Moran, Charles, *Winston Churchill: The Struggle for Survival, 1940–1965* (London, 1966).

Nanda, B.R., *Jawaharlal Nehru: Rebel and Statesman* (New Delhi, 1995).

Pach, Chester and Richardson, Elmo, *The Presidency of Dwight D. Eisenhower* (Lawrence, 1991).

Pandey, Bishwa, *Nehru* (London, 1976).

Pearce, Robert, *Attlee* (London, 1997).

Pearson, Geoffrey, *Seize the Day: Lester B. Pearson and Crisis Diplomacy* (Ottawa, 1993).

Pelling, Henry, *Winston Churchill* (London, 1974).

Perkins, Kevin, *Menzies: The Last of the Queen's Men* (Adelaide, 1968).

Pickett, William, *Dwight David Eisenhower and American Power* (Wheeling, 1995).

Pickett, William, *Eisenhower Decides to Run: Presidential Power and Cold War Strategy* (Chicago, 2000).

Pierpaoli, Paul, *Truman and Korea: The Political Culture of the Early Cold War* (Columbia, 1999).

Pruessen, Ronald, *John Foster Dulles: The Road to Power* (New York, 1982).

Ramachandram, G., *Nehru and World Peace* (London, 1990).

Reddy, E. and Damodaran, A. (eds), *Krishna Menon at the United Nations: India and the World* (London, 1994).

Rothwell, Victor, *Anthony Eden: A Political Biography* (Manchester, 1992).

Sheean, Vincent, *Nehru: The Years of Power* (New York, 1960).

Thompson, Kenneth, *Winston Churchill's World View: Statesmanship and Power* (Baton Rouge, 1983).

Thomson, Dale, *Louis St Laurent: Canadian* (Toronto, 1967).

Thordarson, Bruce, *Lester Pearson: Diplomat and Politician* (Toronto, 1974).

Thorpe, D., *Selwyn Lloyd* (London, 1989).

Toulouse, Mark, *The Transformation of John Foster Dulles: From Prophet of Realism to Priest of Nationalism* (Macon, 1985).

Tyson, Geoffrey, *Nehru: The Years of Power* (London, 1966).

Weiler, Peter, *Ernest Bevin* (Manchester, 1993).

Wilby, Peter, *Eden* (London, 2006).

Williams, Francis, *A Prime Minister Remembers: The War and Post-war Memoirs of the Right Hon. Earl Attlee, Based on His Private Papers and a Series of Recorded Conversations* (London, 1961).

Williams, Francis, *Ernest Bevin: Portrait of a Great Englishman* (London, 1952).

Wolpert, Stanley, *Nehru: A Tryst with Destiny* (New York, 1996).

Young, John, *Winston Churchill's Last Campaign: Britain and the Cold War* (Oxford, 1995).

Zachariah, Benjamin, *Nehru* (New York, 2004).

Secondary books

Acheson, Dean, *The Korean War* (New York, 1969).

Alexander, Bevin, *Korea: The Lost War* (London, 1989).

Anderson, David, *Trapped by Success: The Eisenhower Administration and Vietnam* (New York, 1991).

Appleman, Roy, *East of Chosin: Entrapment and Breakout, 1950* (College Station, 1987).

Appleman, Roy, *Disaster in Korea: The Chinese Confront MacArthur* (College Station, 1989).

Appleman, Roy, *Escaping the Trap: US Army X Corps in Northeast Korea* (College Station, 1990).

Appleman, Roy, *Ridgway Duels for Korea* (College Station, 1990).

Armstrong, Charles, *The North Korean Revolution, 1945–1950* (Ithaca, 2003).

Arnold, James, *The First Domino: Eisenhower, the Military and America's Intervention in Vietnam* (New York, 1991).

Bailey, Sydney, *The Korean Armistice* (Basingstoke, 1992).

Bartlett, C.J., *'The Special Relationship': A Political History of Anglo-American Relations since 1945* (London, 1992).

Baylis, John, *Anglo-American Defence Relations, 1939–1984: The Special Relationship* (London, 1981).

Baylis, John (ed.), *Anglo-American Relations since 1939: The Enduring Alliance* (Manchester, 1997).

Barber, Noel, *The War of the Running Dogs: How Malaya Defeated the Communist Guerrillas, 1948–1960* (London, 1971).

Bassett, Michael, *Confrontation '51: The 1951 Waterfront Dispute* (Wellington, 1972).

Berger, Karl, *Korean Knot: A Military-Political History* (Philadelphia, 1964).

Blair, Clay, *The Forgotten War: America in Korea, 1950–53* (New York, 1987).

Boyd, Andrew, *Fifteen Men on a Powder Keg: A History of the UN Security Council* (London, 1971).

Bramble, Tom (ed.), *Never a White Flag: The Memoirs of Jock Barnes, Waterfront Leader* (Wellington, 1998).

Branch, Daniel, *Defeating Mau Mau, Creating Kenya: Counterinsurgency, Civil War, and Decolonisation* (Cambridge, 2009).

Bull, Hedley and Louis, W.M. Roger (eds), *The Special Relationship: Anglo-American Relations since 1945* (Oxford, 1986).

Burgess, Gregory, *The Attlee Governments in Perspective: Commitment and Detachment in the Writing of Contemporary History* (London, 1994).

Buszynski, Leszek, *SEATO: The Failure of an Alliance Strategy* (Singapore, 1983).

Butler, David, *The British General Election of 1951* (London, 1952).

Cable, James, *The Geneva Conference of 1954 on Indochina* (Basingstoke, 1986).

Camilleri, Joseph, *The Australian-New Zealand-US Alliance: Regional Security in the Nuclear Age* (Boulder, 1987).

Caridi, Ronald, *The Korean War and American Politics: The Republican Party as a Case Study* (Philadelphia, 1969).

Casey, Steven, *Selling the Korean War: Propaganda, Politics and Public Opinion* (Oxford, 2008).

Catchpole, Brian, *The Korean War* (London, 2000).

Charmley, John, *Churchill's Grand Alliance: The Anglo-American Special Relationship, 1940–57* (New York, 1995).

Chen, Jian, *China's Road to the Korean War: The Making of the Sino-American Confrontation* (New York, 1994).

Chernus, Ira, *Eisenhower's Atoms for Peace* (College Station, 2002).

Clark, Nancy and Worger, William, *South Africa: The Rise and Fall of Apartheid* (Harlow, 2004).

Clough, Marshall, *Mau Mau Memoirs: History, Memory and Politics* (London, 1998).

Clough, Ralph, *Embattled Korea: The Rivalry for International Support* (Boulder, 1987).

Clutterbuck, Richard, *The Long Long War: The Emergency in Malaya, 1948–1960* (London, 1967).

Coates, John, *Suppressing Insurgency: An Analysis of the Malayan Emergency, 1948–1954* (Boulder, 1992).

Cohen, Bernard, *The Political Policy and Foreign Policy: The Making of the Japanese Peace Settlement* (Princeton, 1957).

Crampton, Richard, *Eastern Europe in the Twentieth Century and After* (London, 1997).

Crane, Conrad, *American Airpower Strategy in Korea* (Lawrence, 2000).

Cumings, Bruce, *The Origins of the Korean War*, vol. I, *Liberation and the Emergence of Separate Regimes, 1945–1947* (Princeton, 1981).

Cumings, Bruce, *The Origins of the Korean War*, vol. II, *The Roaring of the Cataract, 1947–1950* (Princeton, 1990).

Cumings, Bruce and Halliday, John, *Korea: The Unknown War* (London, 1988).

Cunningham-Boothe, Ashley and Farrar, Peter (eds), *British Forces in the Korean War* (London, 1988).

Danchev, Alex, *On Specialness: Essays in Anglo-American Relations* (Basingstoke, 1998).

Dayal, Shiv, *India's Role in the Korean Question: A Study in the Settlement of International Disputes under the United Nations* (Delhi, 1959).

Divine, Robert, *Foreign Policy and US Presidential Elections, 1952–1960* (New York, 1974).

Dobbs, Charles, *The Unwanted Symbol: American Foreign Policy, the Cold War, and Korea, 1945–1950* (Kent, 1981).

Dockrill, Saki, *Eisenhower's New-Look National Security Policy, 1953–1961* (Basingstoke, 1996).

Dobson, Alan, *Anglo-American Relations in the Twentieth Century: Of friendship, conflict and the rise and decline of superpowers* (London, 1995).

Dalloz, Jacques, *The War in Indochina, 1945–54* (Dublin, 1990).

Dudden, Alexis, *Japan's Colonization of Korea: Discourse and Power* (Honolulu, 2005).

Duignan, Peter, *NATO: Its Past, Present, and Future* (Stanford, 2000).

Eatwell, Roger, *The 1945–51 Labour Governments* (London, 1975).

Edgerton, Robert, *Mau Mau: An African Crucible* (London, 1990).

Edmonds, Robin, *Setting the Mould: The United States and Britain, 1945–1950* (Oxford, 1986).

Farrar-Hockley, Anthony, *The Edge of the Sword* (London, 1954).

Farrar-Hockley, Anthony, *The British Part in the Korean War*, vol. I, *A Distant Obligation* (London, 1990).

Farrar-Hockley, Anthony, *The British Part in the Korean War*, vol. II, *An Honourable Discharge* (London, 1995).

Fitzsimons, Matthew, *The Foreign Policy of the British Labour Government, 1945–1951* (Notre Dame, 1953).

Foot, Rosemary, *The Wrong War: American Policy and the Dimensions of the Korean Conflict, 1950–1953* (Ithaca, 1985).

Foot, Rosemary, *A Substitute for Victory: The Politics of Peacemaking at the Korean Armistice Talks* (Ithaca, 1990).

Fordham, Benjamin, *Building the Cold War Consensus: The Political Economy of US National Security Policy, 1949–51* (Ann Arbor, 1998).

Fried, Richard, *Nightmare in Red: The McCarthy Era in Perspective* (New York, 1990).

Fursdon, Edward, *The European Defence Community: A History* (London, 1980).

Gaddis, John, *Strategies of Containment: A Critical Appraisal of Postwar American National Security Policy* (Oxford, 1982).

Gaddis, John, *The Long Peace: Inquiries into the History of the Cold War* (New York, 1987).

George, Alexander, *The Chinese Communist Army in Action: The Korean War and its Aftermath* (New York, 1967).

Gills, Barry, *Korea versus Korea: A Case of Contested Legitimacy* (London, 1996).

Gleijeses, Piero, *Shattered Hope: The Guatemalan Revolution and the United States, 1944–1954* (Princeton, 1991).

Goncharov, Sergei, Lewis, John and Xue, Litai, *Uncertain Partners: Stalin, Mao, and the Korean War* (Stanford, 1993).

Goodrich, Leland, *Korea: A Study of US Policy in the United Nations* (New York, 1956).

Gordenker, Leon, *The United Nations and the Peaceful Unification of Korea: The Politics of Field Operations* (The Hague, 1959).

Gordon, Michael, *Conflict and Consensus in Labour's Foreign Policy* (Stanford, 1969).

Green, David, *Captured at the Imjin River: The Korean War Memoirs of a Gloster* (Barnsley, 2003).

Greene, John, *The Crusade: The Presidential Election of 1952* (Lanham, 1985).

Griffith, Robert, *The Politics of Fear: Joseph McCarthy and the Senate* (Amherst, 1987).

Hall, H. Duncan, *Commonwealth: A History of the British Commonwealth of Nations* (London, 1971).

Hamilton, W., Robinson, Kenneth and Goodwin, C. (eds), *A Decade of the Commonwealth, 1955–1964* (Durham, NC, 1966).

Hastings, Max, *The Korean War* (London, 1987).

Hathaway, Robert, *Great Britain and the United States: Special Relations since World War II* (Boston, 1990).

Heinzig, Dieter, *The Soviet Union and Communist China 1945–1950: The Arduous Road to the Alliance* (Armonk, 2004).

Heiss, Mary, *Empire and Nationhood: The United States, Great Britain, and Iranian Oil, 1950–1954* (Columbia, 1997).

Hermes, Walter, *Truce Tent and Fighting Front: The United States Army in the Korean War* (Honolulu, 1992).

Hewlett, Richard and Holl, Jack, *Atoms for Peace and War, 1953–1961: Eisenhower and the Atomic Energy Commission* (Berkeley, 1989).

Higgins, Trumbull, *Korea and the Fall of MacArthur: A Precis in Limited War* (Oxford, 1960).

Hogan, Michael, *Cross of Iron: Harry S. Truman and the Origins of the National Security State, 1945–1954* (Cambridge, 1998).

Holloway, David, *Stalin and the Bomb: The Soviet Union and Atomic Energy, 1939–1956* (New Haven, 1994).

Holloway, David, *The Soviet Union and the Arms Race* (New Haven, 1983).

Ismay, Harding, *NATO: The First Five Years, 1949–1954* (Utrecht, 1955).

Jackson, Robert, *The Malayan Emergency: The Commonwealth's Wars, 1948–1966* (London, 1990).

James, D. Clayton with Wells, Anne, *Refighting the Last War: Command and Crisis in Korea, 1950–1953* (New York, 1993).

Jefferys, Kevin, *The Attlee Governments* (London, 1992).

Jones, Matthew, *After Hiroshima: The United States, Race and Nuclear Weapons in Asia, 1945–1965* (Cambridge, 2010).

Kaplan, Lawrence, *NATO and the United States: The Enduring Alliance* (Boston, 1988).

Kaplan, Lawrence, *The Long Entanglement: NATO's First Fifty Years* (Westport, 1999).

Kaplan, Lawrence, *NATO Divided, NATO United: The Evolution of an Alliance* (Westport, 2004).

Kaplan, Lawrence, *The United States and NATO: The Formative Years* (Lexington, 1984).

Kennedy, Paul, *Parliament of Man: The United Nations and the Quest for World Government* (London, 2006).

Kent, John, *British Imperial Strategy and the Origins of the Cold War, 1944–49* (London, 1993).

Kepley, David, *Collapse of the Middle Way: Senate Republicans and the Bipartisanship Foreign Policy, 1948–1952* (London, 1988).

Kershaw, Greet, *Mau Mau from Below* (Oxford, 1997).

Kim, C.I. Eugene and Kim, Han-Kyo, *Korea and the Politics of Imperialism, 1876–1910* (Berkeley, 1967).

Knorr, Klaus, *NATO: Past: Present: Prospect* (Exeter, 1974).

Kogekar, Sadanand and Price, Richard, *Reports of the Indian General Elections, 1951–1952* (Bombay, 1956).

Jain, Rajendra, *Japan's Post-war Peace Settlements* (Atlantic Highlands, 1978).

Joy, C. Turner, *Negotiating While Fighting: The Diary of Admiral C. Turner Joy at the Korean Armistice Conference* (Stanford, 1978).

Leckie, Robert, *The Korean War* (London, 1963).

Lee, Steven, *The Korean War* (Harlow, 2001).

Leffler, Melvyn, *A Preponderance of Power: National Security, the Truman Administration, and the Cold War* (Stanford, 1992).

Louw, P. Eric, *The Rise, Fall and Legacy of Apartheid* (Westport, 2004).

Lowe, Peter, *The Origins of the Korean War* (London, 1986).

Lowe, Peter, *Containing the Cold War in East Asia: British policies towards Japan, China and Korea, 1948–1953* (Manchester, 1997).

Lowe, Peter, *The Korean War* (Basingstoke, 2000).

Luard, Evan, *A History of the United Nations*, vol. I, *The Years of Western Domination, 1945–1955* (London, 1982).

MacDonald, Callum, *Korea: The War Before Vietnam* (Basingstoke, 1986).

MacDonald, Callum, *Britain and the Korean War* (Oxford, 1990).

Manchester, William, *American Caesar: Douglas MacArthur, 1880–1964* (London, 1979).

Mandelbaum, Michael, *The Nuclear Question: The United States and Nuclear Weapons, 1946–1976* (Cambridge, 1979).

Manne, Robert, *The Petrov Affair: Politics and Espionage* (Sydney, 1987).

Mark, Chi-Kwan, *Hong Kong and the Cold War: Anglo-American Relations, 1949–1957* (Oxford, 2004).

Matray, James, *Reluctant Crusade: American Foreign Policy in Korea, 1941–1950* (Honolulu, 1985).

Maurice, Bertrand, *The United Nations: Past, Present and Future* (The Hague, 1997).

McCormack, Gavan, *Cold War, Hot War: An Australian Perspective on the Korean War* (Sydney, 1983).

McCormack, Gavan and Gittings, John, *Crisis in Korea* (Nottingham, 1977).

McGibbon, Ian, *New Zealand and the Korean War*, vol. I, *Politics and Diplomacy* (Auckland, 1992).

McGibbon, Ian, *New Zealand and the Korean War*, vol. II, *Combat Operations* (Auckland, 1996).

McGlothlen, Ronald, *Controlling the Waves: Dean Acheson and US Foreign Policy in Asia* (New York, 1993).

McIntyre, David, *Background to the ANZUS Pact: Policy-Making, Strategy and Diplomacy, 1945–1955* (New York, 1995).

McNamara, Robert, *Britain, Nasser and the Balance of Power in the Middle East, 1952–1967: From the Egyptian Revolution to the Six-Day War* (Portland, 2003).

Meehan, Eugene, *The British Left Wing and Foreign Policy* (New Brunswick, 1960).

Melady, John, *Korea: Canada's Forgotten War* (Toronto, 1998).

Meredith, Martin, *In the Name of Apartheid: South Africa in the Post-war Period* (New York, 1994).

Merrill, John, *Korea: The Peninsular Origins of the War* (Newark, 1989).

Millett, Allan, *The War for Korea, 1945–1950: A House Burning* (Lawrence, 2006).

Millett, Allan, *The War for Korea, 1950–1951: They Came from the North* (Lawrence, 2010).

Milloy, John, *North Atlantic Treaty Organisation, 1948–1957: Community or Alliance?* (Montreal, 2006).

Morgan, Kenneth, *Labour in Power, 1945–1951* (Oxford, 1984).

Morgan, Ted, *Valley of Death: The Tragedy at Dien Bien Phu that Led America into the Vietnam War* (New York, 2010).

Mount, Graeme with Laferriere, Andre, *The Diplomacy of War: The Case for Korea* (Montreal, 2004).

Nordell, John, *Undetected Enemy: French and American Miscalculations at Dien Bien Phu* (College Station, 1995).

O'Ballance, Edgar, *Malaya: The Communist Insurgent War* (London, 1966).

O'Ballance, Edgar, *Korea, 1950–1953* (London, 1969).

O'Neill, Robert, *Australia in the Korean War, 1950–53*, vol. I, *Strategy and Diplomacy* (Canberra, 1991).

O'Neill, Robert, *Australia in the Korean War, 1950–53*, vol. II, *Combat Operations* (Canberra, 1995).

Oakman, Daniel, *Facing Asia: A History of the Colombo Plan* (Canberra, 2005).

Osgood, Robert, *NATO: The Entangling Alliance* (Chicago, 1962).

Ovendale, Ritchie, *The English-Speaking Alliance: Britain, the United States, the Dominions and the Cold War, 1945–1951* (London, 1985).

Paige, Glenn, *The Korean Decision, June 24–30, 1950* (New York, 1968).

Pearlman, Michael, *Truman and MacArthur: Policy, Politics and the Hunger for Honor and Renown* (Bloomington, 2008).

Powaski, Ronald, *The Entangling Alliance: The United States and European Security, 1950–1993* (Westport, 1994).

Ramakrishna, Kumar, *Emergency Propaganda: The Winning of Malayan Hearts and Minds, 1948–1958* (Richmond, 2001).

Rees, David, *Korea: The Limited War* (London, 1964).

Reese, Trevor, *Australia, New Zealand, and the United States: A Survey of International Relations, 1941–1968* (London, 1969).

Renwick, Robin, *Fighting with Allies: America and Britain in Peace and War* (Basingstoke, 1986).

Reynolds, David, *In Command of History: Churchill Fighting and Writing the Second World War* (London, 2004).

Rhodes, Richard, *Dark Sun: The Making of the Hydrogen Bomb* (London, 1995).

Roberts, Adam and Kingsbury, Benedict (eds), *United Nations, Divided World* (Oxford, 1993).

Rotter, Andrew, *The Path to Vietnam: Origins of the American Commitment to Southeast Asia* (London, 1987).

Rovere, Richard, and Schlesinger, Arthur, *The MacArthur Controversy and American Foreign Policy* (1965).

Ryan, Mark, *Chinese Attitudes Toward Nuclear Weapons: China and the United States during the Korean War* (Armonk, 1989).

Salmon, Andrew, *To the Last Round: The Epic British Stand on the Imjin River, Korea 1951* (London, 2009).

Sandler, Stanley, *The Korean War: No Victors, No Vanquished* (Lexington, 1999).

Sandler, Todd and Hartley, Keith, *The Political Economy of NATO: Past, Present and Into the 21st Century* (Cambridge, 1999).

Schaller, Michael, *Douglas MacArthur: The Far Eastern General* (Oxford, 1989).

Schlesinger, Stephen and Kinzer, Stephen, *Bitter Fruit: The Story of the American Coup in Guatemala* (Garden City, 1982).

Schmid, Andre, *Korea Between Empires, 1895–1910* (New York, 2002).

Schnabel, James, *The US Army in the Korean War. Policy and Direction: First Year* (Washington, 1992).

Scott, Dick, *151 Days: Official History of the Great Waterfront Lockout and Supporting Strikes, February 15–July 15, 1951* (Reed, 2001).

Sheng, Michael, *Battling Western Imperialism: Mao, Stalin, and the United States* (Princeton, 1997).

Short, Anthony, *The Communist Insurrection in Malaya, 1948–1960* (London, 1975).

Short, Anthony, *The Origins of the Vietnam War* (London, 1989).

Simmons, Robert, *The Strained Alliance: Peking, Pyongyang, Moscow, and the Politics of the Korean Civil War* (New York, 1995).

Simons, Geoff, *The United Nations: A Chronology of Conflict* (Basingstoke, 1994).

Simpson, Howard, *Dien Bien Phu: The Epic Battle America Forgot* (Washington, 1994).

Singh, Anita Inder, *The Limits of British Influence: South Asia and the Anglo-American Relationship, 1947–56* (London, 1993).

Spanier, John, *The Truman-MacArthur Controversy and the Korean War* (Cambridge, 1959).

Stairs, Denis, *The Diplomacy of Constraint: Canada, the Korean War, and the United States* (Toronto, 1974).

Starke, J.G., *The ANZUS Treaty Alliance* (Melbourne, 1985).

Stone, David, *Dien Bien Phu* (London, 2004).

Stubbs, Richard, *Hearts and Minds in Guerrilla Warfare: The Malayan Emergency, 1948–1960* (Singapore, 1989).

Stueck, William, *The Road to Confrontation: American Policy Toward China and Korea, 1947–1950* (Chapel Hill, 1981).

Stueck, William, *The Korean War: An International History* (Princeton, 1995).

Stueck, William, *Rethinking the Korean War: A New Diplomatic and Strategic History* (Woodstock, 2002).

Stueck, William (ed.), *The Korean War in World History* (Lexington, 2004).

Taratsoo, Nick (ed.), *The Attlee Years* (London, 1991).

Thwaites, Michael, *The Truth Will Out: ASIO and the Petrovs* (Sydney, 1980).

Thornton, Richard, *Odd Man Out: Truman, Stalin, Mao and the Origins of the Korean War* (Washington, 2000).

Trotter, Ann, *New Zealand and Japan, 1945–1952: The Occupation and the Peace Treaty* (London, 1990).

Tucker, Spencer (ed), *Encyclopaedia of the Korean War: A Political, Social, and Military History*, vol. I (Santa Barbara, 2000).

Vatcher, William, *Panmunjom: The Story of the Korean Military Armistice Negotiations* (Westport, 1958).

Wadsworth, James, *The Glass House: The United Nations in Action* (London, 1966).

Walker, Patrick Gordon, *The Commonwealth* (London, 1962).

Weber, Steve, *Multilateralism in NATO: Shaping the Post-war Balance of Power, 1945–1961* (Berkeley, 1991).

Weintraub, Stanley, *MacArthur's War: Korea and the Undoing of an American Hero* (New York, 2000).

Westad, Odd, *Decisive Encounters: The Chinese Civil War, 1946–1950* (Stanford, 2003).

Westerfield, H. Bradford, *Foreign Policy and Party Politics: Pearl Harbour to Korea* (New York, 1972).

Whelan, Richard, *Drawing the Line: The Korean War, 1950–1953* (London. 1990).

Whiting, Allen, *China Crosses the Yalu: The Decision to Enter the Korean War* (Stanford, 1960).

Whitlam, Nicholas and Stubbs, John, *Nest of Traitors: The Petrov Affair* (Brisbane, 1974).

Williamson, Daniel, *Separate Agendas: Churchill, Eisenhower, and Anglo-American Relations, 1953–1955* (Lanham, 2006).

Windrow, Martin, *The Last Valley: Dien Bien Phu and the French Defeat in Vietnam* (London, 2004).

Worth, Richard, *Dien Bien Phu* (Philadelphia, 2002).

Wunyabari, Molaba, *Mau Mau and Kenya: An Analysis of a Peasant Revolt* (Bloomington, 1993).

Yoo, Tae-Ho, *The Korean War and the United Nations: A Legal and Diplomatic Historical Study* (Louvain, 1965).

Yoshitsu, Michael, *Japan and the San Francisco Conference* (New York, 1983).

Zaloga, Steve, *The Kremlin's Nuclear Sword: The Rise and Fall of Russia's Strategic Nuclear Forces, 1945–2000* (Washington, DC, 2002).

Zhang, Shu Guang, *Mao's Military Romanticism: China and the Korean War, 1950–1953* (Lawrence, 1995).

Zhang, Shu Guang, and Chen, Jian, *Chinese Communist Foreign Policy and the Cold War in Asia: New Documentary Evidence, 1944–1950* (Chicago, 1996).

Zhang, Xiaoming, *Red Wings over the Yalu: China, the Soviet Union, and the Air War in Korea* (College Station, 2002).

Zubok, Vladislav and Pleshakov, Konstantin, *Inside the Kremlin's Cold War: From Stalin to Khrushchev* (Cambridge, 1996).

Articles and essays

Adeleke, Ademola, '"Cocksparrow diplomacy": Percy Spender, the Colombo Plan, and Commonwealth relations', *Australian Journal of Politics and History* 54:2 (2008), pp. 174–84.

Afzal, M. Rafique, 'Nazimuddin ministry: reasons for its dismissal', *Pakistan Journal of History and Culture* 15:2 (1994), pp. 47–62.

Armstrong, Charles, 'The cultural Cold War in Korea, 1945–1950', *Journal of Asian Studies* 62:1 (2003), pp. 71–99.

Asselin, Pierre, 'The Democratic Republic of Vietnam and the 1954 Geneva Conference: a revisionist critique', *Cold War History* 11:2 (2011), pp. 155–95.

Bacchus, Wilfrid, 'The relationship between combat and peace negotiations: fighting while talking in Korea, 1953–53', *Orbis* 17:2 (1973), pp. 545–74.

Bajanov, Evgueni, 'Assessing the politics of the Korean War, 1949–51', *Cold War International History Project Bulletin* 6–7 (1995/96), pp. 54, 87–91.

Barclay, Glen and Siracusa, John, 'Australia, the United States, and the Cold War, 1945–1951: from V-J Day to ANZUS', *Diplomatic History* 5:1 (1981), pp. 39–52.

Barnes, Robert, 'Branding an aggressor: the Commonwealth, the United Nations and Chinese intervention in the Korean War, November 1950–January 1951', *Journal of Strategic Studies* 33:2 (2010), pp. 231–253.

Bekes, Csaba, 'East Central Europe, 1953–1962', in M. Leffler and O. Westad (eds), *The Cambridge History of the Cold War*, vol. 1 (Cambridge, 2010).

Bernstein, Barton, 'Election of 1952', in A. Schlesinger (ed.), *History of American Presidential Elections, 1789–1968*, vol. 8 (New York, 1971).

Bernstein, Barton, 'The policy of risk: crossing the 38th parallel and marching to the Yalu', *Foreign Service Journal* 54:3 (1977).

Bernstein, Barton, 'The week we went to war: American intervention in the Korean civil war', *Foreign Service Journal* 54:1 (1977), pp. 6–12.

Bernstein, Barton, 'The struggle over the Korean armistice: prisoners of repatriation?', in B. Cumings (ed.), *Child of Conflict: The Korean-American Relationship, 1943–1953* (Seattle, 1983).

Bernstein, Barton, 'The Truman administration and the Korean War', in M. Lacey (ed.), *The Truman Presidency* (Cambridge, 1989).

Boquerat, Gilles, 'India's commitment to peaceful coexistence and the settlement of the Indochina War', *Cold War History* 5:2 (2005), pp. 211–34.

Botman, Selma, 'Egyptian communists and the Free Officers, 1950–54', *Middle Eastern Studies* 22:3 (1986), pp. 350–66.

Braasch, John, 'Anthony Eden's (Lord Avon) bilary tract saga', *Annals of Surgery* 238:5 (2003), pp. 772–75.

Brain, Russell, 'Encounters with Winston Churchill', *Medical History* 44:1 (2000), pp. 3–20.

Branch, Daniel, 'The enemy within: loyalists and the war against the Mau Mau in Kenya', *Journal of African History* 48:2 (2007), pp. 291–315.

Brands, Henry, 'From ANZUS to SEATO: United States strategic policy towards Australia and New Zealand, 1952–1954', *International History Review* 9:2 (1987), pp. 250–70.

Brands, Henry, 'The Dwight D. Eisenhower administration, Syngman Rhee and the "other" Geneva Conference of 1954', *Pacific Historical Review* 56:1 (1987), pp. 59–85.

Brands, Henry, 'Testing massive retaliation: credibility and crisis management in the Taiwan Strait', *International Security* 12:4 (1998), pp. 124–51.

Brown, Judith, 'Nehru', in S. Casey and J. Wright (eds), *Mental Maps in the Cold War Era* (Basingstoke, 2011).

Casey, Steven, 'Selling NSC-68: the Truman administration, public opinion, and the politics of mobilization, 1950–51', *Diplomatic History* 29:4 (2005), pp. 655–90.

Casey, Steven, 'White House publicity operations during the Korean War, June 1950–June 1951', *Presidential Studies Quarterly* 35:4 (2005), pp. 691–717.

Casey, Steven, 'Casualty reporting and domestic support for war: the US experience during the Korean War', *Journal of Strategic Studies* 33:2 (2010), pp. 291–316.

Chang, Gordon, 'To the nuclear brink: Eisenhower, Dulles, and the Quemoy-Matsu crisis', *International Security* 12:4 (1988), pp. 96–123.

Chen, Jian, 'The myth of America's "lost chance" in China: a Chinese perspective in light of new evidence', *Diplomatic History* 21:1 (1997), pp. 77–86.

Chen, Jian, 'China and the First Indochina War', *China Quarterly* 133 (1993), pp. 85–110.

Chen, Jian and Shen, Zhihua, 'The Geneva Conference of 1954: new evidence from the archives of the Ministry of Foreign Affairs of the People's Republic of China', *Cold War International History Project Bulletin* 16 (2007/8), pp. 7–84.

Chihiro, Hosoya, 'Japan, China, the United States and the United Kingdom, 1951–52: the case of the "Yoshida letter"', *International Affairs* 60:2 (1984), pp. 247–59.

Choi, Chong-Ki, 'The role of the United Nations and the Korean question', in T.H. Kwak, C. Kim and H.N. Kim (eds), *Korean Reunification: New Perspectives and Approaches* (Seoul, 1984).

Christensen, Thomas, 'Threats, assurances, and the last chance for peace: the lessons of Mao's Korean War telegrams', *International Security* 17:1 (1992), pp. 122–54.

Deighton, Anne, 'The last piece of the jigsaw: Britain and the creation of the Western European Union, 1954', *Contemporary European History* 7:2 (1998), pp. 181–96.

Dingman, Roger, 'Atomic diplomacy during the Korean War', *International Security* 13:3 (1988–89), pp. 50–91.

Dingman, Roger, 'John Foster Dulles and the creation of the South-East Asian Treaty Organisation in 1954', *International History Review* 11:3 (1989), pp. 457–77.

Dockrill, Michael, 'The Foreign Office, Anglo-American relations, and the Korean War, June 1950–June 1951', *International Affairs* 62:3 (1986), pp. 459–76.

Dockrill, Michael, 'The Foreign Office, Anglo-American relations and the Korean truce negotiations, July 1951–July 1953', in J. Cotton and I. Neary (eds), *The Korean War in History* (Manchester, 1989).

Dockrill, Saki, 'The evolution of Britain's policy towards a European army, 1950–1954', *Journal of Strategic Studies* 12:1 (1989), pp. 38–62.

Endicott, Stephen, 'Germ warfare and the "plausible denial": the Korean War, 1952–1953', *Modern China* 5:1 (1979), pp. 79–104.

Farrar, Peter, 'A pause for peace negotiations: the British buffer zone plan of November 1950', in J. Cotton and I. Neary (eds), *The Korean War in History* (Manchester, 1989).

Foot, Rosemary, 'Anglo-American relations in the Korean crisis: the British effort to avert an expanded war, December 1950–January 1951', *Diplomatic History* 10:1 (1986), pp. 43–57.

Foot, Rosemary, 'Nuclear coercion and the ending of the Korean conflict', *International Security* 13:3 (1988/9), pp. 92–112.

Foot, Rosemary, 'Making known the unknown war: policy analysis of the Korean War in the last decade', *Diplomatic History* 15 (1991), pp. 411–31.

Foot, Rosemary, 'Negotiating with friends and enemies: the politics of peacemaking in Korea', in C.B. Kim and J. Matray (eds), *Korea and the Cold War: Division, Destruction, and Disarmament* (Claremont, 1993).

Fraser, Andrew, 'Architecture of a broken dream: the CIA and Guatemala, 1952–54', *Intelligence and National Security* 20:3 (2005), pp. 486–508.

Friedman, Edward, 'Nuclear blackmail and the end of the Korean War', *Modern China* 1:1 (1975), pp. 75–91.

Gasiorowski, Mark, 'The 1953 coup d'etat in Iran', *International Journal of Middle East Studies* 10:3 (1987), pp. 261–86.

Gavin, Victor, 'Power through Europe?: the case of the European Defence Community in France (1950–1954)', *French History* 23:1 (2009), pp. 69–87.

Gittings, John, 'Talks, bombs and germs: another look at the Korean War', *Journal of Contemporary Asia* 5:2 (1975), pp. 205–217.

Gray, Collin, 'Strategy in the nuclear age: the United States, 1945–1991', in W. Murray, M. Knox and A. Bernstein (eds), *The Making of Strategy: Rulers, States, and War* (Cambridge, 1994).

Guhin, Michael, 'The United States and the Chinese People's Republic: the non-recognition policy reviewed', *International Affairs* 45:1 (1969), pp. 44–63.

Hao, Yufan and Zhai, Zihai, 'China's decision to enter the Korean War: history revisited', *China Quarterly* 121 (1990), pp. 94–115.

Harry, Ralphy, 'Security treaty between Australia, New Zealand and the United States of America', *Australian Outlook* 35:2 (1981), pp. 201–12.

Herring, George and Immerman, Richard, 'Eisenhower, Dulles, and Dienbienphu: "the day we didn't go to war" revisited', *Journal of American History* 71:2 (1984), pp. 343–63.

Holloway, David, 'Nuclear weapons and the escalation of the Cold War, 1945–1962', in M. Leffler, and O. Westad (eds), *The Cambridge History of the Cold War*, vol. 1 (Cambridge, 2010).

Hopkins, Michael, 'The price of Cold War partnership: Sir Oliver Franks and the British military commitment in the Korean War', *Cold War History* 1:2 (2001), pp. 8–46.

Hughes, Philip, 'Division and discord: British policy, Indochina, and the origins of the Vietnam War, 1954–56', *Journal of Imperial and Commonwealth History* 28:3 (2000), pp. 94–112.

Hunt, Michael, 'Beijing and the Korean crisis, June 1950–June 1951', *Political Science Quarterly* 107:3 (1992), pp. 453–78.

Igarashi, Takeshi, 'Dean Acheson and the Japanese peace treaty', in D. Brinkley (ed.), *Dean Acheson and the Making of US Foreign Policy* (Basingstoke, 1993).

Ivie, Robert, 'Declaring a national emergency: Truman's rhetorical crisis and the great debate of 1951', in A. Kiewe (ed.), *The Modern Presidency and Crisis Rhetoric* (London, 1994), pp. 1–18.

Jackson, Colin, 'Lost chance or lost horizon?: strategic opportunity and escalation risk in the Korean War, April–July 1951', *Journal of Strategic Studies* 33:2 (2010), pp. 255–89.

Jervis, Robert, 'The impact of the Korean War on the Cold War', *Journal of Conflict Resolution* 24:4 (1980), pp. 563–92.

Jones, Matthew, 'Targeting China: US nuclear planning and "massive retaliation" in East Asia, 1953–1955', *Journal of Cold War Studies* 10:4 (2008), pp. 37–65.

Jung, Young-Tae, 'The rise of the Cold War and labor movements in South Korea, 1945–1948', *Asian Perspectives* 13:1 (1989), pp. 151–72.

Keefer, Edward, 'President Eisenhower and the end of the Korean War', *Diplomatic History* 10 (1986), pp. 267–89.

Keefer, Edward, 'The Truman administration and the South Korean political crisis of 1952: democracy's failure?', *Pacific Historical Review* 60:2 (1991), pp. 145–68.

Kim, Chonghan, 'Korean reunification: UN perspectives', in T.H. Kwak, C. Kim and H.N. Kim (eds), *Korean Reunification: New Perspectives and Approaches* (Seoul, 1984).

Lowe, David, 'Percy Spender and the Colombo Plan', *Australian Journal of Politics and History* 40:2 (1994), pp. 162–76.

Lowe, David, 'Mr Spender goes to Washington: an Ambassador's vision of Australian-American relations, 1951–1958', *Journal of Imperial and Commonwealth History* 24:2 (1996), pp. 278–95.

Lowe, David, 'Australia at the United Nations in the 1950s: the paradox of empire', *Australian Journal of International Affairs* 51:2 (1997), pp. 171–81.

Lowe, David, 'Percy Spender's quest', *Australian Journal of International Affairs* 55:2 (2001), pp. 187–98.

Lowe, David, 'Brave new liberal: Percy Spender', *Australian Journal of Politics and History* 51:3 (2005), pp. 389–99.

Lowe, Peter, 'Great Britain, Japan, and the Korean War, 1950–1951', *Proceedings of the British Association for Japanese Studies* 9 (1984), pp. 98–111.

Lowe, Peter, 'The settlement of the Korean War', in J. Young (ed.), *The Foreign Policy of Churchill's Peacetime Administration, 1951–1955* (Leicester, 1988).

Lowe, Peter, 'The frustrations of alliance: Britain, the United States, and the Korean War, 1950–1951', in J. Cotton and I. Neary (eds), *The Korean War in History* (Manchester, 1989).

Lowe, Peter, 'An ally and a recalcitrant general: Great Britain, Douglas MacArthur and the Korean War, 1950–1', *English Historical Review* 115:416 (1990), pp. 624–53.

Lowe, Peter, 'Great Britain and the Japanese peace treaty, 1951', in P. Lowe and H. Moeshart (eds), *Western Interactions with Japan: Expansion, the Armed Forces, and Readjustments, 1859–1956* (Folkestone, 1990).

Lowe, Peter, 'Hopes frustrated: the impact of the Korean War upon Britain's relations with Communist China, 1950–1953', in T. Fraser and K. Jeffery (eds), *Men, Women and War* (Dublin, 1993).

Matsuda, Haruka, 'A clash of empires in East Asia: the Geneva Conference on Korea, 1954', *Seoul Journal of Korean Studies* 20:2 (2007), pp. 193–211.

McAuliffe, Mary, 'Eisenhower, the President', *Journal of American History* 68:3 (1981), pp. 625–32.

McGlothlen, Ronald, 'Acheson, economics and the American commitment in Korea, 1947–1950', *Pacific Historical Review* 58:1 (1989), pp. 23–54.

McLean, David, 'American nationalism, the China myth, and the Truman doctrine: the question of accommodation with Peking, 1949–1950', *Diplomatic History* 10:1 (1986), pp. 25–42.

McLean, David, 'ANZUS origins: a reassessment', *Australian Historical Studies* 24:94 (1990), pp. 64–82.

McLellan, David, 'Dean Acheson and the Korean War', *Political Science Quarterly* 83:1 (1968), pp. 16–39.

McMahon, Robert, 'Food as a diplomatic weapon: the India wheat loan of 1951', *The Pacific Historical Review* 56:3 (1987), pp. 349–77.

Mansourov, Alexandre, 'Stalin, Mao, Kim, and China's decision to enter the Korean War, Sept. 16–Oct. 15, 1950: new evidence from Russian archives', *Cold War International History Project Bulletin* 6/7 (1995/96), pp. 94–119.

Marks, Frederick and Rabe, Stephen, 'The CIA and Castillo Armas in Guatemala, 1954: new clues to an old puzzle', *Diplomatic History* 14:1 (1990), pp. 67–86.

Martin, Allan, 'Sir Robert Gordon Menzies', in Michelle Grattan (ed.), *Australian Prime Ministers* (Sydney, 2001).

Matray, James, 'Hodge podge: American occupation policy in Korea, 1945–1948', *Korean Studies* 19 (1975), pp. 17–38.

Matray, James, 'An end to indifference: America's Korean policy during World War II', *Diplomatic History* 2:2 (1979), pp. 181–96.

Matray, James, 'Truman's plan for victory: national self-determination and the thirty-eighth parallel decision in Korea', *Journal of American History* 66:2 (1979), pp. 314–33.

Matray, James, 'Civil war of a sort: the international origins of the Korean conflict', in D. Meador and J. Monroe (eds), *The Korean War in Retrospect: Lessons for the Future* (Lanham, 1998).

Mawby, Spencer, 'From distrust to despair: Britain and the European army, 1950–1954', *European History Quarterly* 28:4 (1998), pp. 487–508.

Mayall, James, 'Africa in Anglo-American relations', in H. Bull and W. Louis (eds), *The Special Relationship: Anglo-American Relations since 1945* (Oxford, 1986).

Meaney, Neville, 'Look back in fear: Percy Spender, the Japanese peace treaty and the ANZUS pact', *Japan Forum* 15:3 (2003), pp. 399–410.

Medhurst, Martin, 'Text and context in the 1952 presidential campaign: Eisenhower's "I shall go to Korea" speech', *Presidential Studies Quarterly* 30:3 (2000), pp. 464–84.

Miller, J.D.B., 'The "special relationship" in the Pacific', in H. Bull and W. Louis (eds), *The Special Relationship: Anglo-American Relations since 1945* (Oxford, 1986).

Morsy, Laila, 'American support for the 1952 Egyptian coup: why?', *Middle Eastern Studies* 31:5 (1995), pp. 307–16.

Murray, Williamson, 'Dien Bien Phu', *Quarterly Journal of Military History* 9:3 (1997), pp. 40–51.

Niu, Jun, 'The birth of the People's Republic of China and the road to the Korean War', in M. Leffler and O. Westad (eds), *The Cambridge History of the Cold War*, vol. 1 (Cambridge, 2010).

Niu, Jun, 'The origins of the Sino-Soviet alliance', in O. Westad (ed.), *Brothers in Arms: The Rise and Fall of the Sino-Soviet Alliance, 1945–1963* (Stanford, 1998).

Ostermann, Christian, 'New documents on the East German uprising in 1953', *Cold War International History Project Bulletin* 5 (1995), pp. 10–17, 57.

Price, T., 'The South African General Election, 1953', *Parliamentary Affairs* 6:3 (1952), pp. 258–68.

Ra, Jong-Yil, 'Political crisis in Korea, 1952', *Journal of Contemporary History* 27:2 (1992), pp. 301–18.

Ra, Jong-yil, 'The politics of conference: the political conference on Korea in Geneva, 16 April–25 June 1954', *Journal of Contemporary History* 34:3 (1999), pp. 399–416.

Radchenko, Sergei and Wolff, David, 'To the summit via proxy summits: new evidence from Soviet and Chinese archives on Mao's long march to Moscow, 1949', *Cold War International History Project Bulletin* 16 (2008), pp. 105–82.

Rosenberg, David, 'American atomic strategy and the hydrogen bomb decision', *Journal of American History* 66 (1979), pp. 62–87.

Rosenberg, David, 'The origins of overkill: nuclear weapons and American strategy, 1945–1960', *International Security* 7:4 (1983), pp. 3–71.

Ruane, Kevin, 'Anthony Eden, British diplomacy and the origins of the Geneva Conference of 1954', *Historical Journal* 37:1 (1994), pp.153–72.

Ruane, Kevin, 'Refusing to pay the price: British foreign policy and the pursuit of victory in Indochina, 1952–54', *English Historical Review* 110:435 (1995), pp. 70–93.

Ruane, Kevin, 'SEATO, MEDO, and the Baghdad Pact: Anthony Eden, British foreign policy and the collective defence of Southeast Asia and the Middle East, 1952–55', *Diplomacy and Statecraft* 16:1 (2005), pp. 169–80.

Rubin, Barry, 'America and the Egyptian Revolution, 1950–1957', *Political Science Quarterly* 97:1 (1982), pp. 73–90.

Saint Brides, Lord, 'Britain, the United States, and South Asia', in H. Bull and W. Louis (eds), *The Special Relationship: Anglo-American Relations since 1945* (Oxford, 1986).

Schaller, Michael, 'Douglas MacArthur: the China issue, policy conflict, and the Korean War', in C.B. Kim and J. Matray (eds), *Korea and the Cold War: Division, Destruction, and Disarmament* (Claremont, 1993).

Schneer, Jonathan, 'Hopes deferred or shattered: the British Labour left and the third force movement, 1945–1949', *Journal of Modern History* 56:2 (1984), pp. 197–226.

Schonberger, Howard, 'Peacemaking in Asia: the United States, Great Britain, and the Japanese decision to recognize Nationalist China, 1951–1952', *Diplomatic History* 10:1 (1986), pp. 59–73.

Seigen, Miyasoto, 'John Foster Dulles and the peace settlement with Japan', in R. Immerman (ed.), *John Foster Dulles and the Diplomacy of the Cold War* (Princeton, 1989).

Shen, Zhihua, 'Sino-Soviet relations and the origins of the Korean War: Stalin's strategic goals in the Far East', *Journal of Cold War Studies* 2:2 (2000), pp. 44–68.

Shen, Zhihua, 'China and the dispatch of the Soviet air force: the formation of the Chinese-Soviet-Korean alliance in the early stages of the Korean War', *Journal of Strategic Studies* 33:2 (2010), pp. 211–30.

Shin, Gi-Wook, 'The historical making of collective action: the Korean peasant uprisings of 1946', *American Journal of Sociology* 99:6 (1994), pp. 1596–624.

Stueck, William, 'Cold War revisionism and the origins of the Korean War: the Kolko thesis', *Pacific Historical Review* 42:4 (1973), pp. 537–60.

Stueck, William, 'The United States, the Soviet Union, and the division of Korea: a comparative approach', *Journal of American-East Asia Relations* 4:1 (1975), pp. 1–27.

Stueck, William, 'The limits of influence: British policy and American expansion of the war in Korea', *Pacific Historical Review* 55:1 (1986), pp. 65–95.

Stueck, William, 'Introduction' and 'Conclusion', in W. Stueck (ed.), *The Korean War in World History* (Lexington, 2004).

Stueck, William and Yi, Boram, '"An alliance forged in blood": the American occupation of Korea, the Korean War, and the US-South Korean alliance', *Journal of Strategic Studies* 33:2 (2010), pp. 177–209.

Syed, M.M., 'Pakistan: struggle for power, 1947–58', *Pakistan Journal of History and Culture* 15:2 (1994), pp. 85–106.

Tarling, Nicholas, 'The United Kingdom and the origins of the Colombo Plan', *Journal of Commonwealth and Comparative Politics* 24:1 (1986), pp. 3–34.

Taylor, Barry, 'Open road barred (Battle of Imjin River, 1951)', *Military History* 7:6 (1991), pp. 46–52.

Thornhill, Michael, 'Britain, the United States and the rise of an Egyptian leader: the politics and diplomacy of Nasser's consolidation of power, 1952–4', *English Historical Review* 119:483 (2004), pp. 892–904.

Thornton, A.P., 'The transformation of the Commonwealth and the "special relationship"', in H. Bull and W. Louis (eds), *The Special Relationship: Anglo-American Relations since 1945* (Oxford, 1986).

Trachtenberg, Marc, 'A "wasting asset"? American strategy and the shifting nuclear balance, 1949–1954', *International Security* 13:3 (1988/89), pp. 33–49.

Trood, Russell, 'Alliance diplomacy: Australia, the United States and the 1954 Indochina crisis', *Australian Journal of Politics and History* 38:3 (1992), pp. 334–53.

Umetsu, Uroyuki, 'Australia's response to the Indochina crisis of 1954 amidst Anglo-American confrontation', *Australian Journal of Politics and History* 52:3 (2006), pp. 398–416.

Walker, John, 'Five hills at Dien Bien Phu', *Military Heritage* 8:3 (2006), pp. 32–39.

Warner, Geoffrey, 'The Korean War', *International Affairs* 56:1 (1980), pp. 98–107.

Warner, Geoffrey, 'The United States and the rearmament of West Germany, 1950–4', *International Affairs* 61:2 (1985), pp. 279–86.

Waters, Christopher, 'Casey: four decades in the making of Australian foreign policy', *Australian Journal of Politics and History* 51:3 (2005), pp. 380–88.

Weathersby, Kathryn, 'Soviet aims in Korea and the origins of the Korean War, 1945–1950: new evidence from Russian archives', *Cold War International History Project Working Paper* 8 (1993), pp. 1–37.

Weathersby, Kathryn, 'The Soviet role in the early phase of the Korean War: new documentary evidence', *Journal of American-East Asian Relations* 2:4 (1993), pp. 425–58.

Weathersby, Kathryn, 'To attack or not to attack? Stalin, Kim Il Sung, and the prelude to war', *Cold War International History Project Bulletin* 5 (1995), pp. 1–9.

Weathersby, Kathryn, 'New Russian documents on the Korean War: introduction and translations', *Cold War International History Project Bulletin* 6/7 (1995/96), pp. 30–84.

Weiss, Julian, 'The PRC occupation of Tibet', *Journal of Social, Political and Economic Studies* 12:4 (1987), pp. 385–99.

Wells, Samuel, 'Sounding the tocsin: NSC-68 and the Soviet threat,' *International Security* 4:2 (1979), pp. 116–158.

Wells, Samuel, 'The origins of massive retaliation', *Political Science Quarterly* 96:1 (1981), pp. 31–52.

Westad, Odd, 'Introduction', in O. Westad (ed.), *Brothers in Arms: The Rise and Fall of the Sino-Soviet Alliance, 1945–1963* (Stanford, 1998).

Williams, John, 'ANZUS: a blow to Britain's self-esteem', *Review of International Studies* 13:4 (1987), pp. 243–63.

Wilz, John, 'The MacArthur hearings of 1951: the secret testimony,' *Military Affairs* 39:4 (1975), pp. 167–73.

Wiltz, John, 'The Korean War and American society', in F. Heller (ed.), *The Korean War: A 25-Year Perspective* (Lawrence, 1977).

Wiltz, John, 'Truman and MacArthur: the Wake Island meeting', *Military Affairs* 42:4 (1978), pp. 169–76.

Wingrove, Paul, 'Russian documents on the 1954 Geneva Conference', *Cold War International History Project Bulletin* 16 (2007/8), pp. 85–104.

Young, Charles, 'POWs: the hidden reason for forgetting Korea', *Journal of Strategic Studies* 33:2 (2010), pp. 317–32.

Zhang, Shu Guang, 'Constructing "peaceful coexistence": China's diplomacy towards the Geneva and Bandung conferences, 1954–55', *Cold War History* 7:4 (2007), pp. 509–28.

Zhai, Qiang, 'China and the Geneva Conference of 1954', *The China Quarterly* 129 (1992), pp. 103–22.

INDEX

Note: Page numbers for illustrations and maps are given in italic script.

and Indian Resolution, 171, 172
and Jammu and Kashmir, 211
neutrality, 6, 25, 58–9, 242
prisoners of war talks, 153
response to Rhee's prisoners of war
  release, 201–2
Security Council discussions, 41,
  42–3, 70
Soviet peace offensive, 185
and Tibet, 37–8
US food aid, 98–9, 101
Nehru, R.K. 168
Neutral Nations Repatriation Commission (NNRC), 186–7, 207–9,
  223, 226, 228, 229, 231, 270–72
Neutral Nations Supervisory Commission (NNSC), 128, 160–61, 206,
  231
New Zealand
  ANZUS Treaty, 99–100
  General Assembly discussions, 55,
    83, 85, 86
  and Korean War, 8, 72
  military commitment to South
    Korea, 44, 45–6, 48
  and US, 2, 8
  view of the Commonwealth, 23
  waterfront dispute, 98, 122
Newfoundland, 20, 21
NNRC see Neutral Nations Repatria-
  tion Commission (NNRC)
NNSC see Neutral Nations Supervisory
  Commission (NNSC)
Non-Aligned Movement, 242
North Korea see Korea, Democratic
  People's Republic of (DPRK)
  (North)
North Korean People's Army (NKPA),
  11, 31, 32, 112
nuclear weapons see atomic weapons
Nutting, Anthony, 239–40
Nye, Archibald, 41

Officer, Sir Keith, 136

O'Neill, Robert, 8
Ovendale, Ritchie, 9

Padilla Nervo, Luis, 101
Pahlavi, Shah Mohammed Reza, 214
Pakistan
  'aggressor' resolution, 85, 89
  Commonwealth and UN
    membership, 25
  General Assembly discussions, 55
  Khan's assassination, 121–2
  refusal to offer forces, 47
  strategic importance, 2
  tensions, 148
  and US, 183, 210
Pandit, Vijaya Lakshmi
  and food aid, 101
  General Assembly discussions, 88
  General Assembly President, 222,
    228–9
  and Indian Resolution, 159, 161,
    171, 194
  Security Council discussions, 41
  and Zhou En-lai, 153
Panikkar, K.M. 55, 56, 80, 85, 153
Panmunjom, 127, 128
peace negotiations
  Berlin Conference (1954), 228, 229
  Panmunjom US-China talks, 223–4,
    227, 228
  see also armistice negotiations
Pearson, Lester, 24, 46–7, 55, 56, 86,
  101
  ceasefire proposals, 77, 78, 79–81
  'aggressor' resolution, 86
  Chinese proposals, 198
  and Churchill, 121
  and the Commonwealth, 24
  crossing the, 38th parallel, 55, 56
  General Assembly discussions, 55, 56,
    135, 136, 157, 163, 165, 166, 168
  and GOC membership, 101
  and ground forces, 46–7
  and Indian Resolution, 171–2, 193

370   THE US, THE UN AND THE KOREAN WAR